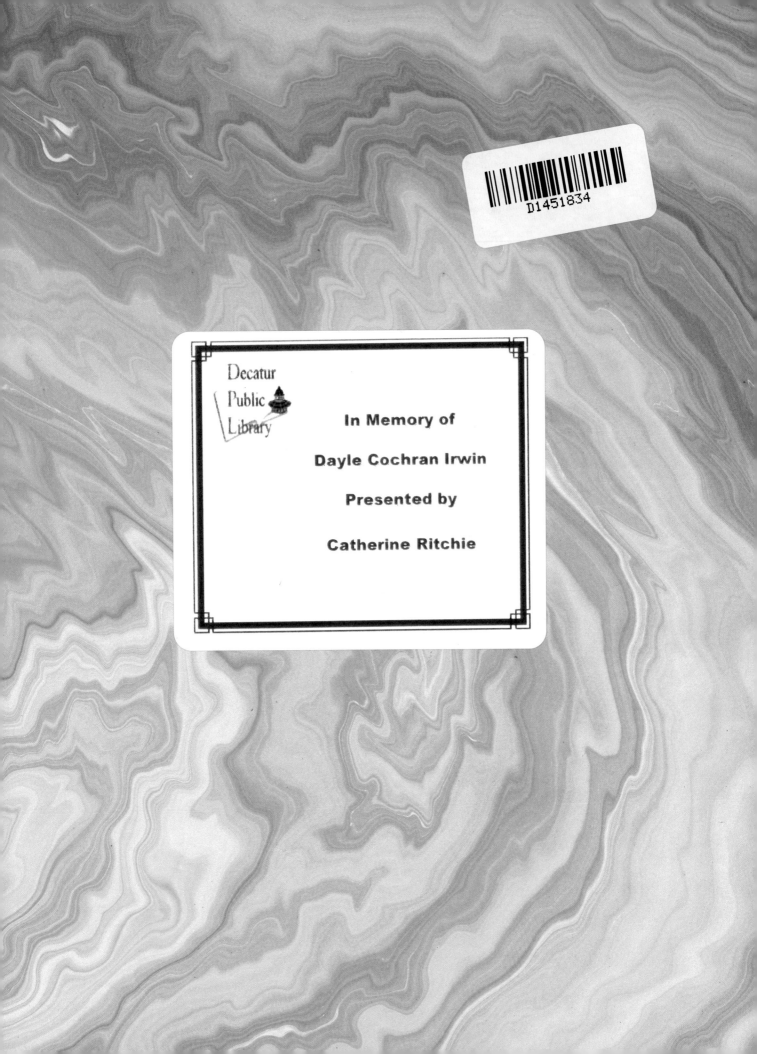

THE CAMP MEN

Also by French MacLean
THE CRUEL HUNTERS: SS-SONDERKOMMANDO DIRLEWANGER

THE CAMP MEN
The SS Officers Who Ran the
Nazi Concentration Camp System

French L. MacLean

Schiffer Military History
Atglen, PA

ACKNOWLEDGMENTS

I could not have completed this work alone. First, I would like to thank Jim Kelling, Niels Cordes and the staff at the National Archives who invariably provided timely assistance in finding specific rolls of the almost 1,000 spools of microfilm needed for this project; many times they were able to recall documents they had seen in their cataloging and reviewing process.

Alex Rossini, Aaron Kornblum, Ron Kurpiers, and the research and photography assistants at the United States Holocaust Memorial Museum opened their extensive document and microfilm files as well as help me navigate through their large library. It is because of their interest that I believed a book this comprehensive not only could be done – it should be done.

Dr. Debórah Dwork, Rose Professor of Holcaust History at Clark University and Dr. Tom Veve, a dedicated historian and college administrator – and a friend of over twenty years – provided much-needed encouragement when I was unsure if the project could ever be finished or subsequently published.

Speaking of publishers, the editors and staff at Schiffer also deserve a great deal of appreciation. They are truly an efficient group and interested in furthering the body of knowledge in this subject. This work marks an expansion from purely military subjects in their Military History Division; expansions of this nature entail a certain willingness to accept a business risk unfortunately found in too few publishers. I hope this work justifies their faith in the importance of this project.

To Michael Tregenza in Poland goes a special word of appreciation. He painstakingly read every word of the huge final draft of this work, offering critical comments and improvements, which have undoubtedly made this a better product. His upcoming work on Belzec reflects the expertise he has acquired as one of the world's most knowledgeable historians on *Operation Reinhard*.

To those sources for photos – both in the United States and in Europe – who expressed their desires to remain anonymous, thank you for your support.

Finally, I would also like to express my immense gratitude to my wife Olga. As initial editor of this book, she organized it's contents in such a way that the book became much more than just separate pools of facts – it has hopefully become a stream of knowledge directed to illuminate this aspect of the Holocaust.

French MacLean
Falls Church, Virginia

Book Design by Robert Biondi.

Printed in the United States of America.
ISBN: 0-7643-0636-7

We are interested in hearing from authors with book ideas on military topics.

Published by Schiffer Publishing Ltd.
4880 Lower Valley Road
Atglen, PA 19310
Phone: (610) 593-1777
FAX: (610) 593-2002
E-mail: Schifferbk@aol.com.
Please write for a free catalog.
This book may be purchased from the publisher.
Please include $3.95 postage.
Try your bookstore first.

CONTENTS

"It is a very simple story. I was a Nazi."

Hans Hüttig
A camp man at:

Buchenwald
Sachsenhausen
Flossenbürg
Natzweiler
Herzogenbusch

INTRODUCTION

I also want to talk to you quite frankly on a very grave matter. Among ourselves it should be mentioned quite frankly and yet we will never speak of it publicly ... I mean the evacuation of the Jews, the extermination of the Jewish race ... This is a page of glory in our history which has never been written and is never to be written.[1]

- Heinrich Himmler

A colleague of mine from the State Department recently asked me how I could remain unemotional enough – given the horrendous attributes of the Holocaust – to do the painstaking research required to produce a book of this nature.

The answer probably relates to the quotation above from Heinrich Himmler, one of the masterminds of the concentration camp system and the mass murder which followed in these locations. I wrote this book because the crime was so immense, so unparalleled, that the SS officers who carried it out deserve to have a concise, centralized place in infamy. All the SS concentration camp officers, not just the leaders, warrant scrutiny. The purpose of this work is first and foremost to serve as a compendium of all *Schutzstaffel* (SS) officers who were assigned to the Nazi concentration camp system during the years of the Third Reich. While several excellent books have specialized in describing one or more of the camp *kommandants* – most notably Tom Segev's *Soldiers of Evil: The Commandants of the Nazi Concentration Camps* and Konnilyn G. Feig's *Hitler's Death Camps: The Sanity of Madness* – none have made the attempt to cover all SS officers who were assigned there. In fact, it has proven quite difficult, even given the huge resources of the United States Holocaust Memorial Museum, to indeed find complete sources listing all SS personnel for even a <u>single</u> camp. But the magnitude of the crimes demands a full accounting of those SS officers involved.

Who were these men? From what areas of Germany did they come? What was their rank structure? Were most married? What were their religious backgrounds? Had any served

in World War I? Did any come from the German nobility? How many were physicians? Were they awarded military decorations by the Nazi government for their activities? Were they members of the Nazi Party? Did most serve in only one camp or did any go on to work in multiple camps during their careers? Did they later fight in front-line *Waffen-SS* combat units and if so, which units? Did many die later during the war in battle or did they survive? If they survived the war, were they prosecuted for their crimes?

While there are many excellent works detailing what went on in the camps, they are somewhat lacking in presenting information on all the perpetrators (most concentrate on the camp *kommandants*) – in fact, most are extremely incomplete when listing which SS officers served at a particular camp. So I have taken what is in existence – from the excellent research center at the United States Holocaust Memorial Museum – and then proceeded to the National Archives. There, I have reviewed a set of records known as Microfilm Publication A3343, *Records of SS Officers from the Berlin Document Center*, Series SSO. These roles of microfilmed SS officers' service records consist of the personnel dossiers for more than 61,000 SS officers with the rank of second lieutenant and above in this large and complex organization. The date span of the records contained in the dossiers extends from 1932 to as late as March 1945 in some cases. There are nine-hundred and nine rolls in this set, parts of most detail the lives of every officer known to be assigned to the concentration camps. These records are truly an open book into the careers of these men and include marital status, religion, court-martial proceedings, promotions, recommendations for awards, transfers, assignment instructions, letters of reprimand, medical histories and family background.

Reviewed is a word that perhaps does not do justice to the effort. There are over nine hundred fifty officers presented in this work. The initial problem was to identify all of them from the literally hundreds of individual camp histories to the large amount of resources at the Simon Wiesenthal Center. Next came a review of each officer's personnel file, on microfilm at the National Archives. Given a examination of perhaps ten to twenty minutes for most officers' files will soon give the reader a feeling that this is certainly not a task to be accomplished over a short period of time. In some instances there was no file to be found; I then turned to alternate sources such as the yearly *Dienstaltersliste der Schutzstaffel der N.S.D.A.P.* – the annual rank lists of the SS – for additional information to piece together this puzzle.

First and foremost then, this work attempts to present information on every single SS officer who served at one time or another in the camp system. The reader will immediately note several names missing from the work. Heinrich Himmler, Ernst Kaltenbrunner, Reinhard Heydrich, Odilo Globocnik and Adolf Eichmann are notable in their absence as are the SS officers who served exclusively in the *Einsatzgruppe* – the battalion-size mobile extermination groups on the eastern front. But as they did not truly serve in the camps, they do not appear here. I wanted to present only those officers who actually carried out the work of the concentration camps or who served in the SS units that guarded these facilities, and even with this limitation, the reader will note the size of the book![2]

The reader may also ask why an attempt was not made to cover all SS personnel and not only the officer corps. First, the nature of the microfilmed records in the National Archives does not support such an effort. The personnel records for officers are relatively complete; those for enlisted personnel are not. Secondly, in most military organizations – and the SS falls into this category – junior officers frequently supervise some twenty to thirty enlisted men. So, even if we could ascertain every enlisted soldier who served in the camps at one time or another, and even if we had complete records for them (again, which we do not), we would be looking at tens of thousands of men.[3] In fact, Wolfgang Sofsky in his work *Die Ordnung des Terrors: Das Konzentrationslager*, states that no fewer than 55,000 SS personnel served in the camp system from 1933 to 1945![4]

The first division of the book features a brief description of the major camps, the SS officer rank system and the authorized SS officer positions in them merely to present a framework for later information. It is short and does not attempt to cover the multitude of activities in each camp. But several ex-

isting sources do a masterful job at this very tragic story. They include Raul Hilberg's *The Destruction of the European Jews (Revised and definitive edition)*, Charles Sydnor Jr.'s *Soldiers of Destruction: The SS Death's Head Division, 1933-1945*, Gerald Reitlinger's *The SS: Alibi of a Nation 1922-1945*, Robert Koehl's *The Black Corps: The Structure and Power Struggles of the Nazi SS*, Yitzak Arad's *Belzec, Sobibór, Treblinka: The Operation Reinhard Death Camps* and Eugen Kogon's, Hermann Langbein's and Adalbert Rückerl's *Nazi Mass Murder*. Additionally, there are numerous books each dealing with a specific camp that do far more justice to what occurred. Many have been written by survivors, and I would not pretend to know more than they do on the subject of prisoner life inside the wire. Several are included in the bibliography as sources for further research by other scholars.

The second, and by far the largest, section of the book contains biographical information on each of the over 900 officers with a microfilm source roll to facilitate further research. Some of the personnel files contained only one summary sheet for an officer, while others feature up to eighty or ninety pages. Additionally, some of the files reveal scant surface information concerning assignments to the camps. Nowhere do officer efficiency reports list specific killings or obvious connections to what would later become known as the Holocaust. The terms that appear in these reports are at first glance benign – "cleansed", "handled", "special action", etc. But the meanings are the same – murder.

The third portion of the book examines significant facets of each officer's career by using a relational database. The reader, I believe, will come to an unusual conclusion, as I did, concerning later assignments in the Waffen-SS – the military arm of the SS that supposedly had no link to the activities that transpired in the camps themselves. Some SS historians, no doubt, will find a few less-than-noble assignments for several officers who went on to have otherwise distinguished military careers – assignments that until now have been hidden, perhaps intentionally, from military biographies.

The photographic section of the book, with well over one hundred photographs – a large portion previously unpublished – is the largest collection of photographs of SS camp personnel ever to appear in one work. The images come from the extensive files of the United States Holocaust Memorial Museum, the Berlin Document Center, Yad Vashem and many other institutional collections. There are additionally photographs from private sources, including almost twenty rare pictures from the Gross-Rosen camp *kommandant's* personal photograph album.

Undoubtedly, some knowledgeable readers will find that I may have missed recording the presence of some SS officers in a camp. With the over 950 officers presented, I believe I am in the ninety percent complete range and welcome any additional information which will be verified and subsequently included in later printings.[5] Others may note that a few SS officers listed here were in fact non-commissioned officers during part of their time in camp service. That is quite correct. I have included all personnel who ultimately held officer ranks; why I did this will become apparent in the analytical section later in the book. Additionally, some officer files are not included in the National Archive holdings. In these cases I was extremely leery of including their names in this work without several corroborating sources – I have no interest in falsely accusing an officer of serving in a camp, when in fact, he was never there. (In some instances, caution caused me to omit names when, in fact, the individuals probably had actually served at a camp.[6])

Along these lines, the reader should keep in mind two points. First, the SS personnel files do not distinguish service, for the most part, between assignment at a main camp – such as Dachau or Mauthausen or Buchenwald – and a sub-camp of a parent camp. So perhaps it is more accurate to say that an officer listed as having served at Dachau actually served in the Dachau system of camps. While he probably spent some time at the main camp in addition to service at a sub-camp, this may not always be the case. Second, this work merely seeks to establish which officers served at the different camps – it does not attempt to assign levels of guilt by specific actions. Some officers were undoubtedly more involved in killing than others. Separate works can attempt to resolve degrees of guilt, I only seek to show who was present at a given camp location, and, if possible, when they were stationed there. Some of the men presented here were personally responsible for hundreds and thousands of deaths. Others, served in support roles which, in a legal sense, would have different degrees of culpability. There may even be a few who actually helped individual inmates – certainly the exception and not the rule. Additionally, this study is unable to determine those officers who volunteered for camp duty as compared to those who were ordered to serve. Motivation rarely appears on a set of assignment orders.

Michael Geyer, in his chapter "German Strategy in the Age of Machine Warfare, 1914-1945" contained in Peter Peret's *Makers of Modern Strategy*, states that German National Socialism had twin strategic goals – the enslavement of eastern European populations and an Armageddon for its perceived mortal enemy, the Jewish minorities of occupied Europe.[7] The men listed in this book ran a concentration/extermination camp system that killed between 3,500,000 and 6,000,000 human beings. It is time their names and careers receive the historical scrutiny they deserve.

French MacLean
Falls Church, Virginia

Notes:

[1] Gerald Reitlinger, *The SS: Alibi of a Nation* (London: Arms and Armour Press, 1981), p.278.

[2] An exception concerns those officers who served at the concentration camp headquarters at Oranienburg. Their role will be described later. Additionally, the author is currently working on a separate study of *Einsatzgruppen* (the mobile SS killing formations primarily on the eastern front) officers using the same computer database techniques.

[3] The private notebook of the *kommandant* of Dachau in 1945 recorded the command, staff and guard force for the camp at 41 officers, 998 non-commissioned officers and 2,814 enlisted men. Source: Paul Berben, *Dachau 1933-1945* (London: The Norfolk Press, 1975).

[4] Wolfgang Sofsky, *Die Ordnung des Terrors: Das Konzentrationslager* (Frankfurt: S. Fischer Verlag, 1993), p.121. Another source states there were 7,400 SS personnel associated with the concentration camps in 1939, 15,000 in 1942 and 35,000 in 1945. Source: Eberhard Kolb, *Bergen Belsen* (Hannover, FRG: Verlag für Literatur und Zeitgeschen, 1962), p.78. A third reference states that of the 35,000 who ultimately served as concentration camp guards, 10,000 were not in the SS. Source: Robert Lewis Koehl, *The Black Corps: The Structure and Power Struggles of the Nazi SS*. (Madison, WI: The University of Wisconsin Press, 1983), p.167.

[5] One concentration camp researcher insists that every SS officer was required to serve at some point in their career in a concentration camp. This patently did not happen and is substantiated in any extensive review of the officer personnel files at the National Archives.

[6] A reference set of books listing SS officers at the United States Holocaust Memorial Museum shows some officers affiliated with a camp if it was their mustering out point from army service before joining the SS. I have not included these officers in this work (unless they some time later served at the camp) as their stay at these locations was only for a few days and even then only for the purpose of formally leaving the army.

[7] Michael Geyer, "German Strategy in the Age of Machine Warfare, 1914-1945" in *Makers of Modern Strategy* ed. Peter Peret (Princeton, NJ: Princeton University Press, 1986), pp. 573-574.

1

THE CONCENTRATION CAMPS

Our system is so terrible that no one in the world will believe it to be possible.[1]

- The Kommandant of Auschwitz

Before we can understand the officers who served this aspect of the SS, we must first examine the concentration camps themselves. The Nazis established an immense camp system before and during World War II; there were at least forty-three <u>types</u> of camps – in total there were well over a thousand camps throughout Europe affecting the lives of millions of people.

Wolfgang Sofsky succinctly describes the central importance that the concentration camps held for the Nazi state:[2]

> The establishment of camps in which inmates were deprived of their liberty, compelled to work at slave labor, and subjected to arbitrary terror was central to the National Socialist apparatus of power. The concentration camps lay at the very center of this network of terror.

There were worker education camps (*Arbeiterziehungslager*), labor camps (*Arbeitslager*), forcible detention camps (*Zwangslager*), punitive camps (*Straflager*), penal servitude camps (*Zwangsarbeitslager*), penal camps for persons refusing to work (*Straflager für Arbeitsverweigerer*), internment camps (*Internierungslager*), assembly camps (*Sammellager*), residence camps (*Wohnlager*), transit camps (*Durchgangslager*) and many other types as the Germans have always had penchant for everything – and everyone – in its proper place. People died, of course, at every type of camp; but the two types of camp that were the most feared and most symbolic of the Nazi regime were the concentration camp and the extermination camp.[3]

Hitler established the first concentration camps in Germany soon after his appointment as chancellor in January 1933.[4] Under a German definition a concentration camp or *Konzentrationslager*, referred to a camp in which people were confined or detained under harsh conditions in situations outside normal due process or the conventional legal norms of arrest. To accomplish this, Hitler instituted the Presidential Emergency Decree of 28 February 1933. This decree was the basis for *Schutzhaft*, or protective custody, which allowed the Gestapo to imprison individuals without judicial proceedings.[5] Prisoners in concentration camps included Communists, Social Democrats, Jehovah's Witnesses, trade unionists, homosexuals, regular criminals, and later Gypsies, clergy and Jews. Even dissident Nazis were sometimes incarcerated. The primary purpose of a concentration camp was punishment. Most concentration camps had subordinate camps known as external camps (*Aussenlager*) and sub-camps (*Nebenlager*). Whenever a concentration camp featured subordinate camps, the main camp (Dachau, Mauthausen, etc.) was known as the *Stammlager*. After 1940-1941 the Germans divided the concentration camps into three categories. Category I consisted of work camps, of which Dachau was termed. Category II camps featured harsher living and working conditions; Buchenwald was initially in this category. Category III camps were termed "*Knochenmühlen*" or "bone mills", and were the harshest of the three categories. Mauthausen, Gross-Rosen and Natzweiler were camps of this classification.[6] Prisoners, within the category of concentration camps, were theoretically eligible to be released from camp detention, if they demonstrated sufficient rehabilitation – although in practice, this only really applied to German nationals.[7] As the war progressed, the camps took on an increasingly economic nature, supporting German armaments and other war-related industry.

The second type of camp that figures significantly in this work is the extermination camp or *Vernichtungslager*. Sometime in 1941, Adolf Hitler, Heinrich Himmler and Reinhard Heydrich arrived at the decision to implement the "Final Solution" and begin full scale exterminations of the Jews.[8] As part of this process in 1942, Himmler instituted *Operation Reinhard* – a plan to kill all Jews in the *Generalgouvernement* (General government) area of captured Poland through the use of extermination camps – namely Belzec, Sobibór and Treblinka. The Germans did not use this term officially as it would reveal the nature of activities at the location. Prisoners in extermination camps were most frequently Jews, but many others perished in these camps as well. The primary purpose of an extermination camp was the rapid death of the victims received, often the same day they arrived. Extermination camps generally did not have subordinate camps, although Auschwitz did; six camps qualify as extermination camps – Belzec, Sobibór, Treblinka, Chelmno/Kulmhof, Majdanek/Lublin and Auschwitz.[9] Within the classification of extermination camps, the only possibility of release for a prisoner – according to the sarcastic humor of guard personnel – was as smoke drifting through the chimneys of the crematoria.

The number of camps generally increased toward the end of the pre-war period and during the war itself because the number of inmates grew quickly. In 1938 roughly 60,000 inmates resided in the camp system. By 1942 this figure climbed to over 100,000. By 1945 more than 715,000 prisoners were in the camp system.[10] The only exception to this increase occurred in the mid-1930s when the Nazis closed several of the initial camps – which were known unofficially as the "Wild Camps" – in an effort to standardize and consolidate the system. The SS officers detailed in this book served in the following fifty of the more significant concentration and extermination camps:[11]

ANKENBUCK

Type of Camp: Early concentration camp; one of the "Wild Camps"
Location: near Villingen, Baden
Opened: April 1933
Closed: 16 January 1934
Victims: Unknown
Remarks: Small camp; held only 125 prisoners. Prisoners did farm work and road construction. Police Captain Franz Mohr and Hans Helwig served as *kommandants*.

ARBEITSDORF

Type: Experimental
Location: near Hannover/Fallersleben
Opened: 8 April 1942
Closed: 11 October 1942
Remarks: Pilot project for utilization of inmates for war industry to include manufacture of Volkswagens. Camp began when prisoners were transferred from Sachsenhausen. At its closure, prisoners transferred to Buchenwald.

AUSCHWITZ/BIRKENAU

Type of Camp: Combined extermination/labor complex
Location: Oswiecim, Poland
Opened: 20 May 1940
Closed: 27 January 1945
Victims: 1,200,000 - 2,500,000
Major sub-camps: Altdorf, Althammer, Babitz, Birkenau (Auschwitz II), Bismarckhuette, Blechhammer, Bobrek, Bruenn, Budy, Charlottengrube, Chiemek, Eintrachthuette, Freudenthal, Fuerstengrube, Gleiwitz, Golleschau, Guenthergrube, Harmense, Hindenburg, Hohenlinde, Janinagrube, Jawischowitz, Kobior, Lagischa, Laurahuette, Lichtewerden, Monowitz (Auschwitz III), Nachhammer, Neudachs, Aneustadt, Plawy, Sosnowitz, Trzebinia and Tschechowitz.
Remarks: Consisted of three major camps: Auschwitz, Birkenau and Monowitz. Site of Nazi medical experiments involving twins, dwarfs, sterilization and hypothermia. Also site for massive war industry sites using prison labor. Held up to 155,000 prisoners at one time. Rudolf Höss, Arthur Liebehenschel, Josef Kramer, Albert Schwarz, Fritz Hartjenstein and Richard Baer served as *kommandants*. SS staff and guards numbered 2,530 on January 15, 1945. Evacuation began January 18, 1945.

BAD SULZA

Type of Camp: Early concentration camp; one of the "Wild Camps"
Location: Thuringia, near Weimar
Opened: July 1933
Closed: July 1937
Victims: Unknown
Remarks: Held 350-400 prisoners. On closure, prisoners transferred to Lichtenburg. Carl Haubenreiser served as *kommandant*.

BELZEC

Type of Camp: Extermination
Location: 100 miles southeast of Warsaw, between Zamosc and Lvov
Opened: March 1942
Closed: 8 May 1943
Victims: 500,000 - 600,000
Remarks: Part of *Operation Reinhard*, the German plan to kill the Jews of the *Generalgouvernement*. Christian Wirth and Gottlieb Hering served as *kommandants*. Between twenty and thirty-five SS men served in the camp at one time. Most of the victims came from Galicia, Krakow and the Lublin areas. Only one prisoner is reported to have survived the camp.

BERGEN-BELSEN

Type of Camp: Prisoner of war/internment/concentration camp
Location: 11 miles north of Celle
Opened: July 1943 (as internment camp)
Closed: 15 April 1945
Victims: 35,000 - 50,000
Remarks: Camp held an average number of 95,000 prisoners. Rudolf Haas and Josef Kramer served as *kommandants*. SS staff and guards numbered 289 on January 15, 1945. Anne Frank died at Bergen-Belsen.

BÖRGERMORR

Type of Camp: Early concentration camp; one of the "Wild Camps"
Location: Westfalen, Surwold District
Opened: 1933
Closed: 1934
Victims: Unknown
Remarks: Had 1,000 prisoners in 1933. Taken over in 1934 by the Ministry of Justice. During WWII used as prison for military offenders.

BRANDENBURG

Type of Camp: Early concentration camp; one of the "Wild Camps"
Location: near Havel River, west of Berlin
Opened: 15 March 1933
Closed: 23 April 1934
Victims: Unknown
Remarks: Later sub-camp of Sachsenhausen

BRAUWEILER

Type of Camp: Early concentration camp; one of the "Wild Camps"
Location: near Cologne
Opened: 1 June 1933
Closed: 8 March 1934
Victims: Unknown
Remarks: Inmates sent to Esterwegen when Brauweiler closed.

BREITENAU

Type of Camp: Early concentration camp; one of the "Wild Camps"
Location: Hesse
Opened: 18 November 1933
Closed: 17 March 1934
Victims: Unknown
Remarks: Held 130 prisoners.

BUCHENWALD

Type of Camp: Concentration camp
Location: near Weimar
Opened: 15 July 1937 as Concentration Camp Ettersberg; name changed to Buchenwald 28 July 1937
Closed: 11 April 1945
Victims: 50,000 - 60,000
Major Sub-camps: Abteroda, Allendorf, Altenburg, Annaburg, Apolda, Arolsen, Aschersleben, Bad Gandersheim, Bad Langensalza, Bad Salzungen, Bensberg, Berga, Berlstedt, Billroda, Blankenburg, Bochum, Boehlen, Braunschweig, Buttelstedt, Colditz, Dernau, Dessau, Dors, Dortmund, Duderstadt, Derendorf, Düsseldorf, Eisenach, Ellrich, Elsnig, Eschershausen, Essen, Flössberg, Gelsenkirchen, Giessen, Goslar, Göttingen, Hadmersleben, Halberstadt, Halle, Hardehausen, Harzungen, Hessisch-Lichenau, Jena, Köln, Langenstain, Lauenberg, Leipzig, Leopoldshall, Lippstadt, Lützekendorf, Magdeburg, Mar Kleeberg, Meuselwitz, Mühlhausen, Neustadt, Niederorschel, Oberndorf, Ohrdruf, Osterode, Penig, Plömitz, Quedlinburg, Raguhn, Rothenburg, Rottleberode, Saalfeld, Schlieben, Schoenbeck, Schwerte, Sennelager, Sömmerda, Sonneberg, Stassfurt, Suhl, Tannenwald, Taucha, Tonndorf, Torgau, Tröglitz, Unna, Wansleben, Weferlingen, Weimar, Wernigerode, Westeregelen, Wewelsburg, Witten and Wolfen.
Remarks: In 1939 had 5,300 inmates. Held up to 86,000 prisoners at one time. Site of Nazi medical experiments involving typhus and other contagious diseases. Karl Koch and Hermann Pister served as *kommandants*. SS staff and guards numbered 6,829 on January 15, 1945.

CHELMNO/KULMHOF
Type of Camp: Extermination
Location: 45 miles west of Lodz
Opened: 7 December 1941
Closed: 17 January 1945
Victims: 152,000 - 310,000
Remarks: Camp used to liquidate the Lodz Ghetto. Herbert Lange and Hans Bothmann served as *kommandants*. Chelmno used gas vans with carbon monoxide rather than gas chambers to kill the victims. Less than ten prisoners are reported to have survived.

COLDITZ
Type of Camp: Early concentration camp; one of the "Wild Camps"
Location: Saxony, 20 miles southeast of Leipzig
Opened: 22 July 1933
Closed: 31 May 1934
Victims: Unknown
Remarks: Became a sub-camp of Buchenwald.

COLUMBIA HAUS
Type of Camp: Early concentration camp; one of the "Wild Camps"
Location: Berlin-Tempelhof
Opened: 8 January 1935
Closed: 5 November 1936
Victims: Unknown, probably in the hundreds
Remarks: Walter Gerlach, Alexander Reiner and Karl Koch served as *kommandants*. Colombia Haus resembled more of a prison than a camp. Location of Gestapo interrogations of early opponents of the Third Reich.

DACHAU
Type of Camp: Concentration camp
Location: 10 miles north of Münich
Opened: 22 March 1933
Closed: 29 April 1945
Victims: 30,000 - 35,000
Major Sub-camps: Ampermoching, Augsburg, Bad Ischl, Bad Toelz, Baeumenheim, Bayrisch Zell, Blaibach, Burgau, Echelsbach, Eching, Ellwangen, Feldafing, Feldmoching, Fischbachau, Fischhorn, Friedrichshafen, Gablingen, Garmisch, Gendorf, Germering, Gmund, Hallein, Haunstettin, Heidenheim, Heppenheim, Innsbruck, Karlsfeld, Kaufbeuren, Kaufering, Kempten, Kottern, Landsberg, Landshut, Lauingen, Moschendorf, Muehldorf, München, Neufahren, Neu-Ulm,

Nürnberg, Oberstdorf, Ottobrunn, Passau, Plansee, Radolfzell, Salzburg, St. Johann, St. Lambrecht, Saulgau, Schliessheim, Seehausen, Stefanskirchen, Steinhoering, Sudelfeld, Trostberg, Tutzing, Ulm, and Ueberlingen.
Remarks: Held 97 prisoners in March 1933; 264 in May 1933. In 1939 had 4,000 inmates. Camp system held up to 160,000 prisoners at one time. Site of Nazi medical experiments involving high altitudes, malaria, tuberculosis and hypothermia. Hilmar Wäckerle, Theodor Eicke, Heinrich Deubel, Alex Piorkowski, Wilhelm Weiter, Hans Loritz and Martin Weiss served as *kommandants*. Closed as a concentration camp from 27 September, 1939 to 18 February, 1940 during which time it was utilized by the Waffen-SS. During this period the prisoners were transferred to Mauthausen. On March 25, 1933 there were fifty-four SS guards at the camp. On 1 January, 1945 the SS staff and guards numbered 3,606. Known as a training camp for many SS personnel who were later stationed at other camps.

DORA-MITTELBAU/NORDHAUSEN
Type of Camp: Concentration camp
Location: 5 miles northwest of Nordhausen
Opened: 28 October 1944
Closed: 9 April 1945
Victims: 20,000
Major Sub-camps: Artern, Ballenstedt, Bischofferode, Blankenburg am Harz, Bleicherode, Ellrich, Göttingen, Grosswerther, Harzungen, Hohlstedt, Ilfeld, Ilsenburg, Kassel, Kelbra, Kleinbodungen, Netzkater, Niedergebra, Niedersachswerfen, Regenstein, Rottleberode, Sollstedt, Stempeda, Trautenstein, Wickerode and Woffleben
Remarks: Camp provided slave labor for underground V2 missile plants. Held an average of 34,000 prisoners; had an extremely high death rate due to hazardous working conditions underground. Otto Förschner and Richard Baer served as *kommandants*. SS staff and guards numbered 3,319 on 15 January, 1945.

ESTERWEGEN
Type of Camp: Early concentration camp; one of the "Wild Camps"
Location: Emsland District
Opened: 4 March 1933
Closed: 5 September 1936
Victims: Unknown
Remarks: 2,500 prisoner capacity. Inmates transferred to Sachsenhausen. Paul Brinkmann, Hans Loritz and Karl Koch served as *kommandants*.

FLOSSENBÜRG

Type of Camp: Concentration Camp
Location: 40 miles east of Nürnberg near Weiden
Opened: 3 May 1938
Closed: 23 April 1945
Victims: 28,000
Major Sub-camps: Altenhammer, Ansbach, Bayreuth, Bruex, Chemnitz, Dresden, Eisenberg, Floeha, Freiberg, Ganacker, Giebelstadt, Grafenreuth, Graslitz, Groeditz, Gundelsdorf, Hainichen, Heidenau, Helmbrechts, Hersbruck, Hertine, Hohenstein, Holleischen, Holysov, Hradischko, Janowitz, Johanngeorgenstadt, Kirschham, Königstein, Krondorf, Leitmeritz, Lengenfeld, Mehltheuer, Meissen, Mittweida, Mockethal, Moschendorf, Mülsen, Neu-Rohlau, Nossen, Nürnberg, Obertraubling, Oederan, Plattling, Plauen, Porschdorf, Poschetzau, Pottenstein, Rabstein, Regensburg, Rochlitz, Saal, St. Georgenthal, Schlackenwerth, Schoenheide, Seifhennersdorf, Siegmar, Stein-Schoenau, Stulln, Teichwolframsdorf, Venusberg, Willischthal, Wolkenburg, Würzburg, Zschachwitz, Zschopau, Zwickau and Zwodau.
Remarks: In 1939 had 1,600 inmates. Held up to 18,000 prisoners at one time. Wilhelm Canaris, former chief of intelligence, executed here by SS April 1945. Jacob Weiseborn, Egon Zill, Karl Fritzsch, Max Koegel and Karl Künstler served as *kommandants*. SS staff and guards numbered 3,079 on 15 January, 1945. Evacuation of the camp began 20 April, 1945.

FUHLSBUETTEL

Type of Camp: Early concentration camp; one of the "Wild Camps"
Location: near Hamburg
Opened: 4 September 1933
Closed: 31 January 1937
Victims: Unknown
Remarks: Site of former prison.

GROSS-ROSEN

Type of Camp: Concentration camp
Location: near Goerlitz, Silesia
Opened: 2 August 1940
Closed: 11 February 1945
Victims: 35,000 - 40,000
Major Sub-camps: Aslau, Bad Salzbrunn, Bad Warmbrunn, Bautzen, Bernsdorf, Birnbaeumel, Bolkenheim, Brandhofen, Breslau, Brieg, Bruennlitz, Bunzlau, Christianstadt, Dyhernfurth, Faulbrueck, Friedland, Fünfteichen, Gabersdorf, Gablonz, Gassen, Gebhardsdorf, Gellenau, Görlitz, Graeben, Grafenort, Gross Koschen, Grünberg, Grulich, Halbau,

Halbstadt, Hartmannsdorf, Hirschberg, Hochweiler, Hohenelbe, Kamenz, Kittlitztreben, Kratzau, Kretschamberg, Landeshut, Langenbielau, Liebau, Liebenau, Maerzdorf, Mittelsteine, Namslau, Neuhammer, Neusalz, Niesky, Ober Altstadt, Parschnitz, peterswaldau, Reichenau, Reichenbach, Sackisch, Schatzlar, Schweidnitz, Treskau, Waldenburg, Weisswasser, Wüstegiersdorf, Zillertal and Zittau.
Remarks: Originally a labor camp to include support to Krupp and I.G. Farben industries. Camp held up to 125,000 prisoners at one time. Johannes Hassebroeck, Arthur Rödl and Wilhelm Gideon served as *kommandants*. SS staff and guards numbered 4,128 on 15 January, 1945. Liberated by Russian Army.

HAMMERSTEIN

Type of Camp: Early concentration camp; one of the "Wild Camps"
Location: Schlochau District of eastern Germany
Opened: 1 August 1933
Closed: 31 March 1935
Victims: Unknown
Remarks: Held 400 - 500 prisoners. Inmates transferred to Dachau on closure.

HERZOGENBUSCH-VUGHT

Type: Concentration camp
Location: Noordbravant, Netherlands
Opened: 5 January 1943
Closed: 5 September 1944
Victims: Unknown
Major Sub-camps: Amersfoort, Arnhem, Breda, Eindhoven, Gilz Rijen, Haaren, Leeuwarden, Moerdijk, Roosendaal, St. Michielsgestel, Valkenburg, Venlo, Zutphen, s'Gravenhage, s'Hertogenbosch
Remarks: Average number of prisoners was 29,000. Hans Hüttig and Adam Grünewald served as *kommandants*.

HEUBERG

Type of Camp: Early concentration camp; one of the "Wild Camps"
Location: Ulm, Baden
Opened: 29 May 1933
Closed: 21 December 1933
Victims: Unknown
Remarks: Held 300 prisoners. Prisoners transferred to Kuhberg when the camp closed. SA officer Kaufmann served as *kommandant*.

HINZERT
Type of Camp: Concentration camp
Location: 18 miles from Trier
Opened: 1 October 1939
Closed: 3 March 1945
Victims: Unknown
Major Sub-camps: Farschweiler, Gelnhausen, Gusterath, Hermeskeil, Konz, Langendiebach, Mainz-Finthen, Nonnweiler, Pluwig, Pölert, Primstal, Reinsfeld, Saarburg, Thalfang, Trier, Wiesbaden, Wittlich, Zeibrücken
Remarks: Hermann Pister, Egon Zill and Paul Sporrenberg served as *kommandants*.

HOHENSTEIN
Type of Camp: Early concentration camp; one of the "Wild Camps"
Location: Saxony
Opened: 29 December 1933
Closed: 15 August 1934
Victims: Unknown
Remarks: SA officers Rudolf Jähnichen and Friedrich served as *kommandants*.

KEMNA
Type of Camp: Early concentration camp; one of the "Wild Camps"
Location: Rhine
Opened: 5 July 1933
Closed: 19 January 1934
Victims: Unknown
Remarks: SA officers Hugo Neuhoff and Alfred Hilgers served as *kommandants*.

KLOOGA
Type of Camp: Concentration camp
Location: Estonia, near Reval
Opened: September 1943
Closed: 19 September 1944
Victims: Unknown
Remarks: Liberated by Russian Army

KOVNO/KAUEN
Type of Camp: Concentration camp
Location: Kovno, Lithuania
Opened: 5 June 1943
Closed: 14 July 1944

Victims: at least 8,000
Remarks: Held up to 14,000 prisoners at one time. Wilhelm Goecke served as *kommandant*.

LICHTENBURG
Type of Camp: Initially one of the "Wild Camps"; remained active for most of the Third Reich
Location: near Torgau
Opened: June 1933
Closed: 9 August 1937; reopened 21 March 1938; 15 May 1939 became sub-camp of Ravensbrück
Victims: Unknown
Remarks: Served as a sorting center for SA prisoners from the Röhm Putsch. All male prisoners sent to Buchenwald on closure of the camp. Bernhard Schmidt, Otto Reich and Hermann Baranowski served as *kommandants*.

MAJDANEK/LUBLIN
Type of Camp: Labor/Extermination
Location: Lublin, Poland
Opened: 8 December 1941
Closed: July 1944
Victims: 120,000 - 200,000
Remarks: Average number of prisoners was 24,000. Began as a prisoner of war camp for captured Poles and Russians. Karl Koch, Hermann Florstedt, Martin Weiss, Arthur Liebehenschel and Max Koegel served as *kommandants*.

MAUTHAUSEN
Type of Camp: Concentration camp
Location: near Linz, Austria
Opened: 8 August 1938
Closed: 5 May 1945
Victims: 71,000 - 120,000
Major Sub-camps: Amstettin, Bretstein, Ebensee, Eisenerz, Enns, Graz, Grein, Grossraming, Gunskirchen, Gusen, Hinterbruehl, Hirtenberg, Jedlesee, Lungitz, St. Georgen, Klagenfurt, Lenzing, Linz, Loibl-Pass, Melk, Neustadt, Passau, Peggau, Perg, St. Aegyd, St. Lambrecht, St. Valentin, Schlier, Schloss Hartheim, Schloss Lind, Schloss Mittersill, Schoenbrunn, Schwechat, Steyr, Ternberg, Vöcklabruck, West-Sauerwerke and Wien
Remarks: In 1939 had 1,500 inmates. Held up to 120,000 prisoners at one time. Site of Nazi medical experiments involving lice infestation, tuberculosis and surgical procedures. Albert Sauer and Franz Ziereis served as *kommandants*. SS camp staff and guards numbered 5,697 on 15 January, 1945.

MORINGEN

Type of Camp: Early concentration camp; one of the "Wild Camps"
Location: near Göttingen
Opened: 16 March 1933
Closed: 29 November 1933
Victims: Unknown
Remarks: Reported to have 800 inmates. One of the initial camps for women. Fritz Flohr served as *kommandant*.

NATZWEILER-STRUTHOF

Type of Camp: Concentration camp
Location: 30 miles southwest of Strasbourg
Opened: 1 May 1941
Closed: September 1944
Victims: at least 17,000
Major Sub-camps: Asbach, Bensheim, Bisingen, Calw, Cochem, Dautmergen, Dormettingen, Echterdingen, Ellwangen, Erzingen, Frankfurt, Frommern, Geisenheim, Geislingen, Hailfingen, Haslach, Heppenheim, Hessental, Iffezheim, Kochendorf, Leonberg, Longwy-Thil, Mannheim, Markirch, Metz, Mühlheim, Pelters, Rastatt, Schömberg, Schörzlingen, Sennheim, Spaichingen, Vaihingen, Unterrexingen, Walldorf, Wasseralfingen and Wesserling.
Remarks: Approximate number of prisoners was 44,000. Site of Nazi medical experiments involving poison gas and typhus. Egon Zill, Fritz Hartjenstein, Hans Hüttig, Heinrich Schwarz and Josef Kramer served as *kommandants*. SS staff and guards numbered 1,644 on 15 January, 1945.

NEUENGAMME

Type of Camp: Concentration camp
Location: Hamburg
Opened: 13 December 1938 as part of Sachsenhausen, became independent 4 June 1940
Closed: 29 April 1945
Victims: 40,000 - 56,000
Major Sub-camps: Ahlen, Alr, Garge, Aurich, Barkhausen, Boizenburg, Braunschweig, Bremen, Druette, Fallersleben, Fuhlsbuettel, Goslar, Hamburg, Hannover, Hausberge, Helmstedt, Hildesheim, Horneburg, Husum, Kaltenkirchen, Ladelund, Langenhagen, Lengerich, Lerbeck, Luebberstedt, Luetjenburg, Meppen-Versen, Misburg, Moelln, Neesen, Obernheide, Porta Westfalica, Salzgitter, Salzwedel, Schandelah, Uelzen, Uphusen, Verden, Waltenstaedt, Wedel, Wilhelmshaven, Wittenberge and Woebbelin.
Remarks: Approximate number of inmates was 36,000. Site of Nazi medical experiments. Martin Weiss and Max Pauly served

as *kommandants*. SS staff and guards numbered 2,452 on 15 January, 1945.

NIEDERHAGEN-WEWELSBURG

Type of Camp: Concentration camp
Location: near Paderborn
Opened: 1 September 1941
Closed: 1 May 1943
Victims: Unknown
Remarks: Became a sub-camp of Buchenwald

OSTHOFEN

Type of Camp: Early concentration camp; one of the "Wild Camps"
Location: Frankfurt
Opened: 15 April 1933
Closed: 3 August 1933
Victims: Unknown
Remarks: Held 345 prisoners. Karl D'Angelo served as *kommandant*.

PAPENBURG

Type of Camp: Concentration camp
Location: Emsland District
Opened: 1934
Closed: 21 April 1945
Victims: Unknown
Major Sub-camps: Aschendorf, Boergermoor, Brual-Rhede, Bathorn, Esterwegen, Lendringsen, Neusustrum, Oberlangen, Strang and Walchum.
Remarks: SA officer Werner Schäfer *kommandant*. Headquarters of a group of camps known as Emsland.

PLASZOW

Type of Camp: Concentration camp
Location: Krakow, Poland
Opened: December 1942
Closed: 15 January 1945
Victims: Unknown, probably thousands
Remarks: Held 25,000 inmates. SS guards numbered 636 on 1 January, 1945. Amon Goeth served as *kommandant*.

RAVENSBRÜCK

Type of Camp: Concentration camp
Location: near Fürstenberg, 56 miles north of Berlin
Opened: 15 May 1939
Closed: 29 April 1945
Victims: at least 92,000
Major Sub-camps: Ansbach, Barth, Belzig, Berlin, Dabelow, Droegen, Eberswalde, Feldberg, Finow, Genthin, Grüneberg, Hagenow, Hohenlychen, Kallies, Karlshagen, Klützow, Königsberg, Malchow, Neubrandenburg, Neustadt, Neustrelitz, Prenzlau, Rechlin, Rostock, Schoenefeld, Stargard and Veltin.
Remarks: Women's camp. In 1939 had 2,500 inmates. Held up to 70,000 prisoners at a time. Site of Nazi medical experiments involving sterilization and treatment of wounds. Max Kögel, Fritz Suhren and Albert Sauer served as *kommandants*. SS staff and guards numbered 1,554 on 15 January, 1945.

RIGA/KAISERWALD/MEZAPARKS

Type of Camp: Concentration camp
Location: Riga, Latvia
Opened: 1942
Closed: 6 August 1944
Victims: Unknown
Remarks: Held up to 15,000 prisoners.

SACHSENBURG

Type of Camp: Early concentration camp; one of the "Wild Camps"
Location: Frankenberg, Saxony
Opened: 3 May 1933
Closed: 9 September 1937
Victims: Unknown
Remarks: Held 40 prisoners in May 1933 and 1,180 prisoners at the end of 1935. SA officer Max Hähnel, Alexander Reiner, Karl Koch and Bernhard Schmidt served as *kommandants*.

SACHSENHAUSEN/ORANIENBURG

Type of Camp: Concentration camp; headquarters for the concentration camp inspectorate
Location: north of Berlin
Opened: August 1936
Closed: 22 April 1945
Victims: 30,000 - 35,000
Major Sub-camps: Bad Saarow, Beerfelde, Belzig, Berlin, Biesenthal, Brandenburg, Briesen, Dammsmuehle, Döberlitz, Droegen, Falkensee, Friedenthal, Fuerstenwalde, Genshagen, Glau-Trebben, Gloewen, Hennigsdorf, Jamlitz, Königs-wusterhausen, Küstrin, Lieberose, Lübben, Niemegk, Potsdam, Prettin, Rathenau, Schwarzheide, Trebnitz, Usedom, Wewelsburg and Wittenberg
Remarks. Oranienburg opened as an SA-run camp in 1933, but was closed in 1934. From 1936, Oranienburg served as the headquarters for the concentration camp inspectorate. Sachsenhausen camp was located very close to Oranienburg and was opened in 1936. In 1939 had 6,500 inmates; in 1942 had 16,577 inmates; in 1943 had 28,224 inmates; and in 1944 had 47,709 inmates. 11,000 Russian POWs murdered there in 1941. Michael Lippert, Hans Hellwig, Karl Koch, Hermann Baranowski, Hans Loritz, Walter Eisfeld, Rudolf Höss and Anton Kaindl served as *kommandants*. SS staff and guards numbered 3,993 on 15 January, 1945.

SOBIBÓR

Type of Camp: Extermination
Location: 42 miles southeast of Warsaw, 3 miles west of Bug River, south of Wlodawa
Opened: April 1942
Closed: October 1943
Victims: 225,000 - 250,000
Remarks: Part of *Operation Reinhard*, the German plan to kill the Jews of the *Generalgouvernement*. Richard Thomalla, Franz Stangl and Franz Reichleitner served as *kommandants*. Between twenty and thirty-five SS men served in the camp at one time. Most of the victims came from Lublin, the Netherlands, Slovakia, France, Minsk and the Reich-Protektorat. The Sobibór Revolt and escape occurred 14 October 1943.

SONNENBURG

Type of Camp: Early concentration camp; one of the "Wild Camps"
Location: near Küstrin, Brandenburg
Opened: April 1933
Closed: 23 April 1934
Victims: Unknown
Remarks: Reported to have 1,200 inmates; previously used as a prison.

STETTIN-BREDOW

Type of Camp: Early concentration camp; one of the "Wild Camps"
Location: Stettin
Opened: 1 October 1933
Closed: 14 March 1934
Victims: Unknown

Remarks: Reported to have 120 inmates. Otto Meier, Karl Salis and Fritz Pleines served as *kommandants*. Previously a factory.

STUTTHOF

Type of Camp: Concentration camp
Location: East of Danzig
Opened: 2 September 1939 as SS civilian prison camp, converted to special SS camp 5 November 1941 and to regular concentration camp 13 January 1942
Closed: 25 January 1945
Victims: 65,000 - 85,000
Major Sub-camps: Adlershorst, Bohnsack, Botschin, Bromberg, Bruss, Burggraben, Chinow, Chorabie, Danzig, Eichwalde, Elbing, Freudendorf, Gartschin, Gerdauen, Goddentow, Gotenhafen, Graudenz, Grenzdorf, Grodno, Guttau, Heiligenbeil, Hopehill, Jesau, Kaesemark, Königsberg, Kolkau, Krumau, Lauenberg, Malken, Matzkau, Merzen, Müggenhahl, Nawitz, Niederfuhr, Poelitz, Praust, Putzig, Quesendorf, Russenschin, Schippembeil, Schirkenpass, Schoenwarling, Seerappen, Stettin, Stolp, Terranowa, Thorn, Tiegenhof, Trutenau, Werderhof and Zeyersniederkampen.
Remarks: Held up to 52,000 prisoners at one time. Max Pauly and Paul Hoppe served as *kommandants*. SS staff and guards numbered 1,056 on 1 January, 1945.

THERESIENSTADT

Type of Camp: Special concentration camp
Location: northwest of Prague
Opened: 24 November 1941
Closed: 7 May 1945
Victims: at least 35,000
Remarks: Nazi propaganda camp for Red Cross inspections. Established for the purpose of receiving transports of Jews evacuated from Germany and other occupied territories. About 140,000 persons were deported to Theresienstadt; 88,000 were subsequently sent to other camps to be killed. Siegfried Seidl, Anton Burger and Karl Rahm served as *kommandants*.

TREBLINKA

Type of Camp: Extermination
Location: 70 miles northeast of Warsaw
Opened: July 1942
Closed: October 1943
Victims: 975,000
Remarks: Part of *Operation Reinhard*, the German plan to kill the Jews of the *Generalgouvernement*. Irmfried Eberl, Franz Stangl and Kurt Franz served as *kommandants*. Between twenty and thirty-five SS men served in the camp at one time. Most of the victims came from Warsaw, Radom, Bialystok, Lublin, Macedonia, Germany and Theresienstadt. Treblinka was a small camp, measuring some 600x400 meters.

ULM-KUHBERG

Type of Camp: Early concentration camp; one of the "Wild Camps"
Location: Ulm
Opened: 1 November 1933
Closed: 31 July 1935
Victims: Unknown
Remarks: A military fort

VIAVARA

Type of Camp: Concentration camp
Location: Viavara, Estonia
Opened: 15 September 1943
Closed: 3 October 1944
Victims: Unknown
Remarks: Hans Aumeier and Helmut Schnabel served as *kommandants*.

WERDEN

Type of Camp: Early concentration camp; one of the "Wild Camps"
Location: Rhine, near Düsseldorf
Opened: 1 June 1933
Closed: 1934
Victims: Unknown
Remarks: Previous detention center

WESTERBORK

Type of Camp: Internment
Location: Northeast Netherlands
Opened: October 1939
Closed: April 1945
Victims: Unknown. The Germans deported 60,000 Jews from Westerbork to Auschwitz, 34,000 to Sobibór, 5,000 to Theresienstadt and 4,000 to Bergen-Belsen.
Remarks: Dutch police helped guard camp

WITTMOOR

Type of Camp: Early concentration camp; one of the "Wild Camps"

Location: near Hamburg

Opened: 10 April 1933

Closed: 17 October 1933

Victims: Unknown

Remarks: Previous factory; prisoners transferred to Fuhlsbuettel when Wittmoor closed.

These then were the major concentration and extermination camps operated by the SS before and during the war. Major camps, sub-camps, and transit camps – not examined in this work, but important cogs in the punishment and extermination machine, none-the-less – all played their role in the political and economic life of the Third Reich. Now that we know the general scope of the camps, the next step is to examine the SS rank structure and the functions of SS officers at these locations to better understand the role these men played in their operations.

Notes:

[1] Richard Breitman, *The Architect of Genocide* (New York: Alfred A. Knopf, 1991), p.4.

[2] Wolfgang Sofsky, *The Order of Terror: The Concentration Camp* Translated by William Templer. (Princeton, NJ: Princeton University Press, 1997), p.13.

[3] Adding to the dread surrounding the concentration camps was the *Nacht-und Nebel Erlass* (the Night and Fog Decree). Hitler issued this order on December 7, 1941 to seize "persons endangering German security", who were not to be executed immediately but rather to vanish without a trace into the night and fog. It is not known how many victims fell as a result of this decree.

[4] The first concentration camps were known as the "Wild Camps", primarily because of their unstructured discipline. They were initially manned and operated by the SA – the brownshirted *Sturmabteilung* (Storm Troops). The Nazis quickly bureaucratized the system under the leadership of Theodor Eicke and standardized the camps; this forced most of the early "Wild Camps" to close by 1937. While the "Wild Camps" account for only a few of the total victims, many SS officers got their training at these early locations.

[5] Office of United States Chief of Counsel For Prosecution of Axis Criminality, *Nazi Conspiracy And Aggression, Volume I* (Washington: United States Government Printing Office, 1946), p.949.

[6] David A. Hackett, ed., *The Buchenwald Report* (Boulder, CO: Westview Press, 1995), p.29.

[7] This does not include the many hundreds of prisoners who were sent to serve in various penal units – the most notorious of which was the Dirlewanger Brigade of the SS.

[8] Breitman, *The Architect of Genocide*, p. 248.

[9] Majdanek/Lublin and Auschwitz were also labor camps as well as destruction.

[10] Martin Weinmann, Anne Kaiser and Ursula Krause-Schmitt, *Das national-sozialistische Lagersystem*. (Frankfurt: Zweitausendeins, 1990), p. 54.

[11] *Kommandants* shown without rank are from the SS and are detailed later in the work. Those *kommandants* shown as police or SA are those men who did not go on to join the SS and therefore are not found again in the book. Additionally, many of the officers listed herein served in the German euthanasia program codenamed *Aktion T4* (due to the street address of the headquarters controlling the operation at *Tiergarten 4*, in Berlin). In October 1939 Hitler ordered that a small group of doctors be commissioned to grant "mercy deaths" to those patients "incurably sick by medical examination." Children appear to have been some of the first victims of this program which was quickly expanded to include those leading "useless lives" in mental hospitals. The program caused the death of 70,273 people, including: 14,072 at Hadamar, 9,839 at Grafeneck, 9,722 at Bernberg, 13,720 at Sonnenstein and 18,269 at Hartheim mental facilities. In 1941 the gassing sites at these locations were used in *Aktion 14f13* – a plan to transport many concentration camp inmates from the camps to mental institutions for gassing. Prisoners were told they were going to a "recovery home" or a "rest home" shortly before being led to their deaths. Source: Michael Burleigh, *Death and Deliverance* (Cambridge, England: Cambridge university Press, 1994), pp.160, 220, and Jeremiah A. Barondess, "Medicine Against Society - Lessons From the Third Reich." *JAMA, The Journal of the American Medical Association* (Chicago, IL: American Medical Association, Vol 276, No.20, November 27, 1996), p.1659.

2

THE SS OFFICERS

We were the best and the toughest.[1]

- The Kommandant of Gross Rosen

SS OFFICER RANKS

Before moving into the officer biographies, we must first examine the overall SS officer rank system used in Heinrich Himmler's huge organization. The SS initially established a rank system in August 1929, and modified the structure on four additional occasions.[2] The officer ranks, from lowest to highest follow in their final form. These ranks belonged to the *Allgemeine-SS* – the general SS, the overall body of the SS, distinct from the Waffen-SS. Officers who also belonged to the *Waffen-SS* – SS field troops – could have a separate rank in that organization. Therefore a colonel in the *Allgemeine-SS*, who volunteered for front-line service in the *Waffen-SS*, might only be a captain in that organization. Not all *Allgemeine-SS* officers were in the *Waffen-SS*.[3]

SS-Untersturmführer – 2nd Lieutenant. The lowest commissioned officer rank in the SS, this position evolved in October 1934 from the original rank called *SS-Sturmführer*. An officer of this rank would command a platoon of approximately thirty men or hold a position of equal responsibility. By July 1935 there were 1,767 officers of this rank.[4] This figure increased to 6,650 by the end of 1938.[5]

SS-Obersturmführer – 1st Lieutenant. This rank was established in May 1933. An officer of this rank could serve as a platoon leader or if necessary a company commander in charge of sev-

enty to one hundred twenty men. As of July 1935 there were 786 *SS-Obersturmführer*; the total increased to 3,449 by 1938.

SS-Hauptsturmführer – Captain. This rank evolved in October 1934 from the position of *SS-Sturmhauptführer*, which had been established in May 1933. This most senior of the company grade ranks would command a *Sturm*, or company, of between seventy and one hundred twenty men.[6] By July 1935 there were 495 officers in this rank. This number more than tripled to 1,855 in 1938.

SS-Sturmbannführer – Major. This was one of the original ranks from 1929 and was the junior field grade rank. He would command a *Sturmbann* (battalion) consisting of three *Sturm*. By July 1935 there were 474 *SS-Sturmbannführer*; by 1938 there were 892.

SS-Obersturmbannführer – Lieutenant Colonel. This rank was instituted in May 1933. An officer of this rank could command a battalion or equivalent level of responsibility. By July 1935 there were 118 officers of this rank in the SS. This total increased to 382 by the end of 1938.

SS-Standartenführer – Colonel. This was one of the original 1929 ranks; this officer would command three or four *Sturmbanne* which made up a *Standarte* or regiment. By July 1935 there were 113 *SS-Standartenführer*; by the end of 1938 there were 307 officers of this rank.

SS-Oberführer – Senior Colonel. This was also one of the original ranks of 1929. This most senior field grade officer would command several *Standarten* which formed an *Untergruppe*. By July 1935 there were 60 officers of this rank. Three years later there were 215.

SS-Brigadeführer – Brigadier General ★. This lowest of the general officer ranks was formed in May 1933; this level officer would command several *Untergruppen* formed into a *Gruppe*. An officer of this rank in the Waffen-SS would be titled *SS-Brigadeführer und Generalmajor der Waffen-SS*.[7] By July 1935 there were 22 *SS-Brigadeführer*. At the end of 1938 there were 49.

SS-Gruppenführer – Major General ★★. This rank was one of the initial positions and its holder would command an *Oberabschnitt* or several *Gruppen*. In the Waffen-SS this rank was *SS-Gruppenführer und Generalleutnant der Waffen-SS*. By July 1935 there were 29 officers of this rank in the SS. This more than doubled to 51 by 1938.

SS-Obergruppenführer – Lieutenant General ★★★. These few individuals served as the corporate heads of the SS. An individual in the Waffen-SS would be titled *SS-Obergruppenführer und General der Waffen-SS*. By July 1935 there were 8 *SS-Obergruppenführer*; three years later there were 17 officers with this rank.

SS-Oberstgruppenführer – General ★★★★ – Colonel General in the German army system of ranks. This rank was introduced in 1942. No officers who ever served in the concentration camps ever achieved this rank.

Reichsführer-SS – Field Marshal ★★★★★. Heinrich Himmler was the exclusive holder of this rank.

Some SS officers who were skilled technicians had temporary specialist rank, known as *Fachman*. Many of the architects in the camp construction departments had a low SS noncommissioned officer rank, for example *SS-Scharführer* (corporal). Because they were, however, employed as architects which demanded a supervisory role, they were given the rank of *SS-Untersturmführer (F)*, which denoted that, for the duration of their appointment as architect, they enjoyed that rank and its salary. If, however, they were transferred to the front, or somewhere else, they would automatically be reduced to their real rank, i.e. *SS-Scharführer*. As a result, these given individuals could, in theory, have three different ranks in the SS: one in the *Allgemeine-SS* (for example *SS-Obersturmführer*), one in the Waffen-SS (for example *SS-Scharführer*), and one

temporary rank in the Waffen-SS as *Fachmann* (*SS-Untersturmführer*).[8]

SS OFFICER POSITIONS

The SS provided relatively few officer positions in each camp considering the size and prisoner population incarcerated in most. Camp administration normally comprised five to seven departments, known as *Abteilungen*. The SS numbered each department with Roman numerals.[9] Officers were found in each department in most, but not all, camps.

The most important SS official in the concentration camp was the *Lagerkommandant* or *kommandant* – the camp commander. The *kommandant* could hold a rank of *SS-Standartenführer* (colonel), *SS-Obersturmbannführer* (lieutenant colonel), *SS-Sturmbannführer* (major) or *SS-Hauptsturmführer* (captain) considering the size and nature of the camp.[10] At the extermination camps of Sobibór and Treblinka there were even instances when an *SS-Obersturmführer* (first lieutenant) and *SS-Untersturmführer* (second lieutenant) held the position of *kommandant*. The *kommandant* had overall responsibility for the camp. *SS-Reichsführer* Heinrich Himmler reportedly interviewed each prospective *kommandant* before his appointment to the position.[11]

The first section (*Abteilung I*) was the Headquarters Department (*Kommandantur*). The deputy camp commandant, or *Adjutant*, oversaw the operation of this segment of the camp. He was responsible for the camp communication, the motor pool and the personnel and legal office. The adjutant normally held the rank of *SS-Hauptsturmführer* or *SS-Obersturmführer*, again depending on the relative size of the camp. The *Kommandantur* laid down the framework for the management of the camp based on the general orders and guidelines sent down by the Central Administration of Concentration Camps.

The second section (*Abteilung II*) served as the Political Department (*Politische Abteilung*), and was an extension of the *Gestapo* (Secret State Police) and *Kripo* (Criminal Police). German personnel in this section conducted registration of prisoners, release of prisoners, documentation of dead prisoners, preparation of prisoner identification, conduct of investigations, surveillance and interrogation of prisoners. Many SS personnel in the camps also believed that this section was also monitoring their own behavior. The chief of the political department could be an *SS-Untersturmführer* or higher. Pure extermination camps did not have this department as their prisoners would not be alive long enough to require these services.[12]

Department III, Camp Administration (*Abteilung III - Schutzhaftlagerführung*) ventured into the area of prisoner affairs/inmate control. Its chief the *Schutzhaftlagerführer* or Camp

Leader, also served as the permanent deputy commandant. The *Schutzhaftelagerführer*, also known as the *Lagerführer*, was generally an *SS-Sturmbannführer* or *SS-Hauptsturmführer*.

In 1942 the SS established an autonomous department *Abteilung IIIa - Arbeitseinsatz*. This new section was in charge of prisoner labor and the formation of labor squads. Positions in this department included Work Recording Officer (*Arbeitsdienstführer*), Work Detail Leader (*Arbeitseinsatzführer*) and Labor Group Supervisor (*Kommandoführer*). These last positions could also be manned by non-commissioned officers.

Department IV, Administration/Economy (*Abteilung IV - Verwaltung*) was a complicated organization responsible for supplies, clothing, laundries and baths, confiscated prisoner property and other prisoner-oriented logistical functions. In larger camps this position, *Verwaltungsführer*, was held by an *SS-Hauptsturmführer* or *SS-Sturmbannführer*.

Camp sanitation was handled by Department V, Camp Physician (*Abteilung V - Standortarzt*). This department could be quite large with numerous doctors, especially if medical experiments were being carried out. Each camp had a chief physician (*Lagerarzt*) plus doctors, doctor's assistants, dentists, pharmacists and medical orderlies. SS doctors in concentration camps were normally *SS-Hauptsturmführer*. In addition to conducting medical duties, these personnel also directed selections of newly arrived prisoners into those who would join the camp work force or those who would go straight to the gas chambers. Medical personnel ironically, also administered the poison gas in the gas chambers.[13] The Health and Hygiene Service Section, another term for this department, did not – as a rule – fall under the authority of the *Lagerführer*.

Department VI, Care and Training of SS Units (*Abteilung VI - Fürsorge, Schulung und Truppenbetreuung*) was responsible for the schooling and cultural life of SS personnel. Some small camps did not have this department; Auschwitz had upwards of 1,800 SS personnel assigned in 1942 and thus had an extensive Department VI.[14]

In 1935, sensing the need for a special branch of the armed SS to perform guard duties in the camps, Himmler charged Theodor Eicke, the Inspector of Concentration Camps and Commander of SS Guard Formations, with forming a guard unit at each camp outside the control of the *Allgemeine-SS*. On March 29, 1936 these units were officially designated as *Totenkopfverbände* (Death's Head Units). There were five of these battalions – with distinct camp affiliation – and were named *Oberbayern* (Dachau), *Elbe* (Lichtenburg), *Sachsen* (Sachsenburg), *Ostfriesland* (Esterwegen) and *Brandenburg* (Columbia Haus, Oranienburg, Sachsenhausen). In 1937 they underwent a reorganization and became *Totenkopfstandarten* (Death's Head Regiments). Originally there were three such units; *Oberbayern* stationed at Dachau, *Thuringia* at Buchenwald and *Brandenburg* at Oranienburg. The SS added more units later and the *Totenkopfstandarten* were given numerical designations.[15] By December 1938 there were 437 officers, 1,571 non-commissioned officers and 6,476 enlisted men in the various *Totenkopf* units.[16] Almost all of the SS officers, assigned to camp duty in the guard force belonged to these units.[17] About seventy-five percent of all SS personnel in a camp were part of the guard forces. The camp guard battalion (*SS-Totenkopfsturmbann*) traditionally had between two to more than a dozen two-hundred man company-size units (*SS-Totenkopfwach-Kompanie*) – again depending on the size of the camp. An *SS-Totenkopfsturmbann* was generally commanded by an *SS-Sturmbannführer* or *SS-Hauptsturmführer*. Before the war, guard troops in the concentration camps were assigned from the various *Totenkopfstandarten*. But as the war progressed many of the men in these units went to the front – especially in the 3rd SS Division "*Totenkopf*" – and SS men unfit for front-line duty, as well as Lithuanians and Ukrainians began to assume guard missions. The overall ratio of camp SS personnel to the SS guard force strength was approximately 1:10.[18]

The following table depicts the various *Totenkopf* units and their commanders during the initial years:[19]

Table 1

SS- TOTENKOPFVERBÄNDE
COMMANDING OFFICERS, 1936[20]

UNIT	COMMANDER
Ist Totenkopfsturmbann *Oberbayern*	Otto-Friedrich Augustini
IInd Totenkopfsturmbann *Elbe*	Erwin Reitz
IIIrd Totenkopfsturmbann *Sachsen*	Max Simon
IVth Totenkopfsturmbann *Ostfriesland*	Otto Reich
Vth Totenkopfsturmbann *Brandenburg*	Michael Lippert

Table 2

SS- TOTENKOPFVERBÄNDE
COMMANDING OFFICERS, 1937[21]

UNIT	COMMANDER
1st Totenkopfstandarte *Oberbayern*	Max Simon
Ist Totenkopfsturmbann	Helmuth Becker
IInd Totenkopfsturmbann	Eduard Deisenhofer
IIIrd Totenkopfsturmbann	Heinrich Scheingraber
2nd Totenkopfstandarte *Brandenburg*	Otto Reich
IVth Totenkopfsturmbann	Marcus Habben
Vth Totenkopfsturmbann	Max Gebhardt
VIth Totenkopfsturmbann	Heinrich Petersen
3rd Totenkopfstandarte *Thüringen*	Paul Nostitz
VIIth Totenkopfsturmbann	Heimo Hierthes

Table 3

SS- TOTENKOPFVERBÄNDE
COMMANDING OFFICERS, 1938[22]

UNIT	COMMANDER
1st Totenkopfstandarte *Oberbayern*	Max Simon
Ist Totenkopfsturmbann	Helmuth Becker
IInd Totenkopfsturmbann	Eduard Deisenhofer
IIIrd Totenkopfsturmbann	Karl Künstler
2nd Totenkopfstandarte *Brandenburg*	Paul Nostitz
Ist Totenkopfsturmbann	Willi Dusenschön
IInd Totenkopfsturmbann	Heinrich Braun
IIIrd Totenkopfsturmbann	Heinrich Petersen
3rd Totenkopfstandarte *Thüringen*	Paul Nostitz
Ist Totenkopfsturmbann	Walther Bellwidt
IInd Totenkopfsturmbann	Kurt Weisse
IIIrd Totenkopfsturmbann	Max Gebhardt
4th Totenkopfstandarte *Ostmarck*	Otto Reich

Other SS agencies operated at concentration camps (but not purely extermination camps). These included Construction Administration (*Bauleitung*), Supply Depots of SS Formations (*SS-Truppen-Wirtschafts-Lager*), the German Mineral and Stone Works (*Deutsche Erd- und Steinwerke GmbH [DEST]*), the German Equipment Works (*Deutsche Ausrüstungswerke [DAW]*), the Union for Textile and Leather Works (*Gesellschaft für Textil- und Lederverwertung GmbH [Texled]*) and the Waffen-SS Institute of Hygiene. Prior to 1942 these organizations were independent of the camp commandants' control; after 1942 they fell under his authority.[23]

The *DEST* operated stone quarries and granite and brick works and were the most notorious prisoner factories in the camp system due to their high mortality rate. The *DEST* operated facilities in and near Flossenbürg, Mauthausen, Gross-Rosen, Natzweiler, Sachsenhausen, Buchenwald, Auschwitz, and Stutthof. The *DAW* specialized in wood and iron manufacture and operated plants near Majdanek/Lublin, Stutthof and Neuengamme. *Texled* operated clothing and textile facilities at Ravensbrück.[24] Not only did these institutions seek to produce goods and make a profit, they also served to eliminate prisoners by simply working them to death.[25]

Both Dachau and Ravensbrück had *SS-Bekleidungslager* (SS Clothing Depot). These institutions used prisoner labor to help make and repair SS uniforms. Dachau additionally featured the *SS-Wirtschaftsbetriebe* (SS Economic Enterprises), which also used prisoner labor.

The Society for Research and Teaching of Ancestral Heritage (*Ahnenerbe Forschungs- und Lehrgemeinschaft*) also paid frequent visits to many concentration camps. The *Ahnenerbe* was an organization devoted to the study of racial doctrine whose purpose was to study early German history in order to prove the value of pure Aryan blood. Administered by the personal staff of Heinrich Himmler, its medical personnel collected forensic specimens of hundreds of non-Aryans at the camps – frequently putting to death those inmates who had "interesting" skeletal features and other valuable physical characteristics – all for the purpose of advancing Nazi racial "science."

SS CAMP STRENGTH

Examining published strength accounts for 1935 to 1938 reveal the increase in SS personnel strength in the camp system. Dachau, the pilot camp, can be seen to be manned to more than double the SS personnel of any other camp. The combined camp and guard personnel strength reported as of December 1935 is as follows:[26]

Dachau 971
Esterwegen 360
Lichtenburg 359
Sachsenburg 473
Columbia Haus 27

In December 1936, Eicke instituted a different reporting system which now positively identified only those SS personnel in the camp staff proper (does not include guard troops). By this date Sachsenhausen entered the scene as the second largest camp in the system.[27]

Dachau 88
Sulza 10
Lichtenburg 34
Sachsenburg 37
Sachsenhausen 70

As of December 1937, in-camp SS personnel strength had grown, and Buchenwald had grown to become the second largest camp:[28]

Dachau 116
Buchenwald 112
Sachsenhausen 109

At the end of 1938, in-camp SS strength again increased. By this date both Sachsenhausen and Buchenwald employed more SS personnel than Dachau.[29]

Dachau 133
Buchenwald 142
Flossenbürg 45
Lichtenburg 19
Mauthausen 66
Sachsenhausen 172

Not all SS concentration camp personnel proved suitable to the task. In 1937, eighty-one men of the SS Death's Head formations applied for and received discharges from the organization, while the SS chain of command discharged sixty-five others for ideological, medical or other official reasons.[30]

OFFICER BIOGRAPHIES

The following pages detail the more important personal and career information of each SS officer who actually worked in the concentration camps. To help standardize the information, and to assist in evaluation of this data which will be accomplished in Chapter 3, the following data-field explanations are provided:

Last Name – self explanatory. This does not account for any officer who may have changed his last name after the war. One SS officer changed his name during the war and is so noted.

First Name – self explanatory.

Date of Birth – self explanatory. The final authority for this information came from the National Archives microfilm collection of the Berlin Document Center collection of SS officer personnel files.

Place of Birth – for officers born inside Germany, the town or city is listed. For those born outside of Germany, the country is included as well. A few of the very small towns could actually have been in Austria but were not so annotated in the file.

Highest SS Rank – denotes the highest rank an officer achieved in the *Allgemeine-SS*. The SS personnel files reliably kept this information only through February/March 1945 (because of the deteriorating military situation), so it is possible an officer could have received a further promotion after this date; there are no SS rank lists (*Dienstaltersliste*) for 1945. This category lists the highest rank achieved; if an officer was subsequently demoted due to a disciplinary infraction, that fact is annotated later in the record under *Notes*. In some instances an officer listed served at a camp as a non-commissioned officer and was later promoted to the officer ranks.

SS Number – denotes the number each SS man received upon entering the organization. The lower the number, the earlier the individual entered the SS. There are a handful of instances where an officer did not have an SS number listed in his file; no two SS personnel had the same number.

NSDAP Number – denotes the number each new member received on joining the National Socialist Workers Party of Germany [*NSDAP*] (the Nazi Party). Again, the smaller the number, the earlier the individual joined. Many SS officers strangely enough, never joined the Nazi Party.

Marital Status – found in the personnel records. If an officer had been divorced and then remarried, he is listed as "Married." Obviously, any change in marital status after the war is not reflected here.

Religion – found in the personnel records. A more detailed explanation of the categories is in Chapter 3.

Camp Service – lists the concentration/extermination camps, and often the years, in which the officer served. The vast majority of this information comes from the personnel records; about ten percent of the information is drawn from other sources. In some instances, service at a camp is missing from the personnel record when in fact we are sure an officer was present due to testimony at post-war judicial proceedings, etc.

Waffen-SS Service – lists the various Waffen-SS divisions, corps and other combat units the individuals served in, either before or after their tour of duty in the concentration camps.

Highest Decoration – this category lists the highest decoration received by each officer during the war. The award does not always specify service at a camp; often the awards were presented for duty in later assignments not connected with the concentration camp system. In Chapter 3 the various types and grades of each award will be discussed in full detail.

Notes – a catch-all category that includes information on the type of position an officer held at a camp, World War I service, occupation, facets of World War II combat service, post-war legal proceedings against the officer and ultimate fate.

National Archives Microfilm Reel – gives the reel number from the set of records known as Microfilm Publication A3343, *Records of SS Officers from the Berlin Document Center,* Series SSO – Officer Personnel Records. These SS officers' service records consist of the personnel dossiers for more than 61,000 SS officers with the rank of second lieutenant and above. The date span of the records contained in the dossiers extends from 1932 to as late as March 1945 in some cases. In those instances where no personnel file exists on microfilm (either the file was destroyed in the war or for some reason was never microfilmed) I have referred to Microfilm Publication A3343, *Records of SS Officers from the Berlin Document Center,* Series RS – SS Race and Settlement Office (*RuSHA, Rasse-und Siedlungshauptamt*). This office had the responsibility of safeguarding the racial purity of the SS – by serving as an oversight board for prospective marriages. The collection has 240,000 dossiers for individual SS personnel and their prospective spouses, who submitted detailed personal and family background information in order to receive permission to marry.

The officer biographies that begin on page 28 are arranged alphabetically.

Notes:

[1] Tom Segev, *Soldiers of Evil* (New York: McGraw-Hill Book Company, 1987), p. 63.

[2] All rank histories come from John Angolia, *Cloth Insignia of the SS* (San Jose, CA: R. James Bender Publishing, 1983), p.21.

[3] The SS Main Office (*SS-Hauptamt* or *SS-HA*) controlled the entire SS establishment to include the Waffen-SS and the *Allgemeine* or General SS. This office evolved in the mid-1930s and controlled such functions as personnel, administration, medical, physical training, education, communications and so forth. As the *SS-HA* controlled all branches of the SS, it grew in both complexity and size. In 1942 it was scaled back somewhat as more and more of the SS became centered around the Waffen-SS. The SS Main Operational Office (*SS-Führungshauptamt* or *SS-FHA*) was essentially the headquarters of the Waffen-SS. Created in August 1940, it was designed to control the organization of field units of the SS and to monitor the training and replacement units of the Waffen-SS. It additionally looked after training schools of the Waffen-SS. The *SS-FHA* had two subordinate branches, the *Kommandoamt Allgemeine-SS*, which dealt with the general SS, and the *Kommandoamt der Waffen-SS*. The *SS-FHA* was independent of the SS Main Office.

[4] All 1935 rank totals come from the *Dienstaltersliste der Schutzstaffel der N.S.D.A.P., Stand vom 1. Juli 1935* (Berlin: Personalkanzlei des Reichsführers-SS, 1935).

[5] All 1938 rank totals come from the *Dienstaltersliste der Schutzstaffel der N.S.D.A.P., Stand vom 1. December 1938.* Berlin: Personalkanzlei des Reichsführers-SS, 1939.

[6] All SS unit descriptions come from Heinz Höhne, *The Order of the Death's Head* Translated by Richard Barry. (New York: Coward-McCann, 1970), p. 58.

[7] In 1940 *Reichsführer-SS* Heinrich Himmler instituted combined titles through the equivalent Army general officer ranks in an effort to further assimilate the Waffen-SS with its Army comrades in arms, and give senior Waffen-SS officers some interservice credibility.

[8] Discussion with Dr. Robert Jan van Pelt, co-author of *Auschwitz: 1270 to the Present*, January 1997.

[9] Israel Gutman and Michael Berenbaum, eds., *Anatomy of the Auschwitz Death Camp* (Bloomington, IN: Indiana University Press in association with the United States Holocaust Memorial Museum, 1994), p.272.

[10] A complete listing of SS ranks and their equivalents is found in Appendix 1.

[11] Segev, *Soldiers of Evil*, p. 23.

[12] Majdanek/Lublin and Auschwitz/Birkenau were classified as combined Labor/Extermination camps.

[13] Either carbon monoxide exhaust gases from a operating engine or Zyklon-B pellets.

[14] Raul Hilberg, *The Destruction of the European Jews* (New York: Holmes & Meier, 1985), p.902.

[15] Höhne, *The Order of the Death's Head,* pp. 454-457.

[16] *Statistisches Jahrbuch der Schutzstaffel der NSDAP 1938* (Berlin, 1939). There had been 216 officers, 976 non-commissioned officers and 3,641 enlisted at the end of 1937.

[17] But not every member of a *Totenkopfstandarten* was assigned to work at a concentration camp as the personnel records so indicate.

[18] Eberhard Kolb, *Bergen Belsen* (Hannover, FRG: Verlag für Literatur und Zeitgeshen, 1962), p.78. Some sources state that several thousand German Army troops helped guard some concentration camps at different periods during the war. During the entire preparation period for this book, the author found no substantiating documents reflecting this claim.

[19] Sources: *Dienstaltersliste der Schutzstaffel der N.S.D.A.P., Stand vom 1. December 1936* (Berlin: Personalkanzlei des Reichsführers-SS, 1937); *Dienstaltersliste der Schutzstaffel der N.S.D.A.P., Stand vom 1. December 1937* (Berlin: Personalkanzlei des Reichsführers-SS, 1938); and *Dienstaltersliste der Schutzstaffel der N.S.D.A.P., Stand vom 1. December 1938* (Berlin: Personalkanzlei des Reichsführers-SS, 1939).

[20] As of 1 December 1936. The SS designated battalion-size elements with Roman numerals. They used arabic numbers for companies, regiments and divisions.

[21] As of 1 December 1937.

[22] As of 1 December 1938.

[23] Wolfgang Sofsky, *The Order of Terror: The Concentration Camp* Translated by William Templer. (Princeton, NJ: Princeton University Press, 1997), pp.176-177.

[24] Ibid.

[25] The Germans referred to this concept as "extermination by work" (*Vernichtung durch Arbeit*).

[26] *Statistisches Jahrbuch der Schutzstaffel der NSDAP 1937* (Berlin, 1938).

[27] Ibid.

[28] Ibid.

[29] *Statistisches Jahrbuch der Schutzstaffel der NSDAP 1938* (Berlin, 1939).

[30] Helmut Krausnick, Hans Buchheim, Martin Broszat and Hans-Adolf Jacobsen, *Anatomy of the SS State*. (New York: Walker and Company, 1968), p.446.

Abraham

First Name:	Dr. Karl	*National Archive File:*	A3343 SSO-001
Birthdate:	2 August 1908	*Birthplace:*	Untergeis
Rank:	SS-Hauptsturmführer	*SS Number:*	167177
NSDAP Number:	Not a member	*Highest Decoration:*	None listed
Religion:	Protestant	*Marital Status:*	Married
Waffen-SS:	No		
Notes:	Dentist		

Camp Service: **Mauthausen, 1940-1941**
Sachsenhausen, 1941-1943
Stutthof, 1943-1944
Flossenbürg, 1944

Adam

First Name:	Dr. Otto	*National Archive File:*	A3343 SSO-002
Birthdate:	28 August 1903	*Birthplace:*	Schumburg, Bohemia
Rank:	SS-Hauptsturmführer	*SS Number:*	347121
NSDAP Number:	Not a member	*Highest Decoration:*	Iron Cross 2nd Class
Religion:	Unknown	*Marital Status:*	Single
Waffen-SS:	SS Infantry Regiment 8, 1941		
	11th SS Division "Nordland", 1943-1944		
Notes:	Doctor		
	Served in SA 1938; acquitted in 1962		

Camp Service: **Sachsenhausen, 1944**   **Dachau, 1944**
Flossenbürg, 1945

Adolph

First Name:	Dr. Benno	*National Archive File:*	A3343 SSO-003
Birthdate:	17 March 1912	*Birthplace:*	Reit im Winkel
Rank:	SS-Hauptsturmführer	*SS Number:*	340774
NSDAP Number:	4411361	*Highest Decoration:*	None listed
Religion:	Agnostic	*Marital Status:*	Married
Waffen-SS:	No		
Notes:	Camp service not listed in personnel file		

Camp Service: **Mauthausen**

Ahlemann

First Name:	Georg	*National Archive File:*	A3343 SSO-003
Birthdate:	15 January 1911	*Birthplace:*	Havelberg
Rank:	SS-Sturmbannführer	*SS Number:*	50686
NSDAP Number:	124829	*Highest Decoration:*	War Service Cross 1st Class
Religion:	Protestant	*Marital Status:*	Married
Waffen-SS:	6th SS Division "Nord", 1941-1942		
	Estonian Legion, 1943-1944		
Notes:	Guard troops at Dachau		
	Wounded in action		

Camp Service: **Dachau, 1937-1938**

Albert

First Name:	Kurt-Oskar	*National Archive File:*	A3343 RS-A040
Birthdate:	9 September 1908	*Birthplace:*	Doermoschel
Rank:	SS-Obersturmführer	*SS Number:*	9230
NSDAP Number:	374739	*Highest Decoration:*	None listed
Religion:	Unknown	*Marital Status:*	Married
Waffen-SS:	Unknown		
Notes:	Adjutant at Dachau		
	Adjutant, 2nd SS Totenkopfstandarte "Brandenburg", 1939		

Camp Service: **Lichtenburg, 1935**
Dachau, 1935-1938
Oranienburg, 1939
Buchenwald, 1940

Albert

First Name:	Roland	*National Archive File:*	A3343 SSO-005
Birthdate:	21 April 1916	*Birthplace:*	Schussburg, Romania
Rank:	SS-Obersturmführer	*SS Number:*	467018
NSDAP Number:	Not a member	*Highest Decoration:*	War Service Cross 1st Class
Religion:	Protestant	*Marital Status:*	Married
Waffen-SS:	No		
Notes:	Served in Romanian Army 1939-1940		
	Wounded in action		

Camp Service: **Auschwitz, 1943**

Albrecht

First Name:	Heinrich	*National Archive File:*	A3343 SSO-006
Birthdate:	2 February 1911	*Birthplace:*	Gelsenkirchen
Rank:	SS-Sturmbannführer	*SS Number:*	11458
NSDAP Number:	593624	*Highest Decoration:*	War Service Cross 2nd Class
Religion:	Agnostic	*Marital Status:*	Married
Waffen-SS:	3rd SS Division "Totenkopf", 1940		
	23rd SS Division "Kama", 1944		
	31st SS Division, 1944		
Notes:	Company commander in Waffen-SS		

Camp Service: **Oranienburg, 1938-1940**

Altfuldisch

First Name:	Johann	*National Archive File:*	A3343 SSO-010
Birthdate:	11 November 1911	*Birthplace:*	Brueckenau
Rank:	SS-Obersturmführer	*SS Number:*	14958
NSDAP Number:	397051	*Highest Decoration:*	War Service Cross 2nd Class
Religion:	Protestant	*Marital Status:*	Married
Waffen-SS:	No		
Notes:	Executed 28 May 1947		

Camp Service: **Mauthausen, 1941-1944**

Amerongen

First Name:	Albert	*National Archive File:*	A3343 SSO-013
Birthdate:	8 August 1911	*Birthplace:*	Dorsten
Rank:	SS-Hauptsturmführer	*SS Number:*	82212
NSDAP Number:	2463600	*Highest Decoration:*	War Service Cross 2nd Class
Religion:	Agnostic	*Marital Status:*	Married
Waffen-SS:	3rd SS Division "Totenkopf", 1939-1940		
Notes:	2nd SS Totenkopfstandarte "Brandenburg"		

Camp Service: **Oranienburg, 1938-1939**

Ammer

First Name:	Dr. Berthold	*National Archive File:*	A3343 SSO-013
Birthdate:	20 March 1907	*Birthplace:*	Eupen, Belgium
Rank:	SS-Obersturmführer	*SS Number:*	308264
NSDAP Number:	4387929	*Highest Decoration:*	None listed
Religion:	Unknown	*Marital Status:*	Single
Waffen-SS:	No		
Notes:	Medical staff		

Camp Service: **Oranienburg, 1938**

Andorfer

First Name:	Herbert	*National Archive File:*	A3343 SSO-014
Birthdate:	3 March 1911	*Birthplace:*	Linz, Austria
Rank:	SS-Obersturmführer	*SS Number:*	309600
NSDAP Number:	610869	*Highest Decoration:*	Iron Cross 2nd Class
Religion:	Agnostic	*Marital Status:*	Married
Waffen-SS:	No		
Notes:	*Kommandant* of Sajmiste		
	Sentenced to 2 1/2 years but released		

Camp Service: **Sajmiste, 1942**

Andresen

First Name:	Otto	*National Archive File:*	A3343 SSO-014
Birthdate:	3 October 1890	*Birthplace:*	Huexmark
Rank:	SS-Sturmbannführer	*SS Number:*	18865
NSDAP Number:	268791	*Highest Decoration:*	None listed
Religion:	Agnostic	*Marital Status:*	Married
Waffen-SS:	2nd SS Division "Das Reich", 1943		
Notes:	Iron Cross 1st Class and Wound Badge WWI		
	Reduced in rank to private, 1942		

Camp Service: **Sachsenhausen, 1941**

Arnold

First Name:	Alfred	*National Archive File:*	A3343 SSO-018
Birthdate:	2 January 1915	*Birthplace:*	Buehlhof/Kunzelsau
Rank:	SS-Sturmbannführer	*SS Number:*	263781
NSDAP Number:	Not a member	*Highest Decoration:*	German Cross in Gold
Religion:	Unknown	*Marital Status:*	Single
Waffen-SS:	SS Infantry Regiment 9, 1940-1943		
	3rd SS Division "Totenkopf", 1943		
	SS Panzer Brigade "Gross", 1944		
Notes:	SS Totenkopfstandarte "Brandenburg" and "Ostfriesland"		
	Killed in action 10 October 1944		

Camp Service: **Oranienburg, 1937**

Arold

First Name:	August	*National Archive File:*	A3343 SSO-018
Birthdate:	4 April 1883	*Birthplace:*	Aschaffenburg
Rank:	SS-Hauptsturmführer	*SS Number:*	74999
NSDAP Number:	3067842	*Highest Decoration:*	None listed
Religion:	Protestant	*Marital Status:*	Married
Waffen-SS:	No		
Notes:	Iron Cross 2nd Class WWI		

Camp Service: **Oranienburg, 1941**

Augustini

First Name:	Otto-Friedrich	*National Archive File:*	A3343 SSO-020
Birthdate:	14 May 1891	*Birthplace:*	Minden
Rank:	SS-Standartenführer	*SS Number:*	49626
NSDAP Number:	266129	*Highest Decoration:*	None
Religion:	Protestant	*Marital Status:*	Married
Waffen-SS:	No		
Notes:	Commander Ist Totenkopfsturmbann, 1st Totenkopfstandarte		
	Released from SS in 1937; Iron Cross 1st Class, Wound Badge WWI		

Camp Service: **Dachau, 1936**

Aumeier

First Name:	Hans	*National Archive File:*	A3343 SSO-021
Birthdate:	20 August 1906	*Birthplace:*	Amberg
Rank:	SS-Sturmbannführer	*SS Number:*	2700
NSDAP Number:	164755	*Highest Decoration:*	War Service Cross 1st Class
Religion:	Catholic	*Marital Status:*	Married
Waffen-SS:	No		
Notes:	Lagerführer at Auschwitz; executed 1948		

Camp Service: **Dachau, 1934-1937, 1944-1945   Buchenwald**
Lichtenburg, 1937   Flossenbürg, 1938-1942
Auschwitz, 1942-1943   Vaivara, 1943-1944

Baader

First Name:	Dr. Fritz	*National Archive File:*	A3343 SSO-023
Birthdate:	9 April 1909	*Birthplace:*	Munich
Rank:	SS-Obersturmbannführer	*SS Number:*	278278
NSDAP Number:	3687942	*Highest Decoration:*	War Service Cross 1st Class
Religion:	Protestant	*Marital Status:*	Married
Waffen-SS:	8th SS Division "Florian Geyer", 1941-1942		
Notes:	Doctor		
	Regimental surgeon in 1st SS Cavalry Regiment		

Camp Service: **Sachsenburg, 1936-1937**
Flossenbürg, 1938-1939

Babor

First Name:	Dr. Karl	*National Archive File:*	A3343 SSO-023
Birthdate:	23 August 1918	*Birthplace:*	Vienna, Austria
Rank:	SS-Hauptsturmführer	*SS Number:*	296670
NSDAP Number:	6242838	*Highest Decoration:*	Iron Cross 1st Class
Religion:	Catholic	*Marital Status:*	Married
Waffen-SS:	2nd SS Division "Das Reich", 1940		
	3rd SS Division "Totenkopf", 1943		
Notes:	Camp doctor; wounded in action		
	Graduated from University of Vienna, 1948; committed suicide in Ethiopia.		

Camp Service: **Gross-Rosen, 1942**　　　　**Dachau, 1942-1943**

Bachmayer

First Name:	Georg	*National Archive File:*	A3343 SSO-025
Birthdate:	12 May 1913	*Birthplace:*	Friedolfing
Rank:	SS-Hauptsturmführer	*SS Number:*	69535
NSDAP Number:	3204530	*Highest Decoration:*	War Service Cross 2nd Class
Religion:	Catholic	*Marital Status:*	Married
Waffen-SS:	No		
Notes:	Lagerführer at Ebensee sub-camp		

Camp Service: **Mauthausen, 1939-1945**

Bachmeier

First Name:	Josef	*National Archive File:*	A3343 SSO-025
Birthdate:	27 October 1908	*Birthplace:*	Dingolfing
Rank:	SS-Hauptsturmführer	*SS Number:*	96239
NSDAP Number:	Not a member	*Highest Decoration:*	Knight's Cross
Religion:	Agnostic	*Marital Status:*	Single
Waffen-SS:	6th SS Division "Nord", 1942-1943		
	11th SS Division "Nordland", 1944		
Notes:	Wounded in action		
	Panzergrenadier battalion commander in 11th SS Division		

Camp Service: **Esterwegen, 1936**　　　　**Oranienburg, 1937**

Back

First Name:	Heinz	*National Archive File:*	A3343 SSO-025
Birthdate:	19 September 1910	*Birthplace:*	Nürnberg
Rank:	SS-Obersturmführer	*SS Number:*	128035
NSDAP Number:	5020630	*Highest Decoration:*	War Service Cross 2nd Class
Religion:	Protestant	*Marital Status:*	Married
Waffen-SS:	3rd SS Division "Totenkopf", 1941-1944		
Notes:	Former salesman		

Camp Service: **Dachau, 1940**

Baer

First Name:	Richard	*National Archive File:*	A3343 SSO-027
Birthdate:	9 September 1911	*Birthplace:*	Floss
Rank:	SS-Sturmbannführer	*SS Number:*	44225
NSDAP Number:	454991	*Highest Decoration:*	Iron Cross 1st Class
Religion:	Protestant	*Marital Status:*	Married
Waffen-SS:	3rd SS Division "Totenkopf", 1940-1942		
Notes:	*Kommandant* at Auschwitz and Dora; Adjutant at Neuengamme		
	Died 17 June 1963		

Camp Service: **Dachau, 1933-1939**   **Columbia Haus, 1934**
Neuengamme, 1942-1943   **Auschwitz, 1944-1945**
Dora, 1945

Baier

First Name:	Lorenz	*National Archive File:*	A3343 SSO-030
Birthdate:	21 December 1911	*Birthplace:*	Munich
Rank:	SS-Sturmbannführer	*SS Number:*	53093
NSDAP Number:	152010	*Highest Decoration:*	Iron Cross 1st Class
Religion:	Agnostic	*Marital Status:*	Single
Waffen-SS:	6th SS Division "Nord", 1942-1943		
	17th SS Division "Götz von Berlichingen", 1943-1944		
	18th SS Division "Horst Wessel", 1944		
Notes:	Guard troops at Sachsenburg; Tank battalion commander in 18th SS Division		

Camp Service: **Sachsenburg, 1935-1936**

Baranowski

First Name:	Hermann	*National Archive File:*	A3343 SSO-032
Birthdate:	11 June 1884	*Birthplace:*	Schwerin
Rank:	SS-Standartenführer	*SS Number:*	24009
NSDAP Number:	345321	*Highest Decoration:*	None listed
Religion:	Protestant	*Marital Status:*	Married
Waffen-SS:	No		
Notes:	Iron Cross 1st Class WWI; *Kommandant* Lichtenburg, Sachsenhausen		
	Died 5 February 1940		

Camp Service: **Lichtenburg, 1936**   **Dachau, 1936-1938**
Sachsenhausen, 1938-1940

Barnewald

First Name: Otto
Birthdate: 10 January 1896
Rank: SS-Sturmbannführer
NSDAP Number: 149640
Religion: Agnostic
Waffen-SS: No
National Archive File: A3343 SSO-033
Birthplace: Leipzig
SS Number: 6469
Highest Decoration: War Service Cross 1st Class
Marital Status: Married
Notes: Administration leader at Neuengamme; Iron Cross 2nd Class and Wound Badge WWI; Sentenced to Death; released 1957

Camp Service: **Mauthausen, 1938-1940   Neuengamme, 1940-1942**
Buchenwald, 1942-1944

Bartenschlager

First Name: Georg
Birthdate: 30 July 1912
Rank: SS-Hauptsturmführer
NSDAP Number: 4340372
Religion: Catholic
Waffen-SS: 6th SS Division "Nord", 1942-1944
National Archive File: A3343 SSO-034
Birthplace: Lindau
SS Number: 77325
Highest Decoration: War Service Cross 1st Class
Marital Status: Married
Notes: Served in Hitler Youth 1931-1933
Spoke English, French and Spanish

Camp Service: **Sachsenhausen, 1938-1940**
Oranienburg, 1941-1942

Bauer

First Name: Rudolf
Birthdate: 14 October 1915
Rank: SS-Untersturmführer
NSDAP Number: Not a member
Religion: Agnostic
Waffen-SS: 3rd SS Division "Totenkopf", 1939-1940
National Archive File: A3343 SSO-041
Birthplace: Grossroehrsdorf
SS Number: 192858
Highest Decoration: None listed
Marital Status: Single
Notes: 3rd SS Totenkopfstandarte "Thüringen"
Killed in action, 24 May 1940 in France

Camp Service: **Buchenwald, 1938-1939**

Baumann

First Name: Richard
Birthdate: 26 December 1913
Rank: SS-Obersturmführer
NSDAP Number: 2530980
Religion: Agnostic
Waffen-SS: 3rd SS Division "Totenkopf", 1941-1942
National Archive File: A3343 SSO-043
Birthplace: Regensburg
SS Number: 71705
Highest Decoration: None listed
Marital Status: Married
Notes: Guard troops at all camps
Killed in action 28 February 1942

Camp Service: **Dachau, 1935**
Sachsenburg, 1935-1936
Lichtenburg, 1937

Baumgart

First Name:	Hans	*National Archive File:*	A3343 SSO-044
Birthdate:	23 April 1905	*Birthplace:*	Freiburg
Rank:	SS-Obersturmführer	*SS Number:*	143890
NSDAP Number:	2261314	*Highest Decoration:*	War Service Cross 2nd Class
Religion:	Catholic	*Marital Status:*	Married
Waffen-SS:	No		
Notes:	Former teacher; Amt D at Oranienburg		

Camp Service: **Oranienburg, 1944**
Dachau, 1944-1945

Baumgartner

First Name:	Ludwig	*National Archive File:*	A3343 SSO-044
Birthdate:	8 November 1909	*Birthplace:*	Nersingen
Rank:	SS-Obersturmführer	*SS Number:*	257276
NSDAP Number:	1497067	*Highest Decoration:*	None listed
Religion:	Catholic	*Marital Status:*	Married
Waffen-SS:	No		
Notes:	Adjutant at Flossenbürg		

Camp Service: **Dachau, 1933**   **Sachsenhausen, 1940**
Flossenbürg, 1940, 1941, 1943, 1944
Auschwitz, 1943

Baumkoether

First Name:	Dr. Heinz	*National Archive File:*	A3343 SSO-044
Birthdate:	7 February 1912	*Birthplace:*	Bergsteinfurt
Rank:	SS-Hauptsturmführer	*SS Number:*	278430
NSDAP Number:	Not a member	*Highest Decoration:*	Iron Cross 2nd Class
Religion:	Catholic	*Marital Status:*	Single
Waffen-SS:	2nd SS Division "Das Reich", 1940-1941		
Notes:	Doctor; sentenced to 8 years – remitted due to POW time in Russia		

Camp Service: **Sachsenhausen, 1942-1945**
Mauthausen, 1941
Natzweiler, 1942

Bause

First Name:	Dr. Karl-Josef	*National Archive File:*	A3343 SSO-045
Birthdate:	6 May 1909	*Birthplace:*	Bacholt
Rank:	SS-Obersturmführer	*SS Number:*	276835
NSDAP Number:	728784	*Highest Decoration:*	None listed
Religion:	Agnostic	*Marital Status:*	Married
Waffen-SS:	No		
Notes:	Possibly at Dachau in 1936-1937		

Camp Service: **Oranienburg, 1938-1939**

Beck

First Name:	Johann	*National Archive File:*	A3343 SSO-047
Birthdate:	22 July 1888	*Birthplace:*	Nürnberg
Rank:	SS-Oberführer	*SS Number:*	179
NSDAP Number:	6911	*Highest Decoration:*	War Service Cross 2nd Class
Religion:	Protestant	*Marital Status:*	Married
Waffen-SS:	No		
Notes:	Iron Cross 2nd Class WWI; Golden Party Badge		

Camp Service: **Sachsenhausen 1940, 1944**
Mauthausen, 1942-1944

Becker

First Name:	Helmuth	*National Archive File:*	A3343 SSO-050
Birthdate:	12 August 1902	*Birthplace:*	Alt-Ruppen
Rank:	SS-Brigadeführer	*SS Number:*	113174
NSDAP Number:	1592593	*Highest Decoration:*	Knight's Cross with Oak Leaves
Religion:	Protestant	*Marital Status:*	Married
Waffen-SS:	3rd SS Division "Totenkopf", 1940-1944		
	16th SS Division "Reichsführer-SS", 1944		
Notes:	Commander 3rd SS Division 1944; died in Soviet POW camp, 28 February 1952		

Camp Service: **Dachau, 1935-1937**

Becker

First Name:	Josef	*National Archive File:*	A3343 SSO-050
Birthdate:	16 August 1884	*Birthplace:*	Feudenheim
Rank:	SS-Hauptsturmführer	*SS Number:*	105804
NSDAP Number:	837549	*Highest Decoration:*	None listed
Religion:	Catholic	*Marital Status:*	Married
Waffen-SS:	No		
Notes:	Iron Cross 2nd Class, Wound Badge WWI; sentenced to Death		

Camp Service: **Dachau, 1942**
Flossenbürg

Becker

First Name:	Dr. Karl	*National Archive File:*	A3343 SSO-050
Birthdate:	5 September 1909	*Birthplace:*	Braunschweig
Rank:	SS-Hauptsturmführer	*SS Number:*	309497
NSDAP Number:	Not a member	*Highest Decoration:*	Iron Cross 1st Class
Religion:	Agnostic	*Marital Status:*	Married
Waffen-SS:	3rd SS Division "Totenkopf", 1940-1942		
	6th SS Division "Nord", 1942-1943		
	13th, 23rd SS Divisions, 1944		
Notes:	Camp doctor		

Camp Service: **Dachau, 1937**   **Buchenwald, 1938**
Mauthausen, 1939

Beer

First Name:	Rudolf	*National Archive File:*	A3343 SSO-051
Birthdate:	17 February 1911	*Birthplace:*	Friedland
Rank:	SS-Obersturmführer	*SS Number:*	322278
NSDAP Number:	6574195	*Highest Decoration:*	None listed
Religion:	Catholic	*Marital Status:*	Married
Waffen-SS:	5th SS Division "Wiking", 1944		
Notes:	Schutzhaftlagerführer Ravensbrück; sentenced to 15 years		

Camp Service: **Dachau, 1940-1941**
Auschwitz, 1941
Ravensbrück, 1941-1944

Beger

First Name:	Dr. Bruno	*National Archive File:*	A3343 SSO-052
Birthdate:	27 April 1911	*Birthplace:*	Frankfurt
Rank:	SS-Hauptsturmführer	*SS Number:*	263712
NSDAP Number:	Not a member	*Highest Decoration:*	War Service Cross 2nd Class
Religion:	Agnostic	*Marital Status:*	Married
Waffen-SS:	No		
Notes:	Ahnenerbe – took part in collection of skeletons		

Camp Service: **Auschwitz, 1943**

Behrndt

First Name:	Harry	*National Archive File:*	A3343 SSO-053
Birthdate:	12 February 1909	*Birthplace:*	Rummelsburg
Rank:	SS-Sturmbannführer	*SS Number:*	174497
NSDAP Number:	Not a member	*Highest Decoration:*	None listed
Religion:	Unknown	*Marital Status:*	Single
Waffen-SS:	15th SS Division, 1943		
Notes:	Pharmacist at Dachau		

Camp Service: **Dachau, 1941**
Sachsenhausen, 1942-1943

Beilhack

First Name:	Armin	*National Archive File:*	A3343 SSO-054
Birthdate:	22 December 1908	*Birthplace:*	Munich
Rank:	SS-Sturmbannführer	*SS Number:*	275452
NSDAP Number:	Not a member	*Highest Decoration:*	Iron Cross 2nd Class
Religion:	Agnostic	*Marital Status:*	Divorced
Waffen-SS:	No		
Notes:	Died of wounds 22 August 1943 from partisan mine explosion		

Camp Service: **Oranienburg, 1937-1940**

Bellwidt

First Name: Walter   *National Archive File:* A3343 SSO-055
Birthdate: 5 May 1900   *Birthplace:* Frankfurt
Rank: SS-Obersturmbannführer   *SS Number:* 15770
NSDAP Number: 271609   *Highest Decoration:* War Service Cross 1st Class
Religion: Protestant   *Marital Status:* Married
Waffen-SS: 3rd SS Division "Totenkopf", 1939-1940
Notes: Commander Ist Totenkopfsturmbann, 3rd Totenkopfstandarte

Camp Service: **Buchenwald, 1938-1939**

Bender

First Name: Dr. August   *National Archive File:* A3343 SSO-055
Birthdate: 2 March 1909   *Birthplace:* Dueren-Kreuzau
Rank: SS-Sturmbannführer   *SS Number:* 194671
NSDAP Number: 2087161   *Highest Decoration:* Iron Cross 2nd Class
Religion: Catholic   *Marital Status:* Married
Waffen-SS: 3rd SS Division "Totenkopf", 1940
Notes: Camp doctor

Camp Service: **Buchenwald, 1938, 1944**

Benedict

First Name: Hugo   *National Archive File:* A3343 SSO-056
Birthdate: 10 January 1898   *Birthplace:* Hamburg
Rank: SS-Obersturmführer   *SS Number:* 174559
NSDAP Number: 1499548   *Highest Decoration:* None listed
Religion: Protestant   *Marital Status:* Single
Waffen-SS: No
Notes: Iron Cross 2nd Class WWI

Camp Service: **Neuengamme, 1942**

Bentele

First Name: Alfons   *National Archive File:* A3343 SSO-056
Birthdate: 2 August 1899   *Birthplace:* Isenbretzhofen
Rank: SS-Hauptsturmführer   *SS Number:* 2843
NSDAP Number: 210411   *Highest Decoration:* None listed
Religion: Catholic   *Marital Status:* Married
Waffen-SS: No
Notes: Lagerführer at Ebensee sub-camp

Camp Service: **Dachau, 1934-1938**
Mauthausen, 1938-1941
Majdanek, 1941-1942
Neuengamme, 1942-1943

Benz

First Name:	Kurt	*National Archive File:*	A3343 SSO-057
Birthdate:	4 June 1899	*Birthplace:*	Munich
Rank:	SS-Hauptsturmführer	*SS Number:*	657
NSDAP Number:	43216	*Highest Decoration:*	Golden Party Badge
Religion:	Protestant	*Marital Status:*	Married
Waffen-SS:	No		
Notes:	Iron Cross 2nd Class WWI; Golden Party Badge		

Camp Service: **Dachau, 1934-1935**
Esterwegen, 1935-1936

Bergel

First Name:	Karl	*National Archive File:*	A3343 SSO-057
Birthdate:	21 March 1902	*Birthplace:*	Dresden
Rank:	SS-Obersturmführer	*SS Number:*	209202
NSDAP Number:	4583089	*Highest Decoration:*	War Service Cross 2nd Class
Religion:	Catholic	*Marital Status:*	Married
Waffen-SS:	No		
Notes:	Sentenced by SS to 4 months confinement		
	Lager inspector at Theresienstadt		

Camp Service: **Theresienstadt, 1942-1945**

Berger

First Name:	Dr. Arno	*National Archive File:*	A3343 SSO-057
Birthdate:	29 August 1912	*Birthplace:*	Stralsund
Rank:	SS-Hauptsturmführer	*SS Number:*	254208
NSDAP Number:	5378961	*Highest Decoration:*	Iron Cross 1st Class
Religion:	Protestant	*Marital Status:*	Married
Waffen-SS:	17th SS Division "Götz von Berlichingen", 1943-1945		
Notes:	Submitted for German Cross in Gold		

Camp Service: **Ravensbrück, 1942**

Berger

First Name:	Franz	*National Archive File:*	A3343 SSO-058
Birthdate:	16 January 1910	*Birthplace:*	Munich
Rank:	SS-Sturmbannführer	*SS Number:*	93920
NSDAP Number:	1722400	*Highest Decoration:*	Iron Cross 2nd Class
Religion:	Catholic	*Marital Status:*	Married
Waffen-SS:	3rd SS Division "Totenkopf", 1940-1941		
Notes:	Father killed in action WWI		
	Acting *kommandant* Flossenbürg; sentenced to 3 1/2 years		

Camp Service: **Lichtenburg, 1934-1937**
Oranienburg, 1938-1939
Flossenbürg, 1945

Bergschmidt

First Name: Robert   *National Archive File:* A3343 SSO-061
Birthdate: 1 August 1893   *Birthplace:* Stettin
Rank: SS-Sturmbannführer   *SS Number:* 53774
NSDAP Number: 312890   *Highest Decoration:* None listed
Religion: Agnostic   *Marital Status:* Married
Waffen-SS: No
Notes: Iron Cross 2nd Class WWI; former salesman

Camp Service: **Oranienburg, 1944-1945**

Berndt

First Name: Dr. Wilhelm   *National Archive File:* A3343 SSO-062
Birthdate: 2 August 1889   *Birthplace:* Hamburg
Rank: SS-Brigadeführer   *SS Number:* 229196
NSDAP Number: 4054776   *Highest Decoration:* Bar to Iron Cross 1st Class
Religion: Agnostic   *Marital Status:* Married
Waffen-SS: 6th SS Division "Nord", 1941-1942
Notes: Iron Cross 1st Class, Wound Badge WWI

Camp Service: **Oranienburg, 1938**

Berning

First Name: Dr. Ferdinand   *National Archive File:* A3343 SSO-063
Birthdate: 15 February 1907   *Birthplace:* Dortmund
Rank: SS-Standartenführer   *SS Number:* 108362
NSDAP Number: 1321636   *Highest Decoration:* War Service Cross 1st Class
Religion: Agnostic   *Marital Status:* Married
Waffen-SS: 2nd SS Division "Das Reich", 1941
Notes: Wounded in action; camp doctor at Esterwegen

Camp Service: **Esterwegen, 1935-1936**   **Columbia Haus, 1936**
Oranienburg, 1936-1937

Bertling

First Name: Heinz   *National Archive File:* A3343 SSO-064
Birthdate: 20 October 1898   *Birthplace:* Kiel
Rank: SS-Oberführer   *SS Number:* 60258
NSDAP Number: 370275   *Highest Decoration:* Bar to Iron Cross 1st Class
Religion: Agnostic   *Marital Status:* Married
Waffen-SS: 3rd SS Division "Totenkopf", 1939-1940
SS Infantry Regiment 10, 1943
Indian Legion, 1944
Notes: Commander VIIIth Totenkopfsturmbann/3rd Totenkopfstandarte "Thüringen"
Commander SS Infantry Regiment 10 and Indian Legion

Camp Service: **Buchenwald, 1938**

Besch

First Name:	Ulrich	*National Archive File:*	A3343 SSO-064
Birthdate:	6 March 1913	*Birthplace:*	Wilhelmshaven
Rank:	SS-Sturmbannführer	*SS Number:*	38112
NSDAP Number:	467223	*Highest Decoration:*	Iron Cross 2nd Class
Religion:	Agnostic	*Marital Status:*	Married
Waffen-SS:	3rd SS Division "Totenkopf", 1941-1942		
	10th SS Division "Frundsberg", 1943		
Notes:	Commander of maintenance battalion in 10th SS Division; wounded in action		

Camp Service: **Sachsenburg, 1937**   **Buchenwald, 1938**

Bessert

First Name:	Arthur	*National Archive File:*	A3343 SSO-064
Birthdate:	4 February 1899	*Birthplace:*	Mositzfelde
Rank:	SS-Hauptsturmführer	*SS Number:*	257406
NSDAP Number:	3527449	*Highest Decoration:*	War Service Cross 2nd Class
Religion:	Protestant	*Marital Status:*	Married
Waffen-SS:	No		
Notes:	Former high school teacher; served in WWI		

Camp Service: **Mauthausen, 1940**

Bestle

First Name:	Karl	*National Archive File:*	A3343 SSO-065
Birthdate:	10 August 1905	*Birthplace:*	Munich
Rank:	SS-Sturmbannführer	*SS Number:*	3932
NSDAP Number:	278831	*Highest Decoration:*	War Service Cross 2nd Class
Religion:	Catholic	*Marital Status:*	Married
Waffen-SS:	No		
Notes:	Served in SA 1921-1923		
	Blood Order #552		

Camp Service: **Dachau, 1934-1939**

Beyer

First Name:	Wilhelm	*National Archive File:*	A3343 SSO-066
Birthdate:	15 April 1894	*Birthplace:*	Groeningen
Rank:	SS-Obersturmführer	*SS Number:*	292029
NSDAP Number:	5720904	*Highest Decoration:*	War Service Cross 2nd Class
Religion:	Protestant	*Marital Status:*	Married
Waffen-SS:	No		
Notes:	Former legal secretary		
	POW in WWI		

Camp Service: **Dachau, 1942**

Biemann

First Name:	Wilhelm	*National Archive File:*	A3343 SSO-068
Birthdate:	9 December 1900	*Birthplace:*	Blumenbach
Rank:	SS-Obersturmführer	*SS Number:*	464390
NSDAP Number:	6449687	*Highest Decoration:*	War Service Cross 2nd Class
Religion:	Agnostic	*Marital Status:*	Married
Waffen-SS:	No		
Notes:	Department DII, Oranienburg		
	Former salesman		

Camp Service: **Oranienburg, 1944**

Biermeier

First Name:	Fritz	*National Archive File:*	A3343 SSO-069
Birthdate:	19 May 1913	*Birthplace:*	Augsburg
Rank:	SS-Sturmbannführer	*SS Number:*	142869
NSDAP Number:	Not a member	*Highest Decoration:*	Knight's Cross with Oak Leaves
Religion:	Agnostic	*Marital Status:*	Married
Waffen-SS:	3rd SS Division "Totenkopf", 1939-1942, 1943-1944		
	2nd SS Division "Das Reich", 1942		
Notes:	Killed in action 10 October 1944 near Warsaw		
	Panzer battalion commander; in Totenkopfverbaende from 1934-1939		

Camp Service: **Dachau, 1934-1937**

Biesemeyer

First Name:	Ernst	*National Archive File:*	A3343 SSO-069
Birthdate:	15 September 1898	*Birthplace:*	Zurich, Switzerland
Rank:	SS-Obersturmbannführer	*SS Number:*	292856
NSDAP Number:	Not a member	*Highest Decoration:*	War Service Cross 1st Class
Religion:	Agnostic	*Marital Status:*	Married
Waffen-SS:	7th SS Division "Prinz Eugen", 1943		
	Vth SS Corps, 1944		
Notes:	Iron Cross 2nd Class WWI		

Camp Service: **Oranienburg, 1938-1940**

Bischoff

First Name:	Karl	*National Archive File:*	A3343 SSO-073
Birthdate:	9 August 1897	*Birthplace:*	Neuhausbach
Rank:	SS-Sturmbannführer	*SS Number:*	419197
NSDAP Number:	Not a member	*Highest Decoration:*	War Service Cross 1st Class
Religion:	Protestant	*Marital Status:*	Married
Waffen-SS:	No		
Notes:	Construction service; Iron Cross 2nd Class WWI		
	Died 2 October 1950		

Camp Service: **Auschwitz, 1941-1944**

Blancke

First Name:	Dr. Max	*National Archive File:*	A3343 SSO-074
Birthdate:	4 May 1909	*Birthplace:*	Heinsberg
Rank:	SS-Hauptsturmführer	*SS Number:*	162897
NSDAP Number:	5309864	*Highest Decoration:*	None listed
Religion:	Protestant	*Marital Status:*	Married
Waffen-SS:	No		
Notes:	Camp doctor at Majdanek, Natzweiler and at Kaufering sub-camp		

Camp Service: **Dachau, 1941**   **Buchenwald, 1941-1942**
Majdanek, 1942-1943   **Oranienburg**
Natzweiler

Blaschke

First Name:	Dr. Otto	*National Archive File:*	A3343 SSO-075
Birthdate:	24 September 1908	*Birthplace:*	Obernith
Rank:	SS-Obersturmführer	*SS Number:*	391852
NSDAP Number:	Not a member	*Highest Decoration:*	None listed
Religion:	Catholic	*Marital Status:*	Single
Waffen-SS:	1st SS Division "Leibstandarte Adolf Hitler", 1942		
Notes:	Doctor; served in Czech army 1936		

Camp Service: **Auschwitz, 1941**
Mauthausen, 1942

Blaser

First Name:	Anton	*National Archive File:*	A3343 SSO-075
Birthdate:	11 January 1899	*Birthplace:*	Stockheim
Rank:	SS-Sturmbannführer	*SS Number:*	260582
NSDAP Number:	Not a member	*Highest Decoration:*	War Service Cross 1st Class
Religion:	Catholic	*Marital Status:*	Married
Waffen-SS:	No		
Notes:	Iron Cross 2nd Class WWI		
	Troop administration at Oranienburg		

Camp Service: **Oranienburg, 1940**

Blei

First Name:	August	*National Archive File:*	A3343 SSO-075
Birthdate:	26 August 1893	*Birthplace:*	Huesten
Rank:	SS-Obersturmführer	*SS Number:*	454747
NSDAP Number:	Not a member	*Highest Decoration:*	None listed
Religion:	Unknown	*Marital Status:*	Married
Waffen-SS:	No		
Notes:	Executed 28 May 1947		

Camp Service: **Mauthausen, 1942**

Blies

First Name:	Dr. Ludwig	*National Archive File:*	A3343 SSO-076
Birthdate:	22 February 1892	*Birthplace:*	Bad Schwalbach
Rank:	SS-Oberführer	*SS Number:*	78004
NSDAP Number:	1662092	*Highest Decoration:*	Bar to Iron Cross 1st Class
Religion:	Protestant	*Marital Status:*	Married
Waffen-SS:	IIIrd SS Panzer Corps		
Notes:	Corps Surgeon		

Camp Service: **Buchenwald, 1940**
Dachau, 1940-1941

Block

First Name:	Hartwig	*National Archive File:*	A3343 SSO-077
Birthdate:	9 February 1894	*Birthplace:*	Radekow
Rank:	SS-Hauptsturmführer	*SS Number:*	276297
NSDAP Number:	165132	*Highest Decoration:*	None listed
Religion:	Agnostic	*Marital Status:*	Married
Waffen-SS:	No		
Notes:	Iron Cross 2nd Class WWI		
	Adjutant at Buchenwald		

Camp Service: **Lichtenburg, 1936**
Buchenwald, 1937-1938

Blumenreuter

First Name:	Dr. Karl	*National Archive File:*	A3343 SSO-079
Birthdate:	16 November 1881	*Birthplace:*	Berlin
Rank:	SS-Gruppenführer	*SS Number:*	276523
NSDAP Number:	5916887	*Highest Decoration:*	War Service Cross 1st Class
Religion:	Protestant	*Marital Status:*	Married
Waffen-SS:	No		
Notes:	Chief Pharmacist Totenkopfverbaende		
	Iron Cross 2nd Class WWI		

Camp Service: **Oranienburg, 1936-1940**

Blumhardt

First Name:	Herbert	*National Archive File:*	A3343 SSO-079
Birthdate:	31 August 1915	*Birthplace:*	Weimar
Rank:	SS-Hauptsturmführer	*SS Number:*	187048
NSDAP Number:	4137045	*Highest Decoration:*	Bar to Iron Cross 1st Class
Religion:	Agnostic	*Marital Status:*	Single
Waffen-SS:	2nd SS Division "Das Reich", 1940-1943		
Notes:	Iron Cross 1st Class WWI		
	Wounded in action in Russia; company commander		

Camp Service: **Sachsenburg, 1934-1935**

Bochmann

First Name:	Georg	*National Archive File:*	A3343 SSO-079
Birthdate:	18 September 1913	*Birthplace:*	Albernau
Rank:	SS-Oberführer	*SS Number:*	122362
NSDAP Number:	1907565	*Highest Decoration:*	Knight's Cross with Oak Leaves and Swords
Religion:	Agnostic	*Marital Status:*	Married
Waffen-SS:	3rd SS Division "Totenkopf", 1939-1943		
	18th SS Division "Horst Wessel", 1945		
Notes:	Commander 18th SS Division; died 8 June 1973		

Camp Service: **Sachsenburg, 1936-1937**   **Dachau, 1937-1938**

Bodmann

First Name:	Dr. Franz von	*National Archive File:*	A3343 SSO-081
Birthdate:	23 March 1908	*Birthplace:*	Zweifaltendorf
Rank:	SS-Obersturmführer	*SS Number:*	263787
NSDAP Number:	1098482	*Highest Decoration:*	War Service Cross 2nd Class
Religion:	Agnostic	*Marital Status:*	Married
Waffen-SS:	5th SS Division "Wiking", 1944-1945		
Notes:	Camp doctor at Majdanek; suicide 25 May 1945		

Camp Service: **Majdanek, 1942-1943**   **Oranienburg, 1942**
Auschwitz   **Natzweiler, 1943**
Viavara, 1944

Boehmichen

First Name:	Dr. Karl	*National Archive File:*	A3343 SSO-083
Birthdate:	31 May 1912	*Birthplace:*	Rheine
Rank:	SS-Hauptsturmführer	*SS Number:*	256732
NSDAP Number:	Not a member	*Highest Decoration:*	None listed
Religion:	Agnostic	*Marital Status:*	Single
Waffen-SS:	No		
Notes:	Camp doctor at Flossenbürg, Kauen; died 1964		

Camp Service: **Flossenbürg, 1940-1941**   **Sachsenhausen**
Neuengamme, 1941-1943   **Kauen, 1943**
Mauthausen, 1944-1945

Boehne

First Name:	Dr. Ludwig	*National Archive File:*	A3343 SSO-083
Birthdate:	21 August 1898	*Birthplace:*	Hahlen-Minderheide
Rank:	SS-Sturmbannführer	*SS Number:*	249802
NSDAP Number:	Not a member	*Highest Decoration:*	War Service Cross 1st Class
Religion:	Unknown	*Marital Status:*	Unknown
Waffen-SS:	No		
Notes:	Veterinarian		
	Iron Cross 2nd Class, WWI		

Camp Service: **Auschwitz, 1943-1944**

Boerner

First Name:	Gerhard	*National Archive File:*	A3343 SSO-084
Birthdate:	28 October 1905	*Birthplace:*	Dresden
Rank:	SS-Obersturmführer	*SS Number:*	3832
NSDAP Number:	295699	*Highest Decoration:*	None listed
Religion:	Agnostic	*Marital Status:*	Married
Waffen-SS:	No		
Notes:	Camp service not listed in personnel file		

Camp Service: **Sobibór, 1942**

Bonin

First Name:	Engelbrecht von	*National Archive File:*	A3343 SSO-090
Birthdate:	13 December 1892	*Birthplace:*	Danzig
Rank:	SS-Hauptsturmführer	*SS Number:*	205878
NSDAP Number:	2650288	*Highest Decoration:*	War Service Cross 2nd Class
Religion:	Catholic	*Marital Status:*	Married
Waffen-SS:	No		
Notes:	Leader of Department IV at Stutthof		

Camp Service: **Stutthof, 1941-1943, 1944-1945**

Boose

First Name:	Dr. Erich	*National Archive File:*	A3343 SSO-090
Birthdate:	11 February 1893	*Birthplace:*	Luettringhausen
Rank:	SS-Hauptsturmführer	*SS Number:*	55389
NSDAP Number:	Not a member	*Highest Decoration:*	War Service Cross 2nd Class
Religion:	Protestant	*Marital Status:*	Married
Waffen-SS:	No		
Notes:	Camp doctor at Hinzert		
	Killed in action 13 May 1942 with Police Battalion 306		

Camp Service: **Hinzert, 1941**

Borell

First Name:	Gustav	*National Archive File:*	A3343 SSO-091
Birthdate:	15 April 1898	*Birthplace:*	Friedrichstahl
Rank:	SS-Obersturmführer	*SS Number:*	244456
NSDAP Number:	4718887	*Highest Decoration:*	War Service Cross 2nd Class
Religion:	Protestant	*Marital Status:*	Married
Waffen-SS:	No		
Notes:	Commander of 2nd Guard Company Majdanek		
	Iron Cross 2nd Class, Silver Wound Badge WWI		

Camp Service: **Hinzert, 1940-1942**
Ravensbrück, 1942
Majdanek, 1942-1943   **Buchenwald**

Bosch

First Name: Jakob
Birthdate: 2 November 1891
Rank: SS-Obersturmführer
NSDAP Number: 742424
Religion: Protestant
Waffen-SS: No
Notes: Iron Cross 2nd Class WWI

National Archive File: A3343 SSO-094
Birthplace: Moerzheim
SS Number: 6959
Highest Decoration: None listed
Marital Status: Married

Camp Service: **Sachsenhausen, 1943-1944**
Dachau, 1944

Bothmann

First Name: Hans
Birthdate: 11 November 1911
Rank: SS-Hauptsturmführer
NSDAP Number: 3601334
Religion: Agnostic
Waffen-SS: No
Notes: *Kommandant* Chelmno
Suicide 4 April 1946

National Archive File: A3343 SSO-095
Birthplace: Sohe
SS Number: 117630
Highest Decoration: War Service Cross 1st Class
Marital Status: Married

Camp Service: **Chelmno, 1941-1943, 1944-1945**

Brachtl

First Name: Dr. Rudolf
Birthdate: 22 April 1909
Rank: SS-Hauptsturmführer
NSDAP Number: 6635612
Religion: Catholic
Waffen-SS: 9th SS Division "Hohenstaufen", 1943
4th SS Division "Polizei", 1944
Notes: Camp doctor at Dachau

National Archive File: A3343 SSO-096
Birthplace: Gaya
SS Number: 327556
Highest Decoration: None listed
Marital Status: Married

Camp Service: **Dachau, 1941-1942**

Braeuning

First Name: Edmund
Birthdate: 2 July 1905
Rank: SS-Hauptsturmführer
NSDAP Number: 1568392
Religion: Agnostic
Waffen-SS: No
Notes: Former salesman

National Archive File: A3343 SSO-097
Birthplace: Naumburg
SS Number: 66975
Highest Decoration: None listed
Marital Status: Married

Camp Service: **Neuengamme, 1940-1941**
Auschwitz, 1941-1943
Ravensbrück, 1943-1944
Buchenwald, 1945

Brandenburg

First Name: Peter
Birthdate: 10 February 1889
Rank: SS-Obersturmführer
NSDAP Number: 1705869
Religion: Catholic
Waffen-SS: No
Notes: Iron Cross 2nd Class WWI

National Archive File: A3343 SSO-098
Birthplace: Hoerde
SS Number: 424556
Highest Decoration: None listed
Marital Status: Married

Camp Service: **Gross-Rosen, 1941-1942**

Brandt

First Name: Alfred
Birthdate: 27 October 1892
Rank: SS-Hauptsturmführer
NSDAP Number: 829713
Religion: Agnostic
Waffen-SS: 10th SS Division "Frundsberg", 1943
Notes: Iron Cross 2nd Class WWI

National Archive File: A3343 SSO-099
Birthplace: Berlin
SS Number: 203705
Highest Decoration: None listed
Marital Status: Married

Camp Service: **Sachsenhausen, 1940-1941**

Brauer

First Name: Karl
Birthdate: 29 September 1893
Rank: SS-Obersturmführer
NSDAP Number: 1105265
Religion: Agnostic
Waffen-SS: No
Notes: Iron Cross 2nd Class, Wound Badge WWI

National Archive File: A3343 SSO-100
Birthplace: Belgern
SS Number: 203635
Highest Decoration: None listed
Marital Status: Married

Camp Service: **Gross-Rosen, 1942**

Bredemeier

First Name: Willi
Birthdate: 21 April 1910
Rank: SS-Hauptsturmführer
NSDAP Number: 396100
Religion: Protestant
Waffen-SS: 5th SS Division "Wiking", 1941
Notes: SS-Heimwehr Danzig
Killed in action 20 September 1941

National Archive File: A3343 SSO-102
Birthplace: Elizenhof
SS Number: 9048
Highest Decoration: Iron Cross 2nd Class
Marital Status: Single

Camp Service: **Dachau, 1936**

Breh

First Name:	Albert	*National Archive File:*	A3343 SSO-103
Birthdate:	22 April 1912	*Birthplace:*	Kempten
Rank:	SS-Obersturmführer	*SS Number:*	33882
NSDAP Number:	864871	*Highest Decoration:*	None listed
Religion:	Catholic	*Marital Status:*	Married
Waffen-SS:	3rd SS Division "Totenkopf", 1941-1943		
Notes:	Court martialled several times during the war		

Camp Service: **Dachau, 1933-1939**

Breimaier

First Name:	Wilhelm	*National Archive File:*	A3343 SSO-103
Birthdate:	26 February 1907	*Birthplace:*	Goenningen
Rank:	SS-Obersturmbannführer	*SS Number:*	11263
NSDAP Number:	357535	*Highest Decoration:*	German Cross in Gold
Religion:	Catholic	*Marital Status:*	Married
Waffen-SS:	Volunteer Legion "Flandern", 1942		
	7th SS Division "Prinz Eugen", 1943		
Notes:	Battalion commander in 7th SS Division		

Camp Service: **Dachau, 1934**
Lichtenburg, 1935-1936

Bremmer

First Name:	Walter	*National Archive File:*	A3343 SSO-104
Birthdate:	4 June 1911	*Birthplace:*	Bad Wildungen
Rank:	SS-Obersturmführer	*SS Number:*	166881
NSDAP Number:	4627251	*Highest Decoration:*	None listed
Religion:	Protestant	*Marital Status:*	Married
Waffen-SS:	8th SS Division "Florian Geyer", 1942-1943		
Notes:	Dentist		

Camp Service: **Buchenwald, 1940-1942**

Brendel

First Name:	Dr. Alfons	*National Archive File:*	A3343 SSO-104
Birthdate:	18 March 1912	*Birthplace:*	Munich
Rank:	SS-Sturmbannführer	*SS Number:*	142204
NSDAP Number:	3203863	*Highest Decoration:*	War Service Cross 1st Class
Religion:	Catholic	*Marital Status:*	Married
Waffen-SS:	5th SS Division "Wiking", 1942-1943		
Notes:	Camp service not listed in personnel file		
	Served in 1st and 4th Totenkopfstandarte in 1939-1940		

Camp Service: **Amersfoort, 1941**

Brendler

First Name: Arnold   *National Archive File:* A3343 SSO-104
Birthdate: 3 October 1916   *Birthplace:* Isabelow
Rank: SS-Obersturmführer   *SS Number:* 384404
NSDAP Number: Not a member   *Highest Decoration:* None listed
Religion: Protestant   *Marital Status:* Married
Waffen-SS: No
Notes: Commander 2nd Guard Company
Camp service not listed in personnel file

Camp Service: **Natzweiler**
Majdanek, 1943-1944

Brenneis

First Name: Otto   *National Archive File:* A3343 SSO-104
Birthdate: 3 July 1900   *Birthplace:* Landau
Rank: SS-Hauptsturmführer   *SS Number:* 73378
NSDAP Number: 2789294   *Highest Decoration:* War Service Cross 2nd Class
Religion: Agnostic   *Marital Status:* Married
Waffen-SS: No
Notes: Former bank official; served in WWI

Camp Service: **Dachau, 1933**   **Flossenbürg, 1938-1943**
Viavara, 1943-1944   **Dora, 1944-1945**

Bretschneider

First Name: Hans-Eberhardt   *National Archive File:* A3343 SSO-105
Birthdate: 14 December 1913   *Birthplace:* Werdau
Rank: SS-Hauptsturmführer   *SS Number:* 177918
NSDAP Number: Not a member   *Highest Decoration:* None listed
Religion: Protestant   *Marital Status:* Single
Waffen-SS: 5th SS Division "Wiking", 1942
Notes: Pharmacist

Camp Service: **Buchenwald, 1942**

Brinkmann

First Name: Heinz   *National Archive File:* A3343 SSO-106
Birthdate: 8 March 1914   *Birthplace:* Wanne
Rank: SS-Sturmbannführer   *SS Number:* 127018
NSDAP Number: Not a member   *Highest Decoration:* Iron Cross 2nd Class
Religion: Agnostic   *Marital Status:* Married
Waffen-SS: 3rd SS Division "Totenkopf", 1940-1941
10th SS Division "Frundsberg", 1943-1944
Notes: Battalion commander in 10th SS Division

Camp Service: **Oranienburg, 1937**

Brinkmann

First Name: Paul
Birthdate: 31 July 1891
Rank: SS-Oberführer
NSDAP Number: 139161
Religion: Agnostic
Waffen-SS: No
Notes: *Kommandant* Esterwegen, Boergermoor
Iron Cross 2nd Class, Wound Badge WWI; died 20 May 1941

National Archive File: A3343 SSO-106
Birthplace: Bochum-Langendreer
SS Number: 3415
Highest Decoration: None listed
Marital Status: Married

Camp Service: **Esterwegen, 1933**
Boergermoor, 1934

Brossmann

First Name: Otto
Birthdate: 1 February 1889
Rank: SS-Hauptsturmführer
NSDAP Number: 6627521
Religion: Catholic
Waffen-SS: SS Infantry Regiment 14, 1941
Notes: *Kommandant* Blechhammer sub-camp; acquitted

National Archive File: A3343 SSO-109
Birthplace: Brawin
SS Number: 352200
Highest Decoration: None listed
Marital Status: Married

Camp Service: **Auschwitz, 1943-1944**

Bruch

First Name: Dr. Kurt aus dem
Birthdate: 10 July 1909
Rank: SS-Hauptsturmführer
NSDAP Number: 5763425
Religion: Protestant
Waffen-SS: 5th SS Division "Wiking", 1941-1943
Notes: Dentist; camp service not mentioned, served in WVHA Amt D

National Archive File: A3343 SSO-109
Birthplace: Yangstze, China
SS Number: 288751
Highest Decoration: Iron Cross 2nd Class
Marital Status: Married

Camp Service: **Mauthausen**
Natzweiler, 1944

Bruder

First Name: Dr. Hugo
Birthdate: 23 December 1901
Rank: SS-Sturmbannführer
NSDAP Number: 3027303
Religion: Protestant
Waffen-SS: No
Notes: Dentist

National Archive File: A3343 SSO-109
Birthplace: London, England
SS Number: 193408
Highest Decoration: None listed
Marital Status: Married

Camp Service: **Oranienburg, 1940-1941**
Majdanek, 1943
Mauthausen

Bucher

First Name:	Josef	*National Archive File:*	A3343 SSO-114
Birthdate:	20 November 1917	*Birthplace:*	Bayrischzell
Rank:	SS-Hauptsturmführer	*SS Number:*	276204
NSDAP Number:	Not a member	*Highest Decoration:*	Iron Cross 1st Class
Religion:	Agnostic	*Marital Status:*	Single
Waffen-SS:	2nd SS Division "Das Reich", 1940-1943		
	3rd SS Division "Totenkopf", 1944		
Notes:	Wounded four times; 2nd guard company at Dachau		

Camp Service: **Dachau, 1934-1935**

Buddensieg

First Name:	Ludwig	*National Archive File:*	A3343 SSO-116
Birthdate:	30 December 1884	*Birthplace:*	Weissenfels
Rank:	SS-Hauptsturmführer	*SS Number:*	3868
NSDAP Number:	68046	*Highest Decoration:*	War Service Cross 2nd Class
Religion:	Agnostic	*Marital Status:*	Married
Waffen-SS:	No		
Notes:	Golden Party Badge; sentenced to Life		

Camp Service: **Flossenbürg, 1939-1941**

Buecker

First Name:	Theo	*National Archive File:*	A3343 SSO-117
Birthdate:	14 August 1914	*Birthplace:*	Rheinbach
Rank:	SS-Obersturmführer	*SS Number:*	270859
NSDAP Number:	2562861	*Highest Decoration:*	Iron Cross 2nd Class
Religion:	Agnostic	*Marital Status:*	Single
Waffen-SS:	3rd SS Division "Totenkopf", 1940-1941		
Notes:	1st SS Totenkopfstandarte "Oberbayern"		
	Killed in action, 28 June 1941 in Russia		

Camp Service: **Dachau, 1938**

Buengeler

First Name:	Heinz	*National Archive File:*	A3343 SSO-118
Birthdate:	29 March 1913	*Birthplace:*	Halle
Rank:	SS-Obersturmführer	*SS Number:*	236287
NSDAP Number:	2451052	*Highest Decoration:*	None listed
Religion:	Agnostic	*Marital Status:*	Single
Waffen-SS:	3rd SS Division "Totenkopf", 1942-1943		
Notes:	Killed in action 4 March 1943 by mine explosion in Russia		

Camp Service: **Sachsenburg, 1936-1937**
Flossenbürg, 1937-1938
Buchenwald, 1938, 1940-1941
Oranienburg, 1941

Buerkle

First Name:	Dr. Herbert	*National Archive File:*	A3343 SSO-119
Birthdate:	9 November 1910	*Birthplace:*	Geislingen
Rank:	SS-Obersturmführer	*SS Number:*	194602
NSDAP Number:	Not a member	*Highest Decoration:*	War Service Cross 2nd Class
Religion:	Agnostic	*Marital Status:*	Married
Waffen-SS:	6th SS Division "Nord", 1942-1944		
Notes:	Dentist		

Camp Service: **Neuengamme, 1942**

Buescher

First Name:	Arnold	*National Archive File:*	A3343 SSO-119
Birthdate:	16 December 1899	*Birthplace:*	Rehme
Rank:	SS-Obersturmführer	*SS Number:*	11862
NSDAP Number:	556757	*Highest Decoration:*	None listed
Religion:	Protestant	*Marital Status:*	Married
Waffen-SS:	No		
Notes:	Iron Cross 2nd Class WWI; commander guard battalion at Buchenwald; disabled		

Camp Service: **Sachsenhausen, 1939-1941**   **Buchenwald, 1941**
Plaszow, 1944   **Neuengamme, 1944**

Burboeck

First Name:	Wilhelm	*National Archive File:*	A3343 SSO-122
Birthdate:	18 May 1907	*Birthplace:*	Knittlefeld, Austria
Rank:	SS-Sturmbannführer	*SS Number:*	46215
NSDAP Number:	1089902	*Highest Decoration:*	Iron Cross 1st Class
Religion:	Agnostic	*Marital Status:*	Married
Waffen-SS:	7th SS Division "Prinz Eugen", 1942-1943		
	11th SS Division "Nordland", 1943		
	5th SS Division "Wiking", 1944		
Notes:	Also served in 22nd SS Division "Maria Theresia"		

Camp Service: **Oranienburg, 1941-1942**

Burger

First Name:	Anton	*National Archive File:*	A3343 SSO-122
Birthdate:	19 November 1911	*Birthplace:*	Neunkirchen, Austria
Rank:	SS-Hauptsturmführer	*SS Number:*	342783
NSDAP Number:	611604	*Highest Decoration:*	None listed
Religion:	Catholic	*Marital Status:*	Married
Waffen-SS:	No		
Notes:	*Kommandant* Theresienstadt		
	Died 1984 (disputed by Simon Wiesenthal)		

Camp Service: **Auschwitz, 1943**
Theresienstadt, 1943-1944

Burger

First Name:	Wilhelm	*National Archive File:*	A3343 SSO-122
Birthdate:	19 April 1904	*Birthplace:*	Munich
Rank:	SS-Sturmbannführer	*SS Number:*	47285
NSDAP Number:	1316366	*Highest Decoration:*	Iron Cross 2nd Class
Religion:	Agnostic	*Marital Status:*	Married
Waffen-SS:	3rd SS Division "Totenkopf", 1941-1942		
Notes:	Camp administration office at Auschwitz; demoted on 21 April 1943 to Office D-IV, WVHA Amt D;Chief, Department DIV at Oranienburg; lived after the war in Dachau		

Camp Service: **Dachau, 1937-1938**   **Auschwitz, 1942-1943**
Oranienburg, 1943-1945

Burk

First Name:	Ewald	*National Archive File:*	A3343 SSO-122
Birthdate:	19 January 1916	*Birthplace:*	Friedensdorf
Rank:	SS-Hauptsturmführer	*SS Number:*	277022
NSDAP Number:	4197094	*Highest Decoration:*	Iron Cross 2nd Class
Religion:	Agnostic	*Marital Status:*	Married
Waffen-SS:	6th SS Division "Nord", 1941-1942		
Notes:	3rd SS Totenkopfstandarte "Thüringen"		
	Wounded in action; missing in action 14 January 1943		

Camp Service: **Buchenwald, 1938**

Burkhardt

First Name:	Johannes	*National Archive File:*	A3343 SSO-123
Birthdate:	31 December 1909	*Birthplace:*	Darmstadt
Rank:	SS-Hauptsturmführer	*SS Number:*	210588
NSDAP Number:	4533792	*Highest Decoration:*	War Service Cross 1st Class
Religion:	Protestant	*Marital Status:*	Married
Waffen-SS:	11th SS Division "Nordland", 1943		
Notes:	Dentist		

Camp Service: **Buchenwald, 1940-1941**

Burkhardt

First Name:	Karl	*National Archive File:*	A3343 SSO-123
Birthdate:	17 July 1900	*Birthplace:*	Schmalkalden
Rank:	SS-Obersturmbannführer	*SS Number:*	52909
NSDAP Number:	44728	*Highest Decoration:*	Iron Cross 1st Class
Religion:	Agnostic	*Marital Status:*	Married
Waffen-SS:	Unknown		
Notes:	Awarded Golden Party Badge		

Camp Service: **Lichtenburg, 1936**
Oranienburg, 1939

Busch

First Name:	Dr. Karl	*National Archive File:*	A3343 SSO-124
Birthdate:	24 November 1908	*Birthplace:*	Gaukoenigshofen
Rank:	SS-Hauptsturmführer	*SS Number:*	208587
NSDAP Number:	Not a member	*Highest Decoration:*	None listed
Religion:	Catholic	*Marital Status:*	Married
Waffen-SS:	Ist SS Corps		
Notes:	Missing in action, 20 August 1944		

Camp Service: **Ravensbrück, 1941-1942**

Busse

First Name:	Dr. Gustav	*National Archive File:*	A3343 SSO-125
Birthdate:	24 January 1911	*Birthplace:*	Bitsch
Rank:	SS-Hauptsturmführer	*SS Number:*	310357
NSDAP Number:	6070497	*Highest Decoration:*	None listed
Religion:	Catholic	*Marital Status:*	Married
Waffen-SS:	25th SS Division "Hunyadi", 1944		
Notes:	Doctor		
	Also served in Police Battalion 304		

Camp Service: **Oranienburg, 1938**

Caesar

First Name:	Joachim	*National Archive File:*	A3343 SSO-125
Birthdate:	30 May 1901	*Birthplace:*	Boppard
Rank:	SS-Obersturmbannführer	*SS Number:*	74704
NSDAP Number:	626589	*Highest Decoration:*	War Service Cross 2nd Class
Religion:	Agnostic	*Marital Status:*	Widower
Waffen-SS:	2nd SS Division "Das Reich", 1940		
Notes:	Head of agricultural enterprises at camp		
	Died 25 January 1974		

Camp Service: **Auschwitz, 1942-1945**

Calebow

First Name:	Erich	*National Archive File:*	A3343 SSO-125
Birthdate:	19 June 1904	*Birthplace:*	Dresden
Rank:	SS-Obersturmbannführer	*SS Number:*	3892
NSDAP Number:	32578	*Highest Decoration:*	Golden Party Badge
Religion:	Protestant	*Marital Status:*	Married
Waffen-SS:	No		
Notes:	Schutzhaftlagerführer Columbia Haus		

Camp Service: **Columbia Haus, 1935**

Calligaro

First Name: Dr. Heinrich *National Archive File:* A3343 SSO-125
Birthdate: 6 February 1907 *Birthplace:* Gietelhausen
Rank: SS-Hauptsturmführer *SS Number:* 87394
NSDAP Number: 724800 *Highest Decoration:* None listed
Religion: Catholic *Marital Status:* Married
Waffen-SS: No
Notes: Doctor
Served in SA 1931-1933

Camp Service: **Dachau, 1935-1936**
Sachsenburg, 1936

Campe

First Name: Hermann *National Archive File:* A3343 SSO-126
Birthdate: 8 November 1910 *Birthplace:* Koebbelitz
Rank: SS-Obersturmführer *SS Number:* 49126
NSDAP Number: Not a member *Highest Decoration:* None listed
Religion: Agnostic *Marital Status:* Married
Waffen-SS: 10th SS Division "Frundsberg", 1945
Notes: Camp doctor at Dachau

Camp Service: **Sachsenhausen, 1941** **Natzweiler, 1943**
Dachau, 1943-1944

Capesius

First Name: Dr. Viktor *National Archive File:* A3343 SSO-126
Birthdate: 7 February 1907 *Birthplace:* Reussmarkt, Romania
Rank: SS-Sturmbannführer *SS Number:* Unknown
NSDAP Number: Not a member *Highest Decoration:* None listed
Religion: Protestant *Marital Status:* Married
Waffen-SS: No
Notes: Pharmacist; sentenced to 9 years imprisonment; died 1985

Camp Service: **Auschwitz, 1944-1945**

Cesinger

First Name: Johann *National Archive File:* A3343 SSO-127
Birthdate: 26 February 1912 *Birthplace:* Augsburg
Rank: SS-Hauptsturmführer *SS Number:* 16332
NSDAP Number: 653130 *Highest Decoration:* War Service Cross 1st Class
Religion: Agnostic *Marital Status:* Married
Waffen-SS: 6th SS Division "Nord", 1942-1944
Notes: Served at Ohrdruf sub-camp

Camp Service: **Buchenwald, 1938-1942, 1944**

Charpentier

First Name: Wilhelm
Birthdate: 22 May 1893
Rank: SS-Untersturmführer
NSDAP Number: 1416701
Religion: Agnostic
Waffen-SS: No
Notes: Former businessman
Served in Navy in WWI

National Archive File: A3343 SSO-127
Birthplace: Bochum
SS Number: 103934
Highest Decoration: None listed
Marital Status: Married

Camp Service: **Hinzert, 1942**

Chmielewski

First Name: Karl
Birthdate: 16 July 1903
Rank: SS-Hauptsturmführer
NSDAP Number: 1508254
Religion: Agnostic
Waffen-SS: No
Notes: 1st Schutzhaftlagerführer at Gusen sub-camp; sentenced to Life

National Archive File: A3343 SSO-127
Birthplace: Frankfurt
SS Number: 63950
Highest Decoration: None listed
Marital Status: Married

Camp Service: **Columbia Haus, 1935-1936**
Sachsenhausen, 1937-1940
Mauthausen, 1940-1943
Herzogenbusch, 1943

Christoffel

First Name: Franz
Birthdate: 18 December 1898
Rank: SS-Sturmbannführer
NSDAP Number: 371233
Religion: Catholic
Waffen-SS: No
Notes: Department I at Stutthof
Iron Cross 2nd Class WWI

National Archive File: A3343 SSO-128
Birthplace: Mittel-Lowitz
SS Number: 5125
Highest Decoration: War Service Cross 2nd Class
Marital Status: Married

Camp Service: **Stutthof**

Clauberg

First Name: Dr. Carl
Birthdate: 28 September 1898
Rank: SS-Brigadeführer
NSDAP Number: Not a member
Religion: Unknown
Waffen-SS: No
Notes: Honorary SS officer; conducted medical research
Died 9 August 1957 in prison

National Archive File: No File
Birthplace: Wupperhof
SS Number: Unknown
Highest Decoration: None listed
Marital Status: Unknown

Camp Service: **Auschwitz, 1942-1944**
Ravensbrück, 1944

Claussen

First Name:	Hinrich	*National Archive File:*	A3343 SSO-129
Birthdate:	25 January 1908	*Birthplace:*	Hemelingen
Rank:	SS-Hauptsturmführer	*SS Number:*	19248
NSDAP Number:	885518	*Highest Decoration:*	None listed
Religion:	Agnostic	*Marital Status:*	Married
Waffen-SS:	No		
Notes:	Sentenced by SS to 1 1/2 years imprisonment		

Camp Service: **Theresienstadt, 1942**

Conrad

First Name:	Siegfried	*National Archive File:*	A3343 SSO-131
Birthdate:	4 June 1915	*Birthplace:*	Regerteln
Rank:	SS-Sturmbannführer	*SS Number:*	258524
NSDAP Number:	4756837	*Highest Decoration:*	German Cross in Silver
Religion:	Agnostic	*Marital Status:*	Single
Waffen-SS:	3rd SS Division "Totenkopf", 1941-1942		
	9th SS Division "Hohenstaufen", 1943-1944		
	11th & 17th SS Divisions, 1944		
Notes:	Administration troops in SS Totenkopfstandarte "Thüringen"		

Camp Service: **Buchenwald, 1938**

Conradi

First Name:	Heinz	*National Archive File:*	A3343 SSO-131
Birthdate:	14 June 1898	*Birthplace:*	Wiesbaden
Rank:	SS-Hauptsturmführer	*SS Number:*	97966
NSDAP Number:	627572	*Highest Decoration:*	Bar to Iron Cross 2nd Class
Religion:	Agnostic	*Marital Status:*	Married
Waffen-SS:	7th SS Division "Prinz Eugen", 1943		
Notes:	Iron Cross 2nd Class, WWI; served in police 1921-1925		

Camp Service: **Mauthausen, 1941-1942**
Flossenbürg, 1942

Czepiczka

First Name:	Herbert	*National Archive File:*	A3343 SSO-132
Birthdate:	24 June 1904	*Birthplace:*	Troppau
Rank:	SS-Sturmbannführer	*SS Number:*	347122
NSDAP Number:	6663730	*Highest Decoration:*	War Service Cross 2nd Class
Religion:	Protestant	*Marital Status:*	Single
Waffen-SS:	4th SS Division "Polizei", 1943-1944		
	VIth SS Corps		
Notes:	Pharmacist at Buchenwald		

Camp Service: **Buchenwald, 1940**
Flossenbürg, 1941-1942

D'Angelo

First Name:	Karl	*National Archive File:*	A3343 SSO-014
Birthdate:	9 September 1890	*Birthplace:*	Osthofen
Rank:	SS-Standartenführer	*SS Number:*	2058
NSDAP Number:	21616	*Highest Decoration:*	Golden Party Badge
Religion:	Protestant	*Marital Status:*	Married
Waffen-SS:	No		

Notes: *Kommandant* Osthofen; Iron Cross 2nd Class, Wound Badge, WWI
Schutzhaftlagerführer at Dachau

Camp Service: **Osthofen, 1933**   **Dachau, 1935-1936**

Dallinger

First Name:	Max	*National Archive File:*	A3343 SSO-134
Birthdate:	18 October 1910	*Birthplace:*	Munich
Rank:	SS-Sturmbannführer	*SS Number:*	11966
NSDAP Number:	194095	*Highest Decoration:*	Iron Cross 1st Class
Religion:	Agnostic	*Marital Status:*	Single
Waffen-SS:	3rd SS Division "Totenkopf", 1939-1940		
	10th SS Division "Frundsberg", 1943		
	16th SS Division "Reichsführer-SS", 1944		

Notes: Guard troops at Dachau; tank battalion commander in 10th SS Division

Camp Service: **Dachau, 1935-1937**

de Martin

First Name:	Franz	*National Archive File:*	A3343 SSO-298A
Birthdate:	1 May 1908	*Birthplace:*	Vienna, Austria
Rank:	SS-Obersturmführer	*SS Number:*	49383
NSDAP Number:	1082925	*Highest Decoration:*	Iron Cross 2nd Class
Religion:	Agnostic	*Marital Status:*	Married
Waffen-SS:	2nd SS Division "Das Reich", 1940		
	36th SS Division "Dirlewanger", 1945		

Notes: Sentenced to serve in the Dirlewanger Brigade 1944

Camp Service: **Esterwegen, 1935-1936**

Degelow

First Name:	Fritz	*National Archive File:*	A3343 SSO-139
Birthdate:	25 February 1892	*Birthplace:*	Gotha
Rank:	SS-Sturmbannführer	*SS Number:*	178978
NSDAP Number:	2196843	*Highest Decoration:*	War Service Cross 1st Class
Religion:	Agnostic	*Marital Status:*	Married
Waffen-SS:	IInd SS Corps, 1943		VIth SS Corps, 1943

Notes: Guard battalion commander at Dachau; executed

Camp Service: **Dachau, 1944**

Deisenhofer

First Name:	Eduard	*National Archive File:*	A3343 SSO-140
Birthdate:	27 June 1909	*Birthplace:*	Freising
Rank:	SS-Oberführer	*SS Number:*	3642
NSDAP Number:	250226	*Highest Decoration:*	Knight's Cross
Religion:	Catholic	*Marital Status:*	Married
Waffen-SS:	3rd SS Division "Totenkopf", 1941-1942		
	10th SS Division "Frundsberg", 1943-1944		
	5th SS Division "Wiking", 1944		
Notes:	Commander IInd Totenkopfsturmbann, 1st Totenkopfstandarte		
	Regimental commander in 10th SS Division; KIA 31 January 1945		

Camp Service: **Columbia Haus, 1935**   **Dachau, 1935**
Sachsenburg, 1936

Dejaco

First Name:	Walter	*National Archive File:*	A3343 SSO-141
Birthdate:	19 June 1909	*Birthplace:*	Muehlau, Austria
Rank:	SS-Obersturmführer (F)	*SS Number:*	295135
NSDAP Number:	Not a member	*Highest Decoration:*	War Service Cross 2nd Class
Religion:	Catholic	*Marital Status:*	Married
Waffen-SS:	No		
Notes:	Construction department Auschwitz; post-war charges dropped in 1972		

Camp Service: **Auschwitz, 1941-1944**

Delitz

First Name:	Dr. Hellmuth	*National Archive File:*	A3343 SSO-141
Birthdate:	18 March 1909	*Birthplace:*	Hoheneiche
Rank:	SS-Hauptsturmführer	*SS Number:*	367740
NSDAP Number:	7286830	*Highest Decoration:*	Iron Cross 1st Class
Religion:	Agnostic	*Marital Status:*	Married
Waffen-SS:	3rd SS Division "Totenkopf", 1941-1943		
	VIIth SS Corps, 1943-1944		
Notes:	Wounded in action		
	Doctor		

Camp Service: **Sachsenhausen, 1943**

Delmotte

First Name:	Hans	*National Archive File:*	A3343 SSO-141
Birthdate:	15 December 1917	*Birthplace:*	Liege, Belgium
Rank:	SS-Obersturmführer	*SS Number:*	313070
NSDAP Number:	Not a member	*Highest Decoration:*	None listed
Religion:	Catholic	*Marital Status:*	Married
Waffen-SS:	No		
Notes:	Doctor, SS Hygiene Institute		
	Committed suicide 1945		

Camp Service: **Auschwitz, 1944**

Demme

First Name:	Karl	*National Archive File:*	A3343 SSO-141
Birthdate:	25 September 1894	*Birthplace:*	Muehlhausen
Rank:	SS-Standartenführer	*SS Number:*	228339
NSDAP Number:	1038060	*Highest Decoration:*	War Service Cross 2nd Class
Religion:	Agnostic	*Marital Status:*	Married
Waffen-SS:	SS Regiment "Deutschland", 1937		
Notes:	Commander SS-Totenkopfstandarte 10		
	Iron Cross 1st Class WWI		

Camp Service: **Buchenwald, 1939-1940**

Deppner

First Name:	Erich	*National Archive File:*	A3343 SSO-143
Birthdate:	8 August 1910	*Birthplace:*	Neuhaldensleben
Rank:	SS-Sturmbannführer	*SS Number:*	177571
NSDAP Number:	1254844	*Highest Decoration:*	None listed
Religion:	Agnostic	*Marital Status:*	Married
Waffen-SS:	No		
Notes:	*Kommandant* Westerbork		
	Camp service not listed in personnel file		

Camp Service: **Westerbork, 1941-1942**

Desch

First Name:	Johann	*National Archive File:*	A3343 SSO-144
Birthdate:	23 December 1885	*Birthplace:*	Worms
Rank:	SS-Obersturmführer	*SS Number:*	14000
NSDAP Number:	73495	*Highest Decoration:*	None listed
Religion:	Agnostic	*Marital Status:*	Married
Waffen-SS:	No		
Notes:	Construction department Auschwitz		
	Iron Cross 1st Class, WWI		

Camp Service: **Auschwitz, 1943-1944**

Detmers

First Name:	Heinrich	*National Archive File:*	A3343 SSO-145
Birthdate:	20 April 1919	*Birthplace:*	Norden
Rank:	SS-Obersturmführer	*SS Number:*	309930
NSDAP Number:	5545920	*Highest Decoration:*	War Service Cross 2nd Class
Religion:	Agnostic	*Marital Status:*	Married
Waffen-SS:	1st SS Infantry Brigade, 1942-1943		
Notes:	Adjutant at Dora		

Camp Service: **Dachau, 1940-1942**
Dora, 1944-1945

Deubel

First Name:	Heinrich	*National Archive File:*	A3343 SSO-145
Birthdate:	19 February 1890	*Birthplace:*	Ortemburg
Rank:	SS-Oberführer	*SS Number:*	186
NSDAP Number:	14178	*Highest Decoration:*	War Service Cross 2nd Class
Religion:	Protestant	*Marital Status:*	Married
Waffen-SS:	No		
Notes:	*Kommandant* Dachau, Columbia Haus; released from SS 1937; died 2 October 1962		
	Iron Cross 1st Class WWI; Golden Party Badge		

Camp Service: **Dachau, 1934-1936**
Columbia Haus, 1936-1937

Diembt

First Name:	Otto	*National Archive File:*	A3343 SSO-149
Birthdate:	18 March 1907	*Birthplace:*	Bad Flinsberg
Rank:	SS-Obersturmführer	*SS Number:*	189176
NSDAP Number:	2196163	*Highest Decoration:*	War Service Cross 2nd Class
Religion:	Agnostic	*Marital Status:*	Married
Waffen-SS:	3rd SS Division "Totenkopf", 1940		
Notes:	Wounded during war		

Camp Service: **Buchenwald, 1941-1944**
Dora, 1944

Dienstbach

First Name:	Dr. Oskar	*National Archive File:*	A3343 SSO-150
Birthdate:	30 September 1910	*Birthplace:*	Usingen
Rank:	SS-Hauptsturmführer	*SS Number:*	101741
NSDAP Number:	2400092	*Highest Decoration:*	None listed
Religion:	Agnostic	*Marital Status:*	Married
Waffen-SS:	1st SS Division "Leibstandarte Adolf Hitler", 1942		
Notes:	Physician for reconnaissance battalion 1st SS Division		
	Died 18 October 1945		

Camp Service: **Mauthausen, 1941**   **Flossenbürg, 1941**
Auschwitz, 1942
Dora, 1945

Dietrich

First Name:	Eugen	*National Archive File:*	A3343 SSO-151
Birthdate:	15 September 1889	*Birthplace:*	Ludwigshafen
Rank:	SS-Obersturmführer	*SS Number:*	262643
NSDAP Number:	400383	*Highest Decoration:*	None listed
Religion:	Catholic	*Marital Status:*	Married
Waffen-SS:	No		
Notes:	Iron Cross 1st Class, Wound Badge WWI		

Camp Service: **Buchenwald, 1942-1944**

Dillmann

First Name:	Herbert	*National Archive File:*	A3343 SSO-154
Birthdate:	31 October 1913	*Birthplace:*	Dresden
Rank:	SS-Obersturmführer	*SS Number:*	270728
NSDAP Number:	5718018	*Highest Decoration:*	War Service Cross 2nd Class
Religion:	Protestant	*Marital Status:*	Married
Waffen-SS:	Volunteer Legion "Norwegen", 1942		
Notes:	Pharmacist		
	Served in SA 1933-1934		

Camp Service: **Mauthausen, 1942**   **Gross-Rosen, 1942-1943**
Natzweiler, 1943-1945

Ding-Schuler

First Name:	Dr. Erwin	*National Archive File:*	A3343 SSO-109B
Birthdate:	19 September 1912	*Birthplace:*	Bitterfeld
Rank:	SS-Sturmbannführer	*SS Number:*	280163
NSDAP Number:	1318211	*Highest Decoration:*	War Service Cross 1st Class
			(from Luftwaffe)
Religion:	Agnostic	*Marital Status:*	Married
Waffen-SS:	3rd SS Division "Totenkopf", 1939-1940		
Notes:	Conducted typhus experiments on prisoners		
	Adopted name of Ding		

Camp Service: **Buchenwald, 1938, 1944**

Dirnagel

First Name:	Rudolf	*National Archive File:*	A3343 SSO-154
Birthdate:	27 January 1912	*Birthplace:*	Memmingen
Rank:	SS-Obersturmbannführer	*SS Number:*	8107
NSDAP Number:	126211	*Highest Decoration:*	Iron Cross 1st Class
Religion:	Agnostic	*Marital Status:*	Married
Waffen-SS:	SS Infantry Regiment 14, 1941		
Notes:	Fined 40 Marks for Assault		
	Battalion commander of a flak unit in 1944		

Camp Service: **Dachau, 1935**
Sachsenburg, 1936

Dittmann

First Name:	Alfred	*National Archive File:*	A3343 SSO-155
Birthdate:	18 November 1906	*Birthplace:*	Neuteich
Rank:	SS-Hauptsturmführer	*SS Number:*	11090
NSDAP Number:	397891	*Highest Decoration:*	War Service Cross 2nd Class
Religion:	Protestant	*Marital Status:*	Single
Waffen-SS:	No		
Notes:	Guard troops at Stutthof		

Camp Service: **Stutthof, 1941**
Ravensbrück, 1941-1944
Mauthausen, 1944

Dolp

First Name:	Hermann	*National Archive File:*	A3343 SSO-160
Birthdate:	12 September 1889	*Birthplace:*	Tuerkheim
Rank:	SS-Sturmbannführer	*SS Number:*	1293
NSDAP Number:	99503	*Highest Decoration:*	Bar to Iron Cross 2nd Class
Religion:	Agnostic	*Marital Status:*	Married
Waffen-SS:	19th SS Division, 1944		
Notes:	Construction Battalion Commander in 19th SS Division		
	Iron Cross 2nd Class WWI; Golden Party Badge		

Camp Service: **Dachau, 1934**　　**Lublin Labor Camp, 1940**
Sachsenhausen, 1940-1943

Dorn

First Name:	Hans	*National Archive File:*	A3343 SSO-161
Birthdate:	13 February 1905	*Birthplace:*	Grohsenbuch
Rank:	SS-Sturmbannführer	*SS Number:*	72910
NSDAP Number:	2552126	*Highest Decoration:*	War Service Cross 1st Class
Religion:	Catholic	*Marital Status:*	Married
Waffen-SS:	2nd SS Division "Das Reich"		
Notes:	Served in Freikorps Oberland, 1923		
	Served in SA 1928-1933		

Camp Service: **Dachau, 1934-1936**

Drees

First Name:	Eduard	*National Archive File:*	A3343 SSO-162
Birthdate:	29 January 1901	*Birthplace:*	Lodbergen
Rank:	SS-Obersturmführer	*SS Number:*	214402
NSDAP Number:	2846257	*Highest Decoration:*	None listed
Religion:	Catholic	*Marital Status:*	Married
Waffen-SS:	No		
Notes:	Transportation department		

Camp Service: **Flossenbürg, 1942**
Auschwitz, 1943
Flossenbürg, 1943-1944

Driemel

First Name:	Alfred	*National Archive File:*	A3343 SSO-164
Birthdate:	24 August 1907	*Birthplace:*	Kuestrin
Rank:	SS-Obersturmführer	*SS Number:*	1848
NSDAP Number:	121168	*Highest Decoration:*	None listed
Religion:	Protestant	*Marital Status:*	Married
Waffen-SS:	8th SS Division "Florian Geyer", 1943		
Notes:	Missing in action 9 December 1943		

Camp Service: **Dachau, 1934-1935**
Sulza, 1937
Buchenwald, 1937-1940

Dueck

First Name:	Walter	*National Archive File:*	A3343 SSO-164
Birthdate:	9 January 1900	*Birthplace:*	Graudenz
Rank:	SS-Hauptsturmführer	*SS Number:*	250074
NSDAP Number:	933214	*Highest Decoration:*	None
Religion:	Agnostic	*Marital Status:*	Married
Waffen-SS:	Unknown		
Notes:	Iron Cross 2nd Class, Wound Badge WWI		
	Died 8 August 1939 in Berlin		

Camp Service: **Dachau, 1936**

Dumboeck

First Name:	Karl	*National Archive File:*	A3343 SSO-165
Birthdate:	19 April 1906	*Birthplace:*	Fomaschow, Poland
Rank:	SS-Obersturmführer	*SS Number:*	267674
NSDAP Number:	50038	*Highest Decoration:*	War Service Cross 2nd Class
Religion:	Protestant	*Marital Status:*	Married
Waffen-SS:	No		
Notes:	Awarded Golden Party Badge		

Camp Service: **Buchenwald, 1938**

Dumm

First Name:	Josef	*National Archive File:*	A3343 SSO-165
Birthdate:	11 August 1908	*Birthplace:*	Mainburg
Rank:	SS-Untersturmführer	*SS Number:*	23050
NSDAP Number:	83080	*Highest Decoration:*	Golden Party Badge
Religion:	Agnostic	*Marital Status:*	Married
Waffen-SS:	No		
Notes:	Former painter; Served in SA 1928-1931		

Camp Service: **Dachau, 1933-1942**

Dusenschoen

First Name:	Willi	*National Archive File:*	A3343 SSO-166
Birthdate:	1 March 1909	*Birthplace:*	Hamburg
Rank:	SS-Obersturmbannführer	*SS Number:*	10984
NSDAP Number:	75582	*Highest Decoration:*	Iron Cross 2nd Class
Religion:	Agnostic	*Marital Status:*	Married
Waffen-SS:	3rd SS Division "Totenkopf", 1940		
	6th SS Division "Nord", 1942-1944		
	2nd SS Division "Das Reich", 1944		
Notes:	Guard company commander; Golden Party Badge		
	Battalion commander in Waffen-SS		

Camp Service: **Fuhlsbuettel, 1933-1934**   **Esterwegen, 1935**
                Sachsenhausen

Eberl

First Name: Dr. Irmfried *National Archive File:* No File
Birthdate: 8 September 1910 *Birthplace:* Bregenz, Austria
Rank: SS-Obersturmführer *SS Number:* Unknown
NSDAP Number: 687095 *Highest Decoration:* None listed
Religion: Protestant *Marital Status:* Married
Waffen-SS: Unknown
Notes: *Kommandant* Treblinka; relieved of command August 1942
Committed suicide February 1948

Camp Service: **Treblinka, 1942**

Eggeling

First Name: Karl *National Archive File:* A3343 SSO-174
Birthdate: 30 May 1912 *Birthplace:* Gadenstedt
Rank: SS-Obersturmführer (F) *SS Number:* 96710
NSDAP Number: Not a member *Highest Decoration:* War Service Cross 2nd Class
Religion: Unknown *Marital Status:* Married
Waffen-SS: No
Notes: Construction department Auschwitz
Engineer

Camp Service: **Auschwitz, 1943**

Ehle

First Name: Paul *National Archive File:* A3343 SSO-175
Birthdate: 22 October 1897 *Birthplace:* Danzig
Rank: SS-Obersturmführer *SS Number:* 153968
NSDAP Number: 1150117 *Highest Decoration:* War Service Cross 2nd Class
Religion: Agnostic *Marital Status:* Married
Waffen-SS: No
Notes: Guard troops at Stutthof; died September 1965

Camp Service: **Stutthof, 1941**

Ehlers

First Name: Ewald *National Archive File:* A3343 SSO-175
Birthdate: 3 January 1910 *Birthplace:* Lelm
Rank: SS-Hauptsturmführer *SS Number:* 309725
NSDAP Number: Not a member *Highest Decoration:* War Service Cross 2nd Class
Religion: Agnostic *Marital Status:* Married
Waffen-SS: 4th SS Division "Polizei", 1943, 1944
3rd SS Division "Totenkopf", 1943
36th SS Division "Dirlewanger", 1944-1945
Notes: Reported killed by own troops, April 1945

Camp Service: **Buchenwald, 1937** **Oranienburg, 1939-1940**

Ehrenberger

First Name:	Dr. Raimond	*National Archive File:*	A3343 SSO-176
Birthdate:	6 August 1893	*Birthplace:*	Vienna, Austria
Rank:	SS-Sturmbannführer	*SS Number:*	308257
NSDAP Number:	1087654	*Highest Decoration:*	None listed
Religion:	Catholic	*Marital Status:*	Married
Waffen-SS:	6th SS Division "Nord", 1943		
	Vth SS Corps, 1943		
Notes:	Doctor and dentist		

Camp Service: **Sachsenhausen, 1941**   **Oranienburg, 1941**
Auschwitz, 1941-1942

Ehrsam

First Name:	Dr. Ludwig	*National Archive File:*	A3343 SSO-178
Birthdate:	31 July 1910	*Birthplace:*	Meiningen
Rank:	SS-Obersturmführer	*SS Number:*	19729
NSDAP Number:	526435	*Highest Decoration:*	Iron Cross 1st Class
Religion:	Unknown	*Marital Status:*	Single
Waffen-SS:	3rd SS Division "Totenkopf", 1941-1943		
	4th SS Division "Polizei", 1945		
Notes:	Wounded in action with 3rd SS Division and lost an eye		

Camp Service: **Dachau, 1936**   **Sachsenhausen, 1936-1937**
Lichtenburg, 1937   **Esterwegen**
Buchenwald

Ehser

First Name:	Max	*National Archive File:*	A3343 SSO-178
Birthdate:	24 March 1893	*Birthplace:*	Eilenburg
Rank:	SS-Obersturmführer	*SS Number:*	9785
NSDAP Number:	256357	*Highest Decoration:*	War Service Cross 2nd Class
Religion:	Agnostic	*Marital Status:*	Married
Waffen-SS:	No		
Notes:	Guard company Flossenbürg; Prisoner of War in WWI		

Camp Service: **Flossenbürg, 1940-1943**
Auschwitz, 1943-1945

Eichele

First Name:	Hans	*National Archive File:*	A3343 SSO-178
Birthdate:	1 May 1901	*Birthplace:*	Munich
Rank:	SS-Standartenführer	*SS Number:*	21640
NSDAP Number:	125994	*Highest Decoration:*	War Service Cross 1st Class
Religion:	Agnostic	*Marital Status:*	Married
Waffen-SS:	No		
Notes:	Administrative officer for 1st Totenkopfstandarte "Oberbayern"		

Camp Service: **Dachau, 1938-1940**

Eichelsdoerfer

First Name:	Johann-Baptist	*National Archive File:*	A3343 SSO-178
Birthdate:	20 January 1890	*Birthplace:*	Dachau
Rank:	SS-Untersturmführer	*SS Number:*	Unknown
NSDAP Number:	Not a member	*Highest Decoration:*	None listed
Religion:	Unknown	*Marital Status:*	Single
Waffen-SS:	No		
Notes:	*Kommandant* of Kaufering sub-camp		
	Executed		

Camp Service: **Dachau**

Eicke

First Name:	Theodor	*National Archive File:*	A3343 SSO-180
Birthdate:	17 October 1892	*Birthplace:*	Hudingen
Rank:	SS-Obergruppenführer	*SS Number:*	2921
NSDAP Number:	114901	*Highest Decoration:*	Knight's Cross with Oak Leaves
Religion:	Agnostic	*Marital Status:*	Married
Waffen-SS:	3rd SS Division "Totenkopf", 1939-1943		
Notes:	*Kommandant* of Dachau, Commander 3rd SS Division		
	Killed in action 26 February 1943 in Russia		

Camp Service: **Dachau, 1933-1934**

Lichtenburg, 1934　　　**Oranienburg, 1934-1939**

Eisele

First Name:	Dr. Hannes	*National Archive File:*	A3343 SSO-182
Birthdate:	13 March 1912	*Birthplace:*	Donauschingen
Rank:	SS-Hauptsturmführer	*SS Number:*	237421
NSDAP Number:	3125695	*Highest Decoration:*	War Service Cross 1st Class
Religion:	Catholic	*Marital Status:*	Married
Waffen-SS:	2nd SS Division "Das Reich", 1942		
Notes:	Camp doctor at Dachau; died 1967		

Camp Service: **Mauthausen, 1940**　　　**Buchenwald, 1941-1942**

Natzweiler, 1942　　　**Dachau**

Eisenhoefer

First Name:	Heinrich	*National Archive File:*	A3343 SSO-182
Birthdate:	19 February 1893	*Birthplace:*	Pirmasens
Rank:	SS-Obersturmführer	*SS Number:*	162304
NSDAP Number:	2266758	*Highest Decoration:*	None listed
Religion:	Protestant	*Marital Status:*	Married
Waffen-SS:	No		
Notes:	Iron Cross 2nd Class WWI		
	Executed April 1947		

Camp Service: **Mauthausen, 1942-1944**

Eisenhut

First Name:	Edmund	*National Archive File:*	A3343 SSO-182
Birthdate:	3 March 1911	*Birthplace:*	Munich
Rank:	SS-Hauptsturmführer	*SS Number:*	88960
NSDAP Number:	2942800	*Highest Decoration:*	War Service Cross 2nd Class
Religion:	Agnostic	*Marital Status:*	Married
Waffen-SS:	6th SS Division "Nord", 1940-1942		
Notes:	Joined SS and NSDAP in 1933		

Camp Service: **Oranienburg, 1938-1940**

Eisfeld

First Name:	Walter	*National Archive File:*	A3343 SSO-182
Birthdate:	11 July 1905	*Birthplace:*	Halle
Rank:	SS-Sturmbannführer	*SS Number:*	1996
NSDAP Number:	4802	*Highest Decoration:*	Golden Party Badge
Religion:	Unknown	*Marital Status:*	Married
Waffen-SS:	No		
Notes:	*Kommandant* Sachsenhausen Died 3 April 1940		

Camp Service: **Sachsenhausen, 1938-1939**   **Dachau**
Neuengamme   **Buchenwald, 1938**

Eisolt

First Name:	Herbert	*National Archive File:*	A3343 SSO-183
Birthdate:	10 June 1914	*Birthplace:*	Muegeln
Rank:	SS-Obersturmführer	*SS Number:*	121357
NSDAP Number:	1559287	*Highest Decoration:*	None listed
Religion:	Agnostic	*Marital Status:*	Married
Waffen-SS:	1st SS Infantry Brigade		
Notes:	Killed in action 2 September 1942 Guard platoon leader		

Camp Service: **Buchenwald, 1938**

Ellenbeck

First Name:	Dr. Hans-Dieter	*National Archive File:*	A3343 SSO-183
Birthdate:	15 June 1912	*Birthplace:*	Duesseldorf
Rank:	SS-Sturmbannführer	*SS Number:*	204652
NSDAP Number:	1777346	*Highest Decoration:*	Iron Cross 1st Class
Religion:	Agnostic	*Marital Status:*	Married
Waffen-SS:	4th SS Division "Polizei", 1941-1942		
Notes:	Conducted blood experiments at Buchenwald		

Camp Service: **Buchenwald, 1944**

Ellenberg

First Name: Gustav *National Archive File:* A3343 SSO-183
Birthdate: 19 July 1912 *Birthplace:* Lehmke
Rank: SS-Obersturmführer *SS Number:* 94884
NSDAP Number: 2624665 *Highest Decoration:* War Service Cross 2nd Class
Religion: Agnostic *Marital Status:* Married
Waffen-SS: 1st SS Infantry Brigade, 1943
Notes: Former bank employee

Camp Service: **Buchenwald, 1941-1943**

Endres

First Name: Hans *National Archive File:* A3343 SSO-186
Birthdate: 22 February 1916 *Birthplace:* Blessenbach
Rank: SS-Sturmbannführer *SS Number:* 256545
NSDAP Number: 3601430 *Highest Decoration:* Iron Cross 1st Class
Religion: Agnostic *Marital Status:* Married
Waffen-SS: 6th SS Division "Nord", 1939-1943
15th SS Division, 1944
Notes: Operations officer (Ia) of 15th SS Division (but rated unsatisfactory in this position)
Died 23 September 1944

Camp Service: **Buchenwald, 1938**

Engelbrecht

First Name: Friedrich *National Archive File:* A3343 SSO-187
Birthdate: 11 June 1905 *Birthplace:* Weiden
Rank: SS-Untersturmführer (F) *SS Number:* 80812
NSDAP Number: Not a member *Highest Decoration:* War Service Cross 2nd Class
Religion: Agnostic *Marital Status:* Married
Waffen-SS: No
Notes: Construction department Auschwitz

Camp Service: **Dachau, 1939-1940**
Auschwitz, 1940-1944

Entress

First Name: Dr. Friedrich *National Archive File:* A3343 SSO-188
Birthdate: 8 December 1904 *Birthplace:* Posen
Rank: SS-Hauptsturmführer *SS Number:* 353124
NSDAP Number: Not a member *Highest Decoration:* None listed
Religion: Unknown *Marital Status:* Married
Waffen-SS: 9th SS Division "Hohenstaufen", 1945
Notes: Camp doctor, conducted prisoner selections
Executed 28 May 1947

Camp Service: **Gross-Rosen, 1941** **Auschwitz, 1941-1943**
Mauthausen, 1943-1944 **Gross-Rosen, 1944-1945**

Entsberger

First Name:	Edgar	*National Archive File:*	No File
Birthdate:	21 July 1897	*Birthplace:*	Boehlitz
Rank:	SS-Obersturmführer	*SS Number:*	133010
NSDAP Number:	347617	*Highest Decoration:*	None listed
Religion:	Unknown	*Marital Status:*	Unknown
Waffen-SS:	Unknown		
Notes:	Adjutant at Neuengamme; shown as dismissed from SS 1935		

Camp Service: **Lichtenburg, 1934**
Neuengamme

Erfurt

First Name:	Hugo	*National Archive File:*	A3343 SSO-189
Birthdate:	30 July 1892	*Birthplace:*	Rettgenstedt
Rank:	SS-Hauptsturmführer	*SS Number:*	133557
NSDAP Number:	2678901	*Highest Decoration:*	None listed
Religion:	Agnostic	*Marital Status:*	Married
Waffen-SS:	No		
Notes:	Former teacher		
	Served in WWI		

Camp Service: **Flossenbürg, 1939-1942**

Ernstberger

First Name:	Walter	*National Archive File:*	A3343 SSO-191
Birthdate:	23 August 1913	*Birthplace:*	Pforzheim
Rank:	SS-Obersturmführer	*SS Number:*	270670
NSDAP Number:	5546899	*Highest Decoration:*	None listed
Religion:	Unknown	*Marital Status:*	Married
Waffen-SS:	No		
Notes:	Lagerführer at Dachau		
	2nd Schutzhaftlagerführer at Mauthausen, Gross-Rosen		

Camp Service: **Mauthausen, 1940**
Dachau
Gross-Rosen, 1942

Erspenmueller

First Name:	Robert	*National Archive File:*	A3343 SSO-191
Birthdate:	4 March 1903	*Birthplace:*	Nürnberg
Rank:	SS-Sturmbannführer	*SS Number:*	3528
NSDAP Number:	247630	*Highest Decoration:*	Iron Cross 1st Class
Religion:	Catholic	*Marital Status:*	Married
Waffen-SS:	2nd SS Division "Das Reich", 1940		
Notes:	Killed in action 25 May 1940; Blood Order		
	Battalion commander artillery		

Camp Service: **Dachau, 1933**

Ertl

First Name:	Fritz	*National Archive File:*	A3343 SSO-191
Birthdate:	31 August 1908	*Birthplace:*	Breitbrunn, Austria
Rank:	SS-Obersturmführer (F)	*SS Number:*	417971
NSDAP Number:	Not a member	*Highest Decoration:*	None listed
Religion:	Unknown	*Marital Status:*	Married
Waffen-SS:	8th SS Division "Florian Geyer", 1943		
Notes:	Construction department Auschwitz		
	Acquitted 1972		

Camp Service: **Auschwitz, 1940-1943**

Euler

First Name:	Emil	*National Archive File:*	A3343 SSO-192
Birthdate:	15 February 1884	*Birthplace:*	Sobernheim
Rank:	SS-Obersturmführer	*SS Number:*	349618
NSDAP Number:	7525307	*Highest Decoration:*	War Service Cross 2nd Class
Religion:	Agnostic	*Marital Status:*	Married
Waffen-SS:	No		
Notes:	Former police official		
	Served in WWI		

Camp Service: **Mauthausen, 1942-1944**

Fasching

First Name:	Alfred	*National Archive File:*	A3343 SSO-197
Birthdate:	12 December 1912	*Birthplace:*	Klosterneuberg, Austria
Rank:	SS-Hauptsturmführer	*SS Number:*	37504
NSDAP Number:	784884	*Highest Decoration:*	Iron Cross 2nd Class
Religion:	Agnostic	*Marital Status:*	Single
Waffen-SS:	6th SS Division "Nord", 1941-1943		
	12th SS Division "Hitlerjugend", 1943-1944		
Notes:	Served in SA 1931-1932		

Camp Service: **Esterwegen, 1935**

Faschingbauer

First Name:	Karl	*National Archive File:*	A3343 SSO-197
Birthdate:	21 May 1904	*Birthplace:*	Nürnberg-Fuerth
Rank:	SS-Hauptsturmführer	*SS Number:*	55074
NSDAP Number:	1175876	*Highest Decoration:*	War Service Cross 2nd Class
Religion:	Protestant	*Marital Status:*	Married
Waffen-SS:	34th SS Division "Landstorm Nederland", 1945		
Notes:	Administration department at Neuengamme		

Camp Service: **Dachau, 1934-1941**
Sachsenhausen, 1941
Neuengamme, 1941
Natzweiler, 1943

Faust

First Name:	Emil	*National Archive File:*	A3343 SSO-198
Birthdate:	3 March 1899	*Birthplace:*	Oberlahnstein
Rank:	SS-Obersturmführer	*SS Number:*	2381
NSDAP Number:	151165	*Highest Decoration:*	None listed
Religion:	Unknown	*Marital Status:*	Married
Waffen-SS:	No		
Notes:	Degraded and thrown out of SS in 1936		
	Kommandant Neusustrum		

Camp Service: **Esterwegen, 1933**
Neusustrum, 1935

Fehrensen

First Name:	Dr. Wilhelm	*National Archive File:*	A3343 SSO-198
Birthdate:	12 December 1898	*Birthplace:*	Hannover
Rank:	SS-Oberführer	*SS Number:*	276829
NSDAP Number:	2703286	*Highest Decoration:*	German Cross in Gold
Religion:	Agnostic	*Marital Status:*	Married
Waffen-SS:	3rd SS Division "Totenkopf", 1940		
	6th SS Division "Nord", 1942-1944		
	IXth SS Corps, 1944		
Notes:	Corps and division doctor		

Camp Service: **Oranienburg, 1938**

Feil

First Name:	Johann von	*National Archive File:*	A3343 SSO-199
Birthdate:	13 June 1896	*Birthplace:*	Leonfelden, Austria
Rank:	SS-Standartenführer	*SS Number:*	41937
NSDAP Number:	900434	*Highest Decoration:*	War Service Cross 1st Class
Religion:	Agnostic	*Marital Status:*	Married
Waffen-SS:	7th SS Division "Prinz Eugen", 1942		
	6th SS Division "Nord", 1942		
Notes:	Guard Battalion Oranienburg		
	Lived in Argentina from 1945 to mid 1950s; died 30 January 1957		

Camp Service: **Oranienburg, 1941**

Filleboeck

First Name:	Sylvester	*National Archive File:*	A3343 SSO-207
Birthdate:	16 June 1896	*Birthplace:*	Pfronten
Rank:	SS-Untersturmführer	*SS Number:*	25250
NSDAP Number:	865608	*Highest Decoration:*	War Service Cross 2nd Class
Religion:	Agnostic	*Marital Status:*	Married
Waffen-SS:	No		
Notes:	Supply officer at Dachau		
	Iron Cross 2nd Class WWI; executed		

Camp Service: **Dachau, 1933-1941**

Finkenzeller

First Name:	Franz	*National Archive File:*	A3343 SSO-207
Birthdate:	1 August 1913	*Birthplace:*	Pfaffenhofen
Rank:	SS-Obersturmführer	*SS Number:*	15185
NSDAP Number:	771317	*Highest Decoration:*	War Service Cross 2nd Class
Religion:	Catholic	*Marital Status:*	Married
Waffen-SS:	No		
Notes:	Prisoner property chief		

Camp Service: **Mauthausen, 1939-1940**
Ravensbrück, 1940

Fischer

First Name:	Dr. Hermann	*National Archive File:*	A3343 SSO-209
Birthdate:	22 March 1883	*Birthplace:*	Coburg
Rank:	SS-Standartenführer	*SS Number:*	19251
NSDAP Number:	1168069	*Highest Decoration:*	War Service Cross 2nd Class
Religion:	Agnostic	*Marital Status:*	Married
Waffen-SS:	No		
Notes:	Iron Cross 2nd Class WWI; Surgeon		
	Had stomach problems at Flossenbürg; sentenced to 3 years		

Camp Service: **Flossenbürg, 1944-1945**   **Beisen, 1944**
Herzogenbusch, 1944

Fischer

First Name:	Dr. Horst	*National Archive File:*	A3343 SSO-209
Birthdate:	31 December 1912	*Birthplace:*	Dresden
Rank:	SS-Hauptsturmführer	*SS Number:*	293937
NSDAP Number:	5370971	*Highest Decoration:*	War Service Cross 2nd Class
Religion:	Protestant	*Marital Status:*	Married
Waffen-SS:	5th SS Division "Wiking", 1941-1942		
Notes:	Doctor		

Camp Service: **Auschwitz, 1942-1944**
Ravensbrück

Fischer

First Name:	Karl-Josef	*National Archive File:*	A3343 SSO-209
Birthdate:	14 March 1904	*Birthplace:*	Graz, Austria
Rank:	SS-Hauptsturmführer	*SS Number:*	324601
NSDAP Number:	Not a member	*Highest Decoration:*	None listed
Religion:	Agnostic	*Marital Status:*	Single
Waffen-SS:	4th SS Division "Polizei", 1942-1943		
	13th SS Division "Handschar", 1944		
Notes:	Stationed at Hohenlychen Clinic 1940		
	Camp doctor at Auschwitz		

Camp Service: **Auschwitz, 1940**   **Sachsenhausen**
Oranienburg, 1942

Flach

First Name:	Dr. Karl	*National Archive File:*	A3343 SSO-211
Birthdate:	5 November 1901	*Birthplace:*	Aschaffenburg
Rank:	SS-Hauptsturmführer	*SS Number:*	102396
NSDAP Number:	Not a member	*Highest Decoration:*	None listed
Religion:	Catholic	*Marital Status:*	Married
Waffen-SS:	10th SS Division "Frundsberg", 1944		
Notes:	Dentist		

Camp Service: **Dachau, 1941**

Fleischhacker

First Name:	Dr. Hans	*National Archive File:*	A3343 SSO-212
Birthdate:	10 March 1912	*Birthplace:*	Toettleben
Rank:	SS-Obersturmführer (F)	*SS Number:*	307399
NSDAP Number:	7501920	*Highest Decoration:*	War Service Cross 2nd Class
Religion:	Agnostic	*Marital Status:*	Married
Waffen-SS:	No		
Notes:	Ahnenerbe		
	Anthropologist (Tuebingen University)		

Camp Service: **Auschwitz, 1943**

Fleitmann

First Name:	Willi	*National Archive File:*	A3343 SSO-212
Birthdate:	31 March 1891	*Birthplace:*	Horneburg
Rank:	SS-Hauptsturmführer	*SS Number:*	2030
NSDAP Number:	166990	*Highest Decoration:*	None listed
Religion:	Agnostic	*Marital Status:*	Married
Waffen-SS:	No		
Notes:	Iron Cross 1st Class Wound Badge WWI		
	Kommandant Boergermoor		

Camp Service: **Esterwegen, 1933**
Boergermoor, 1933

Flohr

First Name:	Fritz	*National Archive File:*	A3343 SSO-213
Birthdate:	24 March 1905	*Birthplace:*	Rethen
Rank:	SS-Sturmbannführer	*SS Number:*	2948
NSDAP Number:	176639	*Highest Decoration:*	None listed
Religion:	Protestant	*Marital Status:*	Married
Waffen-SS:	No		
Notes:	Later served in the army for two years as an enlisted man		

Camp Service: **Moringen, 1933**

Florstedt

First Name:	Hermann	*National Archive File:*	A3343 SSO-213
Birthdate:	18 February 1895	*Birthplace:*	Bitsch
Rank:	SS-Standartenführer	*SS Number:*	8660
NSDAP Number:	488573	*Highest Decoration:*	None listed
Religion:	Protestant	*Marital Status:*	Married
Waffen-SS:	No		
Notes:	*Kommandant* at Majdanek; Iron Cross 2nd Class WWI		
	Executed by SS 15 April 1945 at Buchenwald		

Camp Service: **Buchenwald, 1939**
Sachsenhausen, 1940-1942
Majdanek, 1942-1943

Flothmann

First Name:	Dr. Karl-Heinz	*National Archive File:*	A3343 SSO-213
Birthdate:	3 July 1909	*Birthplace:*	Essen-Kupferdreh
Rank:	SS-Sturmbannführer	*SS Number:*	367749
NSDAP Number:	4776869	*Highest Decoration:*	War Service Cross 2nd Class
Religion:	Protestant	*Marital Status:*	Married
Waffen-SS:	8th SS Division "Florian Geyer", 1942-1943		
Notes:	Served as doctor at Danzig punishment camp for convicted SS soldiers		

Camp Service: **Mauthausen, 1940-1941**

Foerschner

First Name:	Otto	*National Archive File:*	A3343 SSO-214
Birthdate:	4 November 1902	*Birthplace:*	Duerrenzimmern
Rank:	SS-Sturmbannführer	*SS Number:*	191554
NSDAP Number:	Not a member	*Highest Decoration:*	War Service Cross 1st Class
Religion:	Protestant	*Marital Status:*	Married
Waffen-SS:	5th SS Division "Wiking", 1940-1942		
Notes:	*Kommandant* at Dora and at Kaufering sub-camp		
	Executed 28 May 1946		

Camp Service: **Buchenwald, 1942-1944**
Dora, 1944
Dachau, 1945

Foerster

First Name:	Dr. Hans	*National Archive File:*	A3343 SSO-214
Birthdate:	22 April 1913	*Birthplace:*	Murek, Austria
Rank:	SS-Sturmbannführer	*SS Number:*	293746
NSDAP Number:	6218130	*Highest Decoration:*	Iron Cross 1st Class
Religion:	Protestant	*Marital Status:*	Married
Waffen-SS:	3rd SS Division "Totenkopf", 1939-1941		
	6th SS Division "Nord", 1943		
Notes:	Doctor		

Camp Service: **Buchenwald, 1939**

Foerster

First Name:	Heinrich	*National Archive File:*	A3343 SSO-215
Birthdate:	14 January 1897	*Birthplace:*	Langenaltheim
Rank:	SS-Hauptsturmführer	*SS Number:*	36647
NSDAP Number:	829889	*Highest Decoration:*	None listed
Religion:	Protestant	*Marital Status:*	Married
Waffen-SS:	14th SS Division, 1944		
Notes:	Iron Cross 2nd Class WWI		
	2nd Schutzhaftlagerführer at Sachsenhausen		

Camp Service:	**Sachsenhausen, 1938-1942**	**Kauen, 1943**
	Buchenwald, 1943-1944	**Dachau, 1944**

Frank

First Name:	August	*National Archive File:*	A3343 SSO-216
Birthdate:	5 April 1898	*Birthplace:*	Augsburg
Rank:	SS-Obergruppenführer	*SS Number:*	56169
NSDAP Number:	1471185	*Highest Decoration:*	German Cross in Silver
Religion:	Catholic	*Marital Status:*	Married
Waffen-SS:	No		
Notes:	Iron Cross 2nd Class WWI; acting chief WVHA		
	Originally sentenced to Life Imprisonment; sentence reduced to fifteen years		

Camp Service:	**Dachau, 1934**

Frank

First Name:	Dr. Willy	*National Archive File:*	A3343 SSO-217
Birthdate:	9 February 1903	*Birthplace:*	Regensburg
Rank:	SS-Hauptsturmführer	*SS Number:*	289643
NSDAP Number:	2942877	*Highest Decoration:*	War Service Cross 2nd Class
Religion:	Catholic	*Marital Status:*	Married
Waffen-SS:	5th SS Division "Wiking", 1941-1942		
	3rd SS Division "Totenkopf", 1944		
Notes:	Dentist; took part in 9 November 1923 Putsch; Blood Order		
	Sentenced to 7 years imprisonment		

Camp Service:	**Auschwitz, 1943-1944**	**Dachau, 1944**

Franke

First Name:	Kurt	*National Archive File:*	A3343 SSO-218
Birthdate:	13 June 1913	*Birthplace:*	Wurzen
Rank:	SS-Untersturmführer	*SS Number:*	70826
NSDAP Number:	250876	*Highest Decoration:*	Knight's Cross
Religion:	Agnostic	*Marital Status:*	Married
Waffen-SS:	3rd SS Division "Totenkopf", 1940-1945		
Notes:	Possibly served at Sachsenburg		
	Wounded in action; killed in action 19 January 1945		

Camp Service:	**Sachsenburg, 1934**
	Buchenwald, 1936-1938

Franz

First Name:	Kurt	*National Archive File:*	A3343 SSO-219
Birthdate:	17 January 1914	*Birthplace:*	Duesseldorf
Rank:	SS-Untersturmführer	*SS Number:*	316909
NSDAP Number:	Not a member	*Highest Decoration:*	Iron Cross 2nd Class
Religion:	Protestant	*Marital Status:*	Married
Waffen-SS:	1st SS Division "Leibstandarte Adolf Hitler", 1944		
Notes:	*Kommandant* Treblinka; wounded in action 1944 near Trieste		
	Sentenced to Life; released in 1993 after 34 years in prison		

Camp Service:	**Buchenwald, 1938**	**Sobibór, 1942**
	Belzec, 1942	**Treblinka, 1942-1943**

Fredrich

First Name:	Helmut	*National Archive File:*	A3343 SSO-220
Birthdate:	7 April 1915	*Birthplace:*	Zeitz
Rank:	SS-Sturmbannführer	*SS Number:*	113754
NSDAP Number:	3601203	*Highest Decoration:*	Iron Cross 1st Class
Religion:	Agnostic	*Marital Status:*	Married
Waffen-SS:	3rd SS Division "Totenkopf", 1941-1942		
	2nd SS Division "Das Reich", 1944-1945		
Notes:	1st SS Totenkopfstandarte "Oberbayern"		
	Right leg amputated due to combat wound		

Camp Service:	**Dachau, 1938-1939**

Freesemann

First Name:	Heinrich	*National Archive File:*	A3343 SSO-220
Birthdate:	18 October 1914	*Birthplace:*	Voellenerfoehn
Rank:	SS-Obersturmführer	*SS Number:*	270645
NSDAP Number:	5770580	*Highest Decoration:*	Iron Cross 1st Class
Religion:	Agnostic	*Marital Status:*	Engaged
Waffen-SS:	3rd SS Division "Totenkopf", 1939-1942		
Notes:	Wounded in action several times		
	Guard battalion Sachsenhausen; sentenced to Life		

Camp Service:	**Sachsenhausen, 1943**

Frerichs

First Name:	Wilhelm	*National Archive File:*	A3343 SSO-221
Birthdate:	16 August 1900	*Birthplace:*	Salbergen-Ems
Rank:	SS-Hauptsturmführer	*SS Number:*	310578
NSDAP Number:	4293088	*Highest Decoration:*	None listed
Religion:	Protestant	*Marital Status:*	Married
Waffen-SS:	No		
Notes:	Leader of political department at Buchenwald and Bergen-Belsen		

Camp Service:	**Buchenwald, 1939-1942**
	Bergen-Belsen

Frey

First Name:	Walter	*National Archive File:*	A3343 SSO-221
Birthdate:	28 July 1910	*Birthplace:*	Esslingen
Rank:	SS-Untersturmführer	*SS Number:*	249164
NSDAP Number:	5459804	*Highest Decoration:*	Iron Cross 2nd Class
Religion:	Agnostic	*Marital Status:*	Married
Waffen-SS:	Unknown		
Notes:	Construction office at Buchenwald		
	Camp service not listed in personnel file		

Camp Service: **Buchenwald, 1944**

Fricke

First Name:	Gustav	*National Archive File:*	A3343 SSO-222
Birthdate:	17 July 1890	*Birthplace:*	Wittenborn
Rank:	SS-Sturmbannführer	*SS Number:*	34058
NSDAP Number:	1141033	*Highest Decoration:*	War Service Cross 2nd Class
Religion:	Protestant	*Marital Status:*	Married
Waffen-SS:	No		
Notes:	Iron Cross 2nd Class, Silver Wound Badge WWI		

Camp Service: **Flossenbürg, 1939**
Dachau, 1940-1942

Fricke

First Name:	Helmut	*National Archive File:*	A3343 SSO-222
Birthdate:	19 August 1909	*Birthplace:*	Zwichau
Rank:	SS-Sturmbannführer	*SS Number:*	221122
NSDAP Number:	2993034	*Highest Decoration:*	War Service Cross 2nd Class
Religion:	Protestant	*Marital Status:*	Married
Waffen-SS:	4th SS Division "Polizei", 1942-1943		
Notes:	Administration department		

Camp Service: **Oranienburg, 1938-1940**

Friedl

First Name:	Dr. Josef	*National Archive File:*	A3343 SSO-223
Birthdate:	18 December 1907	*Birthplace:*	Althuetten
Rank:	SS-Hauptsturmführer	*SS Number:*	314532
NSDAP Number:	6669413	*Highest Decoration:*	Iron Cross 2nd Class
Religion:	Unknown	*Marital Status:*	Married
Waffen-SS:	6th SS Division "Nord", 1942-1943		
	7th SS Division "Prinz Eugen", 1943		
Notes:	Killed in action 15 November 1943		

Camp Service: **Sachsenhausen, 1941-1942**   **Mauthausen**

Friedrichs

First Name: Hermann *National Archive File:* A3343 SSO-224
Birthdate: 2 November 1914 *Birthplace:* Hannover
Rank: SS-Obersturmführer *SS Number:* 184211
NSDAP Number: 5274268 *Highest Decoration:* Iron Cross 1st Class
Religion: Agnostic *Marital Status:* Married
Waffen-SS: 2nd SS Infantry Brigade, 1942
10th SS Division "Frundsberg", 1943-1944
Notes: Killed in action 10 April 1944
Company commander in 10th SS Division

Camp Service: **Buchenwald, 1938-1939**

Fritzsch

First Name: Karl *National Archive File:* A3343 SSO-226
Birthdate: 10 July 1903 *Birthplace:* Nassengrub
Rank: SS-Hauptsturmführer *SS Number:* 7287
NSDAP Number: 261135 *Highest Decoration:* War Service Cross 2nd Class
Religion: Agnostic *Marital Status:* Married
Waffen-SS: No
Notes: *Kommandant* at Flossenbürg; Killed in action May 1945

Camp Service: **Dachau, 1935-1940**   **Auschwitz, 1940-1942**
Flossenbürg, 1942-1944   **Dora, 1944**

Frommhagen

First Name: Erich *National Archive File:* A3343 SSO-227
Birthdate: 27 February 1912 *Birthplace:* Salzwedel
Rank: SS-Hauptsturmführer *SS Number:* 73754
NSDAP Number: 4330301 *Highest Decoration:* None listed
Religion: Unknown *Marital Status:* Single
Waffen-SS: 3rd SS Division "Totenkopf", 1942-1945
Notes: Adjutant at Auschwitz

Camp Service: **Auschwitz, 1940-1941**
Neuengamme, 1941

Frowein

First Name: Dr. Ernst *National Archive File:* A3343 SSO-227
Birthdate: 25 August 1916 *Birthplace:* Iserlohn
Rank: SS-Hauptsturmführer *SS Number:* 411912
NSDAP Number: Not a member *Highest Decoration:* Wound Badge in Silver
Religion: Unknown *Marital Status:* Single
Waffen-SS: 3rd SS Division "Totenkopf", 1944
Notes: Doctor
Served in Hitler Youth, 1932-1936

Camp Service: **Sachsenhausen**

Fuhrlaender

First Name:	Dr. Wilhelm	*National Archive File:*	A3343 SSO-230
Birthdate:	7 March 1901	*Birthplace:*	Haiger
Rank:	SS-Obersturmbannführer	*SS Number:*	276214
NSDAP Number:	260970	*Highest Decoration:*	None listed
Religion:	Unknown	*Marital Status:*	Married
Waffen-SS:	3rd SS Division "Totenkopf", 1940		
	16th SS Division "Reichsführer-SS", 1944		
Notes:	Education officer for Totenkopfverbaende; served in SA 1932		

Camp Service: **Oranienburg, 1935-1939**

Fuss

First Name:	Ernst	*National Archive File:*	A3343 SSO-231
Birthdate:	24 March 1902	*Birthplace:*	Rothenfels
Rank:	SS-Hauptsturmführer	*SS Number:*	293147
NSDAP Number:	1855924	*Highest Decoration:*	War Service Cross 2nd Class
Religion:	Agnostic	*Marital Status:*	Married
Waffen-SS:	6th SS Division "Nord", 1941-1942		
	34th SS Division "Landstorm Nederland", 1944		
Notes:	Adjutant at Herzogenbusch		

Camp Service: **Oranienburg, 1939**
Herzogenbusch, 1943-1944

Gaberle

First Name:	Dr. Alois	*National Archive File:*	A3343 SSO-001A
Birthdate:	30 September 1907	*Birthplace:*	Oel-Doerberney
Rank:	SS-Untersturmführer	*SS Number:*	363185
NSDAP Number:	6621162	*Highest Decoration:*	None listed
Religion:	Agnostic	*Marital Status:*	Married
Waffen-SS:	No		
Notes:	Assistant physician at Sachsenhausen; sentenced to 3 years		

Camp Service: **Sachsenhausen, 1943-1945**

Gaebler

First Name:	Johannes	*National Archive File:*	A3343 SSO-001A
Birthdate:	12 April 1901	*Birthplace:*	Goeppersdorf
Rank:	SS-Obersturmführer	*SS Number:*	190902
NSDAP Number:	3714580	*Highest Decoration:*	War Service Cross 2nd Class
Religion:	Agnostic	*Marital Status:*	Married
Waffen-SS:	19th SS Division, 1944		
	15th SS Division, 1944-1945		
Notes:	Camp service not listed in personnel file		

Camp Service: **Stutthof, 1941**

Ganninger

First Name:	Heinrich	*National Archive File:*	A3343 SSO-003A
Birthdate:	16 July 1908	*Birthplace:*	Mannheim
Rank:	SS-Obersturmführer	*SS Number:*	102470
NSDAP Number:	4266216	*Highest Decoration:*	War Service Cross 2nd Class
Religion:	Agnostic	*Marital Status:*	Married
Waffen-SS:	No		
Notes:	Platoon leader in 1st Company SS-Totenkopfsturmbann Auschwitz		

Camp Service: **Auschwitz, 1942-1944**
Natzweiler, 1944

Ganz

First Name:	Anton	*National Archive File:*	A3343 SSO-003A
Birthdate:	6 February 1899	*Birthplace:*	Kettershausen
Rank:	SS-Hauptsturmführer	*SS Number:*	34572
NSDAP Number:	672421	*Highest Decoration:*	War Service Cross 2nd Class
Religion:	Catholic	*Marital Status:*	Married
Waffen-SS:	Unknown		
Notes:	Lagerführer at Ebensee sub-camp and Wiener-Neustadt sub-camp		

Camp Service: **Hinzert, 1940-1942**
Mauthausen, 1942-1945

Gast

First Name:	Otto	*National Archive File:*	A3343 SSO-004A
Birthdate:	6 July 1908	*Birthplace:*	Stendal
Rank:	SS-Obersturmführer	*SS Number:*	177886
NSDAP Number:	4641434	*Highest Decoration:*	Iron Cross 2nd Class
Religion:	Agnostic	*Marital Status:*	Married
Waffen-SS:	3rd SS Division "Totenkopf", 1942		
	36th SS Division "Dirlewanger", 1944		
Notes:	Administrative officer in Sonderkommando Dirlewanger		

Camp Service: **Oranienburg, 1941-1942**

Gebhardt

First Name:	Dr. Fritz	*National Archive File:*	A3343 SSO-005A
Birthdate:	3 September 1894	*Birthplace:*	Dresden
Rank:	SS-Obersturmführer	*SS Number:*	121091
NSDAP Number:	1961621	*Highest Decoration:*	None listed
Religion:	Protestant	*Marital Status:*	Divorced
Waffen-SS:	No		
Notes:	Doctor for guard troops at Sachsenburg		

Camp Service: **Sachsenburg, 1935**

Gebhardt

First Name:	Dr. Karl	*National Archive File:*	A3343 SSO-005A
Birthdate:	23 November 1897	*Birthplace:*	Haag
Rank:	SS-Gruppenführer	*SS Number:*	265894
NSDAP Number:	1723317	*Highest Decoration:*	Knight's Cross of the War Service Cross
Religion:	Catholic	*Marital Status:*	Married
Waffen-SS:	2nd SS Division "Das Reich", 1940		
Notes:	Doctor; conducted experiments at Ravensbrück but not permanently assigned there		
	Blood Order; Iron Cross 1st Class and Wound Badge WWI; executed 2 June 1948		

Camp Service: **Ravensbrück, 1942**

Gebhardt

First Name:	Max	*National Archive File:*	A3343 SSO-005A
Birthdate:	6 November 1899	*Birthplace:*	Grafengehaig
Rank:	SS-Sturmbannführer	*SS Number:*	44185
NSDAP Number:	1374719	*Highest Decoration:*	Iron Cross 1st Class
Religion:	Unknown	*Marital Status:*	Married
Waffen-SS:	34th SS Division "Landstorm Nederland"		
Notes:	Died 9 December 1944; Iron Cross 2nd Class and Wound Badge WWI		
	Commander IIIrd Totenkopfsturmbann, 3rd Totenkopfstandarte		

Camp Service: **Esterwegen, 1935**
Oranienburg

Gehrig

First Name:	Christoph	*National Archive File:*	A3343 SSO-006A
Birthdate:	27 October 1890	*Birthplace:*	Laudenbach
Rank:	SS-Sturmbannführer	*SS Number:*	250066
NSDAP Number:	308759	*Highest Decoration:*	War Service Cross 1st Class
Religion:	Catholic	*Marital Status:*	Married
Waffen-SS:	SS Infantry Regiment 8, 1941		
Notes:	Camp Administration at Dachau and Neuengamme		
	Iron Cross 2nd Class WWI		

Camp Service: **Dachau, 1943-1944**
Neuengamme, 1944

Geiger

First Name:	Dr. Hans-Joachim	*National Archive File:*	A3343 SSO-007A
Birthdate:	7 February 1913	*Birthplace:*	Liebenstein
Rank:	SS-Obersturmführer	*SS Number:*	142033
NSDAP Number:	Not a member	*Highest Decoration:*	War Service Cross 2nd Class
Religion:	Protestant	*Marital Status:*	Married
Waffen-SS:	8th SS Division "Florian Geyer", 1942		
	9th SS Division "Hohenstaufen", 1943		
Notes:	Ebensee sub-camp		

Camp Service: **Mauthausen, 1943**

Geisel

First Name:	Heinrich	*National Archive File:*	A3343 SSO-007A
Birthdate:	14 October 1893	*Birthplace:*	Bernsburg
Rank:	SS-Hauptsturmführer	*SS Number:*	4323
NSDAP Number:	230273	*Highest Decoration:*	None listed
Religion:	Agnostic	*Marital Status:*	Married
Waffen-SS:	No		
Notes:	Lagerführer at Hinzert		
	Iron Cross 2nd Class and Wound Badge WWI		

Camp Service: **Hinzert, 1940-1941**
Buchenwald, 1942

Geisler

First Name:	Paul	*National Archive File:*	A3343 SSO-007A
Birthdate:	6 February 1899	*Birthplace:*	Merzdorf
Rank:	SS-Standartenführer	*SS Number:*	127020
NSDAP Number:	854706	*Highest Decoration:*	Bar to Iron Cross 2nd Class
Religion:	Agnostic	*Marital Status:*	Married
Waffen-SS:	3rd SS Division "Totenkopf", 1940		
	5th SS Division "Wiking", 1942		
Notes:	Iron Cross 2nd Class WWI; Blood Order		
	Regimental commander in 5th SS Division		

Camp Service: **Oranienburg, 1937-1938**

Gemmeker

First Name:	Albert	*National Archive File:*	A3343 SSO-008A
Birthdate:	27 September 1907	*Birthplace:*	Duesseldorf
Rank:	SS-Obersturmführer	*SS Number:*	382609
NSDAP Number:	5620430	*Highest Decoration:*	None listed
Religion:	Agnostic	*Marital Status:*	Married
Waffen-SS:	No		
Notes:	*Kommandant* Westerbork		
	Sentenced to 10 years imprisonment		

Camp Service: **Westerbork, 1943**

Gensior

First Name:	Paul	*National Archive File:*	A3343 SSO-008A
Birthdate:	19 August 1902	*Birthplace:*	Koppitz
Rank:	SS-Obersturmführer	*SS Number:*	292156
NSDAP Number:	1738195	*Highest Decoration:*	None listed
Religion:	Agnostic	*Marital Status:*	Married
Waffen-SS:	No		
Notes:	Former electrician		
	Served in *Freikorps*		

Camp Service: **Sachsenhausen, 1944**

Genzken

First Name:	Dr. Karl	*National Archive File:*	A3343 SSO-008A
Birthdate:	8 June 1885	*Birthplace:*	Preetz
Rank:	SS-Gruppenführer	*SS Number:*	207954
NSDAP Number:	39913	*Highest Decoration:*	War Service Cross 1st Class
Religion:	Protestant	*Marital Status:*	Married
Waffen-SS:	3rd SS Division "Totenkopf", 1939-1940		
Notes:	Sterilized habitual criminals at Oranienburg		
	Iron Cross 1st Class WWI; Golden Party Badge		

Camp Service: **Oranienburg, 1937-1939**

Gerber

First Name:	Gerhard	*National Archive File:*	A3343 SSO-009A
Birthdate:	5 August 1915	*Birthplace:*	Strassburg
Rank:	SS-Obersturmführer	*SS Number:*	433204
NSDAP Number:	8734492	*Highest Decoration:*	None listed
Religion:	Agnostic	*Marital Status:*	Married
Waffen-SS:	No		
Notes:	Pharmacist		

Camp Service: **Auschwitz, 1944**
Mauthausen, 1945

Gerlach

First Name:	Walter	*National Archive File:*	A3343 SSO-009A
Birthdate:	25 August 1896	*Birthplace:*	Gusow
Rank:	SS-Oberführer	*SS Number:*	14567
NSDAP Number:	307120	*Highest Decoration:*	War Service Cross 1st Class
Religion:	Protestant	*Marital Status:*	Married
Waffen-SS:	No		
Notes:	Adjutant at Dachau; *Kommandant* at Columbia Haus; Iron Cross 2nd Class WWI;		
	died 31 August 1963		

Camp Service: **Columbia Haus, 1934**   **Sachsenburg, 1934-1935**
Lichtenburg, 1935   **Dachau, 1935-1936**

Gerstein

First Name:	Kurt	*National Archive File:*	A3343 SSO-010A
Birthdate:	11 August 1905	*Birthplace:*	Muenster
Rank:	SS-Obersturmführer	*SS Number:*	417460
NSDAP Number:	Not a member	*Highest Decoration:*	War Service Cross 2nd Class
Religion:	Protestant	*Marital Status:*	Married
Waffen-SS:	No		
Notes:	Disinfectant Officer, SS Hygiene Institute; supplied *Zyklon B* to camps; Visited camps		
	only; attempted to inform Sweden of camp atrocities; suicide 1945		

Camp Service: **Auschwitz, 1942**   **Majdanek, 1942**
Belzec, 1942   **Treblinka, 1942**
Ravensbrück, 1942

Gideon

First Name: Wilhelm	*National Archive File:* A3343 SSO-011A
Birthdate: 15 November 1898	*Birthplace:* Osternburg
Rank: SS-Obersturmführer	*SS Number:* 88569
NSDAP Number: Not a member	*Highest Decoration:* War Service Cross 1st Class
Religion: Protestant	*Marital Status:* Married
Waffen-SS: 3rd SS Division "Totenkopf"	
Notes: *Kommandant* Gross-Rosen; Iron Cross 2nd Class WWI	

Camp Service: **Gross-Rosen, 1942**   **Neuengamme, 1942**
Oranienburg, 1942

Glatz

First Name: Josef	*National Archive File:* A3343 SSO-016A
Birthdate: 3 May 1911	*Birthplace:* Hodosch, Romania
Rank: SS-Obersturmführer	*SS Number:* Unknown
NSDAP Number: Not a member	*Highest Decoration:* None listed
Religion: Unknown	*Marital Status:* Married
Waffen-SS: No	
Notes: Served in Romanian army	
Pharmacist	

Camp Service: **Mauthausen, 1944-1945**

Glode

First Name: Heinz	*National Archive File:* A3343 SSO-017A
Birthdate: 4 March 1914	*Birthplace:* Kolberg
Rank: SS-Obersturmführer	*SS Number:* 159405
NSDAP Number: Not a member	*Highest Decoration:* None listed
Religion: Protestant	*Marital Status:* Single
Waffen-SS: No	
Notes: Died 6 December 1936 of tuberculosis	

Camp Service: **Sachsenburg, 1934-1935**

Gluecks

First Name: Richard	*National Archive File:* A3343 SSO-017A
Birthdate: 22 April 1889	*Birthplace:* Odenkirchen
Rank: SS-Gruppenführer	*SS Number:* 58706
NSDAP Number: 214855	*Highest Decoration:* German Cross in Silver
Religion: Agnostic	*Marital Status:* Married
Waffen-SS: No	
Notes: Replaced Theodor Eicke	
Missing in action May 1945; probable suicide 10 May 1945	

Camp Service: **Oranienburg, 1937-1945**

Goebel

First Name:	Dr. Walter	*National Archive File:*	A3343 SSO-018A
Birthdate:	28 April 1891	*Birthplace:*	Siegen
Rank:	SS-Untersturmführer	*SS Number:*	182700
NSDAP Number:	3003519	*Highest Decoration:*	None listed
Religion:	Protestant	*Marital Status:*	Married
Waffen-SS:	No		
Notes:	Physician; assistant to Dr. Clauberg		
	Iron Cross 2nd Class WWI		

Camp Service: **Auschwitz, 1942-1944**
Ravensbrück, 1944

Goecke

First Name:	Wilhelm	*National Archive File:*	A3343 SSO-018A
Birthdate:	12 February 1898	*Birthplace:*	Schwelm
Rank:	SS-Obersturmbannführer	*SS Number:*	21529
NSDAP Number:	335455	*Highest Decoration:*	German Cross in Gold
Religion:	Agnostic	*Marital Status:*	Married
Waffen-SS:	No		
Notes:	*Kommandant* Kauen; killed in action 22 October 1944 Adriatic Coast		
	Iron Cross 1st Class Silver Wound Badge WWI		

Camp Service: **Mauthausen, 1942** **Kauen, 1943**

Göhler

First Name:	Johannes	*National Archive File:*	A3343 SSO-018A
Birthdate:	15 September 1918	*Birthplace:*	Bischofswerda
Rank:	SS-Sturmbannführer	*SS Number:*	310963
NSDAP Number:	5229214	*Highest Decoration:*	Knight's Cross
Religion:	Agnostic	*Marital Status:*	Married
Waffen-SS:	8th SS Division "Florian Geyer", 1942-1944		
Notes:	Wounded in action; served in Hitler Youth 1933-1936		

Camp Service: **Dachau, 1937-1939**

Göth

First Name:	Amon	*National Archive File:*	A3343 SSO-020A
Birthdate:	11 December 1908	*Birthplace:*	Vienna, Austria
Rank:	SS-Hauptsturmführer	*SS Number:*	43673
NSDAP Number:	510764	*Highest Decoration:*	None listed
Religion:	Catholic	*Marital Status:*	Married
Waffen-SS:	No		
Notes:	*Kommandant* at Plaszow; member of *Operation Reinhard*, Lublin 1942		
	Executed 13 September 1946		

Camp Service: **Plaszow, 1943-1944**

Götz

First Name:	Dr. Hans	*National Archive File:*	A3343 SSO-021A
Birthdate:	24 June 1909	*Birthplace:*	Augezd, Austria
Rank:	SS-Hauptsturmführer	*SS Number:*	336276
NSDAP Number:	6781637	*Highest Decoration:*	Iron Cross 2nd Class
Religion:	Catholic	*Marital Status:*	Married
Waffen-SS:	1st SS Infantry Brigade		
Notes:	Department DIV, Oranienburg		

Camp Service: **Oranienburg, 1940-1941, 1944**

Goroncy

First Name:	Heinz	*National Archive File:*	A3343 SSO-023A
Birthdate:	26 October 1914	*Birthplace:*	Danzig
Rank:	SS-Hauptsturmführer	*SS Number:*	257882
NSDAP Number:	3601505	*Highest Decoration:*	None listed
Religion:	Agnostic	*Marital Status:*	Married
Waffen-SS:	3rd SS Division "Totenkopf", 1940-1942		
Notes:	Platoon leader in 10th Company 1st SS Totenkopfstandarte "Oberbayern"		
	Killed in action 26 April 1942 in Russia		

Camp Service: **Dachau, 1938**

Gossow

First Name:	Erich	*National Archive File:*	A3343 SSO-024A
Birthdate:	13 October 1903	*Birthplace:*	Grueneberg
Rank:	SS-Obersturmführer	*SS Number:*	270203
NSDAP Number:	1994452	*Highest Decoration:*	War Service Cross 2nd Class
Religion:	Protestant	*Marital Status:*	Married
Waffen-SS:	6th SS Division "Nord", 1942		
Notes:	Former teacher		
	Wounded in action		

Camp Service: **Sachsenhausen, 1943-1944**

Gottschalk

First Name:	Gerhard	*National Archive File:*	A3343 SSO-025A
Birthdate:	21 February 1912	*Birthplace:*	Dresden
Rank:	SS-Hauptsturmführer	*SS Number:*	159873
NSDAP Number:	1961601	*Highest Decoration:*	Iron Cross 1st Class
Religion:	Agnostic	*Marital Status:*	Married
Waffen-SS:	8th SS Division "Florian Geyer", 1942-1944		
Notes:	3rd SS Totenkopfstandarte "Thüringen"		

Camp Service: **Buchenwald, 1938**

Grabhorn

First Name:	Dr. Arno	*National Archive File:*	A3343 SSO-026A
Birthdate:	15 May 1887	*Birthplace:*	Muelheim
Rank:	SS-Sturmbannführer	*SS Number:*	144720
NSDAP Number:	2093392	*Highest Decoration:*	War Service Cross 2nd Class
Religion:	Agnostic	*Marital Status:*	Married
Waffen-SS:	No		
Notes:	Doctor		
	Served in WWI		

Camp Service: **Buchenwald, 1941**

Grabner

First Name:	Maximillian	*National Archive File:*	A3343 RS-B5261
Birthdate:	2 October 1905	*Birthplace:*	Vienna, Austria
Rank:	SS-Untersturmführer	*SS Number:*	Unknown
NSDAP Number:	Not a member	*Highest Decoration:*	War Service Cross 2nd Class
Religion:	Agnostic	*Marital Status:*	Married
Waffen-SS:	No		
Notes:	Served in Austrian army; sentenced by SS to 12 years imprisonment in 1944		
	Chief, political section; executed 12 December 1947		

Camp Service: **Auschwitz, 1940-1943**

Grabow

First Name:	Kurt	*National Archive File:*	A3343 SSO-026A
Birthdate:	14 September 1906	*Birthplace:*	Graudenz
Rank:	SS-Hauptsturmführer	*SS Number:*	15847
NSDAP Number:	401665	*Highest Decoration:*	None listed
Religion:	Unknown	*Marital Status:*	Unknown
Waffen-SS:	No		
Notes:	Served in SA 1930-1931		

Camp Service: **Oranienburg, 1937-1938**
Buchenwald, 1938-1939

Gradl

First Name:	Heinrich	*National Archive File:*	A3343 SSO-026A
Birthdate:	27 May 1914	*Birthplace:*	Vienna, Austria
Rank:	SS-Hauptsturmführer	*SS Number:*	132121
NSDAP Number:	612555	*Highest Decoration:*	War Service Cross 2nd Class
Religion:	Agnostic	*Marital Status:*	Married
Waffen-SS:	9th SS Division "Hohenstaufen", 1944		
Notes:	Served in SA 1930-1931		

Camp Service: **Flossenbürg, 1939**

Graeff

First Name:	Dr. Herbert	*National Archive File:*	A3343 SSO-026A
Birthdate:	5 October 1913	*Birthplace:*	Mannheim
Rank:	SS-Obersturmführer	*SS Number:*	200137
NSDAP Number:	4028808	*Highest Decoration:*	None listed
Religion:	Protestant	*Marital Status:*	Married
Waffen-SS:	2nd SS Division "Das Reich", 1942-1944		
Notes:	Missing in action, 5 August 1944		

Camp Service: **Natzweiler, 1941**
Majdanek, 1942

Grams

First Name:	Ruprecht	*National Archive File:*	A3343 SSO-028A
Birthdate:	16 November 1914	*Birthplace:*	Jueterbog
Rank:	SS-Hauptsturmführer	*SS Number:*	150930
NSDAP Number:	4137094	*Highest Decoration:*	Iron Cross 1st Class
Religion:	Agnostic	*Marital Status:*	Single
Waffen-SS:	3rd SS Division "Totenkopf", 1940-1943		
	17th SS Division "Götz von Berlichingen", 1943-1944		
Notes:	Wounded in action, Russia		

Camp Service: **Oranienburg, 1938-1939**

Greb

First Name:	Karl	*National Archive File:*	A3343 SSO-030A
Birthdate:	10 March 1909	*Birthplace:*	Neuburg
Rank:	SS-Untersturmführer	*SS Number:*	179702
NSDAP Number:	4602221	*Highest Decoration:*	None listed
Religion:	Agnostic	*Marital Status:*	Married
Waffen-SS:	No		
Notes:	Former bank teller		

Camp Service: **Hinzert**

Greunuss

First Name:	Dr. Werner	*National Archive File:*	A3343 SSO-031A
Birthdate:	20 February 1908	*Birthplace:*	Unknown
Rank:	SS-Untersturmführer	*SS Number:*	Unknown
NSDAP Number:	98403	*Highest Decoration:*	None listed
Religion:	Unknown	*Marital Status:*	Married
Waffen-SS:	No		
Notes:	Camp doctor at Ohrdruf sub-camp		
	Wife was also a physician		

Camp Service: **Buchenwald, 1945**

Griem

First Name:	Hans	*National Archive File:*	A3343 SSO-031A
Birthdate:	12 May 1902	*Birthplace:*	Berlin-Spandau
Rank:	SS-Obersturmführer	*SS Number:*	15390
NSDAP Number:	319125	*Highest Decoration:*	Iron Cross 2nd Class
Religion:	Protestant	*Marital Status:*	Married
Waffen-SS:	No		
Notes:	*Kommandant* Husum-Schwesing sub-camp		
	Sentenced to Death; escaped, died in 1971		

Camp Service: **Neuengamme, 1940-1945**

Grimm

First Name:	Johannes	*National Archive File:*	A3343 SSO-032A
Birthdate:	5 December 1897	*Birthplace:*	Chemnitz
Rank:	SS-Obersturmführer (F)	*SS Number:*	411946
NSDAP Number:	715638	*Highest Decoration:*	War Service Cross 2nd Class
Religion:	Agnostic	*Marital Status:*	Married
Waffen-SS:	No		
Notes:	Iron Cross 2nd Class, Wound Badge WWI		
	DEST Mauthausen; executed 27 May 1947		

Camp Service: **Mauthausen, 1941-1945**

Grimm

First Name:	Philipp	*National Archive File:*	A3343 SSO-032A
Birthdate:	1 April 1909	*Birthplace:*	Zwiesel
Rank:	SS-Obersturmführer	*SS Number:*	75948
NSDAP Number:	247809	*Highest Decoration:*	War Service Cross 2nd Class
Religion:	Catholic	*Marital Status:*	Married
Waffen-SS:	No		
Notes:	Arbeitseinsatzführer at Neuengamme		
	Acting commander at Buchenwald in 1945		

Camp Service: **Oranienburg, 1943-1944**
Neuengamme, 1944-1945
Buchenwald, 1945

Grosch

First Name:	Wolfgang	*National Archive File:*	A3343 SSO-034A
Birthdate:	15 September 1906	*Birthplace:*	Weimar
Rank:	SS-Sturmbannführer	*SS Number:*	240155
NSDAP Number:	868731	*Highest Decoration:*	Iron Cross 2nd Class
Religion:	Unknown	*Marital Status:*	Married
Waffen-SS:	No		
Notes:	Engineer		

Camp Service: **Buchenwald, 1938-1941**

Gross

First Name: Dr. Karl-Joseph   *National Archive File:* A3343 SSO-036A
Birthdate: 12 October 1907   *Birthplace:* Bad Vellach
Rank: SS-Sturmbannführer   *SS Number:* 314902
NSDAP Number: Not a member   *Highest Decoration:* War Service Cross 2nd Class
Religion: Unknown   *Marital Status:* Single
Waffen-SS: 2nd SS Division "Das Reich", 1939-1942
Notes: Visited Mauthausen to conduct experiments
Died 1 January 1967

Camp Service: **Mauthausen, 1943**

Grossmann

First Name: Hermann   *National Archive File:* A3343 SSO-038A
Birthdate: 21 July 1901   *Birthplace:* Petersdorf
Rank: SS-Obersturmführer   *SS Number:* 150923
NSDAP Number: Not a member   *Highest Decoration:* War Service Cross 2nd Class
Religion: Agnostic   *Marital Status:* Married
Waffen-SS: No
Notes: Executed 19 November 1948

Camp Service: **Buchenwald, 1940**

Groth

First Name: Konrad   *National Archive File:* A3343 SSO-038A
Birthdate: 2 November 1910   *Birthplace:* Eutin
Rank: SS-Hauptsturmführer   *SS Number:* 56733
NSDAP Number: 1390531   *Highest Decoration:* War Service Cross 1st Class
Religion: Agnostic   *Marital Status:* Married
Waffen-SS: 20th SS Division, 1944
17th SS Division "Götz von Berlichingen", 1944-1945
Notes: Former mason

Camp Service: **Dachau, 1938-1939**
Buchenwald, 1939-1940

Gruenberg

First Name: Georg   *National Archive File:* A3343 SSO-039A
Birthdate: 10 October 1906   *Birthplace:* Freiburg
Rank: SS-Obersturmführer   *SS Number:* 23860
NSDAP Number: 690386   *Highest Decoration:* War Service Cross 1st Class
Religion: Protestant   *Marital Status:* Married
Waffen-SS: 3rd SS Division "Totenkopf", 1939-1940
Notes: Engineer

Camp Service: **Sachsenhausen, 1941-1942**   **Auschwitz, 1942-1943**
Dachau, 1943-1944

Gruenewald

First Name:	Adam	*National Archive File:*	A3343 SSO-039A
Birthdate:	20 October 1902	*Birthplace:*	Frickenhausen
Rank:	SS-Sturmbannführer	*SS Number:*	253631
NSDAP Number:	536404	*Highest Decoration:*	None listed
Religion:	Unknown	*Marital Status:*	Married
Waffen-SS:	3rd SS Division "Totenkopf", 1944-1945		
Notes:	Schuetzhaftlagerführer at Dachau; *Kommandant* Herzogenbusch		
	Sentenced by SS to 3 years imprisonment; killed in action Hungary 1945		

Camp Service: **Lichtenburg, 1934-1937**   **Buchenwald, 1938**
Dachau, 1938-1939   **Sachsenhausen, 1942**
Herzogenbusch, 1943-1944

Grueter

First Name:	Heinrich	*National Archive File:*	A3343 SSO-040A
Birthdate:	10 January 1887	*Birthplace:*	Krefeld
Rank:	SS-Obersturmführer	*SS Number:*	40945
NSDAP Number:	1294371	*Highest Decoration:*	None listed
Religion:	Catholic	*Marital Status:*	Married
Waffen-SS:	No		
Notes:	Iron Cross 2nd Class WWI		

Camp Service: **Buchenwald, 1940**   **Niederhagen**

Gudacker

First Name:	Dr. Heinz	*National Archive File:*	A3343 SSO-041A
Birthdate:	8 May 1911	*Birthplace:*	Neidenburg
Rank:	SS-Sturmbannführer	*SS Number:*	347200
NSDAP Number:	Not a member	*Highest Decoration:*	War Service Cross 2nd Class
Religion:	Agnostic	*Marital Status:*	Married
Waffen-SS:	2nd SS Division "Das Reich", 1940-1941, 1943-1944		
	17th SS Division "Götz von Berlichingen", 1944		
Notes:	Doctor		

Camp Service: **Buchenwald, 1940**

Guenther

First Name:	Hans-Ulrich	*National Archive File:*	A3343 SSO-041A
Birthdate:	28 March 1911	*Birthplace:*	Riga, Latvia
Rank:	SS-Untersturmführer	*SS Number:*	67544
NSDAP Number:	1497765	*Highest Decoration:*	None listed
Religion:	Agnostic	*Marital Status:*	Single
Waffen-SS:	No		
Notes:	Former hotel employee		

Camp Service: **Oranienburg**

Guessow

First Name: Dr. Hans   *National Archive File:* A3343 SSO-042A
Birthdate: 19 May 1889   *Birthplace:* Seehausen
Rank: SS-Sturmbannführer   *SS Number:* 135798
NSDAP Number: 2671551   *Highest Decoration:* War Service Cross 2nd Class
Religion: Protestant   *Marital Status:* Married
Waffen-SS: No
Notes: Iron Cross 2nd Class WWI
Dentist at Sachsenhausen

Camp Service: **Sachsenhausen, 1939-1945**

Guessregen

First Name: Georg   *National Archive File:* A3343 SSO-042A
Birthdate: 7 April 1890   *Birthplace:* Bamberg
Rank: SS-Obersturmführer   *SS Number:* 222498
NSDAP Number: 3988326   *Highest Decoration:* War Service Cross 2nd Class
Religion: Agnostic   *Marital Status:* Married
Waffen-SS: No
Notes: Iron Cross 2nd Class WWI

Camp Service: **Sachsenhausen, 1941**   **Gross-Rosen, 1941**
Auschwitz, 1942   **Flossenbürg, 1943**

Gust

First Name: Erich   *National Archive File:* A3343 SSO-044A
Birthdate: 30 August 1909   *Birthplace:* Klein-Boelkau
Rank: SS-Hauptsturmführer   *SS Number:* 54444
NSDAP Number: 465978   *Highest Decoration:* War Service Cross 2nd Class
Religion: Protestant   *Marital Status:* Married
Waffen-SS: No
Notes: Guard troops at Stutthof

Camp Service: **Stutthof, 1941-1942**

Guth

First Name: Michel   *National Archive File:* No File
Birthdate: 26 June 1914   *Birthplace:* Unknown
Rank: SS-Hauptsturmführer   *SS Number:* Unknown
NSDAP Number: Not a member   *Highest Decoration:* None listed
Religion: Unknown   *Marital Status:* Unknown
Waffen-SS: Unknown

Camp Service: **Majdanek, 1944**

Haas

First Name:	Adolf	*National Archive File:*	A3343 SSO-045A
Birthdate:	14 November 1893	*Birthplace:*	Siegen
Rank:	SS-Obersturmbannführer	*SS Number:*	28943
NSDAP Number:	760610	*Highest Decoration:*	War Service Cross 2nd Class
Religion:	Protestant	*Marital Status:*	Married
Waffen-SS:	No		
Notes:	*Kommandant* Bergen-Belsen; Killed in action 31 March 1945		

Camp Service: **Sachsenhausen, 1940**
Wewelsburg, 1940-1943
Bergen-Belsen, 1943-1944

Haas

First Name:	Eberhard	*National Archive File:*	A3343 SSO-046A
Birthdate:	7 October 1913	*Birthplace:*	Unknown
Rank:	SS-Hauptsturmführer	*SS Number:*	268247
NSDAP Number:	Not a member	*Highest Decoration:*	None listed
Religion:	Protestant	*Marital Status:*	Married
Waffen-SS:	No		
Notes:	Camp doctor at Mauthausen		
	Camp service not listed in personnel file		

Camp Service: **Mauthausen, 1940**

Haas

First Name:	Fritz	*National Archive File:*	A3343 SSO-046A
Birthdate:	19 July 1912	*Birthplace:*	Friedberg
Rank:	SS-Sturmbannführer	*SS Number:*	61057
NSDAP Number:	1340872	*Highest Decoration:*	Iron Cross 1st Class
Religion:	Agnostic	*Marital Status:*	Single
Waffen-SS:	3rd SS Division "Totenkopf", 1940-1943		
	10th SS Division "Frundsberg", 1944		
Notes:	Guard troops at Dachau; severe wound to leg		
	Artillery battalion commander in 10th SS Division		

Camp Service: **Dachau, 1937**

Habben

First Name:	Markus	*National Archive File:*	A3343 SSO-047A
Birthdate:	26 October 1903	*Birthplace:*	Nordhausen
Rank:	SS-Sturmbannführer	*SS Number:*	15347
NSDAP Number:	71617	*Highest Decoration:*	Golden Party Badge
Religion:	Lutheran	*Marital Status:*	Married
Waffen-SS:	Yes, unit unknown		
Notes:	Commander IVth Totenkopfsturmbann, 2nd Totenkopfstandarte		
	Reduced to enlisted ranks; killed in action 21 September 1941		

Camp Service: **Lichtenburg, 1935-1936**   **Esterwegen, 1936**
Oranienburg, 1940-1941   **Mauthausen, 1941**

Habersaat

First Name:	Fritz	*National Archive File:*	A3343 SSO-048A
Birthdate:	31 March 1898	*Birthplace:*	Kaihof
Rank:	SS-Hauptsturmführer	*SS Number:*	30878
NSDAP Number:	1047884	*Highest Decoration:*	None listed
Religion:	Lutheran	*Marital Status:*	Married
Waffen-SS:	No		
Notes:	Iron Cross 2nd Class WWI		
	Died 12 April 1937		

Camp Service: **Esterwegen, 1935**

Hackethal

First Name:	Theophil	*National Archive File:*	A3343 SSO-048A
Birthdate:	13 December 1883	*Birthplace:*	Moenchen-Gladbach
Rank:	SS-Sturmbannführer	*SS Number:*	106408
NSDAP Number:	1802808	*Highest Decoration:*	War Service Cross 2nd Class
Religion:	Catholic	*Marital Status:*	Married
Waffen-SS:	No		
Notes:	Iron Cross 2nd Class WWI		
	Doctor		

Camp Service: **Hinzert**

Hackmann

First Name:	Hermann	*National Archive File:*	A3343 SSO-048A
Birthdate:	11 November 1913	*Birthplace:*	Osnabrueck
Rank:	SS-Hauptsturmführer	*SS Number:*	164705
NSDAP Number:	Not a member	*Highest Decoration:*	None listed
Religion:	Agnostic	*Marital Status:*	Single
Waffen-SS:	No		
Notes:	Schutzhaftlagerführer Majdanek		
	Sentenced to 25 years		

Camp Service: **Buchenwald, 1938-1941**
Oranienburg, 1941
Majdanek, 1941-1942

Haefele

First Name:	Alois	*National Archive File:*	A3343 SSO-049A
Birthdate:	5 July 1893	*Birthplace:*	Guendlingen
Rank:	SS-Untersturmführer	*SS Number:*	354180
NSDAP Number:	Unknown	*Highest Decoration:*	None listed
Religion:	Catholic	*Marital Status:*	Married
Waffen-SS:	No		
Notes:	Iron Cross 2nd Class WWI		
	Camp service not listed in personnel file; sentenced to 13 years		

Camp Service: **Chelmno, 1942-1943, 1943-1944**

Haenel

First Name:	Herbert	*National Archive File:*	A3343 SSO-049A
Birthdate:	18 July 1912	*Birthplace:*	Schlettau
Rank:	SS-Obersturmführer	*SS Number:*	121523
NSDAP Number:	1959050	*Highest Decoration:*	None listed
Religion:	Protestant	*Marital Status:*	Married
Waffen-SS:	3rd SS Division "Totenkopf", 1942-1943		
	14th SS Division, 1944		
Notes:	Adjutant at Majdanek		
	Missing in action September 1944		

Camp Service: **Oranienburg, 1941**
Majdanek

Haertel

First Name:	Wilhelm	*National Archive File:*	A3343 SSO-050A
Birthdate:	23 July 1903	*Birthplace:*	Probstzell
Rank:	SS-Untersturmführer	*SS Number:*	107620
NSDAP Number:	597956	*Highest Decoration:*	None listed
Religion:	Agnostic	*Marital Status:*	Married
Waffen-SS:	No		
Notes:	Served in Freikorps after WWI		

Camp Service: **Majdanek, 1943**

Haeusler

First Name:	Willi	*National Archive File:*	A3343 SSO-050A
Birthdate:	9 March 1894	*Birthplace:*	Breslau
Rank:	SS-Untersturmführer	*SS Number:*	187860
NSDAP Number:	1541572	*Highest Decoration:*	War Service Cross 2nd Class
Religion:	Agnostic	*Marital Status:*	Married
Waffen-SS:	No		
Notes:	No mention of *Operation Reinhard* in personnel file; served as chief administration officer for *Operation Reinhard*		

Camp Service: **Buchenwald, 1940**

Haeusser

First Name:	Alfred	*National Archive File:*	A3343 SSO-050A
Birthdate:	29 June 1911	*Birthplace:*	Ludwigshafen
Rank:	SS-Hauptsturmführer	*SS Number:*	123661
NSDAP Number:	5051883	*Highest Decoration:*	War Service Cross 2nd Class
Religion:	Agnostic	*Marital Status:*	Married
Waffen-SS:	IVth SS Corps, 1944-1945		
Notes:	Former bank employee		

Camp Service: **Oranienburg, 1938**

Haeussler

First Name:	Ernst	*National Archive File:*	A3343 SSO-050A
Birthdate:	31 March 1914	*Birthplace:*	Tullau
Rank:	SS-Obersturmbannführer	*SS Number:*	217862
NSDAP Number:	1150866	*Highest Decoration:*	Knight's Cross
Religion:	Agnostic	*Marital Status:*	Single
Waffen-SS:	3rd SS Division "Totenkopf", 1940-1943		
	17th SS Division "Götz von Berlichingen", 1943-1944		
	3rd SS Division "Totenkopf, 1944		
Notes:	Adjutant of Ist Totenkopfsturmbann, SS Totenkopfstandarte 1 "Oberbayern"		
	Died 14 July 1979		

Camp Service: **Dachau, 1938**

Hagel

First Name:	Dr. Heinrich	*National Archive File:*	A3343 SSO-051A
Birthdate:	10 August 1875	*Birthplace:*	Emsdetten
Rank:	SS-Obersturmbannführer	*SS Number:*	382540
NSDAP Number:	4797375	*Highest Decoration:*	War Service Cross 1st Class
Religion:	Catholic	*Marital Status:*	Married
Waffen-SS:	No		
Notes:	Iron Cross 1st Class WWI		

Camp Service: **Wewelsburg, 1940-1942**

Hagen

First Name:	Karl	*National Archive File:*	A3343 SSO-051A
Birthdate:	30 November 1910	*Birthplace:*	Kolberg
Rank:	SS-Hauptsturmführer	*SS Number:*	27587
NSDAP Number:	516097	*Highest Decoration:*	Iron Cross 2nd Class
Religion:	Agnostic	*Marital Status:*	Married
Waffen-SS:	5th SS Division "Wiking", 1944-1945		
	33rd SS Division "Charlemagne", 1945		
Notes:	Administration department		

Camp Service: **Oranienburg, 1942**

Halblieb

First Name:	Franz	*National Archive File:*	A3343 SSO-054A
Birthdate:	30 June 1889	*Birthplace:*	Ried
Rank:	SS-Untersturmführer	*SS Number:*	53215
NSDAP Number:	194751	*Highest Decoration:*	Bar to Iron Cross 2nd Class
Religion:	Catholic	*Marital Status:*	Married
Waffen-SS:	Yes, unit unknown		
Notes:	Commander 4th Guard Company Auschwitz		
	Wounded four times in WWI		

Camp Service: **Buchenwald, 1938**
Flossenbürg, 1939
Auschwitz, 1941-1943

Halfbrodt

First Name:	Heinz	*National Archive File:*	A3343 SSO-054A
Birthdate:	6 May 1912	*Birthplace:*	Braunschweig
Rank:	SS-Hauptsturmführer	*SS Number:*	43005
NSDAP Number:	1358267	*Highest Decoration:*	Iron Cross 2nd Class
Religion:	Protestant	*Marital Status:*	Married
Waffen-SS:	3rd SS Division "Totenkopf", 1943-1944		
Notes:	Wounded		
	Adjutant assault gun battalion 3rd SS Division		

Camp Service: **Neuengamme, 1941**

Hansen

First Name:	Kurt	*National Archive File:*	A3343 SSO-062A
Birthdate:	26 July 1905	*Birthplace:*	Wiesbaden
Rank:	SS-Sturmbannführer	*SS Number:*	3559
NSDAP Number:	35393	*Highest Decoration:*	War Service Cross 1st Class
Religion:	Protestant	*Marital Status:*	Married
Waffen-SS:	8th SS Division "Florian Geyer", 1944		
Notes:	Adjutant at Sachsenhausen and Flossenbürg		
	Golden Party Badge		

Camp Service: **Lichtenburg, 1936**
Sachsenhausen, 1938
Flossenbürg, 1938-1939

Harbaum

First Name:	August	*National Archive File:*	A3343 SSO-063A
Birthdate:	25 March 1913	*Birthplace:*	Guetersloh
Rank:	SS-Sturmbannführer	*SS Number:*	37163
NSDAP Number:	1264669	*Highest Decoration:*	War Service Cross 2nd Class
Religion:	Protestant	*Marital Status:*	Married
Waffen-SS:	No		
Notes:	Adjutant at Flossenbürg; Adjutant for Gluecks at Oranienburg		

Camp Service: **Flossenbürg, 1939-1940**
Oranienburg, 1940-1945

Hardieck

First Name:	Willi	*National Archive File:*	A3343 SSO-063A
Birthdate:	29 December 1912	*Birthplace:*	Guetersloh
Rank:	SS-Obersturmbannführer	*SS Number:*	32786
NSDAP Number:	1112808	*Highest Decoration:*	German Cross in Gold
Religion:	Agnostic	*Marital Status:*	Married
Waffen-SS:	3rd SS Division "Totenkopf", 1939-1941		
	6th SS Division "Nord", 1942-1943		
	12th SS Division "Hitlerjugend", 1944		
Notes:	Regimental commander in 12th SS Division; killed in action 17 December 1944		

Camp Service: **Buchenwald, 1938**

Hartjenstein

First Name:	Friedrich	*National Archive File:*	A3343 SSO-065A
Birthdate:	3 July 1905	*Birthplace:*	Peine
Rank:	SS-Obersturmbannführer	*SS Number:*	327350
NSDAP Number:	Not a member	*Highest Decoration:*	Iron Cross 1st Class
Religion:	Agnostic	*Marital Status:*	Married
Waffen-SS:	3rd SS Division "Totenkopf", 1941-1942		
Notes:	*Kommandant* at Birkenau, Natzweiler and Flossenbürg		
	Died in prison, 20 October 1954		

Camp Service:	**Sachsenhausen, 1938**	**Niedernhagen, 1939**
	Auschwitz, 1942-1944	**Natzweiler, 1944**

Hassebroek

First Name:	Johannes	*National Archive File:*	A3343 SSO-068A
Birthdate:	11 July 1910	*Birthplace:*	Halle
Rank:	SS-Sturmbannführer	*SS Number:*	107426
NSDAP Number:	256527	*Highest Decoration:*	Iron Cross 1st Class
Religion:	Agnostic	*Marital Status:*	Married
Waffen-SS:	3rd SS Division "Totenkopf", 1939-1941		
Notes:	*Kommandant* at Gross-Rosen		
	Sentenced to Death; remitted, released		

Camp Service:	**Esterwegen, 1936**	**Sachsenhausen, 1942-1943**
	Gross-Rosen, 1943-1944	

Hattenkerl

First Name:	Ernst	*National Archive File:*	A3343 SSO-069A
Birthdate:	28 July 1910	*Birthplace:*	Oerlinghausen
Rank:	SS-Untersturmführer	*SS Number:*	309709
NSDAP Number:	818832	*Highest Decoration:*	None listed
Religion:	Agnostic	*Marital Status:*	Married
Waffen-SS:	No		
Notes:	IInd Totenkopfsturmbann/3rd Totenkopfstandarte "Thüringen"		
	Released from SS in 1939		

Camp Service:	**Buchenwald, 1939**

Hattler

First Name:	Josef	*National Archive File:*	No File
Birthdate:	26 December 1912	*Birthplace:*	Unknown
Rank:	SS-Obersturmführer	*SS Number:*	142037
NSDAP Number:	Not a member	*Highest Decoration:*	None listed
Religion:	Unknown	*Marital Status:*	Unknown
Waffen-SS:	Unknown		
Notes:	Doctor at Flossenbürg		

Camp Service:	**Flossenbürg, 1940**
	Sachsenhausen, 1941

Hauck

First Name:	Leander	*National Archive File:*	A3343 SSO-069A
Birthdate:	20 August 1901	*Birthplace:*	Schifferstadt
Rank:	SS-Sturmbannführer	*SS Number:*	14963
NSDAP Number:	401140	*Highest Decoration:*	Iron Cross 2nd Class
Religion:	Agnostic	*Marital Status:*	Married
Waffen-SS:	16th SS Division "Reichsführer-SS", 1944		
	22nd SS Division "Maria Theresia", 1944		
Notes:	Supply officer in 16th and 22nd SS Divisions		

Camp Service: **Dachau, 1934-1938**

Haufschild

First Name:	Fritz	*National Archive File:*	A3343 SSO-069A
Birthdate:	27 February 1895	*Birthplace:*	Unknown
Rank:	SS-Hauptsturmführer	*SS Number:*	Unknown
NSDAP Number:	Not a member	*Highest Decoration:*	None listed
Religion:	Unknown	*Marital Status:*	Unknown
Waffen-SS:	No		
Notes:	Possible honorary SS rank		

Camp Service: **Stutthof, 1945**

Haupt

First Name:	Dr. Willi	*National Archive File:*	A3343 SSO-070A
Birthdate:	8 October 1911	*Birthplace:*	Lahr
Rank:	SS-Hauptsturmführer	*SS Number:*	226781
NSDAP Number:	208509	*Highest Decoration:*	War Service Cross 2nd Class
Religion:	Agnostic	*Marital Status:*	Married
Waffen-SS:	No		
Notes:	Dentist		

Camp Service: **Sachsenhausen, 1941-1942**

Haupt

First Name:	Helmut	*National Archive File:*	A3343 SSO-070A
Birthdate:	20 June 1912	*Birthplace:*	Lauban
Rank:	SS-Hauptsturmführer	*SS Number:*	196189
NSDAP Number:	3529819	*Highest Decoration:*	War Service Cross 1st Class
Religion:	Agnostic	*Marital Status:*	Married
Waffen-SS:	5th SS Division "Wiking", 1940-1943		
	11th SS Division "Nordland", 1943-1944		
	35th SS Division, 1945		
Notes:	Salesman before entering SS		

Camp Service: **Oranienburg, 1938-1940**

Hausamen

First Name:	Dr. Erich	*National Archive File:*	A3343 SSO-070A
Birthdate:	17 March 1907	*Birthplace:*	Neckarburken
Rank:	SS-Hauptsturmführer	*SS Number:*	163077
NSDAP Number:	4271256	*Highest Decoration:*	None listed
Religion:	Protestant	*Marital Status:*	Married
Waffen-SS:	2nd SS Division "Das Reich", 1940-1942		
	Ist SS Corps, 1943-1944		
Notes:	Dentist at Buchenwald		

Camp Service: **Buchenwald, 1940**

Heider

First Name:	Karl	*National Archive File:*	A3343 SSO-075A
Birthdate:	4 January 1909	*Birthplace:*	Wiesenberg
Rank:	SS-Obersturmführer	*SS Number:*	320947
NSDAP Number:	6528048	*Highest Decoration:*	War Service Cross 2nd Class
Religion:	Catholic	*Marital Status:*	Married
Waffen-SS:	No		
Notes:	Engineer		

Camp Service: **Natzweiler, 1943**

Heidingsfelder

First Name:	Johann	*National Archive File:*	A3343 SSO-075A
Birthdate:	18 February 1902	*Birthplace:*	Amberg
Rank:	SS-Obersturmführer	*SS Number:*	1537
NSDAP Number:	137888	*Highest Decoration:*	None listed
Religion:	Catholic	*Marital Status:*	Married
Waffen-SS:	No		
Notes:	Thrown out of Catholic Church		

Camp Service: **Mauthausen, 1939-1940**

Heidl

First Name:	Dr. Otto	*National Archive File:*	A3343 SSO-075A
Birthdate:	8 September 1910	*Birthplace:*	Arnau
Rank:	SS-Hauptsturmführer	*SS Number:*	328012
NSDAP Number:	6749377	*Highest Decoration:*	War Service Cross 2nd Class
Religion:	Agnostic	*Marital Status:*	Married
Waffen-SS:	No		
Notes:	Camp doctor at Stutthof		
	Committed suicide		

Camp Service: **Auschwitz, 1941**
Stutthof, 1942-1945

Heidrich

First Name: Hermann
Birthdate: 23 March 1886
Rank: SS-Obersturmbannführer
NSDAP Number: 35210
Religion: Agnostic
Waffen-SS: No
Notes: Iron Cross 1st Class, Wound Badge WWI; Golden Party Badge

National Archive File: A3343 SSO-075A
Birthplace: Oberstein/Nahe
SS Number: 22606
Highest Decoration: War Service Cross 2nd Class
Marital Status: Married

Camp Service: **Sachsenhausen, 1940**
Kuestrin　　　　　　　　**Falkenhagen**

Heim

First Name: Dr. Aribert
Birthdate: 28 June 1914
Rank: SS-Hauptsturmführer
NSDAP Number: Not a member
Religion: Agnostic
Waffen-SS: 6th SS Division "Nord", 1942
Notes: Doctor; Served in SA 1935-1938

National Archive File: A3343 SSO-076A
Birthplace: Radkersburg
SS Number: 367744
Highest Decoration: None listed
Marital Status: Single

Camp Service: **Mauthausen**
Buchenwald, 1941
Oranienburg, 1941

Heimann

First Name: Karl
Birthdate: 15 May 1891
Rank: SS-Hauptsturmführer
NSDAP Number: 824123
Religion: Protestant
Waffen-SS: No
Notes: Iron Cross 1st Class, Wound Badge WWI

National Archive File: A3343 SSO-077A
Birthplace: Breslau
SS Number: 22219
Highest Decoration: None listed
Marital Status: Married

Camp Service: **Flossenbürg, 1939-1942**
Mauthausen, 1942-1943

Heimann

First Name: Karl
Birthdate: 28 March 1893
Rank: SS-Obersturmführer
NSDAP Number: 2655880
Religion: Protestant
Waffen-SS: No
Notes: Wound Badge WWI

National Archive File: A3343 SSO-077A
Birthplace: Berlin
SS Number: 219906
Highest Decoration: None listed
Marital Status: Married

Camp Service: **Sachsenhausen, 1943-1944**
Ravensbrück, 1944

Heinke

First Name:	Heinrich	*National Archive File:*	A3343 SSO-078A
Birthdate:	28 February 1912	*Birthplace:*	Plauen
Rank:	SS-Sturmbannführer	*SS Number:*	47024
NSDAP Number:	192547	*Highest Decoration:*	German Cross in Gold
Religion:	Agnostic	*Marital Status:*	Single
Waffen-SS:	1st SS Infantry Brigade, 1942		
	18th SS Division "Horst Wessel", 1944		
	10th SS Division "Frundsberg", 1944		
Notes:	Commander 21st SS Grenadier Regiment; wounded in action in Russia		

Camp Service: **Sachsenburg, 1937   Buchenwald, 1937-1940**

Heinrich

First Name:	Alfred	*National Archive File:*	A3343 SSO-078A
Birthdate:	25 January 1896	*Birthplace:*	Namslau
Rank:	SS-Hauptsturmführer	*SS Number:*	259288
NSDAP Number:	1936303	*Highest Decoration:*	None listed
Religion:	Agnostic	*Marital Status:*	Married
Waffen-SS:	No		
Notes:	Iron Cross 2nd Class, Wound Badge WWI		

Camp Service: **Buchenwald, 1940-1941**
                   Oranienburg, 1941-1943

Heinrich

First Name:	Walter	*National Archive File:*	A3343 SSO-078A
Birthdate:	2 January 1910	*Birthplace:*	Myslowitz
Rank:	SS-Hauptsturmführer	*SS Number:*	264110
NSDAP Number:	1594751	*Highest Decoration:*	None listed
Religion:	Agnostic	*Marital Status:*	Married
Waffen-SS:	No		
Notes:	*Kommandant* at Amersfoort		
	Camp service not listed in personnel file		

Camp Service: **Amersfoort, 1942-1943**

Helle

First Name:	Paul Anton	*National Archive File:*	A3343 SSO-081A
Birthdate:	22 September 1898	*Birthplace:*	Rovereto, Austria
Rank:	SS-Sturmbannführer	*SS Number:*	10528
NSDAP Number:	362755	*Highest Decoration:*	War Service Cross 2nd Class
Religion:	Agnostic	*Marital Status:*	Married
Waffen-SS:	SS Infantry Regiment 8, 1939-1941		
Notes:	Commander of guard battalion at Amersfoort		

Camp Service: **Mauthausen, 1939**
                   Oranienburg, 1941
                   Amersfoort, 1941-1944

Hellinger

First Name:	Dr. Martin	*National Archive File:*	A3343 SSO-082A
Birthdate:	17 July 1904	*Birthplace:*	Pirna
Rank:	SS-Hauptsturmführer	*SS Number:*	134328
NSDAP Number:	2969503	*Highest Decoration:*	War Service Cross 2nd Class
Religion:	Agnostic	*Marital Status:*	Married
Waffen-SS:	No		
Notes:	Dentist		

Camp Service: **Sachsenhausen, 1941**
Flossenbürg, 1941-1942
Ravensbrück, 1943-1944

Helmersen

First Name:	Dr. Erwin von	*National Archive File:*	A3343 SSO-083A
Birthdate:	4 November 1914	*Birthplace:*	Bremen
Rank:	SS-Hauptsturmführer	*SS Number:*	372240
NSDAP Number:	4194453	*Highest Decoration:*	Iron Cross 1st Class
Religion:	Agnostic	*Marital Status:*	Married
Waffen-SS:	Fallschirmjaeger Battalion 500, 1943-1944		
Notes:	Executed 12 April 1949		

Camp Service: **Auschwitz, 1944**

Helmling

First Name:	Dr. Alexander	*National Archive File:*	A3343 SSO-083A
Birthdate:	8 May 1892	*Birthplace:*	Bensheim
Rank:	SS-Sturmbannführer	*SS Number:*	77241
NSDAP Number:	507593	*Highest Decoration:*	War Service Cross 2nd Class
Religion:	Agnostic	*Marital Status:*	Married
Waffen-SS:	No		
Notes:	Dentist		
	Iron Cross 2nd Class, WWI		

Camp Service: **Mauthausen, 1940**

Helwig

First Name:	Hans	*National Archive File:*	A3343 SSO-083A
Birthdate:	25 September 1881	*Birthplace:*	Hemsbach
Rank:	SS-Gruppenführer	*SS Number:*	1725
NSDAP Number:	55875	*Highest Decoration:*	War Service Cross 2nd Class
Religion:	Protestant	*Marital Status:*	Married
Waffen-SS:	No		
Notes:	*Kommandant* at Ankenbuck, Sachsenhausen; Iron Cross 2nd Class WWI		
	Died 8 August 1952		

Camp Service: **Ankenbuck, 1934**   **Lichtenburg, 1936-1937**
Sachsenhausen, 1937-1938

Henkel

First Name:	Dr. Wilhelm	*National Archive File:*	A3343 SSO-085A
Birthdate:	14 June 1909	*Birthplace:*	Odenhausen
Rank:	SS-Hauptsturmführer	*SS Number:*	244628
NSDAP Number:	5629125	*Highest Decoration:*	None listed
Religion:	Protestant	*Marital Status:*	Married
Waffen-SS:	3rd SS Division "Totenkopf", 1943		
	11th SS Division "Nordland", 1943		
Notes:	Dentist; executed 28 May 1947		

Camp Service: **Mauthausen, 1941-1943**

Henneberg

First Name:	Waldemar	*National Archive File:*	A3343 SSO-085A
Birthdate:	28 February 1912	*Birthplace:*	Quedlinburg
Rank:	SS-Obersturmführer	*SS Number:*	120283
NSDAP Number:	2001090	*Highest Decoration:*	War Service Cross 2nd Class
Religion:	Agnostic	*Marital Status:*	Married
Waffen-SS:	3rd SS Division "Totenkopf", 1940-1942		
	21st SS Division "Skanderbeg", 1944-1945		
	7th SS Division "Prinz Eugen", 1945		
Notes:	Leader of Administration department		

Camp Service: **Gross-Rosen, 1942-1943**

Hennings

First Name:	Dr. Rudolph	*National Archive File:*	A3343 SSO-087A
Birthdate:	2 May 1912	*Birthplace:*	Duesseldorf
Rank:	SS-Sturmbannführer	*SS Number:*	372353
NSDAP Number:	Not a member	*Highest Decoration:*	Iron Cross 2nd Class
Religion:	Agnostic	*Marital Status:*	Married
Waffen-SS:	3rd SS Division "Totenkopf", 1942		
Notes:	Dentist		

Camp Service: **Niederhagen, 1942**

Henrychowski

First Name:	Rolf	*National Archive File:*	A3343 SSO-087A
Birthdate:	25 August 1911	*Birthplace:*	Posen
Rank:	SS-Hauptsturmführer	*SS Number:*	63244
NSDAP Number:	Not a member	*Highest Decoration:*	None listed
Religion:	Unknown	*Marital Status:*	Single
Waffen-SS:	2nd SS Division "Das Reich", 1940-1941		
Notes:	Dentist at Dachau		

Camp Service: **Dachau, 1940**

Hepburn

First Name:	Dr. Herbert	*National Archive File:*	A3343 SSO-089A
Birthdate:	3 October 1902	*Birthplace:*	Dresden
Rank:	SS-Hauptsturmführer	*SS Number:*	382457
NSDAP Number:	2775123	*Highest Decoration:*	None listed
Religion:	Protestant	*Marital Status:*	Married
Waffen-SS:	Flanders Legion, 1941-1942		
Notes:	Dentist		

Camp Service: **Ravensbrück, 1941**
Neuengamme

Herbet

First Name:	Nikolaus	*National Archive File:*	A3343 SSO-089A
Birthdate:	20 March 1889	*Birthplace:*	Aachen
Rank:	SS-Hauptsturmführer	*SS Number:*	2394
NSDAP Number:	68494	*Highest Decoration:*	War Service Cross 2nd Class
Religion:	Agnostic	*Marital Status:*	Married
Waffen-SS:	No		
Notes:	Awarded Golden Party Badge		
	File shows assignment to a camp at Warsaw in 1943		

Camp Service: **Mauthausen, 1940**

Hering

First Name:	Gottlob	*National Archive File:*	A3343 SSO-090A
Birthdate:	2 June 1887	*Birthplace:*	Warmbrunn
Rank:	SS-Hauptsturmführer	*SS Number:*	Not an official member
NSDAP Number:	Not a member	*Highest Decoration:*	None listed
Religion:	Catholic	*Marital Status:*	Married
Waffen-SS:	No		
Notes:	*Kommandant* Belzec; *kommandant* Sobibór for a short time after camp revolt		
	Career Kripo officer; died 9 October 1945		

Camp Service: **Belzec, 1942-1943**   **Sobibór, 1943**
Poniatowa Labor Camp, 1943   **San Saba, 1944-1945**

Herrmann

First Name:	Alexander	*National Archive File:*	A3343 SSO-091A
Birthdate:	21 August 1916	*Birthplace:*	Plauen
Rank:	SS-Obersturmführer	*SS Number:*	122211
NSDAP Number:	3288213	*Highest Decoration:*	Iron Cross 2nd Class
Religion:	Agnostic	*Marital Status:*	Single
Waffen-SS:	3rd SS Division "Totenkopf", 1939-1941		
Notes:	2nd SS Totenkopfstandarte "Brandenburg"		
	Battalion adjutant in 3rd SS Division; killed in action 20 October 1941		

Camp Service: **Oranienburg, 1938-1939**

Herzum

First Name:	Dr. Erwin	*National Archive File:*	A3343 SSO-093A
Birthdate:	10 November 1915	*Birthplace:*	Reichenberg
Rank:	SS-Hauptsturmführer	*SS Number:*	315565
NSDAP Number:	Not a member	*Highest Decoration:*	War Service Cross 2nd Class
Religion:	Unknown	*Marital Status:*	Single
Waffen-SS:	16th SS Division "Reichsführer-SS", 1944-1945		
Notes:	Camp doctor at Gross-Rosen		

Camp Service: **Gross-Rosen, 1940-1941**
Sachsenhausen, 1941

Heschl

First Name:	Dr. Erwin	*National Archive File:*	A3343 SSO-093A
Birthdate:	28 November 1911	*Birthplace:*	Graz, Austria
Rank:	SS-Hauptsturmführer	*SS Number:*	303997
NSDAP Number:	Not a member	*Highest Decoration:*	Iron Cross 2nd Class
Religion:	Catholic	*Marital Status:*	Married
Waffen-SS:	5th SS Division "Wiking", 1943		
Notes:	Doctor		
	Wounded five times in combat		

Camp Service: **Mauthausen, 1941**
Auschwitz

Heussler

First Name:	Paul	*National Archive File:*	A3343 SSO-095A
Birthdate:	19 January 1890	*Birthplace:*	Rottweil
Rank:	SS-Obersturmführer	*SS Number:*	27301
NSDAP Number:	371798	*Highest Decoration:*	Bar to Iron Cross 2nd Class
Religion:	Catholic	*Marital Status:*	Married
Waffen-SS:	No		
Notes:	Iron Cross 2nd Class WWI		

Camp Service: **Sachsenhausen, 1944**
Ravensbrück, 1944

Heyde

First Name:	Dr. Werner	*National Archive File:*	A3343 SSO-095A
Birthdate:	25 April 1902	*Birthplace:*	Forst/Lausitz
Rank:	SS-Obersturmbannführer	*SS Number:*	276656
NSDAP Number:	3068165	*Highest Decoration:*	None listed
Religion:	Protestant	*Marital Status:*	Married
Waffen-SS:	No		
Notes:	Aktion T4		
	Accused of previous homosexual conduct; suicide 13 February 1964		

Camp Service: **Dachau**   **Sachsenhausen**
Buchenwald   **Oranienburg, 1936-1939**

Hierthes

First Name:	Heinrich	*National Archive File:*	A3343 SSO-096A
Birthdate:	25 July 1897	*Birthplace:*	Neuburg
Rank:	SS-Standartenführer	*SS Number:*	282042
NSDAP Number:	2945974	*Highest Decoration:*	Iron Cross 1st Class
Religion:	Protestant	*Marital Status:*	Married
Waffen-SS:	8th SS Division "Florian Geyer", 1941		
	SS Infantry Regiment 8, 1941-1942		
Notes:	Commander 3rd Totenkopfstandarte "Thüringen"		
	Relieved as commander of SS Cavalry Regiment 2; died in Soviet POW camp 1953		

Camp Service: **Buchenwald, 1937-1940**

Hildebrandt

First Name:	Fritz	*National Archive File:*	A3343 SSO-097A
Birthdate:	6 February 1897	*Birthplace:*	Erfurt
Rank:	SS-Obersturmbannführer	*SS Number:*	10906
NSDAP Number:	498124	*Highest Decoration:*	None listed
Religion:	Protestant	*Marital Status:*	Married
Waffen-SS:	No		
Notes:	Iron Cross 2nd Class WWI		

Camp Service: **Oranienburg, 1938-1940**

Hildebrandt

First Name:	Wilhelm	*National Archive File:*	A3343 SSO-097A
Birthdate:	10 October 1874	*Birthplace:*	Berlin
Rank:	SS-Obersturmführer	*SS Number:*	20974
NSDAP Number:	296956	*Highest Decoration:*	None listed
Religion:	Agnostic	*Marital Status:*	Married
Waffen-SS:	No		
Notes:	Iron Cross 2nd Class WWI		

Camp Service: **Dachau, 1938**
Flossenbürg, 1939-1940

Hintermayer

First Name:	Dr. Fritz	*National Archive File:*	A3343 SSO-100A
Birthdate:	28 October 1911	*Birthplace:*	Markt Grafling
Rank:	SS-Obersturmführer	*SS Number:*	310340
NSDAP Number:	1200381	*Highest Decoration:*	Iron Cross 1st Class
Religion:	Catholic	*Marital Status:*	Married
Waffen-SS:	3rd SS Division "Totenkopf", 1942-1943		
Notes:	Chief doctor at Dachau		
	Executed		

Camp Service: **Oranienburg, 1938**
Dachau, 1944

Hintz

First Name:	Helge	*National Archive File:*	A3343 SSO-100A
Birthdate:	30 August 1908	*Birthplace:*	Budapest, Hungary
Rank:	SS-Hauptsturmführer	*SS Number:*	110435
NSDAP Number:	3091822	*Highest Decoration:*	None listed
Religion:	Agnostic	*Marital Status:*	Married
Waffen-SS:	3rd SS Division "Totenkopf", 1942-1944		
	29th SS Division, 1944		
Notes:	Former mechanic		

Camp Service: **Hinzert, 1940-1941**
Oranienburg, 1941-1942

Hirt

First Name:	Dr. August	*National Archive File:*	A3343 SSO-101A
Birthdate:	29 April 1898	*Birthplace:*	Mannheim
Rank:	SS-Sturmbannführer	*SS Number:*	100414
NSDAP Number:	Not a member	*Highest Decoration:*	None listed
Religion:	Agnostic	*Marital Status:*	Widower
Waffen-SS:	No		
Notes:	Ahnerhebe; Iron Cross 2nd Class, Silver Wound Badge WWI		
	Committed suicide 2 June 1945		

Camp Service: **Natzweiler**

Hock

First Name:	Dr. Oskar	*National Archive File:*	A3343 SSO-102A
Birthdate:	31 January 1898	*Birthplace:*	Babenhausen
Rank:	SS-Brigadeführer	*SS Number:*	276822
NSDAP Number:	97862	*Highest Decoration:*	Iron Cross 1st Class
Religion:	Catholic	*Marital Status:*	Married
Waffen-SS:	3rd SS Division "Totenkopf", 1941-1942		
	IInd SS Corps		
	IIIrd SS Corps		
Notes:	Corps physician IInd SS and IIIrd SS Corps		
	Iron Cross 2nd Class WWI; Golden Party Badge		

Camp Service: **Sachsenhausen, 1936-1937**   **Oranienburg, 1940**

Hoecker

First Name:	Karl	*National Archive File:*	A3343 SSO-102A
Birthdate:	11 December 1911	*Birthplace:*	Engershausen
Rank:	SS-Untersturmführer	*SS Number:*	182961
NSDAP Number:	4444757	*Highest Decoration:*	War Service Cross 2nd Class
Religion:	Protestant	*Marital Status:*	Married
Waffen-SS:	No		
Notes:	Sentenced to 7 years imprisonment		

Camp Service: **Neuengamme, 1939-1942**   **Arbeitsdorf, 1942**
Majdanek, 1943-1944   **Auschwitz, 1944-1945**
Dora, 1945

Hoefle

First Name:	Hermann	*National Archive File:*	No File
Birthdate:	Unknown	*Birthplace:*	Unknown
Rank:	SS-Sturmbannführer	*SS Number:*	Unknown
NSDAP Number:	Not a member	*Highest Decoration:*	None listed
Religion:	Unknown	*Marital Status:*	Unknown
Waffen-SS:	Unknown		

Notes: Administartive head of Operation Reinhard at the Julius Schreck SS barracks at Lublin

Camp Service: **Operation Reinhard**

Hoefle

First Name:	Karl	*National Archive File:*	A3343 SSO-102A
Birthdate:	18 November 1913	*Birthplace:*	Vienna, Austria
Rank:	SS-Obersturmführer	*SS Number:*	272136
NSDAP Number:	4036750	*Highest Decoration:*	Iron Cross 2nd Class
Religion:	Catholic	*Marital Status:*	Married
Waffen-SS:	2nd SS Division "Das Reich", 1943		
	14th SS Division, 1944		

Notes: Wounded during war

Camp Service: **Dachau, 1943-1944**

Hoehn

First Name:	August	*National Archive File:*	A3343 SSO-103A
Birthdate:	19 August 1904	*Birthplace:*	Lipporn
Rank:	SS-Untersturmführer	*SS Number:*	91735
NSDAP Number:	1514767	*Highest Decoration:*	None listed
Religion:	Agnostic	*Marital Status:*	Married
Waffen-SS:	No		

Notes: Sentenced to Life
Camp service not listed in personnel file

Camp Service: **Sachsenhausen, 1939-1945**

Hoeller

First Name:	Dr. Walter	*National Archive File:*	A3343 SSO-104A
Birthdate:	20 October 1908	*Birthplace:*	Windisch-Garsten
Rank:	SS-Hauptsturmführer	*SS Number:*	295116
NSDAP Number:	514230	*Highest Decoration:*	None listed
Religion:	Catholic	*Marital Status:*	Engaged
Waffen-SS:	SS Infantry Regiment 9, 1942		

Notes: Doctor
Served in SA 1931-1933

Camp Service: **Oranienburg, 1941-1942**
Mauthausen

Hoess

First Name:	Rudolf	*National Archive File:*	A3343 SSO-105A
Birthdate:	25 November 1900	*Birthplace:*	Baden-Baden
Rank:	SS-Obersturmbannführer	*SS Number:*	193616
NSDAP Number:		*Highest Decoration:*	War Service Cross 1st Class
Religion:	Agnostic	*Marital Status:*	Married
Waffen-SS:	No		
Notes:	*Kommandant* at Auschwitz; Iron Cross 1st Class, Silver Wound Badge WWI		
	Chief, Department DI, Oranienburg; executed 16 April 1947		

Camp Service: **Dachau, 1934-1938   Sachsenhausen, 1938-1940**
Auschwitz, 1940-1943   Oranienburg, 1943-1945

Hoessler

First Name:	Franz	*National Archive File:*	A3343 SSO-105A
Birthdate:	4 February 1906	*Birthplace:*	Oberdorf
Rank:	SS-Obersturmführer	*SS Number:*	41940
NSDAP Number:	1374713	*Highest Decoration:*	War Service Cross 2nd Class
Religion:	Agnostic	*Marital Status:*	Married
Waffen-SS:	No		
Notes:	Lagerführer at Auschwitz; executed 13 December 1945		

Camp Service: **Auschwitz, 1940-1944   Dachau, 1944**
Dora, 1945   Bergen-Belsen, 1945

Hofer

First Name:	Dr. Peter	*National Archive File:*	A3343 SSO-106A
Birthdate:	19 November 1903	*Birthplace:*	Salzburg, Austria
Rank:	SS-Hauptsturmführer	*SS Number:*	296197
NSDAP Number:	6338766	*Highest Decoration:*	Iron Cross 2nd Class
Religion:	Agnostic	*Marital Status:*	Married
Waffen-SS:	5th SS Division "Wiking", 1942		
	16th SS Division "Reichsführer-SS", 1944		
Notes:	Acting camp doctor at Buchenwald		
	File shows service in WVHA DIII, not at a specific camp		

Camp Service: **Buchenwald**
Oranienburg, 1942-1944

Hoff

First Name:	Erich von dem	*National Archive File:*	A3343 SSO-106A
Birthdate:	6 April 1896	*Birthplace:*	Aachen
Rank:	SS-Obersturmführer	*SS Number:*	134918
NSDAP Number:	2267243	*Highest Decoration:*	None listed
Religion:	Catholic	*Marital Status:*	Married
Waffen-SS:	No		

Camp Service: **Mauthausen, 1944**

Hoffmann

First Name:	Joachim	*National Archive File:*	No File
Birthdate:	1905	*Birthplace:*	Unknown
Rank:	SS-Untersturmführer	*SS Number:*	Unknown
NSDAP Number:	Not a member	*Highest Decoration:*	None
Religion:	Unknown	*Marital Status:*	Unknown
Waffen-SS:	No		
Notes:	Shot in the Röhm Putsch, 1934		

Camp Service: **Stettin-Bredow, 1933**

Hoffmann

First Name:	Karl	*National Archive File:*	A3343 SSO-108A
Birthdate:	7 November 1908	*Birthplace:*	Mainz
Rank:	SS-Obersturmführer	*SS Number:*	127701
NSDAP Number:	Not a member	*Highest Decoration:*	War Service Cross 2nd Class
Religion:	Agnostic	*Marital Status:*	Married
Waffen-SS:	No		
Notes:	Construction Department Auschwitz		

Camp Service: **Oranienburg, 1941**
Buchenwald, 1942-1943
Auschwitz, 1943-1944

Hofinger

First Name:	Wilhelm	*National Archive File:*	A3343 SSO-110A
Birthdate:	6 February 1912	*Birthplace:*	Rosenheim
Rank:	SS-Obersturmführer	*SS Number:*	16366
NSDAP Number:	200947	*Highest Decoration:*	None
Religion:	Agnostic	*Marital Status:*	Married
Waffen-SS:	No		
Notes:	Guard troops at Dachau		
	Released from SS in 1939		

Camp Service: **Dachau, 1936-1939**

Hofmann

First Name:	Albert	*National Archive File:*	A3343 SSO-110A
Birthdate:	6 June 1895	*Birthplace:*	Langenberg
Rank:	SS-Untersturmführer	*SS Number:*	280427
NSDAP Number:	320176	*Highest Decoration:*	None listed
Religion:	Agnostic	*Marital Status:*	Married
Waffen-SS:	No		
Notes:	Gusen sub-camp		
	Iron Cross 2nd Class, Wound Badge WWI		

Camp Service: **Mauthausen, 1944-1945**

Hofmann

First Name:	Franz Johann	*National Archive File:*	A3343 SSO-110A
Birthdate:	5 April 1906	*Birthplace:*	Hof
Rank:	SS-Hauptsturmführer	*SS Number:*	40651
NSDAP Number:	1369617	*Highest Decoration:*	War Service Cross 2nd Class
Religion:	Agnostic	*Marital Status:*	Married
Waffen-SS:	No		
Notes:	Lagerführer at Auschwitz and Natzweiler; sentenced to Life		

Camp Service: **Dachau, 1933-1942**
Auschwitz, 1942-1944
Natzweiler, 1944-1945

Hohenester

First Name:	Pius	*National Archive File:*	A3343 SSO-112A
Birthdate:	25 December 1910	*Birthplace:*	Percha
Rank:	SS-Sturmbannführer	*SS Number:*	277027
NSDAP Number:	873647	*Highest Decoration:*	None listed
Religion:	Agnostic	*Marital Status:*	Married
Waffen-SS:	3rd SS Division "Totenkopf", 1940-1944		
	16th SS Division "Reichsführer-SS", 1944		
Notes:	Guard troops at Dachau		

Camp Service: **Dachau, 1937**

Holzmann

First Name:	Georg	*National Archive File:*	A3343 SSO-114A
Birthdate:	7 May 1887	*Birthplace:*	Diesneck
Rank:	SS-Hauptsturmführer	*SS Number:*	7661
NSDAP Number:	130624	*Highest Decoration:*	None listed
Religion:	Protestant	*Marital Status:*	Married
Waffen-SS:	No		
Notes:	Iron Cross 2nd Class, Wound Badge WWI		

Camp Service: **Sachsenhausen, 1939-1945**

Honig

First Name:	Dr. Fridrich	*National Archive File:*	A3343 SSO-115A
Birthdate:	21 February 1896	*Birthplace:*	Nürnberg
Rank:	SS-Standartenführer	*SS Number:*	254359
NSDAP Number:	2628	*Highest Decoration:*	War Service Cross 2nd Class
Religion:	Protestant	*Marital Status:*	Married
Waffen-SS:	No		
Notes:	Iron Cross 2nd Class, Wound Badge WWI		
	Camp service not listed in personnel file		

Camp Service: **Gross-Rosen**

Hoppe

First Name:	Paul
Birthdate:	28 February 1900
Rank:	SS-Sturmbannführer
NSDAP Number:	1596491
Religion:	Agnostic
Waffen-SS:	3rd SS Division "Totenkopf", 1939-1942
Notes:	*Kommandant* Stutthof; wounded in action
	Sentenced to 9 years - released, died July 1974

National Archive File: A3343 SSO-115A
Birthplace: Berlin
SS Number: 116695
Highest Decoration: Iron Cross 1st Class
Marital Status: Married

Camp Service: **Stutthof, 1942-1945**   **Oranienburg, 1938**

Horstmann

First Name:	Dr. Rudolf
Birthdate:	12 October 1913
Rank:	SS-Hauptsturmführer
NSDAP Number:	4363178
Religion:	Agnostic
Waffen-SS:	8th SS Division "Florian Geyer", 1942-1943
Notes:	Wounded in action

National Archive File: A3343 SSO-116A
Birthplace: Berlin
SS Number: 120026
Highest Decoration: Iron Cross 2nd Class
Marital Status: Married

Camp Service: **Oranienburg, 1943**
Bergen-Belsen, 1945

Hoven

First Name:	Dr. Waldemar
Birthdate:	10 February 1903
Rank:	SS-Hauptsturmführer
NSDAP Number:	Not a member
Religion:	Unknown
Waffen-SS:	No
Notes:	Doctor at Buchenwald
	Executed 2 June 1948

National Archive File: A3343 SSO-117A
Birthplace: Freiburg
SS Number: 244594
Highest Decoration: None listed
Marital Status: Married

Camp Service: **Buchenwald, 1939-1940**

Hoym

First Name:	Gneomar von
Birthdate:	9 November 1909
Rank:	SS-Sturmbannführer
NSDAP Number:	857601
Religion:	Agnostic
Waffen-SS:	3rd SS Division "Totenkopf", 1939-1941
	6th SS Division "Nord", 1941-1942
	10th SS Division "Frundsberg", 1943
Notes:	Wounded in action; battalion commander in artillery

National Archive File: A3343 SSO-118A
Birthplace: Koenigsberg
SS Number: 10124
Highest Decoration: Iron Cross 1st Class
Marital Status: Married

Camp Service: **Oranienburg, 1937-1938**

Huenefeld

First Name:	Wilhelm	*National Archive File:*	A3343 SSO-120A
Birthdate:	20 October 1905	*Birthplace:*	Gross Joerl/Flensburg
Rank:	SS-Obersturmführer	*SS Number:*	7164
NSDAP Number:	278326	*Highest Decoration:*	War Service Cross 1st Class
Religion:	Agnostic	*Marital Status:*	Married
Waffen-SS:	No		
Notes:	Construction office at Buchenwald; Architect		

Camp Service: **Buchenwald, 1944**

Huettig

First Name:	Hans	*National Archive File:*	A3343 SSO-121A
Birthdate:	5 April 1894	*Birthplace:*	Dresden
Rank:	SS-Sturmbannführer	*SS Number:*	127673
NSDAP Number:	1127620	*Highest Decoration:*	None listed
Religion:	Agnostic	*Marital Status:*	Married
Waffen-SS:	34th SS Division "Landstorm Nederland", 1945		
Notes:	*Kommandant* Natzweiler and Herzogenbusch		
	Sentenced to Life - released 1956		

Camp Service: **Lichtenburg, 1936**　　**Sachsenburg, 1937**
　　　　　　　　 Buchenwald, 1938　　**Flossenbürg, 1939-1942**
　　　　　　　　 Natzweiler, 1942　　**Herzogenbusch, 1943-1944**

Huettig

First Name:	Helmut	*National Archive File:*	A3343 SSO-121A
Birthdate:	7 August 1914	*Birthplace:*	Hildesheim
Rank:	SS-Sturmbannführer	*SS Number:*	126046
NSDAP Number:	2638717	*Highest Decoration:*	Iron Cross 1st Class
Religion:	Agnostic	*Marital Status:*	Single
Waffen-SS:	3rd SS Division "Totenkopf", 1941-1943		
Notes:	Signal officer; 3rd SS Totenkopfstandarte "Thuringen"		

Camp Service: **Buchenwald, 1938**

Jaeger

First Name:	Dr. Willy	*National Archive File:*	A3343 SSO-129A
Birthdate:	22 March 1902	*Birthplace:*	Landau
Rank:	SS-Obersturmführer	*SS Number:*	185044
NSDAP Number:	2582822	*Highest Decoration:*	None listed
Religion:	Protestant	*Marital Status:*	Married
Waffen-SS:	No		
Notes:	Dentist		

Camp Service: **Dachau, 1943**　　**Neuengamme, 1943-1944**
　　　　　　　　 Bergen-Belsen

Jakob

First Name:	Franz	*National Archive File:*	A3343 SSO-131A
Birthdate:	23 July 1913	*Birthplace:*	Zerbst
Rank:	SS-Obersturmbannführer	*SS Number:*	40485
NSDAP Number:	640626	*Highest Decoration:*	German Cross in Gold
Religion:	Agnostic	*Marital Status:*	Married
Waffen-SS:	3rd SS Division "Totenkopf", 1939-1944		
	9th SS Division "Hohenstaufen", 1945		
Notes:	Artillery battalion commander; wounded in action		

Camp Service: **Sachsenburg, 1934-1935**
Oranienburg, 1939

Janisch

First Name:	Josef	*National Archive File:*	A3343 SSO-132A
Birthdate:	22 April 1909	*Birthplace:*	Salzburg, Austria
Rank:	SS-Obersturmführer (F)	*SS Number:*	299849
NSDAP Number:	1619295	*Highest Decoration:*	War Service Cross 1st Class
Religion:	Agnostic	*Marital Status:*	Single
Waffen-SS:	No		
Notes:	Construction department Auschwitz		
	Camp service not listed in personnel file		

Camp Service: **Auschwitz, 1941-1943**

Jarolin

First Name:	Josef	*National Archive File:*	A3343 SSO-135A
Birthdate:	6 March 1904	*Birthplace:*	Rehpoint
Rank:	SS-Obersturmführer	*SS Number:*	238596
NSDAP Number:	3205438	*Highest Decoration:*	War Service Cross 2nd Class
Religion:	Agnostic	*Marital Status:*	Single
Waffen-SS:	No		
Notes:	Schutzhaftlagerführer at Dachau		
	Executed 28 May 1946		

Camp Service: **Dachau, 1940-1942**

Joachimsmeyer

First Name:	Willi	*National Archive File:*	A3343 SSO-138A
Birthdate:	1 April 1907	*Birthplace:*	Essen
Rank:	SS-Obersturmführer	*SS Number:*	1277
NSDAP Number:	37245	*Highest Decoration:*	None listed
Religion:	Agnostic	*Marital Status:*	Married
Waffen-SS:	No		
Notes:	Served in SA 1926-1928		

Camp Service: **Sachsenhausen, 1938-1940**

Jobst

First Name:	Dr. Willi	*National Archive File:*	A3343 SSO-139A
Birthdate:	27 October 1912	*Birthplace:*	Egar
Rank:	SS-Hauptsturmführer	*SS Number:*	327636
NSDAP Number:	6749388	*Highest Decoration:*	Wound Badge in Black
Religion:	Catholic	*Marital Status:*	Married
Waffen-SS:	1st SS Division "Leibstandarte Adolf Hitler", 1941-1942		
Notes:	Camp doctor Ebensee sub-camp		
	Executed 28 May 1947		

Camp Service: **Mauthausen**
Gross-Rosen

Joch

First Name:	Hans	*National Archive File:*	A3343 SSO-139A
Birthdate:	4 November 1914	*Birthplace:*	Hamburg
Rank:	SS-Untersturmführer	*SS Number:*	117405
NSDAP Number:	3038141	*Highest Decoration:*	None listed
Religion:	Unknown	*Marital Status:*	Single
Waffen-SS:	No		
Notes:	1st SS Totenkopfstandarte "Oberbayern"		
	Died 31 January 1939		

Camp Service: **Dachau, 1938**

Joebstl

First Name:	Dr. Rudolf	*National Archive File:*	A3343 SSO-139A
Birthdate:	25 March 1903	*Birthplace:*	Steyr, Austria
Rank:	SS-Hauptsturmführer	*SS Number:*	323775
NSDAP Number:	443731	*Highest Decoration:*	War Service Cross 2nd Class
Religion:	Protestant	*Marital Status:*	Married
Waffen-SS:	No		
Notes:	Doctor		
	Served in SA 1932-1936		

Camp Service: **Sachsenhausen, 1941**
Oranienburg, 1944

Joest

First Name:	Dr. Josef	*National Archive File:*	A3343 SSO-139A
Birthdate:	23 May 1907	*Birthplace:*	Untergruene
Rank:	SS-Obersturmbannführer	*SS Number:*	49304
NSDAP Number:	407530	*Highest Decoration:*	War Service Cross 2nd Class
Religion:	Agnostic	*Marital Status:*	Married
Waffen-SS:	3rd SS Division "Totenkopf", 1939-1942		
	VIth SS Corps, 1944		
Notes:	Dentist; Served in SA 1931		

Camp Service: **Columbia Haus, 1935**   **Oranienburg, 1938**

Josten

First Name:	Heinrich
Birthdate:	11 December 1893
Rank:	SS-Obersturmführer
NSDAP Number:	1593636
Religion:	Agnostic
Waffen-SS:	No
Notes:	Iron Cross 2nd Class WWI; executed

National Archive File: A3343 SSO-141A
Birthplace: Malmedy
SS Number: 92316
Highest Decoration: None listed
Marital Status: Married

Camp Service: **Auschwitz, 1941-1944**

Jothann

First Name:	Werner
Birthdate:	18 May 1907
Rank:	SS-Obersturmführer (F)
NSDAP Number:	5037905
Religion:	Protestant
Waffen-SS:	No
Notes:	Construction department Auschwitz

National Archive File: A3343 SSO-141A
Birthplace: Eldenburg
SS Number: 169997
Highest Decoration: War Service Cross 2nd Class
Marital Status: Single

Camp Service: **Auschwitz, 1941-1945**

Jung

First Name:	Dr. Edwin
Birthdate:	11 January 1907
Rank:	SS-Standartenführer
NSDAP Number:	347963
Religion:	Agnostic
Waffen-SS:	3rd SS Division "Totenkopf", 1940-1942
	8th SS Division "Florian Geyer", 1942-1944
	10th SS Division "Frundsberg", 1944
Notes:	Camp Surgeon, Divison Surgeon in 8th and 9th SS Divisions

National Archive File: A3343 SSO-143A
Birthplace: Westerhausen
SS Number: 255916
Highest Decoration: Iron Cross 1st Class
Marital Status: Married

Camp Service: **Columbia Haus, 1935**
Dachau, 1936-1937

Jung

First Name:	Dr. Julius
Birthdate:	29 August 1914
Rank:	SS-Hauptsturmführer
NSDAP Number:	Not a member
Religion:	Unknown
Waffen-SS:	6th SS Division "Nord", 1942-1944
Notes:	Killed in action, 2 October 1944

National Archive File: A3343 SSO-143A
Birthplace: Eltwille
SS Number: 70364
Highest Decoration: None listed
Marital Status: Engaged

Camp Service: **Sachsenhausen, 1941-1942**

Jung

First Name:	Georg	*National Archive File:*	A3343 SSO-143A
Birthdate:	15 February 1893	*Birthplace:*	Zutzendorf/Els
Rank:	SS-Untersturmführer	*SS Number:*	430411
NSDAP Number:	8961479	*Highest Decoration:*	None listed
Religion:	Protestant	*Marital Status:*	Married
Waffen-SS:	No		
Notes:	Iron Cross 2nd Class WWI		

Camp Service: **Dachau, 1943**

Kaether

First Name:	Dr. Hans	*National Archive File:*	A3343 SSO-147A
Birthdate:	2 July 1897	*Birthplace:*	Aachen
Rank:	SS-Obersturmbannführer	*SS Number:*	314114
NSDAP Number:	Not a member	*Highest Decoration:*	None listed
Religion:	Protestant	*Marital Status:*	Married
Waffen-SS:	1st SS Division "Leibstandarte Adolf Hitler", 1941 IInd SS Corps, 1943		
Notes:	Iron Cross 1st Class WWI		

Camp Service: **Sachsenhausen, 1940**

Kahr

First Name:	Dr. Karl	*National Archive File:*	A3343 SSO-148A
Birthdate:	11 September 1914	*Birthplace:*	Fuerstenfell, Austria
Rank:	SS-Hauptsturmführer	*SS Number:*	382463
NSDAP Number:	Not a member	*Highest Decoration:*	None listed
Religion:	Agnostic	*Marital Status:*	Single
Waffen-SS:	4th SS Division "Polizei", 1942		
Notes:	Camp doctor at Dachau		

Camp Service: **Dachau, 1942-1943**
Buchenwald, 1944
Dora, 1945

Kaindl

First Name:	Anton	*National Archive File:*	A3343 SSO-148A
Birthdate:	14 July 1902	*Birthplace:*	Munich
Rank:	SS-Standartenführer	*SS Number:*	241248
NSDAP Number:	4390500	*Highest Decoration:*	War Service Cross 1st Class
Religion:	Catholic	*Marital Status:*	Married
Waffen-SS:	3rd SS Division "Totenkopf", 1939-1941		
Notes:	*Kommandant* Sachsenhausen Sentenced to Life; died November 1947 in prison		

Camp Service: **Oranienburg, 1937**
Sachsenhausen, 1942

Kaltofen

First Name:	Hans	*National Archive File:*	A3343 SSO-150A
Birthdate:	25 April 1909	*Birthplace:*	Riesa
Rank:	SS-Sturmbannführer	*SS Number:*	22226
NSDAP Number:	1005460	*Highest Decoration:*	None listed
Religion:	Agnostic	*Marital Status:*	Married
Waffen-SS:	3rd SS Division "Totenkopf", 1941-1942		
	13th SS Division "Handschar", 1943-1944		
Notes:	Commander Battle Group Kaltofen, 1945		

Camp Service: **Sachsenburg, 1936**

Kamolz

First Name:	Werner	*National Archive File:*	A3343 SSO-151A
Birthdate:	20 January 1910	*Birthplace:*	Posen
Rank:	SS-Obersturmbannführer	*SS Number:*	259367
NSDAP Number:	1422318	*Highest Decoration:*	Iron Cross 2nd Class
Religion:	Agnostic	*Marital Status:*	Married
Waffen-SS:	3rd SS Division "Totenkopf", 1940-1941		
	6th SS Division "Nord", 1943-1945		
	32nd SS Division "30 Januar", 1945		
Notes:	Assistant physician		

Camp Service: **Buchenwald, 1938-1939**

Kantschuster

First Name:	Johann	*National Archive File:*	A3343 SSO-152A
Birthdate:	20 May 1897	*Birthplace:*	Beuerberg
Rank:	SS-Obersturmführer	*SS Number:*	58541
NSDAP Number:	76941	*Highest Decoration:*	Golden Party Badge
Religion:	Agnostic	*Marital Status:*	Married
Waffen-SS:	No		
Notes:	Iron Cross 2nd Class, Wound Badge WWI		
	Discharged 1941 with stomach ailment		

Camp Service: **Dachau, 1933-1939** **Ravensbrück, 1939-1940**
Mauthausen, 1940 **Breendonk**

Kappe

First Name:	Dr. Julius	*National Archive File:*	A3343 SSO-152A
Birthdate:	20 December 1905	*Birthplace:*	Litzum
Rank:	SS-Obersturmführer	*SS Number:*	367748
NSDAP Number:	273537	*Highest Decoration:*	War Service Cross 2nd Class
Religion:	Protestant	*Marital Status:*	Married
Waffen-SS:	8th SS Division "Florian Geyer", 1942-1944		
Notes:	Dentist		
	Served in SA 1932-1936		

Camp Service: **Neuengamme, 1940-1941**

Karl

First Name:	Hubert	*National Archive File:*	A3343 SSO-154A
Birthdate:	3 November 1907	*Birthplace:*	Munich
Rank:	SS-Obersturmführer	*SS Number:*	1339
NSDAP Number:	113509	*Highest Decoration:*	War Service Cross 1st Class
Religion:	Catholic	*Marital Status:*	Married
Waffen-SS:	No		
Notes:	SS Economic Enterprises Dachau		

Camp Service: **Dachau, 1933-1935**

Karschulin

First Name:	Dr. Othmar	*National Archive File:*	A3343 SSO-155A
Birthdate:	1 November 1902	*Birthplace:*	Olmuetz
Rank:	SS-Hauptsturmführer	*SS Number:*	424180
NSDAP Number:	Not a member	*Highest Decoration:*	War Service Cross 2nd Class
Religion:	Catholic	*Marital Status:*	Married
Waffen-SS:	1st SS Infantry Brigade, 1942-1944		
Notes:	Pathologist		

Camp Service: **Buchenwald, 1942**

Kather

First Name:	Dr. Erich	*National Archive File:*	A3343 SSO-157A
Birthdate:	18 July 1908	*Birthplace:*	Hamburg
Rank:	SS-Untersturmführer	*SS Number:*	Unknown
NSDAP Number:	7585459	*Highest Decoration:*	War Service Cross 2nd Class
Religion:	Protestant	*Marital Status:*	Married
Waffen-SS:	No		
Notes:	Doctor		

Camp Service: **Buchenwald, 1943-1944**
Bergen-Belsen, 1944

Katzmann

First Name:	Heinrich	*National Archive File:*	A3343 SSO-157A
Birthdate:	21 January 1899	*Birthplace:*	Bochum-Langendreer
Rank:	SS-Obersturmführer	*SS Number:*	3865
NSDAP Number:	113151	*Highest Decoration:*	War Service Cross 2nd Class
Religion:	Agnostic	*Marital Status:*	Married
Waffen-SS:	No		
Notes:	Iron Cross 2nd Class WWI		
	Camp service not listed in personnel file		

Camp Service: **Esterwegen, 1933**

Kausch

First Name:	Paul-Albert	*National Archive File:*	A3343 SSO-159A
Birthdate:	3 March 1911	*Birthplace:*	Jaedersdorf
Rank:	SS-Obersturmbannführer	*SS Number:*	82578
NSDAP Number:	1736388	*Highest Decoration:*	Knight's Cross with Oak Leaves
Religion:	Agnostic	*Marital Status:*	Married
Waffen-SS:	5th SS Division "Wiking", 1941-1944		
	11th SS Division "Nordland", 1944		
Notes:	Guard troops at Sachsenburg and Buchenwald		
	Tank battalion commander in 11th SS Division		

Camp Service: **Sachsenburg, 1936**   **Buchenwald, 1937**

Keller

First Name:	Emil	*National Archive File:*	A3343 SSO-160A
Birthdate:	30 October 1912	*Birthplace:*	Wuerzburg
Rank:	SS-Hauptsturmführer	*SS Number:*	67804
NSDAP Number:	1543754	*Highest Decoration:*	War Service Cross 1st Class
Religion:	Agnostic	*Marital Status:*	Married
Waffen-SS:	3rd SS Division "Totenkopf", 1939-1940		
Notes:	Later served on Himmler's personal staff		
	Wounded in action several times		

Camp Service: **Dachau, 1933-1937**   **Buchenwald, 1938-1939**

Kempe

First Name:	Kurt	*National Archive File:*	A3343 SSO-162A
Birthdate:	14 June 1913	*Birthplace:*	Loesswnitz
Rank:	SS-Obersturmführer	*SS Number:*	210844
NSDAP Number:	4293153	*Highest Decoration:*	War Service Cross 2nd Class
Religion:	Protestant	*Marital Status:*	Married
Waffen-SS:	No		
Notes:	Former machinist		
	Commander construction brigade Cologne-Deutz		

Camp Service: **Lichtenburg, 1935**
Flossenbürg, 1938
Buchenwald, 1940-1944

Kenn

First Name:	Rudolf	*National Archive File:*	A3343 SSO-163A
Birthdate:	9 October 1914	*Birthplace:*	Berlin
Rank:	SS-Obersturmführer	*SS Number:*	118203
NSDAP Number:	7042707	*Highest Decoration:*	War Service Cross 2nd Class
Religion:	Protestant	*Marital Status:*	Married
Waffen-SS:	No		
Notes:	Former carpenter; Leipzig-Thelka sub-camp		

Camp Service: **Buchenwald, 1939-1944**

Ketterl

First Name:	Hans	*National Archive File:*	A3343 SSO-166A
Birthdate:	20 December 1887	*Birthplace:*	Straubing
Rank:	SS-Standartenführer	*SS Number:*	23080
NSDAP Number:	228746	*Highest Decoration:*	War Service Cross 2nd Class
Religion:	Agnostic	*Marital Status:*	Married
Waffen-SS:	No		

Notes: SS economic enterprises Dachau
Iron Cross 2nd Class WWI

Camp Service: **Dachau, 1943-1945**

Kick

First Name:	Johann	*National Archive File:*	A3343 SSO-166A
Birthdate:	24 November 1901	*Birthplace:*	Waldau
Rank:	SS-Untersturmführer	*SS Number:*	416435
NSDAP Number:	5096990	*Highest Decoration:*	None listed
Religion:	Agnostic	*Marital Status:*	Married
Waffen-SS:	No		

Notes: Leader of political section at Dachau

Camp Service: **Dachau, 1937-1944**

Kiener

First Name:	Hellmuth	*National Archive File:*	A3343 SSO-167A
Birthdate:	16 January 1910	*Birthplace:*	Munich
Rank:	SS-Sturmbannführer	*SS Number:*	208735
NSDAP Number:	4965880	*Highest Decoration:*	War Service Cross 2nd Class
Religion:	Agnostic	*Marital Status:*	Married
Waffen-SS:	No		

Notes: Leader of legal department at concentration camp inspectorate

Camp Service: **Oranienburg, 1938-1944**

Kiesewetter

First Name:	Dr. Hermann	*National Archive File:*	A3343 SSO-168A
Birthdate:	7 January 1912	*Birthplace:*	Hochgarth, Bohemia
Rank:	SS-Hauptsturmführer	*SS Number:*	310402
NSDAP Number:	7930249	*Highest Decoration:*	Iron Cross 1st Class
Religion:	Catholic	*Marital Status:*	Married
Waffen-SS:	5th SS Division "Wiking", 1942-1944		

Notes: Doctor
Served in Czech army 1937-1938

Camp Service: **Oranienburg, 1938**
Ravensbrück, 1941
Mauthausen, 1942

Kiklasch

First Name:	Ernst	*National Archive File:*	A3343 SSO-168A
Birthdate:	29 January 1911	*Birthplace:*	Proskau
Rank:	SS-Sturmbannführer	*SS Number:*	6347
NSDAP Number:	340245	*Highest Decoration:*	Iron Cross 1st Class
Religion:	Agnostic	*Marital Status:*	Married
Waffen-SS:	3rd SS Division "Totenkopf", 1941-1944		
Notes:	Wounded in action; battalion commander		

Camp Service: **Lichtenburg, 1936-1937**   **Sachsenburg, 1937**
Buchenwald, 1938

Kimmel

First Name:	Hermann	*National Archive File:*	A3343 SSO-169A
Birthdate:	15 February 1907	*Birthplace:*	Obermohrau
Rank:	SS-Hauptsturmführer	*SS Number:*	120435
NSDAP Number:	1518420	*Highest Decoration:*	Iron Cross 1st Class
Religion:	Agnostic	*Marital Status:*	Married
Waffen-SS:	3rd SS Division "Totenkopf", 1942-1943		
Notes:	Recommended for posthumous promotion to SS-Sturmbannführer		
	Killed in action 13 July 1943 at Kursk		

Camp Service: **Sachsenburg, 1936**
Buchenwald, 1937-1939

Kinne

First Name:	Rudolf	*National Archive File:*	A3343 SSO-170A
Birthdate:	10 February 1905	*Birthplace:*	Leipzig
Rank:	SS-Hauptsturmführer	*SS Number:*	51383
NSDAP Number:	1369459	*Highest Decoration:*	War Service Cross 2nd Class
Religion:	Agnostic	*Marital Status:*	Married
Waffen-SS:	9th SS Division "Hohenstaufen", 1943		
Notes:	*Kommandant* Elbing Schikau-Werken sub-camp (Stutthof); Former electrician		

Camp Service: **Columbia Haus, 1934-1935**   **Sachsenburg, 1936**
Oranienburg, 1937-1940   **Stutthof, 1944**

Kirchert

First Name:	Dr. Werner	*National Archive File:*	A3343 SSO-171A
Birthdate:	4 October 1906	*Birthplace:*	Halle
Rank:	SS-Obersturmbannführer	*SS Number:*	245540
NSDAP Number:	5020939	*Highest Decoration:*	War Service Cross 2nd Class
Religion:	Agnostic	*Marital Status:*	Married
Waffen-SS:	3rd SS Division "Totenkopf", 1940-1942		
	5th SS Division "Wiking", 1942		
Notes:	Doctor		
	Sentenced to 4 years imprisonment		

Camp Service: **Sachsenburg, 1936-1937**   **Dachau, 1937**
Buchenwald   **Oranienburg, 1940-1941**

Kirschneck

First Name:	Hans	*National Archive File:*	A3343 SSO-172A
Birthdate:	14 June 1909	*Birthplace:*	Eger
Rank:	SS-Obersturmführer (F)	*SS Number:*	328538
NSDAP Number:	Not a member	*Highest Decoration:*	War Service Cross 2nd Class
Religion:	Catholic	*Marital Status:*	Married
Waffen-SS:	No		
Notes:	Construction Department Auschwitz		

Camp Service: **Auschwitz, 1942-1944**

Kitt

First Name:	Dr. Bruno	*National Archive File:*	A3343 SSO-173A
Birthdate:	4 August 1906	*Birthplace:*	Heilsberg
Rank:	SS-Hauptsturmführer	*SS Number:*	246756
NSDAP Number:	Not a member	*Highest Decoration:*	War Service Cross 2nd Class
Religion:	Catholic	*Marital Status:*	Married
Waffen-SS:	No		
Notes:	Head physician at the women's hospital at Birkenau		
	Executed 8 October 1946		

Camp Service: **Auschwitz, 1942-1944**
Neuengamme, 1945

Klapsch

First Name:	Hugo	*National Archive File:*	A3343 SSO-175A
Birthdate:	14 January 1897	*Birthplace:*	Arnoldowo
Rank:	SS-Sturmbannführer	*SS Number:*	40153
NSDAP Number:	874671	*Highest Decoration:*	War Service Cross 2nd Class
Religion:	Protestant	*Marital Status:*	Married
Waffen-SS:	3rd SS Division "Totenkopf", 1940-1941		
Notes:	Iron Cross 2nd Class WWI		
	Former wood salesman		

Camp Service: **Columbia Haus, 1934**
Oranienburg, 1935-1940

Klattenhoff

First Name:	Heinrich	*National Archive File:*	A3343 SSO-175A
Birthdate:	12 May 1907	*Birthplace:*	Delmenhorst
Rank:	SS-Hauptsturmführer	*SS Number:*	270463
NSDAP Number:	3699301	*Highest Decoration:*	War Service Cross 1st Class
Religion:	Protestant	*Marital Status:*	Married
Waffen-SS:	13th SS Division "Handschar", 1943		
Notes:	Former businessman		
	Served in SA 1933-1934		

Camp Service: **Sachsenhausen, 1938-1940**   **Oranienburg, 1940**
Dachau, 1941-1943

Klebeck

First Name:	Kurt	*National Archive File:*	A3343 SSO-176A
Birthdate:	6 March 1906	*Birthplace:*	Berlin
Rank:	SS-Hauptsturmführer	*SS Number:*	129556
NSDAP Number:	2594397	*Highest Decoration:*	War Service Cross 2nd Class
Religion:	Protestant	*Marital Status:*	Divorced
Waffen-SS:	No		
Notes:	Former delivery service worker		

Camp Service: **Sachsenhausen, 1940**
Oranienburg, 1941
Neuengamme

Kleber

First Name:	Wilhelm	*National Archive File:*	A3343 SSO-176A
Birthdate:	27 January 1915	*Birthplace:*	Saarbruecken
Rank:	SS-Hauptsturmführer	*SS Number:*	269170
NSDAP Number:	2680195	*Highest Decoration:*	War Service Cross 2nd Class
Religion:	Agnostic	*Marital Status:*	Married
Waffen-SS:	2nd SS Division "Das Reich", 1942-1944		
Notes:	Leader of Administration Department at Hinzert		
	Killed in action 23 July 1944 in France		

Camp Service: **Hinzert, 1941**

Klein

First Name:	Dr. Fritz	*National Archive File:*	A3343 SSO-177A
Birthdate:	24 November 1888	*Birthplace:*	Zeiden, Romania
Rank:	SS-Untersturmführer	*SS Number:*	Unknown
NSDAP Number:	732	*Highest Decoration:*	None listed
Religion:	Protestant	*Marital Status:*	Divorced
Waffen-SS:	No		
Notes:	Golden Party Badge		
	Executed 13 December 1945		

Camp Service: **Auschwitz, 1944**
Neuengamme, 1944-1945
Bergen-Belsen, 1945

Klimek

First Name:	Dr. Karl	*National Archive File:*	A3343 SSO-179A
Birthdate:	24 July 1905	*Birthplace:*	Maehr-Schoenberg
Rank:	SS-Obersturmführer	*SS Number:*	453191
NSDAP Number:	Not a member	*Highest Decoration:*	None listed
Religion:	Unknown	*Marital Status:*	Married
Waffen-SS:	8th SS Division "Florian Geyer", 1943		
	Vth SS Corps, 1944		
Notes:	Served in Yugoslav army 1926-1940		

Camp Service: **Ravensbrück, 1943**

Klimsza

First Name: Dr. Josef
Birthdate: 8 September 1911
Rank: SS-Sturmbannführer
NSDAP Number: Not a member
Religion: Agnostic
Waffen-SS: 3rd SS Division "Totenkopf", 1942-1943
Notes: Served in Czech army in 1938

National Archive File: A3343 SSO-179A
Birthplace: Neu-Oderberg
SS Number: 310367
Highest Decoration: Iron Cross 2nd Class
Marital Status: Married

Camp Service: **Buchenwald, 1939**

Klinger

First Name: Georg
Birthdate: 10 April 1915
Rank: SS-Obersturmführer
NSDAP Number: 3958897
Religion: Agnostic
Waffen-SS: No
Notes: SS Clothing Works Dachau

National Archive File: A3343 SSO-180A
Birthplace: Munich
SS Number: 156562
Highest Decoration: War Service Cross 2nd Class
Marital Status: Married

Camp Service: **Dachau, 1939**

Klipp

First Name: Kurt
Birthdate: 19 September 1907
Rank: SS-Obersturmführer
NSDAP Number: 5020763
Religion: Agnostic
Waffen-SS: No
Notes: *Kommandant* Blechhammer sub-camp

National Archive File: A3343 SSO-181A
Birthplace: Cologne
SS Number: 293197
Highest Decoration: War Service Cross 2nd Class
Marital Status: Married

Camp Service: **Majdanek, 1943**
Auschwitz, 1944-1945
Bergen-Belsen, 1945

Klug

First Name: Dr. Eduard
Birthdate: 27 March 1901
Rank: SS-Sturmbannführer
NSDAP Number: 6698307
Religion: Catholic
Waffen-SS: 6th SS Division "Nord", 1941
Notes: Camp doctor at Sachsenhausen

National Archive File: A3343 SSO-183A
Birthplace: Leitmeritz
SS Number: 329646
Highest Decoration: Iron Cross 2nd Class
Marital Status: Single

Camp Service: **Sachsenhausen, 1940**

Knapp

First Name:	Dr. Karl	*National Archive File:*	A3343 SSO-184A
Birthdate:	23 March 1913	*Birthplace:*	Hamborn
Rank:	SS-Sturmbannführer	*SS Number:*	226015
NSDAP Number:	2034178	*Highest Decoration:*	Iron Cross 2nd Class
Religion:	Agnostic	*Marital Status:*	Married
Waffen-SS:	3rd SS Division "Totenkopf", 1940-1942		
	1st SS Infantry Brigade, 1942-1944		
Notes:	Doctor		

Camp Service: **Sachsenhausen, 1936-1938**
Mauthausen, 1938-1939
Oranienburg, 1939

Knorr-Krehan

First Name:	Kamillo von	*National Archive File:*	A3343 SSO-188A
Birthdate:	25 March 1899	*Birthplace:*	Plumenau, Austria
Rank:	SS-Hauptsturmführer	*SS Number:*	341937
NSDAP Number:	Not a member	*Highest Decoration:*	War Service Cross 2nd Class
Religion:	Catholic	*Marital Status:*	Married
Waffen-SS:	No		
Notes:	Leader special commando Schloss Eisenberg		

Camp Service: **Buchenwald, 1941-1943**   **Flossenbürg, 1944**

Koch

First Name:	Karl Otto	*National Archive File:*	A3343 SSO-190A
Birthdate:	2 August 1897	*Birthplace:*	Darmstadt
Rank:	SS-Standartenführer	*SS Number:*	14830
NSDAP Number:	475586	*Highest Decoration:*	War Service Cross 2nd Class
Religion:	Agnostic	*Marital Status:*	Married
Waffen-SS:	No		
Notes:	*Kommandant* Columbia Haus, Esterwegen, Sachsenhausen, Majdanek and Buchenwald; executed by SS, 26 April 1945		

Camp Service: **Dachau, 1935**   **Columbia Haus, 1935-1936**
Sachsenhausen, 1936-1937   **Esterwegen, 1937**
Buchenwald, 1937-1941   **Majdanek, 1941-1942**

Koebrich

First Name:	Dr. Konrad	*National Archive File:*	A3343 SSO-190A
Birthdate:	27 February 1885	*Birthplace:*	Trindelburg
Rank:	SS-Hauptsturmführer	*SS Number:*	180209
NSDAP Number:	947278	*Highest Decoration:*	None listed
Religion:	Protestant	*Marital Status:*	Married
Waffen-SS:	No		
Notes:	Iron Cross 2nd Class WWI		
	Doctor at Buchenwald		

Camp Service: **Buchenwald, 1940**

Koegel

First Name:	Max	*National Archive File:*	A3343 SSO-190A
Birthdate:	16 October 1895	*Birthplace:*	Fuessen
Rank:	SS-Obersturmbannführer	*SS Number:*	37644
NSDAP Number:	1179781	*Highest Decoration:*	War Service Cross 1st Class
Religion:	Agnostic	*Marital Status:*	Divorced
Waffen-SS:	No		
Notes:	*Kommandant* Flossenbürg, Ravensbrück and Majdanek; executed 27 April 1947		

Camp Service: **Dachau, 1934-1937** **Columbia Haus, 1937**
Lichtenburg, 1938-1940 **Majdanek, 1942-1943**
Flossenbürg, 1943-1945

Koehn

First Name:	Richard	*National Archive File:*	A3343 SSO-191A
Birthdate:	16 May 1896	*Birthplace:*	Hamburg
Rank:	SS-Sturmbannführer	*SS Number:*	179609
NSDAP Number:	4794692	*Highest Decoration:*	War Service Cross 2nd Class
Religion:	Agnostic	*Marital Status:*	Married
Waffen-SS:	No		
Notes:	Iron Cross 1st Class WWI		

Camp Service: **Sachsenhausen, 1940-1943**

Koelsch

First Name:	Dr. Paul	*National Archive File:*	A3343 SSO-192A
Birthdate:	16 July 1893	*Birthplace:*	Siegen
Rank:	SS-Hauptsturmführer	*SS Number:*	23602
NSDAP Number:	4119394	*Highest Decoration:*	None listed
Religion:	Protestant	*Marital Status:*	Married
Waffen-SS:	No		
Notes:	Iron Cross 2nd Class WWI		

Camp Service: **Oranienburg, 1941-1942**

Koenig

First Name:	Dr. Hans-Wilhelm	*National Archive File:*	A3343 SSO-192A
Birthdate:	13 May 1912	*Birthplace:*	Stuttgart
Rank:	SS-Untersturmführer	*SS Number:*	Unknown
NSDAP Number:	7194323	*Highest Decoration:*	None listed
Religion:	Agnostic	*Marital Status:*	Married
Waffen-SS:	No		
Notes:	Camp physician		

Camp Service: **Auschwitz, 1944**

Koenig

First Name:	Friedrich Otto	*National Archive File:*	A3343 SSO-192A
Birthdate:	25 December 1897	*Birthplace:*	Hohenlimburg
Rank:	SS-Hauptsturmführer	*SS Number:*	42784
NSDAP Number:	Not a member	*Highest Decoration:*	None
Religion:	Agnostic	*Marital Status:*	Married
Waffen-SS:	No		
Notes:	Iron Cross 2nd Class WWI		
	Released from SS in 1940		

Camp Service: **Oranienburg, 1936-1938**
Buchenwald, 1940

Koepfer

First Name:	Hermann	*National Archive File:*	A3343 SSO-193A
Birthdate:	15 September 1900	*Birthplace:*	Schoenau
Rank:	SS-Obersturmführer	*SS Number:*	217750
NSDAP Number:	5611729	*Highest Decoration:*	None listed
Religion:	Catholic	*Marital Status:*	Married
Waffen-SS:	No		
Notes:	Former lawyer; served in WWI		

Camp Service: **Sachsenhausen, 1943**

Koerber

First Name:	Dr. Georg	*National Archive File:*	A3343 RS-D0089
Birthdate:	16 February 1908	*Birthplace:*	Bamberg
Rank:	SS-Untersturmführer	*SS Number:*	67899
NSDAP Number:	3151573	*Highest Decoration:*	None listed
Religion:	Catholic	*Marital Status:*	Married
Waffen-SS:	No		
Notes:	Released from SS, 31 July 1937		

Camp Service: **Papenburg, 1934**
Columbia Haus, 1935

Koermann

First Name:	Edmund	*National Archive File:*	A3343 SSO-193A
Birthdate:	8 May 1890	*Birthplace:*	Langendreer
Rank:	SS-Untersturmführer	*SS Number:*	426509
NSDAP Number:	Not a member	*Highest Decoration:*	None listed
Religion:	Unknown	*Marital Status:*	Single
Waffen-SS:	No		
Notes:	Iron Cross 1st Class WWI		

Camp Service: **Natzweiler, 1942**

Koerner

First Name:	Michael	*National Archive File:*	A3343 SSO-193A
Birthdate:	20 March 1914	*Birthplace:*	Fuerstenhof
Rank:	SS-Obersturmführer	*SS Number:*	327178
NSDAP Number:	1262029	*Highest Decoration:*	War Service Cross 2nd Class
Religion:	Protestant	*Marital Status:*	Married
Waffen-SS:	No		
Notes:	Sentenced to Life		

Camp Service: **Oranienburg, 1941-1944**
Sachsenhausen, 1944

Kolb

First Name:	August	*National Archive File:*	A3343 SSO-196A
Birthdate:	15 August 1893	*Birthplace:*	Roessleinsdorf
Rank:	SS-Hauptsturmführer	*SS Number:*	222497
NSDAP Number:	3958173	*Highest Decoration:*	War Service Cross 2nd Class
Religion:	Agnostic	*Marital Status:*	Married
Waffen-SS:	No		
Notes:	3rd guard company, later 2nd Schutzhaftlagerführer Sachsenhausen; 1st Guard company Arbeitsdorf; Iron Cross 2nd Class, Wound Badge WWI; sentenced to 6 years		

Camp Service: **Sachsenhausen, 1940-1942, 1943-1945**
Arbeitsdorf, 1942

Kollmer

First Name:	Josef	*National Archive File:*	A3343 SSO-197A
Birthdate:	26 February 1901	*Birthplace:*	Haendlern
Rank:	SS-Obersturmführer	*SS Number:*	267573
NSDAP Number:	4263096	*Highest Decoration:*	None listed
Religion:	Agnostic	*Marital Status:*	Married
Waffen-SS:	31st SS Division, 1944-1945		
Notes:	Commander of 7th Guard Company Served 12 years in state police in Munich		

Camp Service: **Auschwitz, 1942**

Konrad

First Name:	Dr. Ladislaus	*National Archive File:*	No File
Birthdate:	28 August 1913	*Birthplace:*	Siegendorf
Rank:	SS-Obersturmführer	*SS Number:*	Unknown
NSDAP Number:	Not a member	*Highest Decoration:*	None listed
Religion:	Unknown	*Marital Status:*	Unknown
Waffen-SS:	No		
Notes:	Killed in action 17 February 1944 Served in Army 10th Panzer Grenadier Regiment		

Camp Service: **Mauthausen, 1941-1942**

Kopff

First Name:	Helmut	*National Archive File:*	A3343 SSO-199A
Birthdate:	24 September 1906	*Birthplace:*	Hamburg
Rank:	SS-Hauptsturmführer	*SS Number:*	361224
NSDAP Number:	999457	*Highest Decoration:*	Iron Cross 2nd Class
Religion:	Unknown	*Marital Status:*	Married
Waffen-SS:	No		
Notes:	Commander IIIrd Totenkopfsturmbann, SS-Totenkopfstandarte 10		
	Served in police units during the war; wounded		

Camp Service: **Buchenwald, 1939-1940**

Korff

First Name:	Werner	*National Archive File:*	A3343 SSO-201A
Birthdate:	12 April 1915	*Birthplace:*	Rinteln
Rank:	SS-Sturmbannführer	*SS Number:*	183211
NSDAP Number:	3601179	*Highest Decoration:*	Iron Cross 1st Class
Religion:	Agnostic	*Marital Status:*	Single
Waffen-SS:	3rd SS Division "Totenkopf", 1939-1943		
	5th SS Division "Wiking", 1945		
Notes:	Adjutant Ist Totenkopfsturmbann/1st SS Totenkopfstandarte		
	Assault gun battalion commander; wounded several times in combat		

Camp Service: **Dachau, 1938**

Kraetzer

First Name:	Theodor	*National Archive File:*	A3343 SSO-205A
Birthdate:	30 October 1914	*Birthplace:*	Nürnberg
Rank:	SS-Obersturmführer	*SS Number:*	276344
NSDAP Number:	4690977	*Highest Decoration:*	War Service Cross 2nd Class
Religion:	Protestant	*Marital Status:*	Married
Waffen-SS:	36th SS Division "Dirlewanger", 1945		
Notes:	Former bank officer		

Camp Service: **Buchenwald, 1939-1941**
Auschwitz, 1941-1945

Kramer

First Name:	Herbert-Guenther	*National Archive File:*	A3343 SSO-206A
Birthdate:	3 April 1906	*Birthplace:*	Berlin
Rank:	SS-Hauptsturmführer	*SS Number:*	18229
NSDAP Number:	372343	*Highest Decoration:*	War Service Cross 2nd Class
Religion:	Agnostic	*Marital Status:*	Married
Waffen-SS:	22nd SS Division "Maria Theresia", 1944		
Notes:	In SA 1929-1931		

Camp Service: **Mauthausen, 1942**   **Auschwitz, 1942-1944**

Kramer

First Name:	Josef	*National Archive File:*	A3343 SSO-206A
Birthdate:	10 November 1906	*Birthplace:*	Munich
Rank:	SS-Hauptsturmführer	*SS Number:*	32217
NSDAP Number:	733597	*Highest Decoration:*	War Service Cross 1st Class
Religion:	Catholic	*Marital Status:*	Married
Waffen-SS:	No		
Notes:	*Kommandant* Birkenau, Natzweiler; Bergen-Belsen; executed 13 December 1945		

Camp Service: **Dachau, 1936-1937   Sachsenhausen, 1937**
Mauthausen, 1938-1940   Auschwitz, 1943
Natzweiler, 1944   Bergen-Belsen, 1944-1945

Kraus

First Name:	Franz-Xaver	*National Archive File:*	A3343 SSO-208A
Birthdate:	27 September 1903	*Birthplace:*	Munich
Rank:	SS-Sturmbannführer	*SS Number:*	16299
NSDAP Number:	405816	*Highest Decoration:*	War Service Cross 2nd Class
Religion:	Catholic	*Marital Status:*	Married
Waffen-SS:	No		
Notes:	Schutzhaftlagerführer at Auschwitz; Blood Order; executed 24 January 1948		

Camp Service: **Esterwegen, 1934-1936   Columbia Haus, 1936**
Sachsenhausen, 1937-1939   Oranienburg, 1941-1943
Auschwitz, 1944

Krauth

First Name:	Heinrich	*National Archive File:*	A3343 SSO-209A
Birthdate:	9 March 1913	*Birthplace:*	Karlsruhe
Rank:	SS-Sturmbannführer	*SS Number:*	13310
NSDAP Number:	Not a member	*Highest Decoration:*	German Cross in Gold
Religion:	Unknown	*Marital Status:*	Married
Waffen-SS:	3rd SS Division "Totenkopf", 1940-1943		
Notes:	Killed in action 21 August 1943		
	Adjutant, IInd Bn/1st Totenkopfstandarte "Oberbayern"		

Camp Service: **Oranienburg, 1936   Dachau, 1937**

Krebsbach

First Name:	Dr. Eduard	*National Archive File:*	A3343 SSO-210A
Birthdate:	8 August 1894	*Birthplace:*	Bonn
Rank:	SS-Sturmbannführer	*SS Number:*	106821
NSDAP Number:	4142556	*Highest Decoration:*	None listed
Religion:	Catholic	*Marital Status:*	Married
Waffen-SS:	3rd SS Division "Totenkopf"		
Notes:	Iron Cross 2nd Class WWI; camp doctor at Riga		
	Executed 28 May 1947		

Camp Service: **Sachsenhausen, 1941   Mauthausen, 1941-1944**
Riga, 1944

Kreibich

First Name:	Dr. Eduard	*National Archive File:*	A3343 SSO-211A
Birthdate:	16 July 1908	*Birthplace:*	Bensen
Rank:	SS-Hauptsturmführer	*SS Number:*	335385
NSDAP Number:	Not a member	*Highest Decoration:*	War Service Cross 2nd Class
Religion:	Catholic	*Marital Status:*	Married
Waffen-SS:	No		
Notes:	Camp doctor		
	Leader of medical training for Department DIII, Oranienburg		

Camp Service: **Sachsenhausen, 1942-1944**
Oranienburg, 1944

Kremer

First Name:	Dr. Johann Paul	*National Archive File:*	A3343 SSO-212A
Birthdate:	26 December 1883	*Birthplace:*	Stelberg/Cologne
Rank:	SS-Obersturmführer	*SS Number:*	262703
NSDAP Number:	1265405	*Highest Decoration:*	None listed
Religion:	Catholic	*Marital Status:*	Divorced
Waffen-SS:	No		
Notes:	Camp doctor at Auschwitz		
	Sentenced to Death, commuted to 10 years; died 1965		

Camp Service: **Auschwitz, 1942**

Kreppel

First Name:	Hans	*National Archive File:*	A3343 SSO-213A
Birthdate:	30 November 1894	*Birthplace:*	Dormitz
Rank:	SS-Sturmbannführer	*SS Number:*	3020
NSDAP Number:	43954	*Highest Decoration:*	War Service Cross 2nd Class
Religion:	Catholic	*Marital Status:*	Married
Waffen-SS:	No		
Notes:	Censor at Dachau		
	Golden Party Badge, Wound Badge WWI		

Camp Service: **Dachau, 1937**

Krieger

First Name:	Dr. Richard	*National Archive File:*	A3343 SSO-214A
Birthdate:	30 October 1876	*Birthplace:*	Kitzingen
Rank:	SS-Sturmbannführer	*SS Number:*	144232
NSDAP Number:	1355645	*Highest Decoration:*	None listed
Religion:	Catholic	*Marital Status:*	Married
Waffen-SS:	No		
Notes:	Iron Cross 2nd Class WWI; Camp doctor at Mauthausen; Bergen-Belsen		

Camp Service: **Mauthausen, 1940**   **Sachsenhausen, 1940-1941**
Niederhagen, 1942   **Natzweiler, 1943**
Auschwitz, 1944   **Dachau, 1944**
Bergen-Belsen, 1945

Krieglstein

First Name:	Dr. Franz	*National Archive File:*	A3343 SSO-214A
Birthdate:	23 February 1912	*Birthplace:*	Graslitz
Rank:	SS-Sturmbannführer	*SS Number:*	310355
NSDAP Number:	Not a member	*Highest Decoration:*	War Service Cross 2nd Class
Religion:	Agnostic	*Marital Status:*	Single
Waffen-SS:	3rd SS Division "Totenkopf", 1940-1943		
Notes:	Served in Czech army 1937-1938		

Camp Service: **Oranienburg, 1938-1940, 1944**

Kriens

First Name:	Dr. Heinrich	*National Archive File:*	A3343 SSO-215A
Birthdate:	2 April 1892	*Birthplace:*	Rumele
Rank:	SS-Sturmbannführer	*SS Number:*	14807
NSDAP Number:	387911	*Highest Decoration:*	None listed
Religion:	Agnostic	*Marital Status:*	Married
Waffen-SS:	SS Police Battalion 13		
Notes:	Doctor; served in WWI		

Camp Service: **Oranienburg, 1940**

Kroeger

First Name:	Johannes	*National Archive File:*	A3343 SSO-215A
Birthdate:	27 April 1921	*Birthplace:*	zu Kropp
Rank:	SS-Untersturmführer	*SS Number:*	413935
NSDAP Number:	Not a member	*Highest Decoration:*	Iron Cross 2nd Class
Religion:	Unknown	*Marital Status:*	Married
Waffen-SS:	1st SS Division "Leibstandarte Adolf Hitler", 1939-1942, 1944		
Notes:	Wounded twice in combat		
	Orders from Buchenwald to 1st SS Division		

Camp Service: **Buchenwald, 1944**

Kroeger

First Name:	Paul	*National Archive File:*	A3343 SSO-215A
Birthdate:	29 January 1901	*Birthplace:*	Tessin
Rank:	SS-Standartenführer	*SS Number:*	25655
NSDAP Number:	1093138	*Highest Decoration:*	War Service Cross 2nd Class
Religion:	Unknown	*Marital Status:*	Unknown
Waffen-SS:	No		
Notes:	Watch leader Buchenwald		

Camp Service: **Buchenwald, 1940-1941**

Kroemer

First Name:	Dr. Friedrich	*National Archive File:*	A3343 SSO-215A
Birthdate:	5 June 1895	*Birthplace:*	Liegnitz
Rank:	SS-Sturmbannführer	*SS Number:*	128182
NSDAP Number:	769276	*Highest Decoration:*	War Service Cross 2nd Class
Religion:	Agnostic	*Marital Status:*	Married
Waffen-SS:	No		
Notes:	Manager of SS pharmacy at Auschwitz; no record of Auschwitz in file		
	Died 18 February 1944		

Camp Service: **Auschwitz, 1942-1943**

Kron

First Name:	Otto	*National Archive File:*	A3343 SSO-216A
Birthdate:	28 February 1911	*Birthplace:*	Speyer
Rank:	SS-Obersturmbannführer	*SS Number:*	31441
NSDAP Number:	3061726	*Highest Decoration:*	Knight's Cross
Religion:	Catholic	*Marital Status:*	Married
Waffen-SS:	3rd SS Division "Totenkopf", 1941-1943		
Notes:	Guard troops		
	Died 8 August 1951		

Camp Service: **Dachau, 1935**

Krone

First Name:	Heinrich	*National Archive File:*	A3343 SSO-217A
Birthdate:	2 February 1901	*Birthplace:*	Lingen
Rank:	SS-Sturmbannführer	*SS Number:*	270465
NSDAP Number:	2845603	*Highest Decoration:*	None listed
Religion:	Agnostic	*Marital Status:*	Married
Waffen-SS:	No		
Notes:	Electrical engineer at Buchenwald		

Camp Service: **Sachsenhausen, 1937**
Buchenwald, 1938-1940

Krueger

First Name:	Bernhard	*National Archive File:*	A3343 SSO-217A
Birthdate:	26 November 1904	*Birthplace:*	Riesa
Rank:	SS-Sturmbannführer	*SS Number:*	15249
NSDAP Number:	4239549	*Highest Decoration:*	War Service Cross 1st Class
Religion:	Agnostic	*Marital Status:*	Married
Waffen-SS:	No		
Notes:	Leader of special counterfeit project located at Sachsenhausen		

Camp Service: **Sachsenhausen, 1942-1944**

Krueger

First Name: Karl
Birthdate: 7 February 1908
Rank: SS-Sturmbannführer
NSDAP Number: Not a member
Religion: Lutheran
Waffen-SS: 3rd SS Division "Totenkopf", 1941
6th SS Division "Nord", 1942-1943
17th SS Division "Götz von Berlichingen", 1943-1944
Notes: Signal officer in SS-TV at camps

National Archive File: A3343 SSO-219A
Birthplace: Braunschweig
SS Number: 292857
Highest Decoration: Iron Cross 2nd Class
Marital Status: Married

Camp Service: **Buchenwald, 1937-1938**
Oranienburg, 1938

Krug

First Name: Felix
Birthdate: 11 December 1908
Rank: SS-Sturmbannführer
NSDAP Number: 315568
Religion: Unknown
Waffen-SS: 5th SS Division "Wiking", 1942-1943
Notes: Former tailor

National Archive File: A3343 SSO-221A
Birthplace: Munich
SS Number: 3933
Highest Decoration: War Service Cross 1st Class
Marital Status: Single

Camp Service: **Dachau, 1934-1939, 1943-1945**
Ravensbrück, 1940-1941

Kruncik

First Name: Eugen
Birthdate: 5 September 1901
Rank: SS-Sturmbannführer
NSDAP Number: 300664
Religion: Agnostic
Waffen-SS: No
Notes: Dentist

National Archive File: A3343 SSO-221A
Birthplace: Vienna, Austria
SS Number: 306507
Highest Decoration: War Service Cross 2nd Class
Marital Status: Married

Camp Service: **Gross-Rosen, 1941**

Kudriawtzow

First Name: Georg
Birthdate: 11 August 1892
Rank: SS-Hauptsturmführer
NSDAP Number: Not a member
Religion: Greek-Orthodox
Waffen-SS: 3rd SS Division "Totenkopf", 1941
2nd SS Infantry Brigade, 1942
Notes: Fought in Russian Army in WWI

National Archive File: A3343 SSO-223A
Birthplace: St. Petersburg, Russia
SS Number: 393296
Highest Decoration: War Service Cross 1st Class
Marital Status: Married

Camp Service: **Auschwitz, 1944**

Kuechle

First Name:	Heinz	*National Archive File:*	A3343 SSO-026C
Birthdate:	6 July 1911	*Birthplace:*	Lenzenfeld
Rank:	SS-Obersturmbannführer	*SS Number:*	134431
NSDAP Number:	2966261	*Highest Decoration:*	Iron Cross 2nd Class
Religion:	Agnostic	*Marital Status:*	Married
Waffen-SS:	3rd SS Division "Totenkopf", 1940-1941		
	6th SS Division "Nord", 1941-1944		
Notes:	Guard troops; killed in action 19 September 1944		

Camp Service: **Sachsenburg, 1935**
Dachau, 1936

Kuehler

First Name:	Heinz	*National Archive File:*	A3343 SSO-224A
Birthdate:	25 May 1911	*Birthplace:*	Essen
Rank:	SS-Obersturmführer	*SS Number:*	264033
NSDAP Number:	Not a member	*Highest Decoration:*	War Service Cross 2nd Class
Religion:	Catholic	*Marital Status:*	Married
Waffen-SS:	No		
Notes:	Administration officer at Plaszow		
	Supply department at Auschwitz		

Camp Service: **Auschwitz, 1943-1944**
Plaszow, 1944

Kuehn

First Name:	Max	*National Archive File:*	A3343 SSO-224A
Birthdate:	25 July 1912	*Birthplace:*	Leobschuetz
Rank:	SS-Sturmbannführer	*SS Number:*	171188
NSDAP Number:	1594583	*Highest Decoration:*	German Cross in Gold
Religion:	Agnostic	*Marital Status:*	Single
Waffen-SS:	3rd SS Division "Totenkopf", 1940-1945		
Notes:	Guard troops at Dachau; acting regimental commander in 3rd SS Division		
	Wounded in action		

Camp Service: **Dachau, 1937**

Kuehne

First Name:	Karl	*National Archive File:*	A3343 SSO-225A
Birthdate:	20 August 1906	*Birthplace:*	Quedlinburg
Rank:	SS-Untersturmführer	*SS Number:*	53672
NSDAP Number:	1400000	*Highest Decoration:*	None
Religion:	Agnostic	*Marital Status:*	Single
Waffen-SS:	No		
Notes:	Thrown out of SS in 1937		

Camp Service: **Dachau, 1935-1936**
Sachsenburg, 1936

Kuenicke

First Name:	Dr. Georg	*National Archive File:*	No file
Birthdate:	13 May 1894	*Birthplace:*	Unknown
Rank:	SS-Untersturmführer	*SS Number:*	Unknown
NSDAP Number:	Not a member	*Highest Decoration:*	None listed
Religion:	Unknown	*Marital Status:*	Unknown
Waffen-SS:	Unknown		
Notes:	Pest control office		

Camp Service: **Auschwitz**

Kuenstler

First Name:	Karl	*National Archive File:*	A3343 SSO-226A
Birthdate:	12 January 1901	*Birthplace:*	Zella
Rank:	SS-Obersturmbannführer	*SS Number:*	40005
NSDAP Number:	1238648	*Highest Decoration:*	Iron Cross 2nd Class
Religion:	Catholic	*Marital Status:*	Married
Waffen-SS:	7th SS Division "Prinz Eugen", 1942-1945		
Notes:	*Kommandant* Flossenbürg; killed in action April 1945		

Camp Service: **Columbia Haus, 1935   Flossenbürg, 1939-1942**

Kuester

First Name:	Otto	*National Archive File:*	A3343 SSO-227A
Birthdate:	8 January 1908	*Birthplace:*	Passendorf
Rank:	SS-Sturmbannführer	*SS Number:*	73841
NSDAP Number:	668271	*Highest Decoration:*	War Service Cross 2nd Class
Religion:	Agnostic	*Marital Status:*	Married
Waffen-SS:	4th SS Division "Polizei", 1942-1943		
	13th SS Division "Handschar", 1943-1944		
	32nd SS Division "30 Januar", 1945		
Notes:	Administration troops		

Camp Service: **Lichtenburg, 1935-1936**
Dachau, 1937-1939

Kuhn

First Name:	Dr. Eugen	*National Archive File:*	A3343 SSO-228A
Birthdate:	1 May 1913	*Birthplace:*	Kienberg
Rank:	SS-Sturmbannführer	*SS Number:*	310341
NSDAP Number:	Not a member	*Highest Decoration:*	Iron Cross 1st Class
Religion:	Unknown	*Marital Status:*	Single
Waffen-SS:	3rd SS Division "Totenkopf", 1939-1942		
Notes:	Doctor		
	Assigned to Adriatic Coast 1944		

Camp Service: **Oranienburg, 1938   Mauthausen, 1939**

Kuiper

First Name:	Bernhard	*National Archive File:*	A3343 SSO-229A
Birthdate:	30 August 1907	*Birthplace:*	Moehlenwarf
Rank:	SS-Obersturmführer	*SS Number:*	270571
NSDAP Number:	1598891	*Highest Decoration:*	War Service Cross 2nd Class
Religion:	Unknown	*Marital Status:*	Married
Waffen-SS:	No		
Notes:	Released from SS 1937		

Camp Service: **Columbia Haus, 1936-1937**

Kurtz

First Name:	Adolf	*National Archive File:*	A3343 SSO-232A
Birthdate:	13 May 1910	*Birthplace:*	Schoenau
Rank:	SS-Obersturmbannführer	*SS Number:*	47703
NSDAP Number:	3016405	*Highest Decoration:*	German Cross in Gold
Religion:	Agnostic	*Marital Status:*	Married
Waffen-SS:	3rd SS Division "Totenkopf", 1941-1942		
Notes:	Guard troops		

Camp Service: **Sachsenburg, 1936**
Dachau, 1936-1937

Kurz

First Name:	Alois	*National Archive File:*	A3343 SSO-232A
Birthdate:	14 July 1917	*Birthplace:*	Saalfelden, Austria
Rank:	SS-Untersturmführer	*SS Number:*	382378
NSDAP Number:	Not a member	*Highest Decoration:*	None listed
Religion:	Agnostic	*Marital Status:*	Married
Waffen-SS:	8th SS Division "Florian Geyer", 1942		
Notes:	Commander 3rd Guard Company Majdanek		

Camp Service: **Majdanek, 1944**
Auschwitz, 1944
Dora, 1944

Lachemair

First Name:	Max von	*National Archive File:*	No File
Birthdate:	31 July 1901	*Birthplace:*	Unknown
Rank:	SS-Untersturmführer	*SS Number:*	67586
NSDAP Number:	1471286	*Highest Decoration:*	Blood Order
Religion:	Unknown	*Marital Status:*	Unknown
Waffen-SS:	Unknown		
Notes:	Released from SS 1937; Blood Order #278		

Camp Service: **Dachau, 1937**

Lachmann

First Name:	Gerhard	*National Archive File:*	No File
Birthdate:	8 February 1920	*Birthplace:*	Niederstrelitz
Rank:	SS-Untersturmführer	*SS Number:*	Unknown
NSDAP Number:	Not a member	*Highest Decoration:*	War Service Cross 2nd Class
Religion:	Unknown	*Marital Status:*	Unknown
Waffen-SS:	Unknown		
Notes:	Political Department		
	One source states he was enlisted only		

Camp Service: **Auschwitz, 1943-1944**

Lange

First Name:	Erich	*National Archive File:*	A3343 SSO-240A
Birthdate:	10 October 1888	*Birthplace:*	Zwickau
Rank:	SS-Sturmbannführer	*SS Number:*	117098
NSDAP Number:	3206314	*Highest Decoration:*	War Service Cross 1st Class
Religion:	Agnostic	*Marital Status:*	Widower
Waffen-SS:	No		
Notes:	Iron Cross 1st Class and Wound Badge WWI		

Camp Service: **Buchenwald, 1944**
Oranienburg, 1944-1945

Lange

First Name:	Herbert	*National Archive File:*	A3343 SSO-240A
Birthdate:	29 September 1909	*Birthplace:*	Menzlin
Rank:	SS-Sturmbannführer	*SS Number:*	93501
NSDAP Number:	1159583	*Highest Decoration:*	War Service Cross 1st Class
Religion:	Protestant	*Marital Status:*	Married
Waffen-SS:	No		
Notes:	*Kommandant* Chelmno		
	Killed in action 20 April 1945 near Berlin		

Camp Service: **Chelmno, 1941-1942**

Lange

First Name:	Kurt	*National Archive File:*	A3343 SSO-240A
Birthdate:	17 September 1911	*Birthplace:*	Stuttgart
Rank:	SS-Hauptsturmführer	*SS Number:*	225256
NSDAP Number:	3233205	*Highest Decoration:*	War Service Cross 2nd Class
Religion:	Agnostic	*Marital Status:*	Married
Waffen-SS:	6th SS Division "Nord", 1941		
Notes:	Guard troops at Lichtenburg		

Camp Service: **Lichtenburg, 1936**

Lange

First Name:	Theodor	*National Archive File:*	A3343 SSO-241A
Birthdate:	28 September 1918	*Birthplace:*	Essen
Rank:	SS-Obersturmführer	*SS Number:*	400103
NSDAP Number:	Not a member	*Highest Decoration:*	Wound Badge in Black
Religion:	Unknown	*Marital Status:*	Single
Waffen-SS:	5th SS Division "Wiking", 1941-1942		
	10th SS Division "Frundsberg", 1944		
Notes:	Commander 8th Guard Company at Auschwitz; missing in action August 1944		

Camp Service: **Auschwitz, 1943-1944**

Langleist

First Name:	Walter-Adolf	*National Archive File:*	A3343 SSO-242A
Birthdate:	5 August 1893	*Birthplace:*	Dresden
Rank:	SS-Hauptsturmführer	*SS Number:*	8980
NSDAP Number:	352801	*Highest Decoration:*	War Service Cross 2nd Class
Religion:	Protestant	*Marital Status:*	Married
Waffen-SS:	No		
Notes:	*Kommandant* Kaufering sub-camp; Commander of guards Majdanek		
	Executed 28 May 1946		

Camp Service: **Buchenwald, 1941-1942**
Majdanek, 1942-1943
Dachau, 1943-1945

Laub

First Name:	Dr. Michael	*National Archive File:*	A3343 SSO-244A
Birthdate:	7 October 1905	*Birthplace:*	St. Hubert
Rank:	SS-Obersturmführer	*SS Number:*	455403
NSDAP Number:	Not a member	*Highest Decoration:*	None listed
Religion:	Catholic	*Marital Status:*	Married
Waffen-SS:	7th SS Division "Prinz Eugen", 1942-1944		
Notes:	Served in Yugoslav army 1932-1933		

Camp Service: **Oranienburg, 1944**   **Mauthausen**
Stutthof, 1945

Lauer

First Name:	Hubert	*National Archive File:*	A3343 SSO-245A
Birthdate:	10 January 1897	*Birthplace:*	Simmern
Rank:	SS-Sturmbannführer	*SS Number:*	291721
NSDAP Number:	Not a member	*Highest Decoration:*	War Service Cross 2nd Class
Religion:	Catholic	*Marital Status:*	Married
Waffen-SS:	No		
Notes:	Administration chief at Lichtenburg and Sachsenhausen		
	Iron Cross 2nd Class Wound Badge WWI		

Camp Service: **Lichtenburg, 1938-1940**
Ravensbrück, 1940
Sachsenhausen, 1940-1944

Lauffs

First Name: Dr. Hans
Birthdate: 12 January 1912
Rank: SS-Hauptsturmführer
NSDAP Number: 5821370
Religion: Protestant
Waffen-SS: No
Notes: SS judge; sentenced to 5 years

National Archive File: A3343 SSO-246A
Birthplace: Leipzig
SS Number: 210397
Highest Decoration: War Service Cross 2nd Class
Marital Status: Single

Camp Service: **Majdanek, 1944**

Launer

First Name: Kurt
Birthdate: 16 September 1906
Rank: SS-Standartenführer
NSDAP Number: 192298
Religion: Protestant
Waffen-SS: 3rd SS Division "Totenkopf", 1939-1944
17th SS Division "Götz von Berlichingen", 1944-1945
Notes: Commander 38th SS Infantry Regiment
Schloss Osterstein sub-camp

National Archive File: A3343 SSO-246A
Birthplace: Zeithain, Saxony
SS Number: 14434
Highest Decoration: Knight's Cross
Marital Status: Married

Camp Service: **Lichtenburg, 1934-1935**
Dachau, 1937

Leipold

First Name: Josef
Birthdate: 10 November 1913
Rank: SS-Obersturmführer
NSDAP Number: 6568081
Religion: Catholic
Waffen-SS: No
Notes: Budzyn sub-camp

National Archive File: A3343 SSO-253A
Birthplace: Altrohlau
SS Number: 344830
Highest Decoration: None listed
Marital Status: Married

Camp Service: **Majdanek, 1942**
Plaszow

Lenkeit

First Name: Friedrich
Birthdate: 23 October 1893
Rank: SS-Untersturmführer
NSDAP Number: 415919
Religion: Protestant
Waffen-SS: No
Notes: Iron Cross 2nd Class WWI

National Archive File: A3343 SSO-255A
Birthplace: Koenigsberg
SS Number: 289947
Highest Decoration: None listed
Marital Status: Married

Camp Service: **Stutthof, 1945**

Lewe

First Name: Dr. Viktor
Birthdate: 19 April 1912
Rank: SS-Obersturmführer
NSDAP Number: 3174312
Religion: Catholic
Waffen-SS: No
Notes: Doctor; Leader pathology section, Sachsenhausen

National Archive File: A3343 SSO-259A
Birthplace: Loeningen
SS Number: 382546
Highest Decoration: War Service Cross 2nd Class
Marital Status: Divorced

Camp Service: **Buchenwald, 1941**
Sachsenhausen, 1941-1942

Liebehenschel

First Name: Arthur
Birthdate: 25 November 1901
Rank: SS-Obersturmbannführer
NSDAP Number: 932766
Religion: Protestant
Waffen-SS: No
Notes: *Kommandant* Auschwitz and Majdanek
Executed 24 January 1948

National Archive File: A3343 SSO-260A
Birthplace: Posen
SS Number: 39254
Highest Decoration: War Service Cross 1st Class
Marital Status: Married

Camp Service: **Columbia Haus, 1934**   **Lichtenburg, 1934-1936**
Oranienburg, 1937   **Auschwitz, 1943-1944**
Majdanek, 1944

Liebermann

First Name: Arthur
Birthdate: 10 September 1893
Rank: SS-Obersturmführer
NSDAP Number: 2730981
Religion: Protestant
Waffen-SS: No
Notes: Construction department Stutthof; camp service not listed in personnel file

National Archive File: A3343 SSO-260A
Birthplace: Tiefenlantor/Coburg
SS Number: Unknown
Highest Decoration: None listed
Marital Status: Married

Camp Service: **Stutthof**

Liesau

First Name: Dr. Karl
Birthdate: 14 March 1911
Rank: SS-Hauptsturmführer
NSDAP Number: 3442659
Religion: Unknown
Waffen-SS: 8th SS Division "Florian Geyer", 1942-1943
Notes: Served in 1942 on Himmler's personal train "Heinrich"
Died of typhus 7 January 1943

National Archive File: A3343 SSO-261A
Birthplace: Frankfurt
SS Number: 77879
Highest Decoration: War Service Cross 2nd Class
Marital Status: Unknown

Camp Service: **Hinzert, 1939-1940**

Linde

First Name:	Dr. Herbert	*National Archive File:*	A3343 SSO-262A
Birthdate:	3 July 1907	*Birthplace:*	Berlin
Rank:	SS-Obersturmführer	*SS Number:*	203212
NSDAP Number:	4827943	*Highest Decoration:*	None listed
Religion:	Unknown	*Marital Status:*	Single
Waffen-SS:	16th SS Division "Reichsführer-SS", 1943-1945		
Notes:	Dentist at sub-camp Gusen		

Camp Service: **Mauthausen, 1942**

Lindenbach

First Name:	Emil	*National Archive File:*	A3343 SSO-263A
Birthdate:	19 December 1888	*Birthplace:*	Haag/Heidelberg
Rank:	SS-Sturmbannführer	*SS Number:*	3457
NSDAP Number:	208657	*Highest Decoration:*	None listed
Religion:	Agnostic	*Marital Status:*	Married
Waffen-SS:	No		
Notes:	Member of a guard company		
	Found unsuitable to serve in concentration camps		

Camp Service: **Dachau, 1939**
Mauthausen, 1940
Buchenwald, 1940

Lindner

First Name:	Alfred	*National Archive File:*	A3343 SSO-263A
Birthdate:	22 May 1904	*Birthplace:*	Koenigsee
Rank:	SS-Obersturmführer	*SS Number:*	47521
NSDAP Number:	1449463	*Highest Decoration:*	War Service Cross 2nd Class
Religion:	Protestant	*Marital Status:*	Married
Waffen-SS:	No		
Notes:	Ebensee sub-camp; former carpenter		

Camp Service: **Mauthausen**
Dachau, 1944

Lindthaler

First Name:	Josef	*National Archive File:*	A3343 SSO-265A
Birthdate:	10 August 1910	*Birthplace:*	Donnawitz/Leoben
Rank:	SS-Hauptsturmführer	*SS Number:*	10531
NSDAP Number:	198535	*Highest Decoration:*	War Service Cross 2nd Class
Religion:	Agnostic	*Marital Status:*	Married
Waffen-SS:	6th SS Division "Nord", 1941-1942		
Notes:	Administration troops		

Camp Service: **Oranienburg, 1937-1938**

Lippert

First Name:	Michael	*National Archive File:*	A3343 SSO-267A
Birthdate:	24 April 1897	*Birthplace:*	Schoenwald
Rank:	SS-Standartenführer	*SS Number:*	2968
NSDAP Number:	246989	*Highest Decoration:*	Iron Cross 1st Class
Religion:	Agnostic	*Marital Status:*	Married
Waffen-SS:	10th SS Division "Frundsberg", 1943-1944		
	34th SS Division "Landstorm Nederland", 1944		
Notes:	Commander Vth Totenkopfsturmbann "Brandenburg"		
	Kommandant Sachsenhausen		

Camp Service: **Dachau, 1933-1934**
Columbia Haus, 1935
Sachsenhausen, 1936

Lippke

First Name:	Erich	*National Archive File:*	A3343 SSO-267A
Birthdate:	2 February 1886	*Birthplace:*	Tilsit
Rank:	SS-Hauptsturmführer	*SS Number:*	215362
NSDAP Number:	2226010	*Highest Decoration:*	None listed
Religion:	Protestant	*Marital Status:*	Married
Waffen-SS:	No		
Notes:	Pharmacist		

Camp Service: **Sachsenhausen, 1940-1941**

Lippmann

First Name:	Arno	*National Archive File:*	A3343 SSO-267A
Birthdate:	25 July 1890	*Birthplace:*	Lippelsdorf
Rank:	SS-Obersturmführer	*SS Number:*	439
NSDAP Number:	8891	*Highest Decoration:*	Golden Party Badge
Religion:	Catholic	*Marital Status:*	Married
Waffen-SS:	No		
Notes:	*Kommandant* at Kaufering sub-camp; executed 29 May 1946		
	Iron Cross 2nd Class WWI; Golden Party Badge		

Camp Service: **Dachau, 1935-1939**   **Flossenbürg, 1941-1943**

Litschel

First Name:	Dr. Gustav	*National Archive File:*	A3343 SSO-268A
Birthdate:	5 February 1903	*Birthplace:*	Vienna, Austria
Rank:	SS-Sturmbannführer	*SS Number:*	308262
NSDAP Number:	Not a member	*Highest Decoration:*	None listed
Religion:	Protestant	*Marital Status:*	Married
Waffen-SS:	3rd SS Division "Totenkopf", 1942-1943		
	4th SS Division "Polizei", 1943		
Notes:	Degree in Forensics		

Camp Service: **Dachau, 1938**
Sachsenhausen, 1938
Flossenbürg, 1939

Lohr

First Name:	Karl	*National Archive File:*	A3343 SSO-274A
Birthdate:	31 December 1885	*Birthplace:*	Munich
Rank:	SS-Untersturmführer	*SS Number:*	41275
NSDAP Number:	87588	*Highest Decoration:*	None listed
Religion:	Agnostic	*Marital Status:*	Married
Waffen-SS:	No		
Notes:	Iron Cross 2nd Class, Wound Badge WWI		
	Company commander in guard troops; found unfit for service		

Camp Service: **Dachau, 1939-1940**

Lolling

First Name:	Dr. Enno	*National Archive File:*	A3343 SSO-275A
Birthdate:	19 July 1888	*Birthplace:*	Cologne
Rank:	SS-Standartenführer	*SS Number:*	179765
NSDAP Number:	4691483	*Highest Decoration:*	War Service Cross 1st Class
Religion:	Protestant	*Marital Status:*	Married
Waffen-SS:	No		
Notes:	Camp doctor at Dachau; Chief Department DIII, Oranienburg		
	Suicide 27 May 1945		

Camp Service: **Dachau, 1937-1941**   **Oranienburg, 1941-1944**

Lonauer

First Name:	Dr. Rudolf	*National Archive File:*	A3343 SSO-275A
Birthdate:	9 January 1907	*Birthplace:*	Linz, Austria
Rank:	SS-Hauptsturmführer	*SS Number:*	308248
NSDAP Number:	Not a member	*Highest Decoration:*	Iron Cross 2nd Class
Religion:	Agnostic	*Marital Status:*	Married
Waffen-SS:	Vth SS Corps, 1943-1944		
Notes:	Aktion T4; doctor; Wounded in action		

Camp Service: **Dachau**
Buchenwald
Sachsenhausen

Loritz

First Name:	Hans	*National Archive File:*	A3343 SSO-278A
Birthdate:	21 December 1895	*Birthplace:*	Augsburg
Rank:	SS-Oberführer	*SS Number:*	4165
NSDAP Number:	298668	*Highest Decoration:*	War Service Cross 1st Class
Religion:	Agnostic	*Marital Status:*	Divorced
Waffen-SS:	No		
Notes:	*Kommandant* Papenburg, Esterwegen, Dachau and Sachsenhausen		
	Wounded several times in WWI; suicide 31 January 1946		

Camp Service: **Papenburg, 1933-1934**   **Esterwegen, 1934-1936**
Dachau, 1936-1939   **Sachsenhausen, 1940-1942**

Lotz

First Name:	Peter	*National Archive File:*	A3343 SSO-278A
Birthdate:	3 July 1913	*Birthplace:*	Battenhausen
Rank:	SS-Hauptsturmführer	*SS Number:*	58282
NSDAP Number:	1803949	*Highest Decoration:*	Iron Cross 2nd Class
Religion:	Agnostic	*Marital Status:*	Married
Waffen-SS:	6th SS Division "Nord", 1942		
	3rd SS Division "Totenkopf", 1943-1944		
Notes:	Court martialed in 1943 and reduced to private; died of wounds, 7 March 1944		

Camp Service:	**Sachsenburg, 1935-1936**	**Buchenwald, 1937**
	Dachau, 1938	

Louis

First Name:	Dr. Herbert	*National Archive File:*	A3343 SSO-279A
Birthdate:	13 September 1908	*Birthplace:*	Dudweiler
Rank:	SS-Hauptsturmführer	*SS Number:*	252490
NSDAP Number:	Not a member	*Highest Decoration:*	None listed
Religion:	Protestant	*Marital Status:*	Married
Waffen-SS:	3rd SS Division "Totenkopf", 1941-1942		
Notes:	Dermatology department at Dachau		
	Camp doctor at Neuengamme		

Camp Service:	**Flossenbürg, 1940**	**Oranienburg, 1940-1941**
	Dachau, 1941	**Neuengamme**

Lucas

First Name:	Dr. Franz	*National Archive File:*	A3343 SSO-279A
Birthdate:	15 September 1911	*Birthplace:*	Osnabrueck
Rank:	SS-Obersturmführer	*SS Number:*	350030
NSDAP Number:	Not a member	*Highest Decoration:*	None listed
Religion:	Unknown	*Marital Status:*	Married
Waffen-SS:	SS Fallschirmjaeger Battalion "Chlum", 1943		
Notes:	Medical Officer; sentenced to 3 years imprisonment; released 1963		

Camp Service:	**Auschwitz, 1943-1944**	**Mauthausen, 1944**
	Stutthof, 1944	**Ravensbrück, 1945**
	Sachsenhausen, 1945	

Ludewig

First Name:	Kurt	*National Archive File:*	A3343 SSO-279A
Birthdate:	4 March 1910	*Birthplace:*	Konradswaldau
Rank:	SS-Obersturmführer	*SS Number:*	41438
NSDAP Number:	84438	*Highest Decoration:*	Golden Party Badge
Religion:	Protestant	*Marital Status:*	Married
Waffen-SS:	SS Infantry Regiment 5, 1941		

Camp Service:	**Oranienburg, 1941**

Ludolph

First Name:	Julius	*National Archive File:*	A3343 SSO-279A
Birthdate:	26 March 1893	*Birthplace:*	Hamburg
Rank:	SS-Obersturmführer	*SS Number:*	114013
NSDAP Number:	2093373	*Highest Decoration:*	None listed
Religion:	Agnostic	*Marital Status:*	Married
Waffen-SS:	No		
Notes:	*Kommandant* Melk sub-camp of Mauthausen; executed 28 May 1947		

Camp Service: **Mauthausen, 1943-1945**

Ludwig

First Name:	Kurt	*National Archive File:*	A3343 SSO-280A
Birthdate:	6 April 1904	*Birthplace:*	Driesen
Rank:	SS-Obersturmführer	*SS Number:*	46798
NSDAP Number:	694538	*Highest Decoration:*	None listed
Religion:	Protestant	*Marital Status:*	Married
Waffen-SS:	No		
Notes:	Dentist		

Camp Service: **Buchenwald, 1941**
Oranienburg, 1941

Lueckert

First Name:	Dr. Walter	*National Archive File:*	A3343 SSO-281A
Birthdate:	7 March 1906	*Birthplace:*	Trubenhausen
Rank:	SS-Hauptsturmführer	*SS Number:*	84576
NSDAP Number:	4625997	*Highest Decoration:*	War Service Cross 2nd Class
Religion:	Agnostic	*Marital Status:*	Married
Waffen-SS:	SS Infantry Regiment 7; Vth SS Corps		
Notes:	Dentist		

Camp Service: **Mauthausen**   **Oranienburg, 1940**

Luetkemeyer

First Name:	Albert	*National Archive File:*	A3343 SSO-282A
Birthdate:	17 June 1911	*Birthplace:*	Wellingholzhausen
Rank:	SS-Hauptsturmführer	*SS Number:*	270485
NSDAP Number:	1598919	*Highest Decoration:*	Iron Cross 2nd Class
Religion:	Agnostic	*Marital Status:*	Married
Waffen-SS:	Yes, unit unknown		
Notes:	Schutzhaftlagerführer at Neuengamme		

Camp Service: **Esterwegen, 1934**
Mauthausen, 1941
Neuengamme, 1941
Gross-Rosen

Luetzelburg

First Name:	Dr. Phillip von	*National Archive File:*	A3343 SSO-283A
Birthdate:	16 July 1880	*Birthplace:*	Landsberg
Rank:	SS-Obersturmbannführer	*SS Number:*	351374
NSDAP Number:	6078766	*Highest Decoration:*	None listed
Religion:	Agnostic	*Marital Status:*	Married
Waffen-SS:	No		
Notes:	Botanist		

Camp Service: **Dachau**

Lutosch

First Name:	Gerhard	*National Archive File:*	A3343 SSO-285A
Birthdate:	8 September 1911	*Birthplace:*	Berlin-Spandau
Rank:	SS-Hauptsturmführer	*SS Number:*	216574
NSDAP Number:	4575899	*Highest Decoration:*	War Service Cross 2nd Class
Religion:	Agnostic	*Marital Status:*	Married
Waffen-SS:	10th SS Division "Frundsberg", 1944		
Notes:	Leader Department 6 at Buchenwald		

Camp Service: **Oranienburg, 1941**
Buchenwald, 1941-1943

Maack

First Name:	Berthold	*National Archive File:*	A3343 SSO-286A
Birthdate:	24 March 1898	*Birthplace:*	Hamburg-Altona
Rank:	SS-Brigadeführer	*SS Number:*	15690
NSDAP Number:	314088	*Highest Decoration:*	Bar to Iron Cross 1st Class
Religion:	Agnostic	*Marital Status:*	Married
Waffen-SS:	5th SS Division "Wiking", 1940-1942		
	6th SS Division "Nord", 1942-1944		
	26th SS Division (ung 2), 1945		
Notes:	Division commander 20th SS Division; died 26 September 1981		

Camp Service: **Dachau, 1934**

Maier

First Name:	Emil	*National Archive File:*	A3343 SSO-289A
Birthdate:	18 December 1895	*Birthplace:*	Freiburg
Rank:	SS-Obersturmführer	*SS Number:*	32185
NSDAP Number:	996728	*Highest Decoration:*	War Service Cross 2nd Class
Religion:	Agnostic	*Marital Status:*	Married
Waffen-SS:	No		
Notes:	Iron Cross 2nd Class WWI; Commander 1st Guard Company		

Camp Service: **Flossenbürg, 1940**
Dachau, 1940-1941
Natzweiler, 1941-1944

Maier

First Name:	Franz-Xaver	*National Archive File:*	A3343 SSO-290A
Birthdate:	7 January 1913	*Birthplace:*	Hausham
Rank:	SS-Untersturmführer	*SS Number:*	69600
NSDAP Number:	1075055	*Highest Decoration:*	None listed
Religion:	Agnostic	*Marital Status:*	Married
Waffen-SS:	No		
Notes:	Second lagerführer; sentenced by SS to 2 years for plundering		

Camp Service: **Buchenwald, 1939-1940**
Auschwitz, 1940-1941

Maier

First Name:	Josef	*National Archive File:*	A3343 SSO-290A
Birthdate:	3 July 1890	*Birthplace:*	Augsburg
Rank:	SS-Untersturmführer	*SS Number:*	141938
NSDAP Number:	3614059	*Highest Decoration:*	None listed
Religion:	Catholic	*Marital Status:*	Married
Waffen-SS:	No		
Notes:	Commanded 3rd Guard Company at Sachsenhausen		

Camp Service: **Sachsenhausen, 1939-1941**

Mann

First Name:	Ludwig	*National Archive File:*	A3343 SSO-295A
Birthdate:	26 January 1913	*Birthplace:*	Kaiserslautern
Rank:	SS-Hauptsturmführer	*SS Number:*	89909
NSDAP Number:	464122	*Highest Decoration:*	War Service Cross 1st Class
Religion:	Agnostic	*Marital Status:*	Married
Waffen-SS:	7th SS Division "Prinz Eugen", 1942-1944		
	XIth SS Corps, 1944-1945		
	36th SS Division "Dirlewanger", 1945		
Notes:	Attached to 545th Volks-Grenadier Division, 1944		

Camp Service: **Oranienburg, 1938-1941**

Marg

First Name:	Karl	*National Archive File:*	A3343 SSO-297A
Birthdate:	21 October 1906	*Birthplace:*	Heyrode
Rank:	SS-Hauptsturmführer	*SS Number:*	2134
NSDAP Number:	180983	*Highest Decoration:*	None listed
Religion:	Unknown	*Marital Status:*	Married
Waffen-SS:	34th SS Division "Landstorm Nederland", 1944		
Notes:	Administration Department Gross Rosen; Schutzhaftlagerführer Sulza		

Camp Service: **Sulza, 1936**   **Sulza, 1936-1937**
Buchenwald, 1937-1941   **Gross-Rosen**
Wewelsburg, 1941

Marquardt

First Name:	Dr. Erich	*National Archive File:*	A3343 SSO-297A
Birthdate:	3 November 1891	*Birthplace:*	Bretnig
Rank:	SS-Hauptsturmführer	*SS Number:*	291952
NSDAP Number:	5488816	*Highest Decoration:*	Bar to Iron Cross 2nd Class
Religion:	Agnostic	*Marital Status:*	Married
Waffen-SS:	Yes, unit unknown		
Notes:	Iron Cross 2nd Class WWI Geologist		

Camp Service: **Oranienburg, 1942-1943**

Martin

First Name:	Karl	*National Archive File:*	A3343 SSO-298A
Birthdate:	15 August 1899	*Birthplace:*	Kaiserslautern
Rank:	SS-Hauptsturmführer	*SS Number:*	15016
NSDAP Number:	289574	*Highest Decoration:*	War Service Cross 2nd Class
Religion:	Protestant	*Marital Status:*	Married
Waffen-SS:	9th SS Division "Hohenstaufen", 1943		
Notes:	Former engineer Prisoner of war in France WWI		

Camp Service: **Hinzert, 1940-1943**

Masarié

First Name:	Azelino	*National Archive File:*	A3343 SSO-298A
Birthdate:	10 October 1912	*Birthplace:*	Nürnberg
Rank:	SS-Sturmbannführer	*SS Number:*	71687
NSDAP Number:	2779402	*Highest Decoration:*	Knight's Cross of the Iron Cross
Religion:	Unknown	*Marital Status:*	Unknown
Waffen-SS:	3rd SS Division "Totenkopf", 1940-1944		
Notes:	Battalion commander; killed in action 9 August 1944		

Camp Service: **Lichtenburg, 1937**
Dachau, 1939

Mathesius

First Name:	Kurt	*National Archive File:*	A3343 SSO-300A
Birthdate:	19 September 1910	*Birthplace:*	Ohra
Rank:	SS-Obersturmführer	*SS Number:*	99130
NSDAP Number:	3396781	*Highest Decoration:*	War Service Cross 2nd Class
Religion:	Protestant	*Marital Status:*	Married
Waffen-SS:	No		
Notes:	Guard troops at Stutthof		

Camp Service: **Stutthof, 1941-1942**

Matt

First Name:	Dr. Karl	*National Archive File:*	A3343 SSO-300A
Birthdate:	20 May 1909	*Birthplace:*	Bruchsal
Rank:	SS-Untersturmführer	*SS Number:*	313560
NSDAP Number:	Not a member	*Highest Decoration:*	None listed
Religion:	Protestant	*Marital Status:*	Married
Waffen-SS:	No		
Notes:	Doctor		

Camp Service: **Oranienburg, 1940-1941**
Auschwitz

Mattner

First Name:	Dr. Walter	*National Archive File:*	A3343 SSO-300A
Birthdate:	31 December 1904	*Birthplace:*	Langenwang
Rank:	SS-Obersturmführer	*SS Number:*	298967
NSDAP Number:	1526106	*Highest Decoration:*	None listed
Religion:	Agnostic	*Marital Status:*	Married
Waffen-SS:	No		
Notes:	Camp doctor at Mauthausen		

Camp Service: **Mauthausen, 1941**

Matz

First Name:	Dr. Karl	*National Archive File:*	A3343 SSO-300A
Birthdate:	21 June 1909	*Birthplace:*	Kiel
Rank:	SS-Obersturmbannführer	*SS Number:*	291210
NSDAP Number:	4358193	*Highest Decoration:*	War Service Cross 1st Class
Religion:	Protestant	*Marital Status:*	Married
Waffen-SS:	13th SS Division "Handschar", 1943-1944		
	21st SS Division "Skanderbeg", 1944		
Notes:	Camp doctor at Mauthausen		

Camp Service: **Neuengamme, 1940**
Mauthausen, 1940-1942

Maurer

First Name:	Gerhard	*National Archive File:*	A3343 SSO-301A
Birthdate:	9 December 1907	*Birthplace:*	Halle
Rank:	SS-Standartenführer	*SS Number:*	12129
NSDAP Number:	387103	*Highest Decoration:*	War Service Cross 1st Class
Religion:	Agnostic	*Marital Status:*	Widower
Waffen-SS:	No		
Notes:	Chief Department DII, Oranienburg; wife and children killed in air raid		
	Executed 2 April 1953		

Camp Service: **Oranienburg, 1942-1945**

Mayer

First Name:	Franz	*National Archive File:*	A3343 SSO-302A
Birthdate:	28 April 1897	*Birthplace:*	Ulm
Rank:	SS-Sturmbannführer	*SS Number:*	21901
NSDAP Number:	340546	*Highest Decoration:*	War Service Cross 2nd Class
Religion:	Agnostic	*Marital Status:*	Married
Waffen-SS:	6th SS Division "Nord", 1941		
Notes:	Iron Cross 2nd Class WWI		
	Guard troops at Dachau		
Camp Service:	**Dachau, 1936-1938**		

Mayr

First Name:	Kurt-Fritz	*National Archive File:*	A3343 SSO-303A
Birthdate:	1 September 1911	*Birthplace:*	Memmingen
Rank:	SS-Sturmbannführer	*SS Number:*	28510
NSDAP Number:	917225	*Highest Decoration:*	Iron Cross 1st Class
Religion:	Agnostic	*Marital Status:*	Married
Waffen-SS:	3rd SS Division "Totenkopf", 1939-1942		
	16th SS Division "Reichsführer-SS", 1944		
Notes:	Division adjutant in 16th SS Division; company commander in 3rd SS Division		
Camp Service:	**Dachau, 1933-1939**		

Meckelburg

First Name:	Otto	*National Archive File:*	A3343 SSO-304A
Birthdate:	14 September 1911	*Birthplace:*	Danzig/Neustadt
Rank:	SS-Sturmbannführer	*SS Number:*	99588
NSDAP Number:	2914799	*Highest Decoration:*	Iron Cross 1st Class
Religion:	Agnostic	*Marital Status:*	Married
Waffen-SS:	5th SS Division "Wiking", 1940-1941		
	7th SS Division "Prinz Eugen", 1942-1944		
Notes:	Battalion commander in 7th SS Division		
	Commended by division commander for operations in Croatia and Montenegro		
Camp Service:	**Oranienburg, 1938-1939**		

Meier

First Name:	Ernst	*National Archive File:*	A3343 SSO-305A
Birthdate:	28 February 1912	*Birthplace:*	Doehren
Rank:	SS-Obersturmführer	*SS Number:*	183127
NSDAP Number:	Not a member	*Highest Decoration:*	Iron Cross 2nd Class
Religion:	Protestant	*Marital Status:*	Married
Waffen-SS:	14th SS Division, 1944		
Notes:	Received Infantry Assault Badge		
Camp Service:	**Ravensbrück, 1943**		

Meier

First Name:	Friedrich	*National Archive File:*	A3343 SSO-305A
Birthdate:	28 May 1911	*Birthplace:*	Marchtrenk
Rank:	SS-Hauptsturmführer	*SS Number:*	33814
NSDAP Number:	513033	*Highest Decoration:*	German Cross in Gold
Religion:	Agnostic	*Marital Status:*	Married
Waffen-SS:	8th SS Division "Florian Geyer", 1942-1944		
Notes:	Guard battalion at Oranienburg		
	Company commander in anti-tank battalion		

Camp Service: **Oranienburg, 1941**

Meier

First Name:	Fritz	*National Archive File:*	A3343 SSO-305A
Birthdate:	29 January 1897	*Birthplace:*	Danzig
Rank:	SS-Obersturmführer	*SS Number:*	54432
NSDAP Number:	1462657	*Highest Decoration:*	War Service Cross 2nd Class
Religion:	Agnostic	*Marital Status:*	Married
Waffen-SS:	No		
Notes:	Camp service not listed in personnel file		

Camp Service: **Stutthof, 1941**

Meimeth

First Name:	Dr. Alfred	*National Archive File:*	A3343 SSO-306A
Birthdate:	11 July 1906	*Birthplace:*	Frankfurt
Rank:	SS-Hauptsturmführer	*SS Number:*	400015
NSDAP Number:	1148463	*Highest Decoration:*	War Service Cross 2nd Class
Religion:	Protestant	*Marital Status:*	Married
Waffen-SS:	3rd SS Division "Totenkopf", 1942-1944		
Notes:	Dentist		

Camp Service: **Auschwitz, 1941**
Oranienburg, 1941

Meinck

First Name:	Dr. Carl-Heinrich	*National Archive File:*	A3343 SSO-306A
Birthdate:	13 September 1906	*Birthplace:*	Schwerin
Rank:	SS-Obersturmführer	*SS Number:*	215846
NSDAP Number:	1725116	*Highest Decoration:*	War Service Cross 1st Class
Religion:	Agnostic	*Marital Status:*	Married
Waffen-SS:	IInd SS Corps, 1944		
Notes:	Dentist		

Camp Service: **Stutthof**
Mauthausen, 1942-1943

Meisse

First Name:	Dr. Albert	*National Archive File:*	A3343 SSO-306A
Birthdate:	22 April 1904	*Birthplace:*	Semlein
Rank:	SS-Hauptsturmführer	*SS Number:*	246383
NSDAP Number:	Not a member	*Highest Decoration:*	War Service Cross 2nd Class
Religion:	Protestant	*Marital Status:*	Married
Waffen-SS:	No		
Notes:	Dentist		

Camp Service: **Majdanek, 1942**

Meixner

First Name:	Dr. Hans	*National Archive File:*	A3343 SSO-307A
Birthdate:	5 November 1906	*Birthplace:*	Reichertshofen
Rank:	SS-Obersturmbannführer	*SS Number:*	3429
NSDAP Number:	707707	*Highest Decoration:*	None listed
Religion:	Catholic	*Marital Status:*	Married
Waffen-SS:	No		
Notes:	Camp doctor at Dachau		
	Also served in *einsatzkommando* on eastern front		

Camp Service: **Dachau, 1933-1934**

Melzer

First Name:	Martin	*National Archive File:*	A3343 SSO-308A
Birthdate:	16 November 1901	*Birthplace:*	Elchesheim
Rank:	SS-Hauptsturmführer	*SS Number:*	172106
NSDAP Number:	3586167	*Highest Decoration:*	War Service Cross 2nd Class
Religion:	Protestant	*Marital Status:*	Married
Waffen-SS:	No		
Notes:	Commander of guards Majdanek		
	Missing in action 24 July 1944		

Camp Service: **Neuengamme, 1940**
Majdanek, 1943-1944

Mengele

First Name:	Josef	*National Archive File:*	A3343 SSO-308A
Birthdate:	16 March 1911	*Birthplace:*	Guenzburg
Rank:	SS-Hauptsturmführer	*SS Number:*	317885
NSDAP Number:	5574974	*Highest Decoration:*	Iron Cross 2nd Class
Religion:	Catholic	*Marital Status:*	Married
Waffen-SS:	5th SS Division "Wiking", 1942		
Notes:	Doctor; wounded in action		
	Died Brazil 7 February 1979		

Camp Service: **Auschwitz, 1943-1945**
Gross-Rosen, 1945

Merbach

First Name:	Hans	*National Archive File:*	A3343 SSO-309A
Birthdate:	10 May 1910	*Birthplace:*	Gotha-Siebleben
Rank:	SS-Obersturmführer	*SS Number:*	3387
NSDAP Number:	259233	*Highest Decoration:*	None listed
Religion:	Protestant	*Marital Status:*	Married
Waffen-SS:	No		
Notes:	Received 14 days punishment for adultery in 1943		
	Executed 14 January 1949		

Camp Service: **Buchenwald, 1940-1942**
Auschwitz, 1944

Merker

First Name:	Karl	*National Archive File:*	A3343 SSO-310A
Birthdate:	14 August 1889	*Birthplace:*	Altenroda
Rank:	SS-Obersturmführer	*SS Number:*	1352
NSDAP Number:	113841	*Highest Decoration:*	None listed
Religion:	Agnostic	*Marital Status:*	Married
Waffen-SS:	No		
Notes:	Wounded in WWI		

Camp Service: **Dachau, 1934, 1937**
Sachsenhausen, 1937-1938

Messerle

First Name:	Friedrich	*National Archive File:*	A3343 SSO-310A
Birthdate:	22 April 1915	*Birthplace:*	Sulzbach-Saar
Rank:	SS-Sturmbannführer	*SS Number:*	268694
NSDAP Number:	Not a member	*Highest Decoration:*	Iron Cross 1st Class
Religion:	Protestant	*Marital Status:*	Single
Waffen-SS:	3rd SS Division "Totenkopf", 1939-1944		
Notes:	Battalion commander in 3rd SS Division artillery regiment		

Camp Service: **Oranienburg, 1938**

Metze

First Name:	Horst	*National Archive File:*	A3343 SSO-311A
Birthdate:	3 July 1911	*Birthplace:*	Bautzen
Rank:	SS-Obersturmführer	*SS Number:*	420734
NSDAP Number:	1254162	*Highest Decoration:*	War Service Cross 2nd Class
Religion:	Protestant	*Marital Status:*	Married
Waffen-SS:	No		
Notes:	Former forest manager		
	Served in SA 1932-1939		

Camp Service: **Sachsenhausen, 1942-1943**

Metzger

First Name:	Dr. Franz	*National Archive File:*	A3343 SSO-311A
Birthdate:	11 July 1911	*Birthplace:*	Saarbruecken
Rank:	SS-Hauptsturmführer	*SS Number:*	367736
NSDAP Number:	Not a member	*Highest Decoration:*	None listed
Religion:	Protestant	*Marital Status:*	Engaged
Waffen-SS:	3rd SS Division "Totenkopf", 1942		
Notes:	Doctor		

Camp Service: **Neuengamme, 1940-1942**
Niederhagen, 1942

Meyer

First Name:	Dr. George Franz	*National Archive File:*	A3343 SSO-313A
Birthdate:	5 September 1917	*Birthplace:*	Vienna, Austria
Rank:	SS-Obersturmführer	*SS Number:*	Unknown
NSDAP Number:	Not a member	*Highest Decoration:*	None listed
Religion:	Catholic	*Marital Status:*	Married
Waffen-SS:	Ist SS Panzer Corps		
Notes:	Camp doctor; retired in Vienna after the war		

Camp Service: **Auschwitz, 1942-1943**
Natzweiler, 1943
Herzogenbusch, 1943

Meyer

First Name:	Hans	*National Archive File:*	No File
Birthdate:	15 May 1904	*Birthplace:*	Unknown
Rank:	SS-Hauptsturmführer	*SS Number:*	48462
NSDAP Number:	731018	*Highest Decoration:*	None listed
Religion:	Unknown	*Marital Status:*	Unknown
Waffen-SS:	Unknown		
Notes:	Platoon leader in guard troops		

Camp Service: **Sachsenburg, 1936**

Meyer

First Name:	Teodor	*National Archive File:*	A3343 SSO-314A
Birthdate:	8 November 1898	*Birthplace:*	Oldenburg
Rank:	SS-Hauptsturmführer	*SS Number:*	340735
NSDAP Number:	2867508	*Highest Decoration:*	War Service Cross 2nd Class
Religion:	Protestant	*Marital Status:*	Married
Waffen-SS:	No		
Notes:	Leader of Department III at Stutthof Executed 13 August 1947		

Camp Service: **Stutthof, 1942-1945**

Meyer

First Name:	Traugott	*National Archive File:*	A3343 SSO-314A
Birthdate:	6 November 1904	*Birthplace:*	Munich
Rank:	SS-Hauptsturmführer	*SS Number:*	16385
NSDAP Number:	771323	*Highest Decoration:*	None listed
Religion:	Agnostic	*Marital Status:*	Married
Waffen-SS:	No		
Notes:	Camp engineer at Neuengamme		

Camp Service: **Dachau, 1938-1940**
Neuengamme, 1940
Ravensbrück, 1941-1942

Meyer

First Name:	Valentin	*National Archive File:*	A3343 SSO-314A
Birthdate:	4 January 1908	*Birthplace:*	Michelstadt
Rank:	SS-Obersturmführer	*SS Number:*	22915
NSDAP Number:	762790	*Highest Decoration:*	War Service Cross 2nd Class
Religion:	Agnostic	*Marital Status:*	Married
Waffen-SS:	4th SS Division "Polizei", 1940-1942		
	26th SS Division, 1945		
Notes:	Economic department		

Camp Service: **Auschwitz, 1944-1945**

Meyer

First Name:	Walter	*National Archive File:*	A3343 SSO-314A
Birthdate:	21 July 1909	*Birthplace:*	Strassburg, France
Rank:	SS-Hauptsturmführer	*SS Number:*	8461
NSDAP Number:	446514	*Highest Decoration:*	Iron Cross 2nd Class
Religion:	Agnostic	*Marital Status:*	Married
Waffen-SS:	11th SS Division "Nordland", 1943-1944		
Notes:	Former bank official; wounded in action		

Camp Service: **Oranienburg, 1938**

Meyr

First Name:	Max	*National Archive File:*	A3343 SSO-315A
Birthdate:	30 July 1915	*Birthplace:*	Noerdlingen
Rank:	SS-Obersturmführer	*SS Number:*	289455
NSDAP Number:	4426588	*Highest Decoration:*	War Service Cross 2nd Class
Religion:	Agnostic	*Marital Status:*	Married
Waffen-SS:	6th SS Division "Nord", 1942-1943		
	27th SS Division "Langemarck", 1945		
Notes:	Camp administration at Auschwitz; camp service not listed in personnel file		

Camp Service: **Oranienburg, 1940**
Neuengamme, 1940
Auschwitz, 1940

The SS Officers

Michl

First Name:	Hermann	*National Archive File:*	A3343 SSO-316A
Birthdate:	23 April 1912	*Birthplace:*	Passau
Rank:	SS-Hauptsturmführer	*SS Number:*	71076
NSDAP Number:	419621	*Highest Decoration:*	War Service Cross 1st Class
Religion:	Catholic	*Marital Status:*	Married
Waffen-SS:	8th SS Division "Florian Geyer", 1942-1944		
Notes:	Administrator at Sachsenhausen; killed in action 21 July 1944 at Lublin		

Camp Service: **Buchenwald, 1939-1940   Sachsenhausen, 1940-1941**
Wewelsburg, 1941-1942   Riga, 1944
Majdanek, 1944

Mickeleit

First Name:	Hans	*National Archive File:*	A3343 SSO-316A
Birthdate:	19 March 1898	*Birthplace:*	Werdohl
Rank:	SS-Sturmbannführer	*SS Number:*	37237
NSDAP Number:	862154	*Highest Decoration:*	War Service Cross 2nd Class
Religion:	Agnostic	*Marital Status:*	Married
Waffen-SS:	No		
Notes:	Reduced in rank and sentenced to 8 months by SS		
	Iron Cross 2nd Class, Wound Badge WWI; Adjutant at Columbia Haus		

Camp Service: **Columbia Haus, 1934-1935   Oranienburg, 1937**
Sachsenhausen, 1938-1939

Miroff

First Name:	Fritz	*National Archive File:*	A3343 SSO-319A
Birthdate:	29 August 1902	*Birthplace:*	Ulm
Rank:	SS-Untersturmführer	*SS Number:*	1511
NSDAP Number:	327386	*Highest Decoration:*	None listed
Religion:	Protestant	*Marital Status:*	Married
Waffen-SS:	No		
Notes:	Executed 19 November 1948		

Camp Service: **Mauthausen, 1941-1944**

Moeckel

First Name:	Karl	*National Archive File:*	A3343 SSO-321A
Birthdate:	9 January 1901	*Birthplace:*	Klingental
Rank:	SS-Oberführer	*SS Number:*	908
NSDAP Number:	22293	*Highest Decoration:*	War Service Cross 1st Class
Religion:	Agnostic	*Marital Status:*	Married
Waffen-SS:	No		
Notes:	Administration and Economy Department at Auschwitz; Golden Party Badge		
	Executed		

Camp Service: **Auschwitz, 1943**

Moehlmann

First Name:	Arie	*National Archive File:*	A3343 SSO-321A
Birthdate:	10 April 1915	*Birthplace:*	Ibbenbueren
Rank:	SS-Hauptsturmführer	*SS Number:*	165026
NSDAP Number:	3568708	*Highest Decoration:*	War Service Cross 2nd Class
Religion:	Protestant	*Marital Status:*	Married
Waffen-SS:	No		
Notes:	Former pastry chef; served in Hitler Youth 1931-1933		

Camp Service: **Auschwitz, 1941**

Moeller

First Name:	Ernst	*National Archive File:*	A3343 SSO-321A
Birthdate:	5 March 1891	*Birthplace:*	Isenbuettal
Rank:	SS-Hauptsturmführer	*SS Number:*	236154
NSDAP Number:	2636297	*Highest Decoration:*	None listed
Religion:	Agnostic	*Marital Status:*	Married
Waffen-SS:	No		
Notes:	Iron Cross 1st Class WWI Wounded in action three times		

Camp Service: **Sachsenhausen, 1941**

Moeser

First Name:	Hans-Karl	*National Archive File:*	A3343 RS-E0029
Birthdate:	7 April 1906	*Birthplace:*	Darmstadt
Rank:	SS-Obersturmführer	*SS Number:*	9555
NSDAP Number:	155301	*Highest Decoration:*	None listed
Religion:	Agnostic	*Marital Status:*	Married
Waffen-SS:	No		
Notes:	Executed		

Camp Service: **Hinzert, 1940**   **Auschwitz**
Dora, 1944

Mohr

First Name:	Christian	*National Archive File:*	A3343 SSO-323A
Birthdate:	29 October 1888	*Birthplace:*	Naila
Rank:	SS-Obersturmbannführer	*SS Number:*	21277
NSDAP Number:	299517	*Highest Decoration:*	War Service Cross 2nd Class
Religion:	Agnostic	*Marital Status:*	Married
Waffen-SS:	6th SS Division "Nord", 1941		
Notes:	Administration department; also served at Sachsenburg, 1936 Blood Order #983		

Camp Service: **Dachau, 1933**   **Oranienburg, 1934**
Columbia Haus, 1934-1936   **Sachsenburg, 1936-1937**
Buchenwald, 1937-1938

Mosenthin

First Name:	Werner	*National Archive File:*	A3343 SSO-325A
Birthdate:	28 March 1911	*Birthplace:*	Berlin
Rank:	SS-Obersturmführer	*SS Number:*	367767
NSDAP Number:	207854	*Highest Decoration:*	Iron Cross 2nd Class
Religion:	Protestant	*Marital Status:*	Married
Waffen-SS:	IIIrd SS Corps, 1943-1944		
Notes:	10 days arrest for an offense in 1943		

Camp Service: **Sachsenhausen, 1940-1941**

Moser

First Name:	Hans	*National Archive File:*	A3343 SSO-325A
Birthdate:	20 November 1907	*Birthplace:*	Celle
Rank:	SS-Standartenführer	*SS Number:*	276746
NSDAP Number:	3958949	*Highest Decoration:*	German Cross in Silver
Religion:	Agnostic	*Marital Status:*	Married
Waffen-SS:	2nd SS Division "Das Reich", 1940-1942		
	IInd SS Corps, 1942-1943		
Notes:	Chief Department DII, Oranienburg		

Camp Service: **Oranienburg, 1944-1945**

Mrugowski

First Name:	Dr. Joachim	*National Archive File:*	A3343 SSO-325A
Birthdate:	15 August 1905	*Birthplace:*	Rathenow
Rank:	SS-Brigadeführer	*SS Number:*	25811
NSDAP Number:	210049	*Highest Decoration:*	Ehrenkreuz der Deutsche Volkspflege
Religion:	Protestant	*Marital Status:*	Married
Waffen-SS:	2nd SS Division "Das Reich", 1940		
Notes:	Worked for only a week at Belsen; executed 2 June 1948		

Camp Service: **Bergen-Belsen, 1945**

Muecke

First Name:	Dr. Alfred	*National Archive File:*	A3343 SSO-326A
Birthdate:	16 January 1899	*Birthplace:*	Oppeln
Rank:	SS-Sturmbannführer	*SS Number:*	206883
NSDAP Number:	3530613	*Highest Decoration:*	Bar to Iron Cross 2nd Class
Religion:	Catholic	*Marital Status:*	Married
Waffen-SS:	9th SS Division "Hohenstaufen", 1944		
Notes:	Dentist		

Camp Service: **Mauthausen, 1940-1941**
Ravensbrück, 1941

Mueller

First Name:	Dr. Gerhard	*National Archive File:*	A3343 SSO-330A
Birthdate:	14 March 1907	*Birthplace:*	Altenberge
Rank:	SS-Hauptsturmführer	*SS Number:*	87181
NSDAP Number:	Not a member	*Highest Decoration:*	None listed
Religion:	Protestant	*Marital Status:*	Married
Waffen-SS:	No		
Notes:	Missing in action		
	Dentist at Buchenwald		

Camp Service: **Buchenwald, 1940**

Mueller

First Name:	Dr. Hans	*National Archive File:*	A3343 SSO-331A
Birthdate:	7 January 1906	*Birthplace:*	Frankfurt
Rank:	SS-Hauptsturmführer	*SS Number:*	248006
NSDAP Number:	1105857	*Highest Decoration:*	None listed
Religion:	Protestant	*Marital Status:*	Married
Waffen-SS:	No		
Notes:	Doctor		

Camp Service: **Buchenwald, 1941-1942**

Mueller

First Name:	Friedrich	*National Archive File:*	A3343 SSO-329A
Birthdate:	13 December 1891	*Birthplace:*	Mainz
Rank:	SS-Sturmbannführer	*SS Number:*	217478
NSDAP Number:	1096885	*Highest Decoration:*	War Service Cross 2nd Class
Religion:	Protestant	*Marital Status:*	Married
Waffen-SS:	No		
Notes:	Iron Cross 1st Class and Wound Badge WWI		

Camp Service: **Hinzert, 1940-1941**

Mueller

First Name:	Karl	*National Archive File:*	A3343 SSO-334A
Birthdate:	5 January 1912	*Birthplace:*	Klein-Raeschen
Rank:	SS-Sturmbannführer	*SS Number:*	147679
NSDAP Number:	1079442	*Highest Decoration:*	Iron Cross 2nd Class
Religion:	Agnostic	*Marital Status:*	Married
Waffen-SS:	8th SS Division "Florian Geyer", 1943		
	9th SS Division "Hohenstaufen", 1943		
	6th SS Division "Nord", 1945		
Notes:	Pharmacist		

Camp Service: **Dachau, 1941**

Mueller

First Name: Paul
Birthdate: 31 January 1896
Rank: SS-Obersturmführer
NSDAP Number: 4486232
Religion: Protestant
Waffen-SS: No
Notes: Iron Cross 2nd Class WWI

National Archive File: A3343 SSO-335A
Birthplace: Kiel
SS Number: 179667
Highest Decoration: War Service Cross 2nd Class
Marital Status: Married three times

Camp Service: **Flossenbürg, 1940**
Auschwitz, 1943

Mueller

First Name: Richard
Birthdate: 7 June 1908
Rank: SS-Sturmbannführer
NSDAP Number: 340451
Religion: Agnostic
Waffen-SS: 2nd SS Division "Das Reich", 1942-1944
7th SS Division "Prinz Eugen", 1944
Notes: Awarded Panzer Assault Badge
Camp Administartion

National Archive File: A3343 SSO-335A
Birthplace: Oberhohndorf
SS Number: 9433
Highest Decoration: War Service Cross 1st Class
Marital Status: Married

Camp Service: **Buchenwald, 1938**

Muellmerstedt

First Name: Dr. Helmut
Birthdate: 28 April 1913
Rank: SS-Hauptsturmführer
NSDAP Number: 651784
Religion: Agnostic
Waffen-SS: 3rd SS Division "Totenkopf", 1943-1944
Notes: Surgeon

National Archive File: A3343 SSO-337A
Birthplace: Offenbach
SS Number: 245841
Highest Decoration: War Service Cross 2nd Class
Marital Status: Engaged

Camp Service: **Dachau, 1941**

Muench

First Name: Dr. Hans
Birthdate: 14 May 1911
Rank: SS-Untersturmführer
NSDAP Number: Not a member
Religion: Agnostic
Waffen-SS: No
Notes: Waffen-SS Hygiene Institute
Acquited 1947

National Archive File: A3343 SSO-337A
Birthplace: Freiburg
SS Number: Unknown
Highest Decoration: War Service Cross 2nd Class
Marital Status: Married

Camp Service: **Auschwitz, 1944**
Dachau, 1945

Muender

First Name:	Ernst	*National Archive File:*	A3343 SSO-337A
Birthdate:	22 July 1888	*Birthplace:*	Feuerbach
Rank:	SS-Obersturmführer	*SS Number:*	55189
NSDAP Number:	774198	*Highest Decoration:*	War Service Cross 2nd Class
Religion:	Protestant	*Marital Status:*	Married
Waffen-SS:	No		
Notes:	Iron Cross 2nd Class WWI; died 2 December 1944		

Camp Service: **Dachau, 1939-1942**

Muetzelfeldt

First Name:	Hans	*National Archive File:*	A3343 SSO-339A
Birthdate:	8 August 1916	*Birthplace:*	Preuss. Oldendorf
Rank:	SS-Sturmbannführer	*SS Number:*	184296
NSDAP Number:	Not a member	*Highest Decoration:*	German Cross in Gold
Religion:	Agnostic	*Marital Status:*	Single
Waffen-SS:	1st SS Division "Leibstandarte Adolf Hitler", 1940-1941		
	2nd SS Division "Das Reich", 1941-1944		
	20th SS Division, 1944		
Notes:	Graduated from Kriegsakademie in 1944 as General Staff Officer		
	Wounded in action several times		

Camp Service: **Oranienburg, 1937-1938**
Buchenwald, 1940

Mulka

First Name:	Robert	*National Archive File:*	A3343 SSO-339A
Birthdate:	12 April 1895	*Birthplace:*	Hamburg
Rank:	SS-Hauptsturmführer	*SS Number:*	Unknown
NSDAP Number:	7848085	*Highest Decoration:*	War Service Cross 2nd Class
Religion:	Unknown	*Marital Status:*	Married
Waffen-SS:	No		
Notes:	Adjutant at Auschwitz		
	Sentenced to 14 years; died 1969		

Camp Service: **Auschwitz, 1942-1943**

Mulsow

First Name:	Dr. Hans	*National Archive File:*	A3343 SSO-339A
Birthdate:	1 February 1913	*Birthplace:*	Raduhn
Rank:	SS-Obersturmführer (F)	*SS Number:*	142421
NSDAP Number:	5637960	*Highest Decoration:*	War Service Cross 2nd Class
Religion:	Unknown	*Marital Status:*	Married
Waffen-SS:	No		
Notes:	Leader of climatology section, Hygiene department Auschwitz		

Camp Service: **Auschwitz, 1943-1944**

Muthig

First Name:	Dr. Julius	*National Archive File:*	A3343 SSO-342A
Birthdate:	9 May 1908	*Birthplace:*	Aschaffenburg
Rank:	SS-Sturmbannführer	*SS Number:*	104518
NSDAP Number:	951631	*Highest Decoration:*	War Service Cross 2nd Class
Religion:	Agnostic	*Marital Status:*	Married
Waffen-SS:	2nd SS Division "Das Reich", 1942-1943		
Notes:	Camp doctor at Dachau		

Camp Service: **Dachau, 1941**
Neuengamme

Neubauer

First Name:	Otto	*National Archive File:*	A3343 SSO-346A
Birthdate:	24 June 1901	*Birthplace:*	Schwintsch
Rank:	SS-Obersturmführer	*SS Number:*	52380
NSDAP Number:	1400855	*Highest Decoration:*	War Service Cross 2nd Class
Religion:	Catholic	*Marital Status:*	Married
Waffen-SS:	No		
Notes:	Department I at Stutthof		

Camp Service: **Stutthof, 1940-1942**

Neumann

First Name:	Dr. Heinz	*National Archive File:*	A3343 SSO-347A
Birthdate:	29 July 1911	*Birthplace:*	Saarbruecken
Rank:	SS-Hauptsturmführer	*SS Number:*	130692
NSDAP Number:	Not a member	*Highest Decoration:*	None listed
Religion:	Unknown	*Marital Status:*	Single
Waffen-SS:	No		
Notes:	Camp doctor at Flossenbürg		

Camp Service: **Buchenwald, 1939**
Flossenbürg, 1940
Oranienburg, 1940-1941

Neumann

First Name:	Dr. Robert	*National Archive File:*	A3343 SSO-348A
Birthdate:	21 August 1902	*Birthplace:*	Nussdorf
Rank:	SS-Obersturmführer	*SS Number:*	203348
NSDAP Number:	5373111	*Highest Decoration:*	None listed
Religion:	Agnostic	*Marital Status:*	Married
Waffen-SS:	No		
Notes:	Camp doctor		

Camp Service: **Auschwitz, 1940**
Buchenwald

Niemann

First Name:	Johann	*National Archive File:*	A3343 SSO-350A
Birthdate:	4 August 1913	*Birthplace:*	Voellen
Rank:	SS-Untersturmführer	*SS Number:*	270600
NSDAP Number:	753836	*Highest Decoration:*	War Service Cross 2nd Class
Religion:	Agnostic	*Marital Status:*	Married
Waffen-SS:	No		
Notes:	Killed at Sobibór 14 October 1943		
	Promoted to officer ranks for *Operation Reinhard*		

Camp Service: **Esterwegen, 1934**   **Sachsenhausen, 1938-1941**
Belzec, 1942   **Sobibór, 1942-1943**

Nommensen

First Name:	Dr. Johannes	*National Archive File:*	A3343 SSO-352A
Birthdate:	26 December 1909	*Birthplace:*	Si-Geempar, Sumatra
Rank:	SS-Hauptsturmführer	*SS Number:*	194673
NSDAP Number:	3970356	*Highest Decoration:*	None listed
Religion:	Protestant	*Marital Status:*	Married
Waffen-SS:	18th SS Division "Horst Wessel", 1945		
Notes:	Camp doctor at Dachau		

Camp Service: **Dachau, 1941**
Neuengamme

Nordhauss

First Name:	Dr. Herbert	*National Archive File:*	A3343 SSO-352A
Birthdate:	20 January 1911	*Birthplace:*	Berlin
Rank:	SS-Hauptsturmführer	*SS Number:*	203977
NSDAP Number:	2850879	*Highest Decoration:*	War Service Cross 2nd Class
Religion:	Unknown	*Marital Status:*	Married
Waffen-SS:	No		
Notes:	Camp doctor at Sachsenhausen		

Camp Service: **Sachsenhausen, 1940**
Hinzert, 1940-1941

Norin

First Name:	Georg	*National Archive File:*	A3343 SSO-353A
Birthdate:	31 August 1909	*Birthplace:*	Essen
Rank:	SS-Sturmbannführer	*SS Number:*	226546
NSDAP Number:	4142648	*Highest Decoration:*	War Service Cross 2nd Class
Religion:	Protestant	*Marital Status:*	Married
Waffen-SS:	No		
Notes:	Pharmacist		

Camp Service: **Oranienburg, 1938-1940**
Sachsenhausen, 1941

Nostitz

First Name:	Paul	*National Archive File:*	A3343 SSO-353A
Birthdate:	25 March 1892	*Birthplace:*	Lyck, East Prussia
Rank:	SS-Standartenführer	*SS Number:*	32617
NSDAP Number:	458596	*Highest Decoration:*	None listed
Religion:	Agnostic	*Marital Status:*	Married
Waffen-SS:	No		
Notes:	Commander 2nd and 3rd Totenkopf Standarten		
	Iron Cross 1st Class, Gold Wound Badge WWI		

Camp Service: **Buchenwald, 1937-1938**

Oberhauser

First Name:	Josef	*National Archive File:*	A3343 SSO-354A
Birthdate:	20 September 1915	*Birthplace:*	Munich-Riem
Rank:	SS-Obersturmführer	*SS Number:*	288121
NSDAP Number:	Not a member	*Highest Decoration:*	Iron Cross 2nd Class
Religion:	Catholic	*Marital Status:*	Married
Waffen-SS:	1st SS Division "Leibstandarte Adolf Hitler", 1944		
Notes:	Promoted to officer rank for *Operation Reinhard*		
	Sentenced to 4 and 1/2 years		

Camp Service: **Oranienburg, 1935-1936**   **Belzec, 1942**
Lublin Airfield Camp, 1942-1943   **San Saba, 1943-1945**

Obermeier

First Name:	Alois	*National Archive File:*	A3343 SSO-354A
Birthdate:	10 April 1901	*Birthplace:*	Landshut
Rank:	SS-Sturmbannführer	*SS Number:*	1885
NSDAP Number:	64542	*Highest Decoration:*	War Service Cross 2nd Class
Religion:	Agnostic	*Marital Status:*	Married
Waffen-SS:	No		
Notes:	Awarded Golden Party Badge		
	Guard battalion commander at Gusen		

Camp Service: **Dachau, 1934-1936, 1937**
Sachsenburg, 1936
Mauthausen, 1940-1944

Oberschmid

First Name:	Albert	*National Archive File:*	A3343 SSO-354A
Birthdate:	29 March 1913	*Birthplace:*	Mindel-Altheim
Rank:	SS-Hauptsturmführer	*SS Number:*	287015
NSDAP Number:	1399108	*Highest Decoration:*	None listed
Religion:	Agnostic	*Marital Status:*	Single
Waffen-SS:	8th SS Division "Florian Geyer", 1942-1943		
Notes:	Assault Gun battalion		

Camp Service: **Oranienburg, 1940-1941**
Sachsenhausen, 1941-1942

Oertli

First Name:	Friedrich	*National Archive File:*	A3343 SSO-355A
Birthdate:	18 May 1906	*Birthplace:*	Bamberg
Rank:	SS-Obersturmführer	*SS Number:*	83673
NSDAP Number:	3211013	*Highest Decoration:*	None listed
Religion:	Catholic	*Marital Status:*	Married
Waffen-SS:	3rd SS Division "Totenkopf", 1942-1943		
Notes:	Administrator at Dachau		

Camp Service: **Dachau, 1939-1941**

Oettler

First Name:	Bruno	*National Archive File:*	A3343 SSO-356A
Birthdate:	24 June 1893	*Birthplace:*	Wuestenwetzdorf
Rank:	SS-Obersturmführer	*SS Number:*	278326
NSDAP Number:	60529	*Highest Decoration:*	War Service Cross 2nd Class
Religion:	Protestant	*Marital Status:*	Married
Waffen-SS:	No		
Notes:	Iron Cross 2nd Class, Black Wound Badge WWI		
	Camp service not listed in personnel file		

Camp Service: **Auschwitz, 1943**

Olm

First Name:	Emil	*National Archive File:*	A3343 SSO-357A
Birthdate:	4 November 1910	*Birthplace:*	Thurow
Rank:	SS-Untersturmführer	*SS Number:*	8206
NSDAP Number:	439734	*Highest Decoration:*	Infantry Assault Badge
Religion:	Protestant	*Marital Status:*	Married
Waffen-SS:	4th SS Division "Polizei", 1942-1943		
	3rd SS Division "Totenkopf", 1944		
Notes:	Wounded in right arm in 1943		

Camp Service: **Neuengamme, 1941-1942**

Opitz

First Name:	Friedrich	*National Archive File:*	A3343 SSO-358A
Birthdate:	7 August 1898	*Birthplace:*	Bergen
Rank:	SS-Hauptsturmführer	*SS Number:*	3533
NSDAP Number:	170897	*Highest Decoration:*	War Service Cross 2nd Class
Religion:	Protestant	*Marital Status:*	Married
Waffen-SS:	No		
Notes:	Former tailor; served in SA 1929-1930		

Camp Service: **Ravensbrück, 1942**

Orendi

First Name:	Dr. Benno	*National Archive File:*	A3343 SSO-358A
Birthdate:	29 March 1918	*Birthplace:*	Hermannstadt, Romania
Rank:	SS-Untersturmführer	*SS Number:*	379245
NSDAP Number:	Not a member	*Highest Decoration:*	War Service Cross 2nd Class
Religion:	Agnostic	*Marital Status:*	Married
Waffen-SS:	No		
Notes:	Camp doctor at Ravensbrück		

Camp Service: **Ravensbrück, 1943**

Orlich

First Name:	Rudolf	*National Archive File:*	No file
Birthdate:	11 December 1910	*Birthplace:*	Hofgastein
Rank:	SS-Untersturmführer	*SS Number:*	297670
NSDAP Number:	1210109	*Highest Decoration:*	None listed
Religion:	Unknown	*Marital Status:*	Unknown
Waffen-SS:	Unknown		

Camp Service: **Auschwitz, 1943**

Ortmann

First Name:	Dr. Gustav	*National Archive File:*	A3343 SSO-359A
Birthdate:	31 January 1904	*Birthplace:*	Gelsenkirchen
Rank:	SS-Obersturmbannführer	*SS Number:*	258144
NSDAP Number:	3460439	*Highest Decoration:*	German Cross in Silver
Religion:	Protestant	*Marital Status:*	Married
Waffen-SS:	3rd SS Division "Totenkopf", 1941-1944		
	IInd SS Corps, 1944		
Notes:	Camp doctor at Sachsenhausen		
	Lived after the war in Baden-Wuerttenberg		

Camp Service: **Oranienburg, 1940**
Sachsenhausen, 1940-1941

Osenbruegge

First Name:	Karl	*National Archive File:*	A3343 SSO-359A
Birthdate:	2 April 1910	*Birthplace:*	Longueville, France
Rank:	SS-Obersturmführer	*SS Number:*	114973
NSDAP Number:	Not a member	*Highest Decoration:*	War Service Cross 2nd Class
Religion:	Unknown	*Marital Status:*	Single
Waffen-SS:	Unknown		
Notes:	Dentist at Sachsenhausen		

Camp Service: **Sachsenhausen, 1940-1941**

Ostermaier

First Name: Dr. Max
Birthdate: 12 March 1907
Rank: SS-Obersturmbannführer
NSDAP Number: 1316542
Religion: Agnostic
Waffen-SS: 5th SS Division "Wiking", 1941-1942
7th SS Division "Prinz Eugen", 1942-1944
Notes: Camp doctor at Dachau

National Archive File: A3343 SSO-360A
Birthplace: Munich
SS Number: 63959
Highest Decoration: War Service Cross 1st Class
Marital Status: Married

Camp Service: **Dachau, 1935**   **Esterwegen, 1936**
Oranienburg, 1937

Otto

First Name: Dr. Johannes
Birthdate: 24 June 1908
Rank: SS-Hauptsturmführer
NSDAP Number: Not a member
Religion: Protestant
Waffen-SS: 5th SS Division "Wiking", 1943
6th SS Division "Nord", 1943
Notes: Doctor

National Archive File: A3343 SSO-362A
Birthplace: Meiningen
SS Number: 367737
Highest Decoration: None listed
Marital Status: Married

Camp Service: **Oranienburg, 1941**
Stutthof, 1942

Otto

First Name: Herbert
Birthdate: Unknown
Rank: SS-Obersturmführer
NSDAP Number: 97592
Religion: Unknown
Waffen-SS: 7th SS Division "Prinz Eugen", 1943
Notes: Helped shut down camp in 1943; killed in action 6 May 1945 near Prague

National Archive File: No File
Birthplace: Unknown
SS Number: 11544
Highest Decoration: Golden Party Badge
Marital Status: Unknown

Camp Service: **Chelmno, 1941-1943**

Otto

First Name: Hermann
Birthdate: 3 November 1911
Rank: SS-Sturmbannführer
NSDAP Number: Not a member
Religion: Agnostic
Waffen-SS: 3rd SS Division "Totenkopf", 1939-1940
6th SS Division "Nord", 1941-1942
23rd SS Division "Kama", 1944
Notes: 2nd SS Totenkopfstandarte "Brandenburg"
Engineer Battalion commander in 23rd SS Division

National Archive File: A3343 SSO-362A
Birthplace: Hamburg
SS Number: 286861
Highest Decoration: Iron Cross 1st Class
Marital Status: Married

Camp Service: **Oranienburg, 1938-1939**

Otto

First Name:	Johannes	*National Archive File:*	A3343 SSO-362A
Birthdate:	24 December 1906	*Birthplace:*	Oederan
Rank:	SS-Obersturmführer	*SS Number:*	292442
NSDAP Number:	2442274	*Highest Decoration:*	War Service Cross 2nd Class
Religion:	Protestant	*Marital Status:*	Married
Waffen-SS:	No		
Notes:	Served in SA 1933-1935		
	Married after birth of first child		

Camp Service: **Oranienburg, 1942-1943**

Otto

First Name:	Kurt	*National Archive File:*	A3343 RS-E0439
Birthdate:	7 November 1910	*Birthplace:*	Duesseldorf
Rank:	SS-Hauptsturmführer	*SS Number:*	19341
NSDAP Number:	559416	*Highest Decoration:*	None listed
Religion:	Agnostic	*Marital Status:*	Married
Waffen-SS:	No		
Notes:	Guard company commander at Auschwitz		
	Committed suicide 1943		

Camp Service: **Sachsenburg, 1936**
Auschwitz, 1943

Overhoff

First Name:	Dr. Wilhelm	*National Archive File:*	A3343 SSO-362A
Birthdate:	25 August 1912	*Birthplace:*	Dessau
Rank:	SS-Sturmbannführer	*SS Number:*	210780
NSDAP Number:	5472825	*Highest Decoration:*	Iron Cross 2nd Class
Religion:	Protestant	*Marital Status:*	Married
Waffen-SS:	3rd SS Division "Totenkopf", 1940-1941		
	10th SS Division "Frundsberg", 1943		
Notes:	Battalion physician for engineer battalion, 3rd SS Division		

Camp Service: **Oranienburg, 1938-1939; 1941-1942**

Pachen

First Name:	Hermann	*National Archive File:*	A3343 SSO-362A
Birthdate:	9 August 1898	*Birthplace:*	Metz, France
Rank:	SS-Hauptsturmführer	*SS Number:*	1804
NSDAP Number:	153331	*Highest Decoration:*	War Service Cross 2nd Class
Religion:	Agnostic	*Marital Status:*	Married
Waffen-SS:	No		
Notes:	Sentenced to Life		
	Iron Cross 2nd Class WWI		

Camp Service: **Flossenbürg**

Painter

First Name: Josef   *National Archive File:* A3343 SSO-363A
Birthdate: 13 November 1903   *Birthplace:* Ettenkofen
Rank: SS-Hauptsturmführer   *SS Number:* 10013
NSDAP Number: 14292   *Highest Decoration:* War Service Cross 1st Class
Religion: Agnostic   *Marital Status:* Married
Waffen-SS: 7th SS Division "Prinz Eugen", 1942
Notes: IInd Totenkopfsturmbann Elbe, 1936-1938
Gold Party Badge, Blood Order #1241

Camp Service: **Dachau, 1936**

Palfner

First Name: Gerhard   *National Archive File:* A3343 SSO-363A
Birthdate: 26 February 1908   *Birthplace:* Unknown
Rank: SS-Untersturmführer   *SS Number:* 205909
NSDAP Number: 3757575   *Highest Decoration:* None listed
Religion: Unknown   *Marital Status:* Married
Waffen-SS: Unknown
Notes: Dentist

Camp Service: **Buchenwald, 1944**

Panitz

First Name: Julius   *National Archive File:* A3343 SSO-364A
Birthdate: 8 July 1892   *Birthplace:* Pforzheim
Rank: SS-Obersturmführer   *SS Number:* 262366
NSDAP Number: 4028994   *Highest Decoration:* War Service Cross 2nd Class
Religion: Protestant   *Marital Status:* Married
Waffen-SS: No
Notes: Iron Cross 2nd Class WWI

Camp Service: **Dachau, 1940**

Pauly

First Name: Max   *National Archive File:* A3343 SSO-367A
Birthdate: 1 June 1907   *Birthplace:* Wesselburen
Rank: SS-Obersturmbannführer   *SS Number:* 5448
NSDAP Number: 106204   *Highest Decoration:* Iron Cross 1st Class
Religion: Protestant   *Marital Status:* Widower
Waffen-SS: No
Notes: *Kommandant* Neuengamme and Stutthof
Executed October 1948

Camp Service: **Stutthof, 1941-1942**
Neuengamme, 1942-1945

Pauly

First Name:	Richard	*National Archive File:*	A3343 SSO-367A
Birthdate:	21 December 1913	*Birthplace:*	Kriensen
Rank:	SS-Sturmbannführer	*SS Number:*	128581
NSDAP Number:	3037646	*Highest Decoration:*	Iron Cross 1st Class
Religion:	Agnostic	*Marital Status:*	Single
Waffen-SS:	3rd SS Division "Totenkopf", 1941-1942		
	9th SS Division "Hohenstaufen", 1943		
	5th SS Division "Wiking", 1944		
Notes:	Wounded in action		
	Attended General Staff training in 1944; operations officer 5th SS Division		

Camp Service: **Oranienburg, 1937**   **Buchenwald, 1938-1939**

Pausch

First Name:	Max	*National Archive File:*	A3343 SSO-367A
Birthdate:	22 April 1894	*Birthplace:*	Gehren
Rank:	SS-Hauptsturmführer	*SS Number:*	54021
NSDAP Number:	1440350	*Highest Decoration:*	None listed
Religion:	Protestant	*Marital Status:*	Married
Waffen-SS:	No		
Notes:	Iron Cross 2nd Class WWI; executed 12 November 1948		

Camp Service: **Mauthausen**   **Oranienburg, 1943**

Peters

First Name:	Dr. Max	*National Archive File:*	A3343 SSO-372A
Birthdate:	29 January 1908	*Birthplace:*	Remscheid
Rank:	SS-Sturmbannführer	*SS Number:*	323791
NSDAP Number:	3964775	*Highest Decoration:*	Iron Cross 2nd Class
Religion:	Unknown	*Marital Status:*	Single
Waffen-SS:	3rd SS Division "Totenkopf", 1940-1942		
Notes:	Doctor		

Camp Service: **Sachsenhausen, 1939-1940**

Peters

First Name:	Heinrich	*National Archive File:*	A3343 SSO-372A
Birthdate:	22 August 1890	*Birthplace:*	Auenbuettel
Rank:	SS-Obersturmführer	*SS Number:*	139396
NSDAP Number:	959262	*Highest Decoration:*	None listed
Religion:	Agnostic	*Marital Status:*	Married
Waffen-SS:	No		
Notes:	Company commander of guard company at Arbeitsdorf		
	Iron Cross 1st Class WWI		

Camp Service: **Sachsenhausen, 1939-1941**
Natzweiler, 1941
Arbeitsdorf, 1942
Ravensbrück, 1942-1944

Petersen

First Name:	Heinrich	*National Archive File:*	A3343 SSO-373A
Birthdate:	31 March 1904	*Birthplace:*	Sonderburg
Rank:	SS-Standartenführer	*SS Number:*	134299
NSDAP Number:	1964574	*Highest Decoration:*	Knight's Cross
Religion:	Agnostic	*Marital Status:*	Married
Waffen-SS:	3rd SS Division "Totenkopf", 1941-1942		
	7th SS Division "Prinz Eugen", 1943-1944		
	18th SS Division "Horst Wessel", 1944		
Notes:	Commander IIIrd Totenkopfsturmbann, 2nd Totenkopf Standarte		
	Regimental commander in 7th & 18th SS Division; suicide 9 May 1945		

Camp Service: **Oranienburg, 1937-1939**

Pfitzner

First Name:	Dr. Walter	*National Archive File:*	A3343 SSO-377A
Birthdate:	23 April 1910	*Birthplace:*	Rotterdam, Netherlands
Rank:	SS-Obersturmbannführer	*SS Number:*	223210
NSDAP Number:	5718253	*Highest Decoration:*	Iron Cross 2nd Class
Religion:	Protestant	*Marital Status:*	Married
Waffen-SS:	3rd SS Division "Totenkopf", 1940-1943		
	20th SS Division, 1944		
Notes:	Doctor		

Camp Service: **Oranienburg, 1938**   **Lichtenburg, 1939**
                  Ravensbrück, 1939-1940

Pflaum

First Name:	Guntram	*National Archive File:*	A3343 SSO-377A
Birthdate:	13 April 1903	*Birthplace:*	Freistadt
Rank:	SS-Standartenführer	*SS Number:*	39477
NSDAP Number:	1200703	*Highest Decoration:*	War Service Cross 2nd Class
Religion:	Agnostic	*Marital Status:*	Divorced
Waffen-SS:	No		
Notes:	Camp service not listed in personnel file		

Camp Service: **Auschwitz, 1944**

Pfuetze

First Name:	Bruno	*National Archive File:*	A3343 SSO-378A
Birthdate:	9 July 1912	*Birthplace:*	Nerchau
Rank:	SS-Obersturmführer	*SS Number:*	81491
NSDAP Number:	1737180	*Highest Decoration:*	War Service Cross 2nd Class
Religion:	Agnostic	*Marital Status:*	Married
Waffen-SS:	No		
Notes:	*Kommandant* Jaworzno sub-camp		
	Camp service not listed in personnel file		

Camp Service: **Auschwitz, 1943**

Piefke

First Name:	Ernst	*National Archive File:*	A3343 SSO-379A
Birthdate:	22 January 1885	*Birthplace:*	Posen
Rank:	SS-Hauptsturmführer	*SS Number:*	275574
NSDAP Number:	Not a member	*Highest Decoration:*	None listed
Religion:	Protestant	*Marital Status:*	Married
Waffen-SS:	No		
Notes:	Gestapo; served in WWI		

Camp Service: **Oranienburg, 1937-1938**

Pietzsch

First Name:	Kurt	*National Archive File:*	A3343 SSO-380A
Birthdate:	12 August 1905	*Birthplace:*	Dresden
Rank:	SS-Hauptsturmführer	*SS Number:*	249
NSDAP Number:	4898	*Highest Decoration:*	War Service Cross 2nd Class
Religion:	Protestant	*Marital Status:*	Married
Waffen-SS:	No		
Notes:	Administration		
	Original SS number was 1664, but this changed in 1938		

Camp Service: **Oranienburg, 1938-1940**

Pinnow

First Name:	Willi	*National Archive File:*	A3343 SSO-380A
Birthdate:	14 November 1898	*Birthplace:*	Kolberg
Rank:	SS-Obersturmführer	*SS Number:*	12922
NSDAP Number:	144103	*Highest Decoration:*	War Service Cross 2nd Class
Religion:	Agnostic	*Marital Status:*	Married
Waffen-SS:	No		
Notes:	Iron Cross 2nd Class, WWI		

Camp Service: **Auschwitz, 1943**

Piorkowski

First Name:	Alex	*National Archive File:*	A3343 SSO-381A
Birthdate:	11 October 1904	*Birthplace:*	Bremen
Rank:	SS-Obersturmbannführer	*SS Number:*	8737
NSDAP Number:	161437	*Highest Decoration:*	None listed
Religion:	Protestant	*Marital Status:*	Married
Waffen-SS:	No		
Notes:	*Kommandant* Dachau		
	Executed 22 October 1948		

Camp Service: **Sachsenburg, 1937**
Lichtenburg, 1938
Dachau, 1939

Pister

First Name:	Hermann	*National Archive File:*	A3343 SSO-381A
Birthdate:	21 February 1885	*Birthplace:*	Luebeck
Rank:	SS-Oberführer	*SS Number:*	29842
NSDAP Number:	918391	*Highest Decoration:*	War Service Cross 1st Class
Religion:	Catholic	*Marital Status:*	Divorced
Waffen-SS:	No		
Notes:	*Kommandant* Buchenwald		
	Sentenced to Death; died in prison 28 September 1948		

Camp Service: **Hinzert, 1941**   **Buchenwald, 1941**

Pittschellis

First Name:	Adolf	*National Archive File:*	A3343 SSO-382A
Birthdate:	28 October 1914	*Birthplace:*	Homburg
Rank:	SS-Sturmbannführer	*SS Number:*	52819
NSDAP Number:	1492016	*Highest Decoration:*	Knight's Cross
Religion:	Agnostic	*Marital Status:*	Married
Waffen-SS:	3rd SS Division "Totenkopf", 1940-1945		
Notes:	Assault gun battalion commander; wounded several times		
	Killed in action 26 January 1945 in Hungary		

Camp Service: **Sachsenburg, 1937**
Buchenwald, 1938

Plaettig

First Name:	Dr. Richard	*National Archive File:*	A3343 SSO-382A
Birthdate:	3 May 1909	*Birthplace:*	Dortmund
Rank:	SS-Hauptsturmführer	*SS Number:*	136785
NSDAP Number:	5845468	*Highest Decoration:*	None listed
Religion:	Unknown	*Marital Status:*	Single
Waffen-SS:	No		
Notes:	Camp doctor		

Camp Service: **Ravensbrück, 1943-1944**
Mauthausen, 1944

Plaul

First Name:	Wolfgang	*National Archive File:*	A3343 SSO-383A
Birthdate:	5 April 1909	*Birthplace:*	Freiburg
Rank:	SS-Obersturmführer	*SS Number:*	13679
NSDAP Number:	576791	*Highest Decoration:*	None listed
Religion:	Catholic	*Marital Status:*	Married
Waffen-SS:	No		
Notes:	Deputy *kommandant* at Buchenwald		

Camp Service: **Sachsenhausen, 1939**
Buchenwald
Wewelsburg

Plaza

First Name:	Dr. Heinrich	*National Archive File:*	A3343 SSO-383A
Birthdate:	10 July 1912	*Birthplace:*	Hultschin
Rank:	SS-Hauptsturmführer	*SS Number:*	352853
NSDAP Number:	6446500	*Highest Decoration:*	None listed
Religion:	Catholic	*Marital Status:*	Married
Waffen-SS:	No		
Notes:	Camp doctor		

Camp Service: **Sachsenhausen, 1942**
Buchenwald, 1944

Ploetz

First Name:	Karl	*National Archive File:*	A3343 SSO-384A
Birthdate:	25 March 1892	*Birthplace:*	Ploetzkau
Rank:	SS-Hauptsturmführer	*SS Number:*	270458
NSDAP Number:	2909047	*Highest Decoration:*	War Service Cross 1st Class
Religion:	Agnostic	*Marital Status:*	Married
Waffen-SS:	4th SS Division "Polizei", 1943-1944		
	16th SS Division "Reichsführer-SS", 1944-1945		
Notes:	Iron Cross 2nd Class WWI		
	Armorer in guard troops		

Camp Service: **Sachsenhausen, 1938-1941**

Pohle

First Name:	Walter	*National Archive File:*	A3343 SSO-388A
Birthdate:	6 January 1910	*Birthplace:*	Obergruenberg
Rank:	SS-Obersturmführer	*SS Number:*	236288
NSDAP Number:	486601	*Highest Decoration:*	Iron Cross 2nd Class
Religion:	Unknown	*Marital Status:*	Married
Waffen-SS:	No		
Notes:	Postal Department at Buchenwald		

Camp Service: **Buchenwald, 1939-1941**

Polenz

First Name:	Walter	*National Archive File:*	A3343 SSO-388A
Birthdate:	18 December 1906	*Birthplace:*	Marienwerder
Rank:	SS-Hauptsturmführer	*SS Number:*	85132
NSDAP Number:	324670	*Highest Decoration:*	War Service Cross 2nd Class
Religion:	Protestant	*Marital Status:*	Married
Waffen-SS:	3rd SS Division "Totenkopf", 1941-1942		
Notes:	Former machinest		

Camp Service: **Auschwitz, 1942-1943**

Pollok

First Name:	Josef	*National Archive File:*	A3343 SSO-388A
Birthdate:	13 November 1908	*Birthplace:*	Charlottenhof
Rank:	SS-Obersturmführer (F)	*SS Number:*	170897
NSDAP Number:	Not a member	*Highest Decoration:*	None listed
Religion:	Agnostic	*Marital Status:*	Married
Waffen-SS:	No		
Notes:	Adjutant of Auschwitz Construction Department		
	Camp service not listed in personnel file		

Camp Service: **Auschwitz, 1942-1943**

Pongs

First Name:	Dr. Walter	*National Archive File:*	A3343 SSO-389A
Birthdate:	14 June 1911	*Birthplace:*	Wies
Rank:	SS-Hauptsturmführer	*SS Number:*	104849
NSDAP Number:	Not a member	*Highest Decoration:*	War Service Cross 2nd Class
Religion:	Unknown	*Marital Status:*	Single
Waffen-SS:	6th SS Division "Nord", 1942		
Notes:	Dentist		

Camp Service: **Buchenwald, 1941-1942**

Pook

First Name:	Dr. Hermann	*National Archive File:*	A3343 SSO-389A
Birthdate:	1 May 1901	*Birthplace:*	Berlin
Rank:	SS-Obersturmbannführer	*SS Number:*	155870
NSDAP Number:	2645140	*Highest Decoration:*	None listed
Religion:	Agnostic	*Marital Status:*	Married
Waffen-SS:	9th SS Division "Hohenstaufen", 1943		
Notes:	Chief dentist 9th SS Division; chief dentist Section DIII		
	Sentenced to ten years; released in 1951; resumed dental practice in Berlin		

Camp Service: **Oranienburg, 1939-1941, 1943-1944**

Popiersch

First Name:	Dr. Max	*National Archive File:*	A3343 RS-E5130
Birthdate:	26 May 1893	*Birthplace:*	Pless
Rank:	SS-Sturmbannführer	*SS Number:*	176467
NSDAP Number:	Not a member	*Highest Decoration:*	None listed
Religion:	Agnostic	*Marital Status:*	Single
Waffen-SS:	No		
Notes:	Camp doctor at Auschwitz; died 21 April 1942 of typhus		
	Iron Cross 2nd Class WWI		

Camp Service: **Flossenbürg, 1939-1940** **Buchenwald, 1940**
Auschwitz, 1940-1942 **Majdanek, 1943**

Pork

First Name:	Dr. Karl	*National Archive File:*	A3343 SSO-389A
Birthdate:	17 February 1889	*Birthplace:*	Muenster
Rank:	SS-Hauptsturmführer	*SS Number:*	163282
NSDAP Number:	3394168	*Highest Decoration:*	None listed
Religion:	Protestant	*Marital Status:*	Married
Waffen-SS:	No		
Notes:	Dentist		

Camp Service: **Buchenwald**

Post

First Name:	Dr. Ernst	*National Archive File:*	A3343 SSO-390A
Birthdate:	1 January 1901	*Birthplace:*	Tilsit
Rank:	SS-Sturmbannführer	*SS Number:*	6649
NSDAP Number:	229089	*Highest Decoration:*	Iron Cross 2nd Class
Religion:	Agnostic	*Marital Status:*	Widower
Waffen-SS:	Unknown		
Notes:	Dentist		

Camp Service: **Sachsenhausen, 1941-1942**

Prauss

First Name:	Artur	*National Archive File:*	A3343 SSO-391A
Birthdate:	18 November 1892	*Birthplace:*	Berlin
Rank:	SS-Untersturmführer	*SS Number:*	220790
NSDAP Number:	5372634	*Highest Decoration:*	None listed
Religion:	Unknown	*Marital Status:*	Unknown
Waffen-SS:	No		

Notes: Iron Cross 1st Class, Wound Badge WWI
Camp service not listed in personnel file

Camp Service: **Sachsenhausen** **Breendonk**

Precht

First Name:	Dr. Elimar	*National Archive File:*	A3343 SSO-391A
Birthdate:	25 May 1912	*Birthplace:*	Unknown
Rank:	SS-Hauptsturmführer	*SS Number:*	233392
NSDAP Number:	Not a member	*Highest Decoration:*	War Service Cross 2nd Class
Religion:	Unknown	*Marital Status:*	Married
Waffen-SS:	No		
Notes:	Dentist		

Camp Service: **Dachau, 1943**
Natzweiler, 1943
Auschwitz, 1944-1945

Preissel

First Name:	Dr. Rolf	*National Archive File:*	A3343 SSO-392A
Birthdate:	14 February 1912	*Birthplace:*	Unknown
Rank:	SS-Hauptsturmführer	*SS Number:*	28963
NSDAP Number:	1122100	*Highest Decoration:*	Iron Cross 2nd Class
Religion:	Unknown	*Marital Status:*	Single
Waffen-SS:	1st SS Division "Leibstandarte Adolf Hitler", 1942		
Notes:	Doctor; wounded in action		

Camp Service: **Oranienburg, 1941**
Dachau, 1942

Puetz

First Name:	Dr. Heinrich	*National Archive File:*	A3343 SSO-396A
Birthdate:	1 September 1908	*Birthplace:*	Essen
Rank:	SS-Hauptsturmführer	*SS Number:*	237817
NSDAP Number:	2210355	*Highest Decoration:*	None listed
Religion:	Catholic	*Marital Status:*	Married
Waffen-SS:	3rd SS Division "Totenkopf", 1941		
Notes:	Dentist		

Camp Service: **Flossenbürg, 1940**
Oranienburg, 1940-1941
Stutthof, 1944

Puhr

First Name:	Dr. Fridolin	*National Archive File:*	A3343 SSO-396A
Birthdate:	30 April 1913	*Birthplace:*	Gaungs
Rank:	SS-Hauptsturmführer	*SS Number:*	295858
NSDAP Number:	6206449	*Highest Decoration:*	Iron Cross 1st Class
Religion:	Agnostic	*Marital Status:*	Single
Waffen-SS:	3rd SS Division "Totenkopf", 1941-1943		
	16th SS Division "Reichsführer-SS", 1944		
Notes:	Camp doctor at Dachau		
	Sentenced to 20 years		

Camp Service: **Dachau, 1944**   **Oranienburg, 1944**

Pusch

First Name:	Hermann	*National Archive File:*	A3343 SSO-397A
Birthdate:	19 January 1913	*Birthplace:*	Hamm
Rank:	SS-Hauptsturmführer	*SS Number:*	273442
NSDAP Number:	4261327	*Highest Decoration:*	Iron Cross 2nd Class
Religion:	Agnostic	*Marital Status:*	Married
Waffen-SS:	4th SS Division "Polizei", 1942-1943		
	17th SS Division "Götz von Berlichingen", 1944		
Notes:	Wounded in 1943; commander guard battalion at Amersfoort		

Camp Service: **Amersfoort, 1943-1944**

Quirsfeld

First Name:	Eberhard	*National Archive File:*	A3343 SSO-399A
Birthdate:	29 March 1899	*Birthplace:*	Salzburg, Austria
Rank:	SS-Standartenführer	*SS Number:*	23029
NSDAP Number:	512528	*Highest Decoration:*	Iron Cross 1st Class
Religion:	Agnostic	*Marital Status:*	Married
Waffen-SS:	6th SS Division "Nord", 1941		
	7th SS Division "Prinz Eugen", 1942		
Notes:	Blood Order #454		
	Artillery Regiment Commander in 7th SS Division		

Camp Service: **Dachau, 1937-1938**   **Mauthausen, 1938-1939**
Buchenwald, 1939-1940

Rachel

First Name:	Albert	*National Archive File:*	A3343 SSO-001B
Birthdate:	11 December 1911	*Birthplace:*	Karlsruhe
Rank:	SS-Untersturmführer	*SS Number:*	111850
NSDAP Number:	Not a member	*Highest Decoration:*	None listed
Religion:	Catholic	*Marital Status:*	Married
Waffen-SS:	No		
Notes:	Camp doctor at Mauthausen		

Camp Service: **Oranienburg, 1940**
Mauthausen, 1940

Rahm

First Name:	Karl	*National Archive File:*	A3343 SSO-004B
Birthdate:	2 April 1907	*Birthplace:*	Klosternenburg, Austria
Rank:	SS-Obersturmführer	*SS Number:*	296534
NSDAP Number:	6222124	*Highest Decoration:*	War Service Cross 2nd Class
Religion:	Catholic	*Marital Status:*	Married
Waffen-SS:	No		
Notes:	*Kommandant* Theresienstadt; camp service not confirmed in personnel file		
	Executed 1947		

Camp Service: **Theresienstadt, 1944-1945**

Rahn

First Name:	Helmuth	*National Archive File:*	A3343 SSO-004B
Birthdate:	2 August 1913	*Birthplace:*	Dampen
Rank:	SS-Sturmbannführer	*SS Number:*	283080
NSDAP Number:	3163941	*Highest Decoration:*	Iron Cross 2nd Class
Religion:	Agnostic	*Marital Status:*	Married
Waffen-SS:	3rd SS Division "Totenkopf", 1940-1941		
	6th SS Division "Nord", 1941-1943		
Notes:	1st SS Totenkopfstandarte "Oberbayern"; reconnaissance battalion commander		
	Killed in action 24 June 1943 in aircraft shootdown		

Camp Service: **Dachau, 1938**

Ramsauer

First Name:	Siegbert	*National Archive File:*	A3343 SSO-006B
Birthdate:	19 October 1909	*Birthplace:*	Klagenfurt, Austria
Rank:	SS-Hauptsturmführer	*SS Number:*	301007
NSDAP Number:	6103648	*Highest Decoration:*	None listed
Religion:	Catholic	*Marital Status:*	Married
Waffen-SS:	8th SS Division "Florian Geyer", 1941		
Notes:	Sentenced to Life		
	Camp doctor of Sub-Camp Loiblpass		

Camp Service: **Oranienburg, 1941**
Dachau
Mauthausen, 1943

Rascher

First Name:	Dr. Sigmund	*National Archive File:*	A3343 SSO-007B
Birthdate:	12 February 1909	*Birthplace:*	Munich
Rank:	SS-Hauptsturmführer	*SS Number:*	347142
NSDAP Number:	3092414	*Highest Decoration:*	War Service Cross 1st Class
Religion:	Agnostic	*Marital Status:*	Married
Waffen-SS:	No		
Notes:	Conducted medical experiments at Dachau		
	Executed by the SS 26 April 1945 at Dachau		

Camp Service: **Dachau, 1942-1944**

Rautenberg

First Name:	Herbert	*National Archive File:*	A3343 SSO-011B
Birthdate:	19 January 1908	*Birthplace:*	Berlin
Rank:	SS-Sturmbannführer	*SS Number:*	2297
NSDAP Number:	33842	*Highest Decoration:*	Iron Cross 2nd Class
Religion:	Agnostic	*Marital Status:*	Married
Waffen-SS:	Unknown		
Notes:	Commander of Druette sub-camp of Neuengamme		
	Wounded in 1941; Golden Party Badge		

Camp Service: **Dachau, 1937**
Majdanek, 1943
Neuengamme, 1943-1944

Reddig

First Name:	Richard	*National Archive File:*	A3343 SSO-012B
Birthdate:	27 September 1896	*Birthplace:*	Siddau
Rank:	SS-Hauptsturmführer	*SS Number:*	17791
NSDAP Number:	719892	*Highest Decoration:*	War Service Cross 2nd Class
Religion:	Protestant	*Marital Status:*	Married
Waffen-SS:	No		
Notes:	Commander 1st Guard Company and acting commander 2nd Guard Battalion		

Camp Service: **Stutthof, 1942-1945**

Reder

First Name:	Walter	*National Archive File:*	A3343 SSO-013B
Birthdate:	4 February 1915	*Birthplace:*	Freiwaldau
Rank:	SS-Sturmbannführer	*SS Number:*	58074
NSDAP Number:	Not a member	*Highest Decoration:*	Knight's Cross
Religion:	Agnostic	*Marital Status:*	Married
Waffen-SS:	3rd SS Division "Totenkopf", 1941-1943		
	16th SS Division "Reichsführer-SS", 1943-1945		
Notes:	Guard troops at Dachau		
	Sentenced to Life Imprisonment in Italy; died 1992		

Camp Service: **Dachau, 1936, 1938-1940**

Redwitz

First Name:	Michael	*National Archive File:*	A3343 SSO-013B
Birthdate:	14 August 1900	*Birthplace:*	Bayreuth
Rank:	SS-Hauptsturmführer	*SS Number:*	327349
NSDAP Number:	17607	*Highest Decoration:*	War Service Cross 2nd Class
Religion:	Protestant	*Marital Status:*	Married
Waffen-SS:	Ist SS Panzer Corps		
Notes:	Schutzhaftlagerführer at Dachau and Mauthausen-Gusen sub-camp		
	Golden Party Badge; executed 29 May 1946		

Camp Service: **Mauthausen, 1938-1941**   **Ravensbrück, 1941-1942**
Buchenwald, 1944   **Dachau, 1944**

Rehn

First Name:	Ludwig	*National Archive File:*	A3343 SSO-015B
Birthdate:	7 July 1910	*Birthplace:*	Saarbruecken
Rank:	SS-Obersturmführer	*SS Number:*	269927
NSDAP Number:	Not a member	*Highest Decoration:*	War Service Cross 2nd Class
Religion:	Catholic	*Marital Status:*	Married
Waffen-SS:	No		
Notes:	Arbeitseinsatzführer at Neuengamme		
	Sentenced to Life		

Camp Service: **Neuengamme, 1942**
Sachsenhausen

Reich

First Name:	Otto	*National Archive File:*	A3343 SSO-016B
Birthdate:	5 December 1891	*Birthplace:*	Waldhausen
Rank:	SS-Oberführer	*SS Number:*	9948
NSDAP Number:	289356	*Highest Decoration:*	Iron Cross 1st Class
Religion:	Agnostic	*Marital Status:*	Married
Waffen-SS:	SS Legion "Flandern", 1941-1942		
Notes:	Commander SS Police Regiment 4, 1943-1944		
	Kommandant Lichtenburg; died 20 September 1955		

Camp Service: **Lichtenburg, 1935-1936**

Reichherzer

First Name:	Emil	*National Archive File:*	A3343 RS-E5329
Birthdate:	1 May 1911	*Birthplace:*	Munich
Rank:	SS-Hauptsturmführer	*SS Number:*	32502
NSDAP Number:	320705	*Highest Decoration:*	None listed
Religion:	Agnostic	*Marital Status:*	Married
Waffen-SS:	Yes, unit unknown		
Notes:	Adjutant at Sachsenhausen		
	Killed in action 23 January 1943		

Camp Service: **Sachsenburg, 1936**   **Dachau, 1936**
Neuengamme, 1939   **Buchenwald, 1939**
Sachsenhausen, 1940

Reichleitner

First Name:	Franz	*National Archive File:*	No File
Birthdate:	2 December 1906	*Birthplace:*	Ried, Austria
Rank:	SS-Hauptsturmführer	*SS Number:*	357065
NSDAP Number:	6369213	*Highest Decoration:*	War Service Cross 1st Class
Religion:	Unknown	*Marital Status:*	Married
Waffen-SS:	No		
Notes:	*Kommandant* Sobibór; killed in action 3 January 1944 near Fiume		

Camp Service: **Sobibór, 1942-1943**

Reim

First Name:	Dr. Heinrich	*National Archive File:*	A3343 SSO-018B
Birthdate:	8 April 1915	*Birthplace:*	Weissenstein
Rank:	SS-Hauptsturmführer	*SS Number:*	382467
NSDAP Number:	7073610	*Highest Decoration:*	Iron Cross 1st Class
Religion:	Catholic	*Marital Status:*	Married
Waffen-SS:	5th SS Division "Wiking", 1943		
	9th SS Division "Hohenstaufen", 1944		
Notes:	Doctor		

Camp Service: **Dachau, 1941**

Reimer

First Name:	Guido	*National Archive File:*	A3343 SSO-019B
Birthdate:	31 July 1901	*Birthplace:*	Ronsperg
Rank:	SS-Obersturmführer	*SS Number:*	305116
NSDAP Number:	Not a member	*Highest Decoration:*	None listed
Religion:	Agnostic	*Marital Status:*	Married
Waffen-SS:	No		
Notes:	Commander guard battalion at Buchenwald		
	Sentenced to Life; released 1950		

Camp Service: **Buchenwald, 1939-1944**

Reiner

First Name:	Dr. Alexander	*National Archive File:*	A3343 SSO-020B
Birthdate:	4 March 1885	*Birthplace:*	Panschwitz
Rank:	SS-Oberführer	*SS Number:*	49294
NSDAP Number:	577431	*Highest Decoration:*	None listed
Religion:	Catholic	*Marital Status:*	Married
Waffen-SS:	No		
Notes:	*Kommandant* Columbia Haus, Sachsenburg; Dismissed from SS in 1935		
	Dentist		

Camp Service: **Dachau, 1934**   **Sachsenburg, 1934**
Columbia Haus, 1934-1935

Reinicke

First Name:	Otto	*National Archive File:*	A3343 SSO-021B
Birthdate:	1 January 1908	*Birthplace:*	Steigra
Rank:	SS-Untersturmführer	*SS Number:*	156653
NSDAP Number:	218819	*Highest Decoration:*	None listed
Religion:	Agnostic	*Marital Status:*	Married
Waffen-SS:	No		
Notes:	Reporting officer at Auschwitz		

Camp Service: **Buchenwald, 1937-1938**
Flossenbürg, 1938-1940
Auschwitz, 1940-1942

Reischenbeck

First Name:	Wilhelm	*National Archive File:*	A3343 SSO-021B
Birthdate:	23 June 1902	*Birthplace:*	Munich
Rank:	SS-Obersturmführer	*SS Number:*	3926
NSDAP Number:	348592	*Highest Decoration:*	None listed
Religion:	Catholic	*Marital Status:*	Married
Waffen-SS:	No		
Notes:	Organized evacuation of Auschwitz; guard company commander; sentenced to 10 years		

Camp Service: **Auschwitz, 1944-1945**
Mauthausen, 1945

Reiss

First Name:	Paul	*National Archive File:*	A3343 SSO-022B
Birthdate:	12 October 1888	*Birthplace:*	Altersdorf
Rank:	SS-Sturmbannführer	*SS Number:*	260567
NSDAP Number:	Not a member	*Highest Decoration:*	War Service Cross 2nd Class
Religion:	Protestant	*Marital Status:*	Married
Waffen-SS:	No		
Notes:	Former cabinet maker; SS economic enterprises at Dachau		
	Iron Cross 2nd Class, Wound Badge WWI		

Camp Service: **Dachau, 1942-1945**

Reitz

First Name:	Erwin	*National Archive File:*	A3343 SSO-022B
Birthdate:	4 January 1892	*Birthplace:*	Jevelsberg
Rank:	SS-Obersturmbannführer	*SS Number:*	223918
NSDAP Number:	3472358	*Highest Decoration:*	None listed
Religion:	Unknown	*Marital Status:*	Married
Waffen-SS:	SS Infantry Regiment 8, 1941-1942		
Notes:	Commander IInd Totenkopfsturmbann "Elbe"		
	Iron Cross 1st Class WWI; relieved of command in 1942		

Camp Service: **Lichtenburg, 1936-1937**

Remmert

First Name:	Heinrich	*National Archive File:*	A3343 SSO-023B
Birthdate:	1 September 1905	*Birthplace:*	Ennigloh
Rank:	SS-Obersturmbannführer	*SS Number:*	253680
NSDAP Number:	19110	*Highest Decoration:*	War Service Cross 2nd Class
Religion:	Protestant	*Marital Status:*	Married
Waffen-SS:	No		
Notes:	Letter from SA in personnel file describing his brutality in early camps		
	Golden Party Badge		

Camp Service: **Papenburg, 1934**
Esterwegen, 1934
Lichtenburg, 1935-1936

Renner

First Name:	Dr. Ferdinand	*National Archive File:*	A3343 SSO-023B
Birthdate:	22 February 1911	*Birthplace:*	Munich-Deining
Rank:	SS-Sturmbannführer	*SS Number:*	313906
NSDAP Number:	4332084	*Highest Decoration:*	War Service Cross 1st Class
Religion:	Catholic	*Marital Status:*	Married
Waffen-SS:	3rd SS Division "Totenkopf", 1941-1944		
Notes:	Battalion physician in 3rd SS Division		
	Wounded in action		

Camp Service: **Dachau, 1939-1941**

Rett

First Name:	Dr. Andreas	*National Archive File:*	A3343 SSO-024B
Birthdate:	20 April 1909	*Birthplace:*	Ingolstadt
Rank:	SS-Obersturmführer	*SS Number:*	411930
NSDAP Number:	Not a member	*Highest Decoration:*	None listed
Religion:	Protestant	*Marital Status:*	Married
Waffen-SS:	No		
Notes:	Dentist		

Camp Service: **Auschwitz, 1942**

Reutter

First Name: Dr. Paul
Birthdate: 14 October 1911
Rank: SS-Sturmbannführer
NSDAP Number: 1795672
Religion: Agnostic
Waffen-SS: 5th SS Division "Wiking", 1941-1942
IVth SS Corps, 1943
Notes: Dentist
Leading dentist in Department DIII, Oranienburg

National Archive File: A3343 SSO-025B
Birthplace: Bad Homburg
SS Number: 55447
Highest Decoration: None listed
Marital Status: Married

Camp Service: **Dachau, 1941**
Oranienburg, 1943

Richter

First Name: Dr. Hermann
Birthdate: 13 August 1915
Rank: SS-Obersturmführer
NSDAP Number: 6380626
Religion: Protestant
Waffen-SS: No
Notes: Diagnosed with mental problems (schizophrenia, accoustical hallucinations)

National Archive File: A3343 SSO-027B
Birthplace: Linz, Austria
SS Number: 340076
Highest Decoration: None listed
Marital Status: Married

Camp Service: **Mauthausen, 1942-1943**　　**Oranienburg, 1944**
Dachau, 1944

Rieck

First Name: Willi
Birthdate: 3 March 1914
Rank: SS-Hauptsturmführer
NSDAP Number: 1671286
Religion: Protestant
Waffen-SS: 15th SS Division, 1944
Notes: Administration department at Auschwitz

National Archive File: A3343 SSO-028B
Birthplace: Jueterbog
SS Number: 63900
Highest Decoration: War Service Cross 2nd Class
Marital Status: Married

Camp Service: **Dachau, 1939-1940**
Auschwitz, 1940-1943

Riedl

First Name: Robert
Birthdate: 30 July 1912
Rank: SS-Sturmbannführer
NSDAP Number: 2336309
Religion: Agnostic
Waffen-SS: No
Notes: Construction engineer; designed headquarters at Oranienburg
Architect after the war in West Germany

National Archive File: A3343 SSO-030B
Birthplace: Rhoenwald
SS Number: 96363
Highest Decoration: War Service Cross 1st Class
Marital Status: Married

Camp Service: **Dachau, 1935-1936**　　**Sachsenhausen, 1936-1937**
Buchenwald, 1937-1938　**Oranienburg, 1938-1939**

Riek

First Name:	Dr. Gustav	*National Archive File:*	A3343 SSO-031B
Birthdate:	23 May 1900	*Birthplace:*	Stuttgart
Rank:	SS-Obersturmführer	*SS Number:*	289678
NSDAP Number:	142933	*Highest Decoration:*	None listed
Religion:	Protestant	*Marital Status:*	Married
Waffen-SS:	No		
Notes:	Department VI at Hinzert		
	Geologist		

Camp Service: **Hinzert, 1940-1941**

Riem

First Name:	Erich	*National Archive File:*	No File
Birthdate:	26 December 1900	*Birthplace:*	Unknown
Rank:	SS-Obersturmführer	*SS Number:*	65228
NSDAP Number:	1731737	*Highest Decoration:*	None listed
Religion:	Unknown	*Marital Status:*	Unknown
Waffen-SS:	Unknown		

Camp Service: **Lichtenburg, 1936**

Riemer

First Name:	Otto	*National Archive File:*	A3343 SSO-032B
Birthdate:	19 May 1897	*Birthplace:*	Rastatt
Rank:	SS-Obersturmführer	*SS Number:*	13599
NSDAP Number:	552630	*Highest Decoration:*	War Service Cross 2nd Class
Religion:	Agnostic	*Marital Status:*	Married
Waffen-SS:	No		
Notes:	Lagerführer at Ebensee sub-camp		
	Iron Cross 2nd Class WWI		

Camp Service: **Mauthausen, 1942-1944**

Rieth

First Name:	Arthur	*National Archive File:*	A3343 SSO-032B
Birthdate:	14 April 1890	*Birthplace:*	Pforzheim
Rank:	SS-Untersturmführer	*SS Number:*	233111
NSDAP Number:	5611759	*Highest Decoration:*	None listed
Religion:	Protestant	*Marital Status:*	Married
Waffen-SS:	No		
Notes:	Prisoner of war in France during WWI		

Camp Service: **Dachau, 1943**

Rinck

First Name:	Willi Klaus	*National Archive File:*	A3343 SSO-033B
Birthdate:	10 October 1905	*Birthplace:*	Hamburg
Rank:	SS-Hauptsturmführer	*SS Number:*	179300
NSDAP Number:	575244	*Highest Decoration:*	War Service Cross 2nd Class
Religion:	Agnostic	*Marital Status:*	Married
Waffen-SS:	5th SS Division "Wiking", 1942-1943		
Notes:	Administrator at Neuengamme		

Camp Service: **Neuengamme, 1940-1942**
Oranienburg, 1944

Rindfleisch

First Name:	Dr. Heinrich	*National Archive File:*	A3343 SSO-033B
Birthdate:	3 March 1916	*Birthplace:*	Strassburg
Rank:	SS-Obersturmführer	*SS Number:*	289832
NSDAP Number:	Not a member	*Highest Decoration:*	None listed
Religion:	Protestant	*Marital Status:*	Married
Waffen-SS:	No		
Notes:	Camp doctor at Majdanek		

Camp Service: **Ravensbrück, 1942**
Sachsenhausen
Majdanek, 1943
Gross-Rosen, 1944

Rink

First Name:	Otto	*National Archive File:*	A3343 SSO-034B
Birthdate:	15 June 1888	*Birthplace:*	Brueck
Rank:	SS-Untersturmführer	*SS Number:*	259562
NSDAP Number:	5537551	*Highest Decoration:*	None listed
Religion:	Protestant	*Marital Status:*	Married
Waffen-SS:	No		
Notes:	Iron Cross 2nd Class and Wound Badge WWI		

Camp Service: **Flossenbürg, 1944**

Ritterbusch

First Name:	Fritz	*National Archive File:*	A3343 SSO-036B
Birthdate:	11 January 1894	*Birthplace:*	Zschockau
Rank:	SS-Hauptsturmführer	*SS Number:*	9107
NSDAP Number:	6317	*Highest Decoration:*	War Service Cross 2nd Class
Religion:	Protestant	*Marital Status:*	Married
Waffen-SS:	No		
Notes:	Iron Cross 1st Class WWI; Golden Party Badge		
	Commander 3rd Guard Company Flossenbürg		

Camp Service: **Flossenbürg, 1939-1941**
Gross-Rosen, 1944-1945

Rittinghaus

First Name:	Helmut	*National Archive File:*	A3343 SSO-036B
Birthdate:	25 August 1908	*Birthplace:*	Dahlbruch
Rank:	SS-Hauptsturmführer	*SS Number:*	291339
NSDAP Number:	178369	*Highest Decoration:*	War Service Cross 2nd Class
Religion:	Agnostic	*Marital Status:*	Engaged
Waffen-SS:	20th SS Division, 1944		
Notes:	Pharmacist		

Camp Service: **Ravensbrück, 1942**   **Majdanek, 1943-1944**

Ritzheimer

First Name:	Heinz	*National Archive File:*	A3343 SSO-037B
Birthdate:	14 July 1900	*Birthplace:*	Worms
Rank:	SS-Hauptsturmführer	*SS Number:*	9204
NSDAP Number:	650608	*Highest Decoration:*	None listed
Religion:	Catholic	*Marital Status:*	Married
Waffen-SS:	4th SS Division "Polizei", 1940		
Notes:	Former iron worker		

Camp Service: **Dachau, 1935-1936**
Lichtenburg, 1936-1937
Buchenwald, 1937-1938
Flossenbürg, 1938-1939
Auschwitz, 1941-1942

Roederer

First Name:	Dr. Rudolf	*National Archive File:*	A3343 SSO-039B
Birthdate:	7 October 1910	*Birthplace:*	Mannheim
Rank:	SS-Untersturmführer	*SS Number:*	200198
NSDAP Number:	Not a member	*Highest Decoration:*	None listed
Religion:	Agnostic	*Marital Status:*	Married
Waffen-SS:	No		
Notes:	Dentist		

Camp Service: **Sachsenhausen, 1941**

Rödl

First Name:	Arthur	*National Archive File:*	A3343 SSO-039B
Birthdate:	13 May 1898	*Birthplace:*	Munich
Rank:	SS-Standartenführer	*SS Number:*	1240
NSDAP Number:	98023	*Highest Decoration:*	War Service Cross 1st Class
Religion:	Agnostic	*Marital Status:*	Married
Waffen-SS:	9th SS Division "Hohenstaufen", 1943		
	15th SS Division, 1944		
Notes:	*Kommandant* Lichtenburg and Gross-Rosen; Blood Order #216		
	Golden Party Badge; suicide April 1945		

Camp Service: **Lichtenburg, 1934-1935**   **Sachsenburg, 1935-1937**
Buchenwald, 1937-1940   **Gross-Rosen, 1941-1942**

Roetzel

First Name:	Willy	*National Archive File:*	No File
Birthdate:	Unknown	*Birthplace:*	Unknown
Rank:	SS-Untersturmführer	*SS Number:*	7084
NSDAP Number:	317474	*Highest Decoration:*	None listed
Religion:	Unknown	*Marital Status:*	Unknown
Waffen-SS:	Unknown		
Notes:	Thrown out of SS in 1936		

Camp Service: **Columbia Haus, 1936**

Rohde

First Name:	Dr. Werner	*National Archive File:*	A3343 SSO-043B
Birthdate:	11 June 1904	*Birthplace:*	Marburg
Rank:	SS-Untersturmführer	*SS Number:*	283486
NSDAP Number:	1663050	*Highest Decoration:*	None listed
Religion:	Protestant	*Marital Status:*	Married
Waffen-SS:	No		
Notes:	Camp physician		
	Executed 11 October 1946		

Camp Service: **Auschwitz, 1943**
Natzweiler, 1944

Rokita

First Name:	Richard	*National Archive File:*	A3343 SSO-045B
Birthdate:	8 October 1894	*Birthplace:*	Aschersleben
Rank:	SS-Obersturmführer (F)	*SS Number:*	53796
NSDAP Number:	1106724	*Highest Decoration:*	Bar to Iron Cross 2nd Class
Religion:	Agnostic	*Marital Status:*	Married
Waffen-SS:	No		
Notes:	Former musician; served in 309th Infantry Regiment in the army 1939		
	Served in SA 1931-1932; after the war assumed name of Domagala		

Camp Service: **Janowska**

Roschmann

First Name:	Dr. August	*National Archive File:*	A3343 SSO-046B
Birthdate:	26 September 1902	*Birthplace:*	Augsburg
Rank:	SS-Obersturmbannführer	*SS Number:*	42666
NSDAP Number:	1232743	*Highest Decoration:*	Iron Cross 1st Class
Religion:	Catholic	*Marital Status:*	Married
Waffen-SS:	2nd SS Division "Das Reich", 1940-1944		
Notes:	Missing in action 29 July 1944 in Normandy		

Camp Service: **Sachsenhausen, 1940**

Rosenbusch

First Name:	Erich	*National Archive File:*	A3343 SSO-047B
Birthdate:	18 January 1913	*Birthplace:*	Kloster Veilsdorf
Rank:	SS-Obersturmbannführer	*SS Number:*	102899
NSDAP Number:	2280754	*Highest Decoration:*	German Cross in Gold
Religion:	Agnostic	*Marital Status:*	Married
Waffen-SS:	3rd SS Division "Totenkopf", 1940		
	5th SS Division "Wiking", 1940-1942		
Notes:	Wounded in action several times		

Camp Service: **Sachsenburg, 1937**
Buchenwald, 1938

Rosenthal

First Name:	Dr. Rolf	*National Archive File:*	A3343 SSO-047B
Birthdate:	22 January 1911	*Birthplace:*	Braunschweig
Rank:	SS-Obersturmführer	*SS Number:*	31442
NSDAP Number:	112187	*Highest Decoration:*	None listed
Religion:	Unknown	*Marital Status:*	Married
Waffen-SS:	No		
Notes:	Thrown out of SS and sentenced to 8 years imprisonment for performing an abortion		
	Committed suicide in 1972		

Camp Service: **Ravensbrück, 1941-1943**

Rossner

First Name:	Emil	*National Archive File:*	A3343 SSO-048B
Birthdate:	2 September 1906	*Birthplace:*	Hof
Rank:	SS-Obersturmführer	*SS Number:*	3777
NSDAP Number:	315783	*Highest Decoration:*	War Service Cross 2nd Class
Religion:	Agnostic	*Marital Status:*	Married
Waffen-SS:	No		
Notes:	Prisoner administration		
	Served in SA 1922-1924		

Camp Service: **Columbia Haus, 1936**
Sachsenhausen, 1938-1944

Rouenhoff

First Name:	Gerhard	*National Archive File:*	A3343 SSO-050B
Birthdate:	20 October 1901	*Birthplace:*	Duesseldorf
Rank:	SS-Obersturmbannführer	*SS Number:*	51480
NSDAP Number:	425786	*Highest Decoration:*	War Service Cross 2nd Class
Religion:	Catholic	*Marital Status:*	Married
Waffen-SS:	No		
Notes:	Worked on Globocnik's staff at Lublin, 1940		

Camp Service: **Sachsenhausen, 1941**

Ruehs

First Name:	Walter	*National Archive File:*	A3343 SSO-054B
Birthdate:	3 May 1914	*Birthplace:*	Seestadt-Rostock
Rank:	SS-Hauptsturmführer	*SS Number:*	120030
NSDAP Number:	Not a member	*Highest Decoration:*	None listed
Religion:	Agnostic	*Marital Status:*	Married
Waffen-SS:	6th SS Division "Nord", 1941-1944		
Notes:	Received three weeks confinement in 1942 for adultery		

Camp Service: **Buchenwald, 1938-1941**

Rumpenhorst

First Name:	Julius	*National Archive File:*	A3343 SSO-55B
Birthdate:	9 August 1904	*Birthplace:*	Ahlen-Westphalia
Rank:	SS-Obersturmführer	*SS Number:*	96637
NSDAP Number:	2169614	*Highest Decoration:*	War Service Cross 1st Class
Religion:	Agnostic	*Marital Status:*	Married
Waffen-SS:	6th SS Division "Nord", 1943 26th SS Division (Ung. Nr. 2), 1945		
Notes:	Former salesman		

Camp Service: **Oranienburg, 1943-1945**

Ruopp

First Name:	Dr. Karl	*National Archive File:*	A3343 SSO-056B
Birthdate:	24 April 1891	*Birthplace:*	Mengen
Rank:	SS-Untersturmführer	*SS Number:*	225554
NSDAP Number:	3224308	*Highest Decoration:*	None listed
Religion:	Protestant	*Marital Status:*	Married
Waffen-SS:	No		
Notes:	Iron Cross 1st Class, Wound Badge WWI Medical discharge		

Camp Service: **Mauthausen, 1939-1940**

Ruppert

First Name:	Wilhelm	*National Archive File:*	A3343 SSO-056B
Birthdate:	2 February 1905	*Birthplace:*	Frankenthal
Rank:	SS-Obersturmführer	*SS Number:*	7282
NSDAP Number:	414280	*Highest Decoration:*	None listed
Religion:	Agnostic	*Marital Status:*	Married
Waffen-SS:	No		
Notes:	Electrical engineer at Dachau Executed 28 May 1946		

Camp Service: **Dachau, 1933-1942** **Majdanek, 1942-1944**
Dachau, 1944-1945

Saalbach

First Name:	Rudolf	*National Archive File:*	A3343 SSO-057B
Birthdate:	18 March 1911	*Birthplace:*	Grossenhain
Rank:	SS-Sturmbannführer	*SS Number:*	127697
NSDAP Number:	1375011	*Highest Decoration:*	Knight's Cross
Religion:	Agnostic	*Marital Status:*	Married
Waffen-SS:	5th SS Division "Wiking", 1942-1943		
	11th SS Division "Nordland", 1944		
Notes:	Reconnaissance battalion commander; missing in action April 1945		

Camp Service: **Elbe, 1935-1937**
Dachau, 1938

Sack

First Name:	Gerhard	*National Archive File:*	A3343 SSO-058B
Birthdate:	2 March 1909	*Birthplace:*	Leipzig
Rank:	SS-Sturmbannführer	*SS Number:*	17980
NSDAP Number:	321288	*Highest Decoration:*	Iron Cross 1st Class
Religion:	Agnostic	*Marital Status:*	Single
Waffen-SS:	16th SS Division "Reichsführer-SS", 1943-1944		
Notes:	Battery commander in 16th SS Division artillery		

Camp Service: **Sachsenburg, 1934**

Sand

First Name:	Michael	*National Archive File:*	A3343 SSO-060B
Birthdate:	20 December 1916	*Birthplace:*	Leoben, Austria
Rank:	SS-Hauptsturmführer	*SS Number:*	276953
NSDAP Number:	Not a member	*Highest Decoration:*	War Service Cross 2nd Class
Religion:	Protestant	*Marital Status:*	Married
Waffen-SS:	10th SS Division "Frundsberg", 1943-1944		
	17th SS Division "Götz von Berlichingen", 1944		
Notes:	Former salesman		
	Served in Hitler Youth 1932-1936		

Camp Service: **Sachsenhausen, 1939-1940**
Oranienburg, 1940-1941
Mauthausen, 1941-1943

Sansoni

First Name:	Richard	*National Archive File:*	A3343 SSO-061B
Birthdate:	7 January 1902	*Birthplace:*	Eisleben
Rank:	SS-Standartenführer	*SS Number:*	261907
NSDAP Number:	519295	*Highest Decoration:*	Iron Cross 2nd Class
Religion:	Protestant	*Marital Status:*	Divorced
Waffen-SS:	3rd SS Division "Totenkopf", 1939-1941		
Notes:	Commander 3rd SS Division signal battalion		

Camp Service: **Oranienburg, 1937**

Sator

First Name:	Emil-Adolf	*National Archive File:*	A3343 SSO-062B
Birthdate:	26 July 1905	*Birthplace:*	Wuerzburg
Rank:	SS-Obersturmbannführer	*SS Number:*	11736
NSDAP Number:	597947	*Highest Decoration:*	None listed
Religion:	Agnostic	*Marital Status:*	Married
Waffen-SS:	No		
Notes:	Guard troops at Dachau		

Camp Service: **Dachau, 1936-1937**

Sauer

First Name:	Albert	*National Archive File:*	A3343 SSO-063B
Birthdate:	17 August 1898	*Birthplace:*	Misdroy
Rank:	SS-Sturmbannführer	*SS Number:*	19180
NSDAP Number:	862698	*Highest Decoration:*	None listed
Religion:	Lutheran	*Marital Status:*	Married
Waffen-SS:	No		
Notes:	*Kommandant* Mauthausen, Riga, Sulza and Ravensbrück		
	Killed in action 3 May 1945		

Camp Service: **Columbia Haus, 1935** **Sulza, 1937**
Sachsenhausen, 1937-1938 **Mauthausen, 1938-1939**
Auschwitz, 1943 **Ravensbrück, 1945**

Sauer

First Name:	Julius	*National Archive File:*	A3343 SSO-063B
Birthdate:	4 December 1905	*Birthplace:*	Waldbuettelbrunn
Rank:	SS-Untersturmführer	*SS Number:*	67798
NSDAP Number:	2677170	*Highest Decoration:*	War Service Cross 2nd Class
Religion:	Catholic	*Marital Status:*	Married
Waffen-SS:	No		
Notes:	Works department at Dachau		

Camp Service: **Dachau, 1943**

Sautter

First Name:	Dr. Erich	*National Archive File:*	A3343 SSO-063B
Birthdate:	8 August 1905	*Birthplace:*	Bad Cannstatt
Rank:	SS-Hauptsturmführer	*SS Number:*	143341
NSDAP Number:	2875526	*Highest Decoration:*	None listed
Religion:	Protestant	*Marital Status:*	Married
Waffen-SS:	No		
Notes:	Dentist at Auschwitz		

Camp Service: **Auschwitz, 1942**

Schaaf

First Name:	Hans	*National Archive File:*	A3343 SSO-063B
Birthdate:	4 January 1906	*Birthplace:*	Koblenz-Wallersheim
Rank:	SS-Obersturmführer	*SS Number:*	75254
NSDAP Number:	1834448	*Highest Decoration:*	War Service Cross 2nd Class
Religion:	Catholic	*Marital Status:*	Single
Waffen-SS:	2nd SS Division "Das Reich", 1942		
Notes:	Assigned to the butcher company supply unit in "Das Reich"		

Camp Service: **Dachau, 1944**
Bergen-Belsen, 1944

Scharf

First Name:	Norbert	*National Archive File:*	A3343 SSO-070B
Birthdate:	7 January 1901	*Birthplace:*	Breslau
Rank:	SS-Standartenführer	*SS Number:*	2473
NSDAP Number:	67694	*Highest Decoration:*	War Service Cross 2nd Class
Religion:	Agnostic	*Marital Status:*	Married
Waffen-SS:	7th SS Division "Prinz Eugen", 1943		
Notes:	Guard troops at Buchenwald; Golden Party Badge		

Camp Service: **Dachau, 1934**
Buchenwald, 1940-1941
Oranienburg, 1941

Schattenberg

First Name:	Dr. Heinz	*National Archive File:*	A3343 SSO-071B
Birthdate:	26 January 1906	*Birthplace:*	Nienhagen
Rank:	SS-Obersturmführer (F)	*SS Number:*	Unknown
NSDAP Number:	Not a member	*Highest Decoration:*	None listed
Religion:	Agnostic	*Marital Status:*	Married
Waffen-SS:	No		
Notes:	Economist; camp service not listed in personnel file		

Camp Service: **Auschwitz, 1943-1944**

Schatz

First Name:	Dr. Willi	*National Archive File:*	A3343 SSO-071B
Birthdate:	1 February 1905	*Birthplace:*	Hannover
Rank:	SS-Untersturmführer	*SS Number:*	Unknown
NSDAP Number:	Not a member	*Highest Decoration:*	None listed
Religion:	Agnostic	*Marital Status:*	Married
Waffen-SS:	No		
Notes:	Dentist; camp service not listed in personnel file; thrown out of NSDAP in 1937 Acquitted in post-war trial		

Camp Service: **Auschwitz, 1944**
Neuengamme, 1944-1945

Scheffe

First Name:	Walter	*National Archive File:*	A3343 SSO-72B
Birthdate:	3 January 1908	*Birthplace:*	Mudersbach
Rank:	SS-Obersturmführer	*SS Number:*	456854
NSDAP Number:	3029789	*Highest Decoration:*	War Service Cross 2nd Class
Religion:	Agnostic	*Marital Status:*	Married
Waffen-SS:	No		
Notes:	Former salesman; guards detachment Natzweiler		

Camp Service: **Oranienburg, 1944**
Natzweiler, 1944

Scheingraber

First Name:	Heinrich	*National Archive File:*	A3343 SSO-073B
Birthdate:	8 February 1900	*Birthplace:*	Munich
Rank:	SS-Obersturmbannführer	*SS Number:*	10000
NSDAP Number:	571915	*Highest Decoration:*	Iron Cross 1st Class
Religion:	Agnostic	*Marital Status:*	Married
Waffen-SS:	27th SS Division "Langemarck", 1944		
Notes:	Commander IIIrd Totenkopfsturmbann, 1st Totenkopfstandarte		

Camp Service: **Dachau, 1934-1935**

Schellong

First Name:	Konrad	*National Archive File:*	A3343 SSO-074B
Birthdate:	7 February 1910	*Birthplace:*	Dresden
Rank:	SS-Obersturmbannführer	*SS Number:*	135553
NSDAP Number:	1428412	*Highest Decoration:*	Knight's Cross
Religion:	Agnostic	*Marital Status:*	Married
Waffen-SS:	27th SS Division "Langemarck", 1944		
Notes:	Commander Sturmbrigade Langemarck		
	Wounded in action three times		

Camp Service: **Sachsenburg, 1935**

Schemmel

First Name:	Alfred	*National Archive File:*	A3343 SSO-074B
Birthdate:	29 July 1905	*Birthplace:*	Hermannstadt, Romania
Rank:	SS-Hauptsturmführer	*SS Number:*	430416
NSDAP Number:	Not a member	*Highest Decoration:*	War Service Cross 2nd Class
Religion:	Protestant	*Marital Status:*	Married
Waffen-SS:	27th SS Division "Langemarck", 1944		
Notes:	7th SS Sturmbann guard unit at Auschwitz		

Camp Service: **Auschwitz, 1942-1944**

Schenck

First Name: Dr. Ernst-Guenther　　*National Archive File:* A3343 SSO-074B
Birthdate: 3 August 1904　　*Birthplace:* Marburg
Rank: SS-Obersturmbannführer　　*SS Number:* 353139
NSDAP Number: Not a member　　*Highest Decoration:* Iron Cross 2nd Class
Religion: Protestant　　*Marital Status:* Single
Waffen-SS: 1st SS Division "Leibstandarte Adolf Hitler", 1941-1942
Notes: Visited Mauthausen to conduct medical experiments

Camp Service: **Mauthausen**

Schenk

First Name: Dr. Werner von　　*National Archive File:* A3343 SSO-074B
Birthdate: 27 July 1912　　*Birthplace:* Heilbronn
Rank: SS-Untersturmführer　　*SS Number:* 252362
NSDAP Number: 7278391　　*Highest Decoration:* Iron Cross 2nd Class
Religion: Protestant　　*Marital Status:* Married
Waffen-SS: No
Notes: Camp doctor at Stutthof

Camp Service: **Stutthof, 1939-1941**

Scherbel

First Name: Dr. Kurt　　*National Archive File:* A3343 SSO-075B
Birthdate: 28 January 1912　　*Birthplace:* Kronach
Rank: SS-Hauptsturmführer　　*SS Number:* 83734
NSDAP Number: 3213992　　*Highest Decoration:* War Service Cross 2nd Class
Religion: Catholic　　*Marital Status:* Single
Waffen-SS: 9th SS Division "Hohenstaufen", 1943-1944
18th SS Division "Horst Wessel", 1945
Notes: Camp service not listed in personnel file

Camp Service: **Auschwitz, 1942**

Scheungraber

First Name: Wilhelm　　*National Archive File:* A3343 SSO-076B
Birthdate: 1 July 1911　　*Birthplace:* Munich
Rank: SS-Sturmbannführer　　*SS Number:* 31077
NSDAP Number: 935628　　*Highest Decoration:* Iron Cross 2nd Class
Religion: Agnostic　　*Marital Status:* Married
Waffen-SS: 3rd SS Division "Totenkopf", 1941-1944
Notes: 1st Schutzhaftlagerführer at Mauthausen

Camp Service: **Lichtenburg, 1935**　　**Mauthausen, 1938-1939**

Schiedlausky

First Name:	Dr. Gerhard	*National Archive File:*	A3343 SSO-076B
Birthdate:	14 January 1906	*Birthplace:*	Berlin
Rank:	SS-Hauptsturmführer	*SS Number:*	213323
NSDAP Number:	617194	*Highest Decoration:*	War Service Cross 1st Class
Religion:	Protestant	*Marital Status:*	Married
Waffen-SS:	No		
Notes:	Sentenced to death		
	Camp doctor Mauthausen, Ravensbrück		

Camp Service: **Dachau, 1941** **Mauthausen, 1941**
Ravensbrück, 1941-1943 **Natzweiler, 1943**
Buchenwald, 1943

Schildbach

First Name:	Dr. Fritz	*National Archive File:*	A3343 SSO-077B
Birthdate:	24 September 1913	*Birthplace:*	Dresden
Rank:	SS-Hauptsturmführer	*SS Number:*	367764
NSDAP Number:	Not a member	*Highest Decoration:*	Iron Cross 2nd Class
Religion:	Unknown	*Marital Status:*	Single
Waffen-SS:	16th SS Division "Reichsführer-SS", 1944		
Notes:	Served 6 weeks arrest for having sexual relations with a Polish women		

Camp Service: **Dachau**
Mauthausen

Schindler

First Name:	Hans	*National Archive File:*	A3343 SSO-078B
Birthdate:	15 June 1907	*Birthplace:*	Amstetten
Rank:	SS-Obersturmführer	*SS Number:*	300975
NSDAP Number:	614858	*Highest Decoration:*	War Service Cross 2nd Class
Religion:	Agnostic	*Marital Status:*	Unknown
Waffen-SS:	No		
Notes:	Adjutant Guard Battalion		
	Camp service not listed in personnel file		

Camp Service: **Auschwitz, 1942-1943**

Schippel

First Name:	Helmut	*National Archive File:*	A3343 SSO-079B
Birthdate:	17 September 1913	*Birthplace:*	Oberschlemm
Rank:	SS-Obersturmführer	*SS Number:*	282228
NSDAP Number:	2960646	*Highest Decoration:*	Iron Cross 2nd Class
Religion:	Protestant	*Marital Status:*	Married
Waffen-SS:	Yes, unit unknown		
Notes:	Former draftsman		
	Wounded in action three times; served in SA 1933-1935		

Camp Service: **Auschwitz, 1943-1944**

Schitli

First Name:	Wilhelm	*National Archive File:*	A3343 SSO-079B
Birthdate:	26 June 1912	*Birthplace:*	Osnabrueck
Rank:	SS-Hauptsturmführer	*SS Number:*	88647
NSDAP Number:	2907236	*Highest Decoration:*	War Service Cross 1st Class
Religion:	Catholic	*Marital Status:*	Married
Waffen-SS:	20th SS Division		
Notes:	Schutzhaftlagerführer at Neuengamme		
	Kommandant for one month Arbeitsdorf		

Camp Service: **Sachsenhausen, 1938-1940   Neuengamme, 1940-1942**
Arbeitsdorf, 1942

Schlachter

First Name:	August	*National Archive File:*	A3343 SSO-079B
Birthdate:	25 January 1901	*Birthplace:*	Barabein
Rank:	SS-Hauptsturmführer	*SS Number:*	128820
NSDAP Number:	2339579	*Highest Decoration:*	None listed
Religion:	Catholic	*Marital Status:*	Married
Waffen-SS:	No		
Notes:	Construction office		

Camp Service: **Auschwitz, 1940**
Natzweiler, 1942-1943
Dora, 1945

Schlechl

First Name:	Johann	*National Archive File:*	A3343 SSO-80B
Birthdate:	4 February 1897	*Birthplace:*	Innsbruck, Austria
Rank:	SS-Standartenführer	*SS Number:*	17065
NSDAP Number:	624164	*Highest Decoration:*	War Service Cross 1st Class
Religion:	Agnostic	*Marital Status:*	Married
Waffen-SS:	5th SS Division "Wiking", 1941-1944		
	8th SS Division "Florian Geyer", 1944		
Notes:	Wounded in WWI; wounded in action WWII		

Camp Service: **Esterwegen, 1934-1935**
Buchenwald, 1939

Schlegel

First Name:	Dr. Wolfgang	*National Archive File:*	A3343 SSO-080B
Birthdate:	7 April 1913	*Birthplace:*	Gelsenkirchen
Rank:	SS-Sturmbannführer	*SS Number:*	323799
NSDAP Number:	968345	*Highest Decoration:*	Iron Cross 2nd Class
Religion:	Agnostic	*Marital Status:*	Married
Waffen-SS:	3rd SS Division "Totenkopf", 1941		
	13th SS Division "Handschar", 1943-1944		
Notes:	Prior army service as regimental doctor 28th Mountain Regiment		

Camp Service: **Dachau, 1939-1941**

Schleifenbaum

First Name:	Hermann	*National Archive File:*	A3343 SSO-080B
Birthdate:	8 May 1908	*Birthplace:*	Weidenau
Rank:	SS-Sturmbannführer	*SS Number:*	309085
NSDAP Number:	Not a member	*Highest Decoration:*	Iron Cross 1st Class
Religion:	Catholic	*Marital Status:*	Married
Waffen-SS:	3rd SS Division "Totenkopf", 1939-1940		
	8th SS Division "Florian Geyer", 1942		
	6th SS Division "Nord", 1942		
Notes:	Dismissed from SS in 1942; recommended for German Cross in Gold		

Camp Service: **Oranienburg, 1939**

Schlorf

First Name:	Dr. Joachim	*National Archive File:*	A3343 SSO-081B
Birthdate:	6 February 1908	*Birthplace:*	Roebel
Rank:	SS-Hauptsturmführer	*SS Number:*	68519
NSDAP Number:	998963	*Highest Decoration:*	None listed
Religion:	Protestant	*Marital Status:*	Married
Waffen-SS:	No		
Notes:	Dentist		

Camp Service: **Neuengamme, 1942-1943**

Schlosser

First Name:	Dr. Hans	*National Archive File:*	A3343 SSO-081B
Birthdate:	3 November 1901	*Birthplace:*	Ulbersdorf
Rank:	SS-Standartenführer	*SS Number:*	58529
NSDAP Number:	1024025	*Highest Decoration:*	War Service Cross 2nd Class
Religion:	Agnostic	*Marital Status:*	Married
Waffen-SS:	3rd SS Division "Totenkopf", 1941		
	2nd SS Infantry Brigade, 1942-1943		
	11th SS Division "Nordland", 1943-1944		
Notes:	Division surgeon, 11th SS Division		

Camp Service: **Buchenwald, 1939-1941**

Schlueter

First Name:	Dr. Friedrich	*National Archive File:*	A3343 SSO-082B
Birthdate:	12 May 1913	*Birthplace:*	Essen
Rank:	SS-Hauptsturmführer	*SS Number:*	347132
NSDAP Number:	Not a member	*Highest Decoration:*	Iron Cross 1st Class
Religion:	Protestant	*Marital Status:*	Married
Waffen-SS:	1st SS Infantry Brigade		
Notes:	Doctor		

Camp Service: **Auschwitz, 1941**

Schmelz

First Name:	Dr. Kurt	*National Archive File:*	A3343 SSO-083B
Birthdate:	5 October 1907	*Birthplace:*	Frankfurt
Rank:	SS-Hauptsturmführer	*SS Number:*	122511
NSDAP Number:	536315	*Highest Decoration:*	None listed
Religion:	Protestant	*Marital Status:*	Married
Waffen-SS:	8th SS Division "Florian Geyer", 1942-1944		
Notes:	Dentist		

Camp Service: **Dachau, 1941**

Schmick

First Name:	Dr. Hugo	*National Archive File:*	A3343 SSO-083B
Birthdate:	30 March 1909	*Birthplace:*	Gelsenkirchen
Rank:	SS-Obersturmbannführer	*SS Number:*	84693
NSDAP Number:	3681138	*Highest Decoration:*	Iron Cross 2nd Class
Religion:	Protestant	*Marital Status:*	Married
Waffen-SS:	5th SS Division "Wiking", 1943		
	6th SS Division "Nord", 1944		
	3rd SS Division "Totenkopf"		
Notes:	Camp doctor at Dachau		

Camp Service: **Dachau**   **Sachsenhausen, 1939**

Schmid

First Name:	Emeran	*National Archive File:*	A3343 SSO-083B
Birthdate:	22 December 1901	*Birthplace:*	Munich
Rank:	SS-Obersturmbannführer	*SS Number:*	34
NSDAP Number:	5428	*Highest Decoration:*	Golden Party Badge
Religion:	Catholic	*Marital Status:*	Widower
Waffen-SS:	No		
Notes:	One of the earliest SS members; member 34; Blood Order #601 Schutzhaftlagerführer at Esterwegen		

Camp Service: **Esterwegen, 1935-1936**

Schmid

First Name:	Hanns	*National Archive File:*	No File
Birthdate:	23 June 1903	*Birthplace:*	Munich
Rank:	SS-Untersturmführer	*SS Number:*	18977
NSDAP Number:	676617	*Highest Decoration:*	None listed
Religion:	Unknown	*Marital Status:*	Unknown
Waffen-SS:	Unknown		

Camp Service: **Columbia Haus, 1934**

Schmid

First Name:	Max	*National Archive File:*	A3343 SSO-083B
Birthdate:	28 April 1907	*Birthplace:*	Munich
Rank:	SS-Obersturmführer	*SS Number:*	19692
NSDAP Number:	786907	*Highest Decoration:*	War Service Cross 2nd Class
Religion:	Catholic	*Marital Status:*	Married
Waffen-SS:	No		
Notes:	Missing in action 5 January 1944 due to partisan action		
	Guard troops at Dachau		

Camp Service: **Dachau, 1933-1940**

Schmidetzki

First Name:	Walter	*National Archive File:*	A3343 SSO-084B
Birthdate:	5 January 1913	*Birthplace:*	Sohrau
Rank:	SS-Untersturmführer	*SS Number:*	224469
NSDAP Number:	Not a member	*Highest Decoration:*	War Service Cross 2nd Class
Religion:	Catholic	*Marital Status:*	Married
Waffen-SS:	No		
Notes:	In charge of depot where victims belongings were held; executed		

Camp Service: **Hinzert, 1944**　　　　**Flossenbürg, 1944**
　　　　　　　　Auschwitz, 1944　　　**Natzweiler, 1945**

Schmidt

First Name:	Bernhard	*National Archive File:*	A3343 SSO-084B
Birthdate:	18 April 1890	*Birthplace:*	Pegnitz
Rank:	SS-Standartenführer	*SS Number:*	2069
NSDAP Number:	14699	*Highest Decoration:*	War Service Cross 2nd Class
Religion:	Agnostic	*Marital Status:*	Married
Waffen-SS:	No		
Notes:	Iron Cross 1st Class WWI; Golden Party Badge		
	Kommandant Lichtenburg, Sachsenburg		

Camp Service: **Lichtenburg, 1934-1935**　　　**Sachsenburg, 1936-1937**
　　　　　　　　Sachsenhausen, 1937-1938　　　**Dachau, 1938**

Schmidt

First Name:	Dr. Fritz	*National Archive File:*	A3343 SSO-085B
Birthdate:	2 September 1902	*Birthplace:*	Wesel
Rank:	SS-Obersturmführer	*SS Number:*	223104
NSDAP Number:	2335276	*Highest Decoration:*	War Service Cross 2nd Class
Religion:	Catholic	*Marital Status:*	Married
Waffen-SS:	No		
Notes:	Former lawyer		
	Spoke English and French		

Camp Service: **Sachsenhausen, 1943-1944**

Schmidt

First Name:	Dr. Heinrich	*National Archive File:*	A3343 SSO-086B
Birthdate:	27 March 1912	*Birthplace:*	Altenburg
Rank:	SS-Hauptsturmführer	*SS Number:*	23069
NSDAP Number:	555294	*Highest Decoration:*	War Service Cross 2nd Class
Religion:	Protestant	*Marital Status:*	Married
Waffen-SS:	No		
Notes:	Doctor		
	Served in Hitler Youth 1931		

Camp Service: **Buchenwald, 1942**
Majdanek, 1943-1944
Dora, 1944

Schmidt

First Name:	Dr. Karl	*National Archive File:*	A3343 SSO-086B
Birthdate:	15 April 1913	*Birthplace:*	Riebelsdorf
Rank:	SS-Untersturmführer	*SS Number:*	350471
NSDAP Number:	2828748	*Highest Decoration:*	None listed
Religion:	Agnostic	*Marital Status:*	Married
Waffen-SS:	No		
Notes:	Dentist		

Camp Service: **Auschwitz**
Gross-Rosen, 1944

Schmidt

First Name:	Hans-Theodor	*National Archive File:*	A3343 SSO-085B
Birthdate:	25 December 1899	*Birthplace:*	Hoexter
Rank:	SS-Hauptsturmführer	*SS Number:*	115662
NSDAP Number:	1246794	*Highest Decoration:*	War Service Cross 2nd Class
Religion:	Protestant	*Marital Status:*	Married
Waffen-SS:	No		
Notes:	Iron Cross 2nd Class WWI; Guard troops at Buchenwald; adjutant at Hinzert		
	Executed 7 June 1951		

Camp Service: **Hinzert, 1940-1941**
Buchenwald, 1941

Schmidt

First Name:	Wilhelm	*National Archive File:*	A3343 SSO-088B
Birthdate:	29 February 1912	*Birthplace:*	Bretten
Rank:	SS-Obersturmführer	*SS Number:*	165775
NSDAP Number:	4271515	*Highest Decoration:*	Wound Badge in Black
Religion:	Protestant	*Marital Status:*	Married
Waffen-SS:	Italian Volunteer Legion, 1944		
Notes:	Wounded in action		
	Spoke English and French		

Camp Service: **Sachsenhausen, 1943**

Schmitt

First Name:	Philipp	*National Archive File:*	A3343 SSO-089B
Birthdate:	20 November 1902	*Birthplace:*	Bad Kissingen
Rank:	SS-Sturmbannführer	*SS Number:*	44291
NSDAP Number:	19192	*Highest Decoration:*	None listed
Religion:	Agnostic	*Marital Status:*	Married
Waffen-SS:	No		
Notes:	Also served in Jewish collection camp at Necheln		
	Executed 1950		

Camp Service: **Breendonk, 1940-1944**

Schmitz

First Name:	Dr. Emil	*National Archive File:*	A3343 SSO-089B
Birthdate:	1 July 1914	*Birthplace:*	Remscheid
Rank:	SS-Obersturmführer	*SS Number:*	162492
NSDAP Number:	2879347	*Highest Decoration:*	None listed
Religion:	Unknown	*Marital Status:*	Single
Waffen-SS:	No		
Notes:	Doctor		

Camp Service: **Sachsenhausen, 1942**

Schmorell

First Name:	Hermann	*National Archive File:*	A3343 SSO-090B
Birthdate:	12 August 1910	*Birthplace:*	Orenburg, Russia
Rank:	SS-Sturmbannführer	*SS Number:*	2255
NSDAP Number:	192527	*Highest Decoration:*	Iron Cross 2nd Class
Religion:	Protestant	*Marital Status:*	Married
Waffen-SS:	1st SS Infantry Brigade, 1941		
	6th SS Division "Nord", 1941		
	3rd SS Division "Totenkopf", 1943		
Notes:	Received Silver Wound Badge; severely wounded in the head		
	Battalion commander and division adjutant 3rd SS Division		

Camp Service: **Columbia Haus, 1935**
Dachau, 1935

Schmutzler

First Name:	Kurt	*National Archive File:*	A3343 SSO-090B
Birthdate:	17 November 1895	*Birthplace:*	Elsterberg/Plauen
Rank:	SS-Hauptsturmführer	*SS Number:*	153980
NSDAP Number:	5101486	*Highest Decoration:*	War Service Cross 2nd Class
Religion:	Protestant	*Marital Status:*	Married
Waffen-SS:	Unknown		
Notes:	Iron Cross 2nd Class WWI; executed 29 October 1948		

Camp Service: **Mauthausen, 1940**

Schnabel

First Name:	Dr. Alfred	*National Archive File:*	A3343 SSO-090B
Birthdate:	11 March 1888	*Birthplace:*	Wuenschelburg
Rank:	SS-Sturmbannführer	*SS Number:*	188285
NSDAP Number:	1937902	*Highest Decoration:*	War Service Cross 2nd Class
Religion:	Catholic	*Marital Status:*	Married
Waffen-SS:	No		
Notes:	Iron Cross 2nd Class WWI		

Camp Service: **Flossenbürg, 1942-1944**
Bergen-Belsen, 1944

Schnabel

First Name:	Helmut	*National Archive File:*	No File
Birthdate:	Unknown	*Birthplace:*	Unknown
Rank:	Unknown	*SS Number:*	Unknown
NSDAP Number:	Not a member	*Highest Decoration:*	None listed
Religion:	Unknown	*Marital Status:*	Unknown
Waffen-SS:	Unknown		

Camp Service: **Viavara**

Schneider

First Name:	Jakob	*National Archive File:*	A3343 SSO-092B
Birthdate:	17 December 1903	*Birthplace:*	Schlitz
Rank:	SS-Obersturmführer	*SS Number:*	9332
NSDAP Number:	391340	*Highest Decoration:*	War Service Cross 2nd Class
Religion:	Protestant	*Marital Status:*	Married
Waffen-SS:	16th SS Division "Reichsführer-SS", 1943		
Notes:	Served in SA 1930-1931		

Camp Service: **Hinzert, 1940**
Mauthausen

Schneider

First Name:	Max	*National Archive File:*	A3343 SSO-092B
Birthdate:	5 June 1910	*Birthplace:*	Freiburg
Rank:	SS-Obersturmführer	*SS Number:*	262531
NSDAP Number:	4719248	*Highest Decoration:*	War Service Cross 2nd Class
Religion:	Protestant	*Marital Status:*	Married
Waffen-SS:	No		
Notes:	Former typesetter		

Camp Service: **Buchenwald**
Natzweiler, 1942
Mauthausen, 1943

Schneider

First Name:	Oswald	*National Archive File:*	A3343 SSO-092B
Birthdate:	28 July 1912	*Birthplace:*	Neu Titschein
Rank:	SS-Untersturmführer	*SS Number:*	12016
NSDAP Number:	611189	*Highest Decoration:*	War Service Cross 1st Class
Religion:	Agnostic	*Marital Status:*	Married
Waffen-SS:	9th SS Division "Hohenstaufen", 1944		
Notes:	Served in Hitler Youth 1927-1929 Served in SA 1929-1931		

Camp Service: **Oranienburg, 1937-1940**

Schneider

First Name:	Rudolf	*National Archive File:*	A3343 SSO-092B
Birthdate:	2 October 1910	*Birthplace:*	Essen
Rank:	SS-Obersturmbannführer	*SS Number:*	33064
NSDAP Number:	1292445	*Highest Decoration:*	German Cross in Gold
Religion:	Agnostic	*Marital Status:*	Married
Waffen-SS:	3rd SS Division "Totenkopf", 1941-1943		
Notes:	Killed in action 6 July 1943 at Kursk Battalion commander in 3rd SS Division		

Camp Service: **Sachsenhausen, 1938**

Schneider

First Name:	Wolfram	*National Archive File:*	A3343 SSO-093B
Birthdate:	12 November 1912	*Birthplace:*	Plauen
Rank:	SS-Surmbannführer	*SS Number:*	23593
NSDAP Number:	819945	*Highest Decoration:*	Iron Cross 1st Class
Religion:	Agnostic	*Marital Status:*	Married
Waffen-SS:	3rd SS Division "Totenkopf", 1940-1943		
Notes:	Wound Badge in Silver; left arm amputated		

Camp Service: **Dachau, 1935**
Sachsenburg, 1936
Oranienburg, 1937-1939

Schneier

First Name:	Reinhold	*National Archive File:*	A3343 SSO-093B
Birthdate:	18 November 1895	*Birthplace:*	Stettin
Rank:	SS-Obersturmführer	*SS Number:*	278952
NSDAP Number:	3779803	*Highest Decoration:*	War Service Cross 2nd Class
Religion:	Agnostic	*Marital Status:*	Married
Waffen-SS:	1st SS Division "Leibstandarte Adolf Hitler", 1941 6th SS Division "Nord", 1944		
Notes:	Camp service not listed in personnel file		

Camp Service: **Auschwitz**

Schnettler

First Name:	Wittekind	*National Archive File:*	A3343 SSO-093A
Birthdate:	25 July 1914	*Birthplace:*	Hamburg
Rank:	SS-Sturmbannführer	*SS Number:*	48264
NSDAP Number:	1502195	*Highest Decoration:*	Iron Cross 1st Class
Religion:	Agnostic	*Marital Status:*	Married
Waffen-SS:	2nd SS Division "Das Reich", 1939-1941		
	5th SS Division "Wiking", 1941-1942		
Notes:	Guard troops at Dachau; adjutant IIIrd Bn, 1st Totenkopfstandarte "Oberbayern"		
	Wounded in action		

Camp Service: **Dachau, 1936-1937**

Schobert

First Name:	Max	*National Archive File:*	A3343 SSO-094B
Birthdate:	25 December 1904	*Birthplace:*	Wuerzburg
Rank:	SS-Sturmbannführer	*SS Number:*	3531
NSDAP Number:	317486	*Highest Decoration:*	War Service Cross 1st Class
Religion:	Protestant	*Marital Status:*	Widower
Waffen-SS:	No		
Notes:	Schutzhaftlagerführer at Dachau; wife and five children killed in air raid		
	Executed 19 November 1948		

Camp Service: **Dachau, 1935**   **Flossenbürg, 1938-1939**
              Buchenwald, 1939-1941

Schoeffel

First Name:	Hans	*National Archive File:*	A3343 SSO-095B
Birthdate:	1 October 1912	*Birthplace:*	Wolgast
Rank:	SS-Hauptsturmführer	*SS Number:*	67753
NSDAP Number:	1997993	*Highest Decoration:*	None listed
Religion:	Agnostic	*Marital Status:*	Married
Waffen-SS:	3rd SS Division "Totenkopf", 1944		
Notes:	Received Gold Honor Badge of Hitler Youth		

Camp Service: **Oranienburg, 1937-1940**

Schoening

First Name:	Fritz	*National Archive File:*	A3343 SSO-097B
Birthdate:	10 March 1890	*Birthplace:*	Hamburg
Rank:	SS-Hauptsturmführer	*SS Number:*	207630
NSDAP Number:	3300084	*Highest Decoration:*	War Service Cross 2nd Class
Religion:	Protestant	*Marital Status:*	Married
Waffen-SS:	No		
Notes:	Iron Cross 2nd Class WWI		

Camp Service: **Sachsenhausen, 1940**
              Oranienburg
              Flossenbürg

Schoenlein

First Name:	Heinz	*National Archive File:*	A3343 SSO-097B
Birthdate:	12 January 1907	*Birthplace:*	Radebeul
Rank:	SS-Obersturmführer	*SS Number:*	4730
NSDAP Number:	302423	*Highest Decoration:*	None listed
Religion:	Agnostic	*Marital Status:*	Married
Waffen-SS:	3rd SS Division "Totenkopf", 1942-1944		
Notes:	Camp service not listed in personnel file		

Camp Service: **Auschwitz**

Schoenthaler

First Name:	Dr. Friedrich	*National Archive File:*	A3343 SSO-097B
Birthdate:	29 February 1887	*Birthplace:*	Karlsruhe
Rank:	SS-Obersturmbannführer	*SS Number:*	148981
NSDAP Number:	5200222	*Highest Decoration:*	None listed
Religion:	Protestant	*Marital Status:*	Married
Waffen-SS:	No		
Notes:	Iron Cross 2nd Class WWI		

Camp Service: **Niederhagen, 1942**

Schoenwetter

First Name:	Karl	*National Archive File:*	A3343 SSO-097B
Birthdate:	18 August 1902	*Birthplace:*	Neufraunhofen, Austria
Rank:	SS-Sturmbannführer	*SS Number:*	17166
NSDAP Number:	865256	*Highest Decoration:*	None listed
Religion:	Agnostic	*Marital Status:*	Married
Waffen-SS:	No		
Notes:	Camp service not listed in personnel file		

Camp Service: **Breendonk, 1944-1945**

Schoepperle

First Name:	Karl	*National Archive File:*	A3343 SSO-097B
Birthdate:	23 June 1892	*Birthplace:*	Triberg
Rank:	SS-Obersturmführer	*SS Number:*	110510
NSDAP Number:	1817025	*Highest Decoration:*	War Service Cross 2nd Class
Religion:	Catholic	*Marital Status:*	Married
Waffen-SS:	No		
Notes:	Iron Cross 2nd Class WWI		
	Executed 12 November 1948		

Camp Service: **Mauthausen, 1940**

Schoettl

First Name:	Vinzenz	*National Archive File:*	A3343 SSO-097B
Birthdate:	30 June 1905	*Birthplace:*	Appersdorf
Rank:	SS-Obersturmführer	*SS Number:*	5630
NSDAP Number:	104083	*Highest Decoration:*	War Service Cross 2nd Class
Religion:	Catholic	*Marital Status:*	Married
Waffen-SS:	No		
Notes:	Lagerführer at Kaufering sub-camp; executed 28 May 1946		

Camp Service: **Neuengamme, 1941**
Auschwitz, 1944-1945
Dachau, 1945

Schoor

First Name:	Otto	*National Archive File:*	A3343 SSO-098B
Birthdate:	28 January 1909	*Birthplace:*	Wuerzburg
Rank:	SS-Sturmbannführer	*SS Number:*	337715
NSDAP Number:	Not a member	*Highest Decoration:*	Iron Cross 1st Class
Religion:	Agnostic	*Marital Status:*	Married
Waffen-SS:	3rd SS Division "Totenkopf", 1941-1945		
Notes:	Camp dentist at Dachau; Wounded in action several times in Russia		

Camp Service: **Oranienburg, 1940**
Dachau, 1940-1941

Schorsten

First Name:	Guenther	*National Archive File:*	A3343 SSO-099B
Birthdate:	12 April 1916	*Birthplace:*	Hermannstadt, Romania
Rank:	SS-Hauptsturmführer	*SS Number:*	382544
NSDAP Number:	Not a member	*Highest Decoration:*	Iron Cross 2nd Class
Religion:	Protestant	*Marital Status:*	Single
Waffen-SS:	SS Infantry Regiment 9, 1942		
Notes:	Doctor		

Camp Service: **Dachau, 1941**

Schott

First Name:	Martin	*National Archive File:*	A3343 SSO-099B
Birthdate:	25 January 1900	*Birthplace:*	Dittersbach-Gruessau
Rank:	SS-Untersturmführer	*SS Number:*	340059
NSDAP Number:	Not a member	*Highest Decoration:*	None listed
Religion:	Protestant	*Marital Status:*	Married
Waffen-SS:	No		
Notes:	Served in police 1923-1935		

Camp Service: **Buchenwald, 1939-1942**

Schottes

First Name:	Michael	*National Archive File:*	A3343 SSO-099B
Birthdate:	6 March 1903	*Birthplace:*	Grossmoyeuvre
Rank:	SS-Sturmbannführer	*SS Number:*	262220
NSDAP Number:	2881338	*Highest Decoration:*	War Service Cross 1st Class
Religion:	Catholic	*Marital Status:*	Married
Waffen-SS:	8th SS Division "Florian Geyer", 1941-1942		
	1st SS Infantry Brigade, 1942-1943		
	18th SS Division "Horst Wessel", 1944		
Notes:	Administration troops		

Camp Service: **Esterwegen, 1936**   **Sachsenburg, 1937**
Buchenwald, 1938

Schrader

First Name:	Kurt	*National Archive File:*	A3343 SSO-099B
Birthdate:	21 October 1911	*Birthplace:*	Koeslin
Rank:	SS-Hauptsturmführer	*SS Number:*	403609
NSDAP Number:	5970733	*Highest Decoration:*	None listed
Religion:	Agnostic	*Marital Status:*	Married
Waffen-SS:	24th SS Division, 1944		
	6th SS Division "Nord"		
Notes:	Pharmacist		

Camp Service: **Ravensbrück, 1941**

Schramm

First Name:	Kuno	*National Archive File:*	A3343 SSO-100B
Birthdate:	11 May 1905	*Birthplace:*	Zella
Rank:	SS-Obersturmführer	*SS Number:*	71638
NSDAP Number:	2553999	*Highest Decoration:*	Iron Cross 2nd Class
Religion:	Agnostic	*Marital Status:*	Single
Waffen-SS:	No		
Notes:	Vernehmungsführer at Dachau		
	Arbeitseinsatzführer at Neuengamme		

Camp Service: **Dachau, 1941**   **Gross-Rosen, 1941**
Majdanek, 1942   **Neuengamme, 1943-1944**

Schroedel

First Name:	Wilfried	*National Archive File:*	A3343 SSO-101B
Birthdate:	30 October 1913	*Birthplace:*	Darmstadt
Rank:	SS-Obersturmführer	*SS Number:*	131288
NSDAP Number:	5546240	*Highest Decoration:*	Iron Cross 1st Class
Religion:	Agnostic	*Marital Status:*	Single
Waffen-SS:	3rd SS Division "Totenkopf", 1940-1941		
Notes:	Killed in action 17 August 1941 in Russia		

Camp Service: **Oranienburg, 1938**

Schroeder

First Name:	Dr. Otto	*National Archive File:*	A3343 SSO-102B
Birthdate:	23 August 1903	*Birthplace:*	Quern
Rank:	SS-Hauptsturmführer	*SS Number:*	50450
NSDAP Number:	992544	*Highest Decoration:*	None listed
Religion:	Protestant	*Marital Status:*	Married
Waffen-SS:	No		
Notes:	Chief doctor at Lichtenburg		

Camp Service: **Lichtenburg, 1935-1936**
Sachsenhausen, 1936
Oranienburg, 1937

Schroeder

First Name:	Hermann	*National Archive File:*	A3343 SSO-102B
Birthdate:	20 November 1895	*Birthplace:*	Bantorf
Rank:	SS-Obersturmbannführer	*SS Number:*	270783
NSDAP Number:	2081265	*Highest Decoration:*	War Service Cross 1st Class
Religion:	Unknown	*Marital Status:*	Married
Waffen-SS:	No		
Notes:	Training and Education Officer at Buchenwald		
	Later commander of an SS technical engineer school		

Camp Service: **Buchenwald, 1939-1941**

Schubert

First Name:	Alois	*National Archive File:*	A3343 SSO-103B
Birthdate:	13 May 1912	*Birthplace:*	Bergan-Wildschuetz
Rank:	SS-Obersturmführer	*SS Number:*	Unknown
NSDAP Number:	6735807	*Highest Decoration:*	None listed
Religion:	Catholic	*Marital Status:*	Married
Waffen-SS:	No		
Notes:	Leader of work commando Steinbruch at Flossenbürg; Executed 3 October 1947		
	Served in Czech army 1934-1936		

Camp Service: **Flossenbürg**

Schuettauf

First Name:	Erich	*National Archive File:*	A3343 SSO-107B
Birthdate:	21 February 1887	*Birthplace:*	Dresden
Rank:	SS-Obersturmführer	*SS Number:*	172513
NSDAP Number:	530214	*Highest Decoration:*	War Service Cross 2nd Class
Religion:	Protestant	*Marital Status:*	Married
Waffen-SS:	No		
Notes:	Iron Cross 2nd Class WWI; Guard Company commander at Gusen sub-camp of Mauthausen; died in prison 1 January 1952		

Camp Service: **Flossenbürg, 1940-1941   Mauthausen, 1941-1944**

Schuetz

First Name:	Walter	*National Archive File:*	A3343 SSO-108B
Birthdate:	24 July 1904	*Birthplace:*	Coburg
Rank:	SS-Hauptsturmführer	*SS Number:*	104277
NSDAP Number:	2529810	*Highest Decoration:*	War Service Cross 2nd Class
Religion:	Protestant	*Marital Status:*	Married
Waffen-SS:	No		
Notes:	Joined SS in 1933; served in SA 1923-1925		

Camp Service: **Oranienburg, 1941   Mauthausen, 1941-1944   Auschwitz, 1944**

Schuetze

First Name:	Bruno	*National Archive File:*	A3343 SSO-108B
Birthdate:	15 September 1914	*Birthplace:*	Braunschweig
Rank:	SS-Hauptsturmführer	*SS Number:*	131659
NSDAP Number:	4198106	*Highest Decoration:*	Iron Cross 2nd Class
Religion:	Agnostic	*Marital Status:*	Married
Waffen-SS:	3rd SS Division "Totenkopf", 1939-1940		
	6th SS Division "Nord", 1942-1944		
	17th SS Division "Götz von Berlichingen", 1945		
Notes:	Company commander in 6th SS Division; wounded in action 1944		
	2nd SS Totenkopfstandarte "Brandenburg"		

Camp Service: **Oranienburg, 1938-1939**

Schuller

First Name:	Dr. Andreas	*National Archive File:*	A3343 SSO-110B
Birthdate:	22 November 1913	*Birthplace:*	Petersberg, Romania
Rank:	SS-Sturmbannführer	*SS Number:*	310483
NSDAP Number:	Not a member	*Highest Decoration:*	War Service Cross 1st Class
Religion:	Protestant	*Marital Status:*	Married
Waffen-SS:	No		
Notes:	Later served in field laboratory for bacteriology in the Ukraine		

Camp Service: **Sachsenhausen, 1939**

Schulte

First Name:	Dr. Wilhelm	*National Archive File:*	A3343 SSO-110B
Birthdate:	27 March 1907	*Birthplace:*	Elberfeld
Rank:	SS-Hauptsturmführer	*SS Number:*	236174
NSDAP Number:	5379284	*Highest Decoration:*	War Service Cross 2nd Class
Religion:	Protestant	*Marital Status:*	Married
Waffen-SS:	19th SS Division, 1944		
Notes:	Dentist		

Camp Service: **Auschwitz, 1941-1942**

Schultz

First Name:	Dr. Carl	*National Archive File:*	A3343 SSO-111B
Birthdate:	24 December 1910	*Birthplace:*	Hamburg
Rank:	SS-Hauptsturmführer	*SS Number:*	179483
NSDAP Number:	4491341	*Highest Decoration:*	War Service Cross 2nd Class
Religion:	Protestant	*Marital Status:*	Married
Waffen-SS:	8th SS Division "Florian Geyer", 1942		
	IInd SS Corps, 1944		
Notes:	Camp doctor at Neuengamme		

Camp Service: **Neuengamme, 1940**
Wewelsburg, 1941-1942

Schultz

First Name:	Dr. Erich	*National Archive File:*	No File
Birthdate:	Unknown	*Birthplace:*	Unknown
Rank:	SS-Obersturmführer	*SS Number:*	250187
NSDAP Number:	Not a member	*Highest Decoration:*	None listed
Religion:	Unknown	*Marital Status:*	Unknown
Waffen-SS:	Unknown		
Notes:	Camp doctor at Neuengamme		

Camp Service: **Neuengamme, 1940**

Schultz

First Name:	Ernst	*National Archive File:*	A3343 SSO-111B
Birthdate:	13 March 1908	*Birthplace:*	Berlin
Rank:	SS-Obersturmführer	*SS Number:*	382533
NSDAP Number:	Not a member	*Highest Decoration:*	None listed
Religion:	Agnostic	*Marital Status:*	Single
Waffen-SS:	3rd SS Division "Totenkopf", 1940-1944		
Notes:	Former mechanic		

Camp Service: **Oranienburg, 1944-1945**

Schulz

First Name:	Karl	*National Archive File:*	A3343 SSO-113B
Birthdate:	9 September 1902	*Birthplace:*	Eberswalde
Rank:	SS-Obersturmführer	*SS Number:*	400037
NSDAP Number:	Not a member	*Highest Decoration:*	None listed
Religion:	Agnostic	*Marital Status:*	Married
Waffen-SS:	No		
Notes:	Leader of Poloitical department at Mauthausen		

Camp Service: **Mauthausen, 1941**

Schulze

First Name:	Ernst	*National Archive File:*	A3343 SSO-115B
Birthdate:	18 July 1899	*Birthplace:*	Koenigshuette
Rank:	SS-Obersturmbannführer	*SS Number:*	308278
NSDAP Number:	4358364	*Highest Decoration:*	None listed
Religion:	Agnostic	*Marital Status:*	Married
Waffen-SS:	No		
Notes:	Released from SS in 1936; rejoined		
	Iron Cross 2nd Class, Wound Badge WWI		

Camp Service: **Dachau, 1936**

Schulze

First Name:	Richard	*National Archive File:*	A3343 SSO-117B
Birthdate:	2 October 1914	*Birthplace:*	Berlin-Spandau
Rank:	SS-Obersturmführer	*SS Number:*	264059
NSDAP Number:	Not a member	*Highest Decoration:*	German Cross in Gold
Religion:	Agnostic	*Marital Status:*	Single
Waffen-SS:	1st SS Division "Leibstandarte Adolf Hitler"		
Notes:	Served as Eicke's adjutant		
	Later SS adjutant to von Ribbentrop		

Camp Service: **Lichtenburg, 1937**   **Oranienburg, 1938**
                 Buchenwald, 1939

Schumacher

First Name:	Erwin	*National Archive File:*	A3343 SSO-117B
Birthdate:	29 May 1913	*Birthplace:*	Ebingen
Rank:	SS-Obersturmbannführer	*SS Number:*	111811
NSDAP Number:	5020931	*Highest Decoration:*	Iron Cross 2nd Class
Religion:	Agnostic	*Marital Status:*	Single
Waffen-SS:	3rd SS Division "Totenkopf", 1941-1943		
	IIIrd SS Corps, 1943-1944		
Notes:	Communications officer		
	Signal battalion commander in IIIrd SS Corps		

Camp Service: **Dachau, 1937-1939**

Schumann

First Name:	Dr. Horst	*National Archive File:*	No File
Birthdate:	11 May 1906	*Birthplace:*	Halle
Rank:	SS-Sturmbannführer	*SS Number:*	Unknown
NSDAP Number:	190002	*Highest Decoration:*	None listed
Religion:	Unknown	*Marital Status:*	Unknown
Waffen-SS:	No		
Notes:	Conducted medical experiments at Auschwitz		
	Died 5 May 1983		

Camp Service: **Auschwitz, 1942, 1944**

Schurz

First Name: Hans
Birthdate: 28 December 1913
Rank: SS-Untersturmführer
NSDAP Number: Not a member
Religion: Catholic
Waffen-SS: No
Notes: Auschwitz political department
Missing in action December 1944

National Archive File: A3343 SSO-119B
Birthplace: St. Salvator, Austria
SS Number: 385370
Highest Decoration: War Service Cross 2nd Class
Marital Status: Single

Camp Service: **Auschwitz, 1943-1944**

Schwald

First Name: Anton
Birthdate: 13 March 1892
Rank: SS-Obersturmführer
NSDAP Number: 39362
Religion: Agnostic
Waffen-SS: 13th SS Division "Handschar", 1944
Notes: Iron Cross 2nd Class WWI

National Archive File: A3343 SSO-121B
Birthplace: Ludwigsburg
SS Number: 284525
Highest Decoration: Golden Party Badge
Marital Status: Married

Camp Service: **Sachsenhausen, 1941-1942**
Auschwitz, 1942

Schwartz

First Name: Albert
Birthdate: 11 May 1905
Rank: SS-Hauptsturmführer
NSDAP Number: 228771
Religion: Agnostic
Waffen-SS: No
Notes: Sentenced to Life imprisonment; released

National Archive File: A3343 SSO-121B
Birthplace: Schwarzenau
SS Number: 6532
Highest Decoration: War Service Cross 2nd Class
Marital Status: Married

Camp Service: **Stutthof, 1941**
Buchenwald

Schwarz

First Name: Gottfried
Birthdate: Unknown
Rank: SS-Untersturmführer
NSDAP Number: Not a member
Religion: Unknown
Waffen-SS: Unknown
Notes: Promoted to officer rank for *Operation Reinhard*

National Archive File: A3343 SSO-121B
Birthplace: Unknown
SS Number: Unknown
Highest Decoration: None listed
Marital Status: Unknown

Camp Service: **Belzec, 1942**

Schwarz

First Name:	Heinrich	*National Archive File:*	A3343 SSO-122B
Birthdate:	14 June 1906	*Birthplace:*	Munich
Rank:	SS-Hauptsturmführer	*SS Number:*	19691
NSDAP Number:	786871	*Highest Decoration:*	War Service Cross 1st Class
Religion:	Catholic	*Marital Status:*	Married
Waffen-SS:	No		
Notes:	*Kommandant* Natzweiler and Auschwitz-Monowitz; executed 20 March 1947		

Camp Service: **Mauthausen, 1939-1941** **Oranienburg, 1941**
Auschwitz, 1941-1945 **Natzweiler, 1945**

Schwarz

First Name:	Ludwig	*National Archive File:*	A3343 SSO-122B
Birthdate:	21 May 1899	*Birthplace:*	Unknown
Rank:	SS-Hauptsturmführer	*SS Number:*	Unknown
NSDAP Number:	Not a member	*Highest Decoration:*	None listed
Religion:	Catholic	*Marital Status:*	Unknown
Waffen-SS:	No		
Notes:	Executed 3 October 1947		
	Kommandant Hersbruck sub-camp		

Camp Service: **Flossenbürg**
Dachau

Schwarzhuber

First Name:	Johann	*National Archive File:*	A3343 SSO-123B
Birthdate:	28 August 1904	*Birthplace:*	Tuetzing
Rank:	SS-Obersturmführer	*SS Number:*	142388
NSDAP Number:	1929969	*Highest Decoration:*	War Service Cross 2nd Class
Religion:	Agnostic	*Marital Status:*	Married
Waffen-SS:	No		
Notes:	Lagerführer at Auschwitz		
	Executed 3 May 1947		

Camp Service: **Sachsenhausen, 1938-1942** **Dachau, 1944**
Auschwitz, 1944-1945 **Ravensbrück, 1945**

Schwela

First Name:	Dr. Siegfried	*National Archive File:*	A3343 SSO-125B
Birthdate:	3 May 1905	*Birthplace:*	Cottbus
Rank:	SS-Hauptsturmführer	*SS Number:*	Unknown
NSDAP Number:	Not a member	*Highest Decoration:*	None listed
Religion:	Unknown	*Marital Status:*	Unknown
Waffen-SS:	No		
Notes:	Died of typhus at Auschwitz 10 May 1942		

Camp Service: **Auschwitz, 1941-1942**

Schwoegler

First Name:	Robert	*National Archive File:*	A3343 SSO-127B
Birthdate:	13 July 1901	*Birthplace:*	Mannheim
Rank:	SS-Untersturmführer	*SS Number:*	276190
NSDAP Number:	5020937	*Highest Decoration:*	None listed
Religion:	Unknown	*Marital Status:*	Married
Waffen-SS:	No		
Notes:	Died in an automobile accident 2 July 1939		

Camp Service: **Dachau, 1937**
Buchenwald, 1938

Seehaus

First Name:	Martin	*National Archive File:*	A3343 SSO-128B
Birthdate:	29 November 1898	*Birthplace:*	Bieberstein
Rank:	SS-Untersturmführer	*SS Number:*	27565
NSDAP Number:	621521	*Highest Decoration:*	None listed
Religion:	Unknown	*Marital Status:*	Married
Waffen-SS:	No		
Notes:	Degraded and thrown out of the SS in 1938		

Camp Service: **Esterwegen, 1933**

Seel

First Name:	Wilhelm	*National Archive File:*	A3343 SSO-129B
Birthdate:	2 August 1885	*Birthplace:*	Aglasterhausen
Rank:	SS-Obersturmführer	*SS Number:*	4672
NSDAP Number:	166139	*Highest Decoration:*	None listed
Religion:	Catholic	*Marital Status:*	Married
Waffen-SS:	No		
Notes:	Iron Cross 2nd Class WWI		

Camp Service: **Dachau, 1939-1944**

Seidl

First Name:	Dr. Siegfried	*National Archive File:*	A3343 SSO-131B
Birthdate:	24 August 1911	*Birthplace:*	Tulln, Austria
Rank:	SS-Hauptsturmführer	*SS Number:*	46106
NSDAP Number:	300738	*Highest Decoration:*	None listed
Religion:	Catholic	*Marital Status:*	Married
Waffen-SS:	No		
Notes:	*Kommandant* Theresienstadt		
	Executed February 1947		

Camp Service: **Theresienstadt, 1941-1943**
Bergen-Belsen, 1943

Seidler

First Name:	Fritz	*National Archive File:*	A3343 SSO-131B
Birthdate:	18 July 1907	*Birthplace:*	Werdau
Rank:	SS-Hauptsturmführer	*SS Number:*	135387
NSDAP Number:	3693999	*Highest Decoration:*	None listed
Religion:	Protestant	*Marital Status:*	Married
Waffen-SS:	No		
Notes:	Camp engineer		

Camp Service: **Sachsenhausen, 1938-1940**
Auschwitz, 1940
Mauthausen, 1944

Seifert

First Name:	Dr. Gustav	*National Archive File:*	A3343 SSO-131B
Birthdate:	11 April 1885	*Birthplace:*	Neundorf
Rank:	SS-Hauptsturmführer	*SS Number:*	128213
NSDAP Number:	3388	*Highest Decoration:*	War Service Cross 2nd Class
Religion:	Protestant	*Marital Status:*	Married
Waffen-SS:	No		
Notes:	Awarded Golden Party Badge		

Camp Service: **Mauthausen, 1940-1944**
Neuengamme, 1944

Seitschek

First Name:	Dr. Robert	*National Archive File:*	A3343 SSO-132B
Birthdate:	29 July 1917	*Birthplace:*	Vienna, Austria
Rank:	SS-Hauptsturmführer	*SS Number:*	367375
NSDAP Number:	Not a member	*Highest Decoration:*	Iron Cross 2nd Class
Religion:	Catholic	*Marital Status:*	Married
Waffen-SS:	2nd SS Infantry Brigade, 1942		
	10th SS Division "Frundsberg", 1943-1944		
Notes:	Wounded 1944		

Camp Service: **Oranienburg, 1941**   **Flossenbürg, 1941**
Mauthausen, 1941

Seitz

First Name:	Kurt	*National Archive File:*	A3343 SSO-132B
Birthdate:	9 June 1907	*Birthplace:*	Karlsruhe
Rank:	SS-Hauptsturmführer	*SS Number:*	14405
NSDAP Number:	473319	*Highest Decoration:*	War Service Cross 2nd Class
Religion:	Protestant	*Marital Status:*	Married
Waffen-SS:	No		
Notes:	Administration leader at Ravensbrück		

Camp Service: **Sulza, 1936-1937**   **Sachsenhausen, 1937-1938**
Lichtenburg, 1938-1939   **Ravensbrück, 1940-1943**
Herzogenbusch, 1943-1944

Sell

First Name:	Max	*National Archive File:*	A3343 SSO-133B
Birthdate:	8 January 1893	*Birthplace:*	Kiel
Rank:	SS-Obersturmführer	*SS Number:*	35889
NSDAP Number:	704095	*Highest Decoration:*	War Service Cross 2nd Class
Religion:	Protestant	*Marital Status:*	Married
Waffen-SS:	No		
Notes:	Iron Cross 2nd Class WWI		

Camp Service: **Ravensbrück, 1942**
Auschwitz, 1943
Dora, 1945

Semenow

First Name:	Nikolai	*National Archive File:*	A3343 SSO-133B
Birthdate:	17 February 1901	*Birthplace:*	Dorpat, Russia
Rank:	SS-Hauptsturmführer	*SS Number:*	Unknown
NSDAP Number:	Not a member	*Highest Decoration:*	War Service Cross 2nd Class
Religion:	Protestant	*Marital Status:*	Married
Waffen-SS:	No		
Notes:	Camp service not listed in personnel file		

Camp Service: **Auschwitz, 1943**

Sendel

First Name:	Wilhelm	*National Archive File:*	A3343 RS-F5281
Birthdate:	26 March 1913	*Birthplace:*	Recklinghausen
Rank:	SS-Obersturmführer	*SS Number:*	4346
NSDAP Number:	371897	*Highest Decoration:*	None listed
Religion:	Catholic	*Marital Status:*	Married
Waffen-SS:	Unknown		

Camp Service: **Columbia Haus, 1935**

Sette

First Name:	Ernst	*National Archive File:*	A3343 SSO-134B
Birthdate:	3 October 1893	*Birthplace:*	Unknown
Rank:	SS-Hauptsturmführer	*SS Number:*	Unknown
NSDAP Number:	Not a member	*Highest Decoration:*	None listed
Religion:	Unknown	*Marital Status:*	Unknown
Waffen-SS:	No		
Notes:	Probably honorary SS member		

Camp Service: **Stutthof, 1944-1945**

Sewera

First Name:	Joseph	*National Archive File:*	A3343 SSO-134B
Birthdate:	22 November 1905	*Birthplace:*	Winterberg
Rank:	SS-Hauptsturmführer	*SS Number:*	334818
NSDAP Number:	Not a member	*Highest Decoration:*	War Service Cross 2nd Class
Religion:	Catholic	*Marital Status:*	Single
Waffen-SS:	No		
Notes:	Former teacher		
	Served in Czech army 1925-1927		

Camp Service: **Oranienburg, 1940-1943**

Sibeth

First Name:	Dr. Fedor	*National Archive File:*	A3343 SSO-134B
Birthdate:	3 October 1907	*Birthplace:*	Gleiwitz
Rank:	SS-Sturmbannführer	*SS Number:*	277251
NSDAP Number:	482892	*Highest Decoration:*	None listed
Religion:	Agnostic	*Marital Status:*	Single
Waffen-SS:	7th SS Division "Prinz Eugen", 1942		
	3rd Estonian SS Brigade, 1943		
	XIIth SS Corps, 1944		
Notes:	Camp doctor at Lichtenburg		

Camp Service: **Lichtenburg, 1938**
Dachau, 1941

Siedler

First Name:	Johann	*National Archive File:*	A3343 SSO-135B
Birthdate:	27 December 1894	*Birthplace:*	Troppau, Austria
Rank:	SS-Obersturmführer	*SS Number:*	331666
NSDAP Number:	Not a member	*Highest Decoration:*	None listed
Religion:	Catholic	*Marital Status:*	Married
Waffen-SS:	12th SS Division "Hitlerjugend", 1944		
Notes:	Former teacher at girl's school; wounded in WWI		

Camp Service: **Buchenwald, 1939-1941**

Siegmann

First Name:	Wilhelm	*National Archive File:*	A3343 SSO-135B
Birthdate:	16 August 1898	*Birthplace:*	Oebisfelde
Rank:	SS-Hauptsturmführer	*SS Number:*	49125
NSDAP Number:	413945	*Highest Decoration:*	None listed
Religion:	Protestant	*Marital Status:*	Married
Waffen-SS:	No		
Notes:	Department VI at Majdanek; Iron Cross 2nd Class WWI		

Camp Service: **Neuengamme, 1941**
Auschwitz, 1941
Ravensbrück, 1941
Majdanek, 1943

Sieling

First Name: Heinz
Birthdate: 2 May 1914
Rank: SS-Untersturmführer
NSDAP Number: 4137222
Religion: Agnostic
Waffen-SS: No
Notes: Court-martialed during war

National Archive File: A3343 SSO-136B
Birthplace: Berlin
SS Number: 256271
Highest Decoration: None listed
Marital Status: Married

Camp Service: **Buchenwald, 1938**

Siggelkow

First Name: Herbert
Birthdate: 17 November 1906
Rank: SS-Hauptsturmführer
NSDAP Number: 914845
Religion: Unknown
Waffen-SS: No
Notes: Pharmacist in Department DIII, Oranienburg

National Archive File: A3343 SSO-137B
Birthplace: Schleswig
SS Number: 222606
Highest Decoration: None listed
Marital Status: Unknown

Camp Service: **Oranienburg, 1943**

Simke

First Name: Willi
Birthdate: 26 January 1914
Rank: SS-Obersturmführer
NSDAP Number: Not a member
Religion: Agnostic
Waffen-SS: SS Infantry Regiment 4, 1940-1942
2nd SS Division "Das Reich, 1942-1944
Notes: Wounded in action

National Archive File: A3343 SSO-137B
Birthplace: Belgern
SS Number: 133099
Highest Decoration: Knight's Cross
Marital Status: Married

Camp Service: **Lichtenburgk, 1933**
Buchenwald, 1938-1939
Oranienburg, 1939

Simon

First Name: Josef
Birthdate: 7 January 1906
Rank: SS-Untersturmführer
NSDAP Number: 6484347
Religion: Agnostic
Waffen-SS: Yes, unknown
Notes: Dental technician; wounded in action

National Archive File: A3343 SSO-138B
Birthplace: Gablonz
SS Number: 315500
Highest Decoration: Iron Cross 2nd Class
Marital Status: Married

Camp Service: **Auschwitz, 1942-1943**
Dachau, 1943

Simon

First Name:	Max	*National Archive File:*	A3343 SSO-138B
Birthdate:	6 January 1899	*Birthplace:*	Breslau
Rank:	SS-Gruppenführer	*SS Number:*	83086
NSDAP Number:	1359567	*Highest Decoration:*	Knight's Cross with Oak Leaves
Religion:	Protestant	*Marital Status:*	Married

Waffen-SS: 3rd SS Division "Totenkopf", 1941-1943
16th SS Division "Reichsführer-SS", 1943-1944
XIIIth SS Corps, 1944-1945

Notes: Commander 16th SS Division and XIIIth SS Corps; died February 2, 1961

Camp Service: **Sachsenburg, 1935-1937**   **Dachau, 1937-1939**

Sitzmann

First Name:	Richard	*National Archive File:*	A3343 SSO-139B
Birthdate:	30 April 1903	*Birthplace:*	Forchheim
Rank:	SS-Obersturmführer	*SS Number:*	107552
NSDAP Number:	Not a member	*Highest Decoration:*	None listed
Religion:	Unknown	*Marital Status:*	Unknown
Waffen-SS:	No		

Notes: Construction Department Stutthof
Camp service not listed in personnel file

Camp Service: **Stutthof**

Skierka

First Name:	Bruno	*National Archive File:*	A3343 SSO-139B
Birthdate:	3 March 1897	*Birthplace:*	Danzig
Rank:	SS-Untersturmführer	*SS Number:*	166786
NSDAP Number:	2273409	*Highest Decoration:*	War Service Cross 2nd Class
Religion:	Agnostic	*Marital Status:*	Married
Waffen-SS:	No		

Notes: Guard company commander; Iron Cross 2nd Class, Silver Wound Badge WWI
Executed 3 October 1947

Camp Service: **Flossenbürg, 1945**

Soeldner

First Name:	Otto	*National Archive File:*	A3343 RS-F5361
Birthdate:	4 June 1895	*Birthplace:*	Bamberg
Rank:	SS-Obersturmführer	*SS Number:*	277085
NSDAP Number:	Not a member	*Highest Decoration:*	None listed
Religion:	Agnostic	*Marital Status:*	Married
Waffen-SS:	No		

Notes: Arbeiteinsatzführer at Neuengamme; acting kommandant at Ravensbrück
Died 9 July 1943

Camp Service: **Flossenbürg, 1938**   **Ravensbrück, 1940-1941**
Neuengamme, 1941-1943

Sommer

First Name:	Karl	*National Archive File:*	A3343 SSO-142B
Birthdate:	25 March 1915	*Birthplace:*	Cologne
Rank:	SS-Hauptsturmführer	*SS Number:*	130199
NSDAP Number:	Not a member	*Highest Decoration:*	War Service Cross 1st Class
Religion:	Agnostic	*Marital Status:*	Married
Waffen-SS:	Unknown		

Notes: Received Iron Cross 2nd Class and Wound Badge for combat early in the war
Served as acting chief Department DII, Oranienburg
Originally sentenced to Death; sentence reduced to twenty years

Camp Service: **Sachsenhausen**   **Oranienburg**

Sommerfeld

First Name:	Hermann	*National Archive File:*	A3343 SSO-142B
Birthdate:	31 October 1891	*Birthplace:*	Eichfier
Rank:	SS-Obersturmführer	*SS Number:*	Unknown
NSDAP Number:	Not a member	*Highest Decoration:*	None listed
Religion:	Unknown	*Marital Status:*	Married
Waffen-SS:	No		

Notes: Evacuated prisoners from Flossenbürg at end of war
Sentenced to 15 years imprisonment

Camp Service: **Flossenbürg, 1945**

Sonntag

First Name:	Dr. Walter	*National Archive File:*	A3343 SSO-143B
Birthdate:	13 May 1907	*Birthplace:*	Meto
Rank:	SS-Hauptsturmführer	*SS Number:*	257328
NSDAP Number:	2683413	*Highest Decoration:*	War Service Cross 2nd Class
Religion:	Catholic	*Marital Status:*	Single
Waffen-SS:	3rd SS Division "Totenkopf", 1941-1942		

Notes: Dentist

Camp Service: **Sachsenhausen, 1939**
Ravensbrück, 1940-1941

Sorge

First Name:	Alfred	*National Archive File:*	A3343 SSO-143B
Birthdate:	15 August 1911	*Birthplace:*	Lueckow
Rank:	SS-Hauptsturmführer	*SS Number:*	34915
NSDAP Number:	182477	*Highest Decoration:*	War Service Cross 1st Class
Religion:	Agnostic	*Marital Status:*	Married
Waffen-SS:	No		

Notes: Construction department at Buchenwald

Camp Service: **Buchenwald**
Sachsenhausen

Sorge

First Name:	Dr. Hans-Hermann	*National Archive File:*	A3343 SSO-143B
Birthdate:	4 April 1912	*Birthplace:*	Koenigsee
Rank:	SS-Hauptsturmführer	*SS Number:*	411935
NSDAP Number:	Not a member	*Highest Decoration:*	None listed
Religion:	Unknown	*Marital Status:*	Single
Waffen-SS:	No		
Notes:	Doctor		

Camp Service: **Sachsenhausen, 1941-1942**

Speck

First Name:	Friedrich	*National Archive File:*	A3343 SSO-145B
Birthdate:	14 July 1889	*Birthplace:*	Pforzheim
Rank:	SS-Untersturmführer	*SS Number:*	6072
NSDAP Number:	270768	*Highest Decoration:*	None listed
Religion:	Protestant	*Marital Status:*	Married
Waffen-SS:	No		
Notes:	Former goldsmith		

Camp Service: **Dachau, 1940**

Sperling

First Name:	Herbert	*National Archive File:*	A3343 SSO-146B
Birthdate:	1 January 1914	*Birthplace:*	Berlin-Spandau
Rank:	SS-Sturmbannführer	*SS Number:*	83427
NSDAP Number:	Not a member	*Highest Decoration:*	Iron Cross 1st Class
Religion:	Agnostic	*Marital Status:*	Married
Waffen-SS:	5th SS Division "Wiking", 1941		
	2nd SS Division "Das Reich", 1942-1944		
	3rd SS Division "Totenkopf", 1944		
Notes:	2nd Administration officer at Sachsenhausen and Mauthausen		
	Awarded Panzer Badge in Bronze		

Camp Service: **Sachsenhausen, 1938**
Mauthausen, 1938-1940

Spiess

First Name:	Georg	*National Archive File:*	No File
Birthdate:	12 June 1900	*Birthplace:*	Unknown
Rank:	SS-Obersturmführer	*SS Number:*	9199
NSDAP Number:	454568	*Highest Decoration:*	None listed
Religion:	Unknown	*Marital Status:*	Unknown
Waffen-SS:	Unknown		

Camp Service: **Dachau, 1935**

Sporrenberg

First Name: Paul
Birthdate: 27 March 1896
Rank: SS-Hauptsturmführer
NSDAP Number: 25561
Religion: Agnostic
Waffen-SS: Unknown
Notes: *Kommandant* Hinzert
Iron Cross 2nd Class WWI; Golden Party Badge; died 1961

National Archive File: A3343 SSO-147B
Birthplace: Venlo, Netherlands
SS Number: 180233
Highest Decoration: Iron Cross 1st Class
Marital Status: Married

Camp Service: **Hinzert, 1940**

Stahlmann

First Name: Albert
Birthdate: 28 January 1911
Rank: SS-Sturmbannführer
NSDAP Number: 231401
Religion: Agnostic
Waffen-SS: 2nd SS Division "Das Reich", 1941-1942
Notes: Wounded in action
Education Officer, 3rd SS Totenkopfstandarte

National Archive File: A3343 SSO-148B
Birthplace: Mannheim
SS Number: 11199
Highest Decoration: War Service Cross 2nd Class
Marital Status: Married

Camp Service: **Buchenwald, 1938-1939**

Stangl

First Name: Franz
Birthdate: 26 March 1898
Rank: SS-Hauptsturmführer
NSDAP Number: 6370447
Religion: Catholic
Waffen-SS: No
Notes: *Kommandant* Sobibór and Treblinka
Died 28 June 1971 in prison

National Archive File: A3343 SSO-149B
Birthplace: Altmuenster, Austria
SS Number: 296569
Highest Decoration: War Service Cross 1st Class
Marital Status: Married

Camp Service: **Sobibór, 1942**
Treblinka, 1942-1943

Stark

First Name: Hans
Birthdate: 14 June 1921
Rank: SS-Untersturmführer
NSDAP Number: Not a member
Religion: Protestant
Waffen-SS: No
Notes: Taught agriculture after the war
Sentenced to 10 years imprisonment

National Archive File: A3343 SSO-150B
Birthplace: Darmstadt
SS Number: 319998
Highest Decoration: War Service Cross 2nd Class
Marital Status: Single

Camp Service: **Buchenwald, 1937**   **Oranienburg, 1938**
Dachau, 1938   **Auschwitz, 1940-1943**

Steffen

First Name:	Georg	*National Archive File:*	A3343 SSO-151B
Birthdate:	27 April 1910	*Birthplace:*	Berlin
Rank:	SS-Obersturmführer	*SS Number:*	219473
NSDAP Number:	4157286	*Highest Decoration:*	War Service Cross 2nd Class
Religion:	Protestant	*Marital Status:*	Married
Waffen-SS:	9th SS Division "Hohenstaufen", 1945		
Notes:	Served in HSSPF Ostland in 1943-1944		

Camp Service: **Ravensbrück, 1944-1945**

Stehno

First Name:	Anton	*National Archive File:*	A3343 SSO-151B
Birthdate:	3 August 1913	*Birthplace:*	Laubheim
Rank:	SS-Hauptsturmführer	*SS Number:*	143448
NSDAP Number:	3939091	*Highest Decoration:*	Iron Cross 1st Class
Religion:	Agnostic	*Marital Status:*	Married
Waffen-SS:	6th SS Division "Nord", 1941-1944		
	17th SS Division "Götz von Berlichingen", 1944		
Notes:	3rd SS Totenkopfstandarte "Thüringen"		
	Killed in action 10 July 1944 in France		

Camp Service: **Buchenwald, 1938**

Steiner

First Name:	Bartholomaeus	*National Archive File:*	A3343 SSO-153B
Birthdate:	20 September 1907	*Birthplace:*	Wolferts
Rank:	SS-Hauptsturmführer	*SS Number:*	4841
NSDAP Number:	414277	*Highest Decoration:*	None listed
Religion:	Agnostic	*Marital Status:*	Married
Waffen-SS:	No		
Notes:	Guard troops at Dachau		

Camp Service: **Dachau, 1933-1934**

Steinert

First Name:	Fritz	*National Archive File:*	A3343 SSO-154B
Birthdate:	4 November 1909	*Birthplace:*	Wiesbaden
Rank:	SS-Sturmbannführer	*SS Number:*	293538
NSDAP Number:	65652	*Highest Decoration:*	Iron Cross 1st Class
Religion:	Agnostic	*Marital Status:*	Single
Waffen-SS:	5th SS Division "Wiking", 1941-1942		
Notes:	Awarded Golden Party Badge; battalion commander in 5th SS Division		
	Died of wounds 7 October 1942		

Camp Service: **Dachau, 1938-1939**

Steinhoff

First Name:	Alexander	*National Archive File:*	A3343 SSO-155B
Birthdate:	17 September 1884	*Birthplace:*	Berlin
Rank:	SS-Sturmbannführer	*SS Number:*	276906
NSDAP Number:	1145720	*Highest Decoration:*	War Service Cross 2nd Class
Religion:	Protestant	*Marital Status:*	Married
Waffen-SS:	No		
Notes:	Iron Cross 1st Class WWI		

Camp Service: **Oranienburg, 1940**

Stenger

First Name:	Franz	*National Archive File:*	A3343 SSO-157B
Birthdate:	8 May 1897	*Birthplace:*	Aschaffenburg
Rank:	SS-Obersturmführer	*SS Number:*	464033
NSDAP Number:	Not a member	*Highest Decoration:*	None listed
Religion:	Catholic	*Marital Status:*	Married
Waffen-SS:	No		
Notes:	Iron Cross 1st Class WWI		
	Commander 7th Guard Company		

Camp Service: **Auschwitz, 1943**

Stephan

First Name:	Dr. Werner	*National Archive File:*	A3343 SSO-157B
Birthdate:	27 February 1911	*Birthplace:*	Posen
Rank:	SS-Untersturmführer	*SS Number:*	291664
NSDAP Number:	601213	*Highest Decoration:*	None
Religion:	Protestant	*Marital Status:*	Single
Waffen-SS:	No		
Notes:	Dismissed from SS in 1939		

Camp Service: **Buchenwald, 1938**
Oranienburg, 1938

Stieger

First Name:	Dr. Wilhelm	*National Archive File:*	A3343 SSO-160B
Birthdate:	12 June 1910	*Birthplace:*	Essen-Werden
Rank:	SS-Obersturmführer (F)	*SS Number:*	102603
NSDAP Number:	3435642	*Highest Decoration:*	None listed
Religion:	Catholic	*Marital Status:*	Single
Waffen-SS:	3rd SS Division "Totenkopf", 1939-1940		
Notes:	Former lawyer		
	Guard battalion at Flossenbürg		

Camp Service: **Flossenbürg, 1941**

Stiller

First Name:	Edgar	*National Archive File:*	A3343 SSO-161B
Birthdate:	25 January 1904	*Birthplace:*	Hermannseifen
Rank:	SS-Untersturmführer	*SS Number:*	298149
NSDAP Number:	1622724	*Highest Decoration:*	None listed
Religion:	Protestant	*Marital Status:*	Married
Waffen-SS:	No		
Notes:	Served in police 1927-1940		

Camp Service: **Dachau, 1943**

Stocker

First Name:	Emil	*National Archive File:*	A3343 SSO-162B
Birthdate:	12 March 1902	*Birthplace:*	Zuerich, Switzerland
Rank:	SS-Hauptsturmführer	*SS Number:*	34081
NSDAP Number:	473630	*Highest Decoration:*	Iron Cross 2nd Class
Religion:	Protestant	*Marital Status:*	Married
Waffen-SS:	2nd SS Division "Das Reich", 1938-1942		
	6th SS Division "Nord", 1942		
Notes:	Former bank official		

Camp Service: **Auschwitz, 1943**   **Herzogenbusch, 1943-1944**

Stoetzler

First Name:	Wilhelm	*National Archive File:*	A3343 SSO-163B
Birthdate:	1 October 1893	*Birthplace:*	Friedrichstadt
Rank:	SS-Hauptsturmführer	*SS Number:*	225183
NSDAP Number:	3949261	*Highest Decoration:*	War Service Cross 2nd Class
Religion:	Protestant	*Marital Status:*	Married
Waffen-SS:	No		
Notes:	Iron Cross 2nd Class WWI		

Camp Service: **Sachsenhausen, 1939-1941**   **Neuengamme, 1941**
Gross-Rosen, 1944   **Kauen, 1944**

Stoever

First Name:	Johann	*National Archive File:*	A3343 SSO-163B
Birthdate:	9 August 1899	*Birthplace:*	Unknown
Rank:	SS-Untersturmführer	*SS Number:*	51190
NSDAP Number:	Not a member	*Highest Decoration:*	None listed
Religion:	Unknown	*Marital Status:*	Unknown
Waffen-SS:	No		
Notes:	1st Shutzhaftlagerführer Amersfoort		
	Honorary SS member; camp service not listed		

Camp Service: **Amersfoort, 1943**

Stoltz

First Name:	August	*National Archive File:*	A3343 SSO-163B
Birthdate:	26 November 1889	*Birthplace:*	Karlsruhe
Rank:	SS-Untersturmführer	*SS Number:*	244374
NSDAP Number:	2332868	*Highest Decoration:*	War Service Cross 2nd Class
Religion:	Protestant	*Marital Status:*	Widower
Waffen-SS:	No		
Notes:	Iron Cross 1st Class WWI		

Camp Service: **Dachau, 1943**

Stoppel

First Name:	Otto	*National Archive File:*	A3343 SSO-164B
Birthdate:	13 September 1902	*Birthplace:*	Klammer
Rank:	SS-Sturmbannführer	*SS Number:*	25564
NSDAP Number:	1050628	*Highest Decoration:*	War Service Cross 2nd Class
Religion:	Agnostic	*Marital Status:*	Married
Waffen-SS:	1st SS Division "Leibstandarte Adolf Hitler", 1941-1942		
Notes:	Served in Reichswehr 1919-1931		

Camp Service: **Auschwitz, 1943**
Gross-Rosen, 1944

Storch

First Name:	Henry	*National Archive File:*	A3343 SSO-164B
Birthdate:	7 November 1910	*Birthplace:*	Husum
Rank:	SS-Hauptsturmführer	*SS Number:*	288218
NSDAP Number:	Not a member	*Highest Decoration:*	None listed
Religion:	Protestant	*Marital Status:*	Married
Waffen-SS:	4th SS Division "Polizei", 1942-1944		
	16th SS Division "Reichsführer-SS", 1944-1945		
Notes:	Pharmacist		

Camp Service: **Auschwitz, 1941**
Dachau, 1942

Storch

First Name:	Otto	*National Archive File:*	A3343 SSO-164B
Birthdate:	25 May 1901	*Birthplace:*	Bad Liebenstein
Rank:	SS-Obersturmbannführer	*SS Number:*	13743
NSDAP Number:	259421	*Highest Decoration:*	Iron Cross 2nd Class
Religion:	Agnostic	*Marital Status:*	Married
Waffen-SS:	SS Infantry Regiment 10, 1941-1942		
Notes:	Wounded in action		
	Former book seller		

Camp Service: **Buchenwald, 1940**

Strathmann

First Name:	Horst	*National Archive File:*	A3343 SSO-164B
Birthdate:	17 May 1899	*Birthplace:*	Bad Essen
Rank:	SS-Standartenführer	*SS Number:*	25885
NSDAP Number:	261557	*Highest Decoration:*	War Service Cross 2nd Class
Religion:	Agnostic	*Marital Status:*	Married
Waffen-SS:	7th SS Division "Prinz Eugen", 1942-1943		
Notes:	Commander IInd Totenkopfsturmbann, SS-Totenkopfstandarte 10		
	Killed in action 26 November 1943; infantry battalion commander		

Camp Service: **Buchenwald, 1939-1940**

Strauss

First Name:	Xaver	*National Archive File:*	A3343 SSO-165B
Birthdate:	29 May 1910	*Birthplace:*	Velburg
Rank:	SS-Hauptsturmführer	*SS Number:*	161264
NSDAP Number:	Not a member	*Highest Decoration:*	War Service Cross 2nd Class
Religion:	Catholic	*Marital Status:*	Married
Waffen-SS:	1st SS Infantry Brigade, 1942		
Notes:	Administration leader at Mauthausen		

Camp Service: **Dachau, 1938**
Flossenbürg, 1938-1940
Mauthausen, 1940-1942

Streibel

First Name:	Karl	*National Archive File:*	A3343 SSO-166B
Birthdate:	11 October 1903	*Birthplace:*	Neustadt
Rank:	SS-Sturmbannführer	*SS Number:*	60152
NSDAP Number:	554023	*Highest Decoration:*	None listed
Religion:	Agnostic	*Marital Status:*	Married
Waffen-SS:	No		
Notes:	*Kommandant* of Trawniki		

Camp Service: **Trawniki, 1942-1944**

Streitwieser

First Name:	Anton	*National Archive File:*	A3343 SSO-166B
Birthdate:	3 July 1916	*Birthplace:*	Surheim
Rank:	SS-Untersturmführer	*SS Number:*	276125
NSDAP Number:	Not a member	*Highest Decoration:*	Iron Cross 2nd Class
Religion:	Catholic	*Marital Status:*	Divorced
Waffen-SS:	5th SS Division "Wiking", 1941-1942		
Notes:	Wounded in action; *kommandant* Melk sub-camp of Mauthausen; died 17 July 1972		

Camp Service: **Dachau, 1934-1935**   **Sachsenhausen, 1935-1936**
Esterwegen, 1936   **Sachsenhausen, 1936-1937**
Mauthausen, 1938 and 1942-1944

Strese

First Name:	Gustav	*National Archive File:*	A3343 SSO-166B
Birthdate:	29 November 1893	*Birthplace:*	Greifenhagen
Rank:	SS-Untersturmführer	*SS Number:*	27669
NSDAP Number:	470794	*Highest Decoration:*	War Service Cross 2nd Class
Religion:	Agnostic	*Marital Status:*	Widower
Waffen-SS:	No		
Notes:	Iron Cross 2nd Class WWI; butcher by trade		

Camp Service: **Niederhagen, 1942**

Strippel

First Name:	Arnold	*National Archive File:*	A3343 SSO-166B
Birthdate:	2 June 1911	*Birthplace:*	Unhausen
Rank:	SS-Obersturmführer	*SS Number:*	236290
NSDAP Number:	4330442	*Highest Decoration:*	War Service Cross 1st Class
Religion:	Agnostic	*Marital Status:*	Married
Waffen-SS:	No		
Notes:	Schutzhaftlagerführer Majdanek and Wewelsburg		
	Kommandant of two sub-camps of Neuengamme; sentenced to 10 years		

Camp Service: **Buchenwald, 1937-1941**   **Natzweiler, 1941**
Majdanek, 1941-1943   **Herzogenbusch, 1943-1944**
Neuengamme, 1944-1945

Stumpf

First Name:	Wolfgang	*National Archive File:*	A3343 SSO-168B
Birthdate:	6 August 1910	*Birthplace:*	Schesslitz/Bamberg
Rank:	SS-Obersturmführer	*SS Number:*	40629
NSDAP Number:	1320436	*Highest Decoration:*	War Service Cross 2nd Class
Religion:	Catholic	*Marital Status:*	Widower
Waffen-SS:	11th SS Division "Nordland", 1943		
	IIIrd SS Corps, 1943		
Notes:	Former salesman		

Camp Service: **Oranienburg, 1941-1942, 1943**   **Dachau, 1942**

Sturm

First Name:	Dr. Franz	*National Archive File:*	A3343 SSO-169B
Birthdate:	7 January 1908	*Birthplace:*	Troschwitz, Czechoslovakia
Rank:	SS-Sturmbannführer	*SS Number:*	310424
NSDAP Number:	Not a member	*Highest Decoration:*	None listed
Religion:	Catholic	*Marital Status:*	Married
Waffen-SS:	3rd SS Division "Totenkopf", 1942		
	10th SS Division "Frundsberg", 1943-1944		
	25th SS Division "Hunyadi", 1944-1945		
Notes:	Division doctor 25th SS Division; served in Czech Army, 1936-1938		

Camp Service: **Dachau, 1939**
Oranienburg, 1942

Stutz

First Name: Hans
Birthdate: 15 June 1910
Rank: SS-Sturmbannführer
NSDAP Number: Not a member
Religion: Unknown
Waffen-SS: 3rd SS Division "Totenkopf", 1942-1944
Notes: Surgeon

National Archive File: A3343 SSO-169B
Birthplace: Groetzingen
SS Number: 245919
Highest Decoration: German Cross in Silver
Marital Status: Single

Camp Service: **Oranienburg, 1940**

Suhren

First Name: Fritz
Birthdate: 10 June 1908
Rank: SS-Sturmbannführer
NSDAP Number: 109561
Religion: Agnostic
Waffen-SS: No
Notes: *Kommandant* Ravensbrück
Executed 12 June 1950

National Archive File: A3343 SSO-170B
Birthplace: Varel
SS Number: 14682
Highest Decoration: War Service Cross 1st Class
Marital Status: Married

Camp Service: **Sachsenhausen, 1941-1942**
Ravensbrück, 1942-1945

Sulzbach

First Name: Otto
Birthdate: 18 May 1909
Rank: SS-Sturmbannführer
NSDAP Number: 61317
Religion: Agnostic
Waffen-SS: 14th SS Division
Notes: Administration officer at Sachsenburg
Golden Party Badge

National Archive File: A3343 SSO-170B
Birthplace: Darmstadt
SS Number: 1364
Highest Decoration: Iron Cross 2nd Class
Marital Status: Single

Camp Service: **Sachsenburg, 1934-1936**

Suttrop

First Name: Rudolf-Heinrich
Birthdate: 17 July 1911
Rank: SS-Obersturmführer
NSDAP Number: 4330444
Religion: Protestant
Waffen-SS: No
Notes: Adjutant at Dachau and Gross-Rosen
Enlisted guard at Wewelsburg; executed

National Archive File: A3343 SSO-170B
Birthplace: Luenen-Horstmar
SS Number: 230953
Highest Decoration: None listed
Marital Status: Married

Camp Service: **Wewelsburg, 1940** **Gross-Rosen, 1941-1942, 1944-1945**
Dachau, 1942-1944

Taeger

First Name:	Heinrich	*National Archive File:*	A3343 SSO-171B
Birthdate:	23 February 1897	*Birthplace:*	Lippstadt
Rank:	SS-Obersturmführer	*SS Number:*	249766
NSDAP Number:	3131462	*Highest Decoration:*	None listed
Religion:	Agnostic	*Marital Status:*	Married
Waffen-SS:	No		
Notes:	Iron Cross 2nd Class WWI		

Camp Service: **Auschwitz, 1940**
Flossenbürg, 1942-1943

Tamaschke

First Name:	Guenther	*National Archive File:*	A3343 SSO-172B
Birthdate:	26 February 1896	*Birthplace:*	Berlin
Rank:	SS-Standartenführer	*SS Number:*	851
NSDAP Number:	36978	*Highest Decoration:*	Golden Party Badge
Religion:	Agnostic	*Marital Status:*	Married
Waffen-SS:	No		
Notes:	Iron Cross 1st Class WWI		

Camp Service: **Dachau, 1934**
Oranienburg, 1937
Lichtenburg, 1938-1939

Tauber

First Name:	Dr. Karl-Heinz	*National Archive File:*	No File
Birthdate:	16 December 1907	*Birthplace:*	Glogau
Rank:	SS-Hauptsturmführer	*SS Number:*	Unknown
NSDAP Number:	Not a member	*Highest Decoration:*	None listed
Religion:	Unknown	*Marital Status:*	Unknown
Waffen-SS:	Unknown		
Notes:	Dentist; served 6 years imprisonment; died 15 June 1961		

Camp Service: **Dachau, 1941-1942**
Auschwitz, 1942-1943

Taus

First Name:	Karl	*National Archive File:*	A3343 SSO-174B
Birthdate:	24 September 1893	*Birthplace:*	Gleisdorf
Rank:	SS-Brigadeführer	*SS Number:*	6786
NSDAP Number:	301353	*Highest Decoration:*	War Service Cross 1st Class
Religion:	Protestant	*Marital Status:*	Married
Waffen-SS:	No		
Notes:	Assigned to Higher SS and Police Leader Adriatic Coast 1944		
	Schutzhaftlagerfuehrer at Buchenwald		

Camp Service: **Oranienburg, 1938**
Dachau, 1938
Buchenwald, 1938

Thaler

First Name:	Dr. Hans
Birthdate:	22 January 1907
Rank:	SS-Untersturmführer
NSDAP Number:	1305717
Religion:	Agnostic
Waffen-SS:	No
Notes:	Doctor, Ohrdruf sub-camp; served in SA 1933-1937

National Archive File:	A3343 SSO-176B
Birthplace:	Mollbruecke, Austria
SS Number:	295822
Highest Decoration:	None listed
Marital Status:	Married

Camp Service: **Buchenwald, 1945**

Thate

First Name:	Werner
Birthdate:	12 January 1912
Rank:	SS-Obersturmführer
NSDAP Number:	245575
Religion:	Agnostic
Waffen-SS:	No
Notes:	Released from SS 1937
	Father killed at Verdun in WWI

National Archive File:	A3343 RS-G0201
Birthplace:	Karlsruhe
SS Number:	2971
Highest Decoration:	None listed
Marital Status:	Married

Camp Service: **Columbia Haus, 1935**

Thernes

First Name:	Anton
Birthdate:	8 February 1892
Rank:	Unknown
NSDAP Number:	Not a member
Religion:	Unknown
Waffen-SS:	Unknown
Notes:	Executed 3 December 1944

National Archive File:	No File
Birthplace:	Unknown
SS Number:	Unknown
Highest Decoration:	None listed
Marital Status:	Unknown

Camp Service: **Majdanek, 1942-1944**

Thilo

First Name:	Dr. Heinz
Birthdate:	8 October 1911
Rank:	SS-Hauptsturmführer
NSDAP Number:	404295
Religion:	Protestant
Waffen-SS:	No
Notes:	Conducted prisoner selections
	Died 13 May 1945

National Archive File:	A3343 SSO-179B
Birthplace:	Elberfeld
SS Number:	126436
Highest Decoration:	War Service Cross 2nd Class
Marital Status:	Married

Camp Service: **Auschwitz, 1942-1944**
Gross-Rosen, 1944

Thomalla

First Name:	Richard	*National Archive File:*	A3343 SSO-180B
Birthdate:	23 October 1903	*Birthplace:*	Annahof
Rank:	SS-Hauptsturmführer	*SS Number:*	41206
NSDAP Number:	1238872	*Highest Decoration:*	War Service Cross 1st Class
Religion:	Catholic	*Marital Status:*	Widower; remarried
Waffen-SS:	No		
Notes:	Construction supervisor Sobibór, Belzec and Treblinka		
	Executed by Soviet NKVD 12 May 1945, Czechoslovakia		

Camp Service: **Sobibór, 1942**   **Belzec, 1942**
Treblinka, 1942

Thomsen

First Name:	Reinhard	*National Archive File:*	A3343 SSO-181B
Birthdate:	7 February 1901	*Birthplace:*	Eckernfoerde
Rank:	SS-Obersturmführer	*SS Number:*	146483
NSDAP Number:	3144330	*Highest Decoration:*	War Service Cross 2nd Class
Religion:	Agnostic	*Marital Status:*	Married
Waffen-SS:	No		
Notes:	Commander of a guard company at Auschwitz		

Camp Service: **Auschwitz, 1940-1944**

Thumann

First Name:	Anton	*National Archive File:*	A3343 SSO-182B
Birthdate:	31 October 1912	*Birthplace:*	Pfaffenhofen
Rank:	SS-Obersturmführer	*SS Number:*	27444
NSDAP Number:	1726633	*Highest Decoration:*	None listed
Religion:	Agnostic	*Marital Status:*	Married
Waffen-SS:	No		
Notes:	Leader of guard dog company at Auschwitz; Schutzhaftlagerführer Majdanek		
	Executed 8 October 1946		

Camp Service: **Esterwegen**   **Auschwitz**
Dachau   **Gross-Rosen, 1941-1943**
Majdanek, 1943-1944   **Neuengamme, 1944-1945**

Thumstaedter

First Name:	Dr. Heinz	*National Archive File:*	A3343 SSO-182B
Birthdate:	26 April 1907	*Birthplace:*	Frankenberg
Rank:	SS-Obersturmbannführer	*SS Number:*	314179
NSDAP Number:	1739445	*Highest Decoration:*	Iron Cross 2nd Class
Religion:	Agnostic	*Marital Status:*	Married
Waffen-SS:	4th SS Division "Polizei", 1940		
	11th SS Division "Nordland", 1943		
	20th SS Division, 1944		
Notes:	Wounded in action		

Camp Service: **Buchenwald, 1939-1940**

Thun

First Name:	Erich	*National Archive File:*	A3343 SSO-182B
Birthdate:	15 December 1893	*Birthplace:*	Danzig
Rank:	SS-Untersturmführer	*SS Number:*	280221
NSDAP Number:	371262	*Highest Decoration:*	None listed
Religion:	Catholic	*Marital Status:*	Married
Waffen-SS:	No		
Notes:	Leader of Political department at Stutthof; sentenced to Life		

Camp Service: **Stutthof, 1944-1945**

Thunecke

First Name:	Friedrich-Wilhelm	*National Archive File:*	A3343 SSO-182B
Birthdate:	17 April 1899	*Birthplace:*	Magdeburg
Rank:	SS-Untersturmführer	*SS Number:*	132746
NSDAP Number:	1984323	*Highest Decoration:*	None listed
Religion:	Protestant	*Marital Status:*	Widower
Waffen-SS:	No		
Notes:	Iron Cross 2nd Class WWI		
	Son Detlef killed in action 1942; wife died of tuberculosis in 1942		

Camp Service: **Dachau, 1942**

Thurnher

First Name:	Dr. Viktor	*National Archive File:*	A3343 SSO-183B
Birthdate:	4 February 1903	*Birthplace:*	Dornbirn
Rank:	SS-Sturmbannführer	*SS Number:*	298221
NSDAP Number:	Not a member	*Highest Decoration:*	None listed
Religion:	Catholic	*Marital Status:*	Married
Waffen-SS:	3rd SS Division "Totenkopf", 1942		
Notes:	Doctor		

Camp Service: **Oranienburg, 1940**
Sachsenhausen, 1941

Tietze

First Name:	Walter	*National Archive File:*	A3343 SSO-183B
Birthdate:	24 April 1911	*Birthplace:*	Lissa/Posen
Rank:	SS-Untersturmführer	*SS Number:*	420956
NSDAP Number:	Not a member	*Highest Decoration:*	None listed
Religion:	Catholic	*Marital Status:*	Single
Waffen-SS:	5th SS Division "Wiking", 1944		
Notes:	Killed in action January 1945		

Camp Service: **Majdanek, 1943**

Toeppner

First Name:	Robert	*National Archive File:*	A3343 SSO-185B
Birthdate:	12 October 1889	*Birthplace:*	Cunow
Rank:	SS-Obersturmführer	*SS Number:*	24706
NSDAP Number:	559377	*Highest Decoration:*	None listed
Religion:	Protestant	*Marital Status:*	Married
Waffen-SS:	No		
Notes:	Iron Cross 2nd Class WWI		

Camp Service: **Sachsenhausen, 1939**
Flossenbürg, 1943

Totzauer

First Name:	Karl	*National Archive File:*	A3343 SSO-187B
Birthdate:	15 June 1909	*Birthplace:*	Udritsch
Rank:	SS-Obersturmführer	*SS Number:*	383925
NSDAP Number:	6732186	*Highest Decoration:*	None listed
Religion:	Catholic	*Marital Status:*	Married
Waffen-SS:	No		
Notes:	Adjutant at Neuengamme		

Camp Service: **Neuengamme, 1940-1944**

Treite

First Name:	Dr. Percival	*National Archive File:*	A3343 SSO-189B
Birthdate:	10 September 1911	*Birthplace:*	Berlin
Rank:	SS-Untersturmführer	*SS Number:*	220796
NSDAP Number:	5386859	*Highest Decoration:*	None listed
Religion:	Protestant	*Marital Status:*	Married
Waffen-SS:	No		
Notes:	Gynecologist		

Camp Service: **Ravensbrück, 1943**

Trischkat

First Name:	Dr. Hans	*National Archive File:*	A3343 SSO-190B
Birthdate:	19 October 1908	*Birthplace:*	Solingen
Rank:	SS-Hauptsturmführer	*SS Number:*	312912
NSDAP Number:	Not a member	*Highest Decoration:*	None listed
Religion:	Protestant	*Marital Status:*	Married
Waffen-SS:	4th SS Division "Polizei", 1943-1944		
Notes:	Doctor		

Camp Service: **Oranienburg, 1941**
Flossenbürg, 1941
Dachau, 1941

Trommer

First Name:	Dr. Richard	*National Archive File:*	A3343 SSO-190B
Birthdate:	16 June 1910	*Birthplace:*	Muennerstadt
Rank:	SS-Hauptsturmführer	*SS Number:*	106394
NSDAP Number:	Not a member	*Highest Decoration:*	War Service Cross 2nd Class
Religion:	Catholic	*Marital Status:*	Married
Waffen-SS:	No		
Notes:	Made selections for executions at Ravensbrück		

Camp Service: **Flossenbürg, 1941**
Neuengamme, 1942
Ravensbrück, 1943-1945

Trzebinski

First Name:	Alfred	*National Archive File:*	A3343 SSO-191B
Birthdate:	29 August 1902	*Birthplace:*	Jotruschin/Posen
Rank:	SS-Hauptsturmführer	*SS Number:*	133574
NSDAP Number:	1447570	*Highest Decoration:*	None listed
Religion:	Catholic	*Marital Status:*	Married
Waffen-SS:	No		
Notes:	Doctor at Neuengamme; executed 8 October 1946		

Camp Service: **Auschwitz, 1941**
Majdanek, 1941-1943
Neuengamme, 1943-1945

Tschesny

First Name:	Paul	*National Archive File:*	A3343 SSO-192B
Birthdate:	13 June 1895	*Birthplace:*	Unknown
Rank:	SS-Hauptsturmführer	*SS Number:*	Unknown
NSDAP Number:	Not a member	*Highest Decoration:*	None listed
Religion:	Unknown	*Marital Status:*	Unknown
Waffen-SS:	No		
Notes:	Honorary SS member		

Camp Service: **Stutthof, 1945**

Tschimpke

First Name:	Erich	*National Archive File:*	A3343 SSO-192B
Birthdate:	11 March 1898	*Birthplace:*	Breslau
Rank:	SS-Oberführer	*SS Number:*	40065
NSDAP Number:	1191365	*Highest Decoration:*	Bar to Iron Cross 1st Class
Religion:	Catholic	*Marital Status:*	Married
Waffen-SS:	3rd SS Division "Totenkopf", 1940		
Notes:	Iron Cross 1st Class WWI; seriously wounded in WWI		
	Received War Service Cross 1st Class		

Camp Service: **Oranienburg, 1938-1939**

Turek

First Name:	Dr. Friedrich	*National Archive File:*	A3343 SSO-193B
Birthdate:	16 January 1912	*Birthplace:*	Vienna, Austria
Rank:	SS-Obersturmführer	*SS Number:*	298218
NSDAP Number:	Not a member	*Highest Decoration:*	War Service Cross 2nd Class
Religion:	Unknown	*Marital Status:*	Married
Waffen-SS:	8th SS Division "Florian Geyer", 1942-1943		
	36th SS Division "Dirlewanger", 1944-1945		
Notes:	Veterinarian		

Camp Service: **Auschwitz, 1943-1944**

Uhlenbrock

First Name:	Dr. Kurt	*National Archive File:*	A3343 SSO-195B
Birthdate:	2 March 1908	*Birthplace:*	Rostock
Rank:	SS-Sturmbannführer	*SS Number:*	391825
NSDAP Number:	3982886	*Highest Decoration:*	War Service Cross 2nd Class
Religion:	Protestant	*Marital Status:*	Married
Waffen-SS:	4th SS Division "Polizei", 1942		
	5th SS Division "Wiking", 1942-1943		
Notes:	Garrison physician at Auschwitz; selected unfit prisoners for gas chambers		
	Charged but never tried after the war		

Camp Service: **Auschwitz, 1942-1943**

Ulbrich

First Name:	Karl	*National Archive File:*	A3343 SSO-196B
Birthdate:	16 February 1898	*Birthplace:*	Freiwaldau
Rank:	SS-Hauptsturmführer	*SS Number:*	26827
NSDAP Number:	372367	*Highest Decoration:*	War Service Cross 2nd Class
Religion:	Agnostic	*Marital Status:*	Married
Waffen-SS:	No		
Notes:	1st Guard Company commander Majdanek		

Camp Service: **Buchenwald, 1940-1943**
Majdanek, 1943
Gross-Rosen, 1944

Ulrich

First Name:	Hans-Guenther	*National Archive File:*	A3343 SSO-197B
Birthdate:	9 June 1913	*Birthplace:*	Rosian
Rank:	SS-Hauptsturmführer	*SS Number:*	293971
NSDAP Number:	1807376	*Highest Decoration:*	Iron Cross 1st Class
Religion:	Agnostic	*Marital Status:*	Single
Waffen-SS:	4th SS Division "Polizei", 1941-1942		
	17th SS Division "Götz von Berlichingen", 1943-1944		
Notes:	Former police officer; received second degree frostbite on Russian Front		
	Missing in action 23 October 1944		

Camp Service: **Buchenwald, 1938**

Unger

First Name:	Walter	*National Archive File:*	A3343 SSO-199B
Birthdate:	22 June 1917	*Birthplace:*	Lauter
Rank:	SS-Obersturmführer	*SS Number:*	288093
NSDAP Number:	5961560	*Highest Decoration:*	War Service Cross 2nd Class
Religion:	Protestant	*Marital Status:*	Married
Waffen-SS:	No		
Notes:	Adjutant at Stutthof; Department DI/1 Oranienburg		
	Camp service not listed in personnel file		

Camp Service: **Stutthof, 1943-1944**
Oranienburg, 1944

Unsin

First Name:	Andreas	*National Archive File:*	A3343 SSO-200B
Birthdate:	23 June 1911	*Birthplace:*	Fuessen
Rank:	SS-Obersturmführer	*SS Number:*	87304
NSDAP Number:	1884043	*Highest Decoration:*	None
Religion:	Catholic	*Marital Status:*	Single
Waffen-SS:	No		
Notes:	Died 29 March 1940		

Camp Service: **Oranienburg, 1937-1940**

Urbanczyk

First Name:	Walter	*National Archive File:*	A3343 SSO-200B
Birthdate:	12 June 1901	*Birthplace:*	Takczany, Hungary
Rank:	SS-Obersturmführer (F)	*SS Number:*	249022
NSDAP Number:	6987652	*Highest Decoration:*	War Service Cross 2nd Class
Religion:	Agnostic	*Marital Status:*	Married
Waffen-SS:	No		
Notes:	Construction Department Auschwitz; supervised construction of crematoria		

Camp Service: **Buchenwald, 1939**
Auschwitz, 1940-1942

Urbanietz

First Name:	Erich	*National Archive File:*	A3343 SSO-200B
Birthdate:	7 July 1909	*Birthplace:*	Rybnik
Rank:	SS-Sturmbannführer	*SS Number:*	155412
NSDAP Number:	Not a member	*Highest Decoration:*	Iron Cross 1st Class
Religion:	Agnostic	*Marital Status:*	Single
Waffen-SS:	1st SS Division "Leibstandarte Adolf Hitler", 1941-1943		
	12th SS Division "Hitlerjugend", 1944		
	17th SS Division "Götz von Berlichingen", 1945		
Notes:	Guard troops at Dachau		
	Artillery battalion commander		

Camp Service: **Dachau, 1937**

Vaernet

First Name:	Dr. Carl	*National Archive File:*	No File
Birthdate:	28 April 1893	*Birthplace:*	Netherlands
Rank:	SS-Sturmbannführer	*SS Number:*	Unknown
NSDAP Number:	Not a member	*Highest Decoration:*	None listed
Religion:	Unknown	*Marital Status:*	Unknown
Waffen-SS:	Unknown		
Notes:	Conducted experiments on homosexuality at Buchenwald		

Camp Service: **Buchenwald, 1944**

Vaessen

First Name:	Heinz	*National Archive File:*	A3343 SSO-202B
Birthdate:	11 May 1892	*Birthplace:*	Aachen
Rank:	SS-Obersturmführer	*SS Number:*	230457
NSDAP Number:	3980048	*Highest Decoration:*	None listed
Religion:	Catholic	*Marital Status:*	Divorced
Waffen-SS:	No		
Notes:	Iron Cross 1st Class WWI; POW in WWI		
	Guard company commander		

Camp Service: **Mauthausen, 1939-1944**

Verbruggen

First Name:	Alfons	*National Archive File:*	A3343 SSO-204B
Birthdate:	21 October 1902	*Birthplace:*	Munich
Rank:	SS-Hauptsturmführer	*SS Number:*	121790
NSDAP Number:	4821184	*Highest Decoration:*	None listed
Religion:	Agnostic	*Marital Status:*	Married
Waffen-SS:	No		
Notes:	Pest control		

Camp Service: **Auschwitz, 1944**

Vetter

First Name:	Dr. Helmuth	*National Archive File:*	A3343 SSO-205B
Birthdate:	21 March 1910	*Birthplace:*	Rastenburg
Rank:	SS-Obersturmführer	*SS Number:*	126917
NSDAP Number:	5393805	*Highest Decoration:*	War Service Cross 2nd Class
Religion:	Protestant	*Marital Status:*	Married
Waffen-SS:	No		
Notes:	Tested medicines on prisoners		
	Executed 2 February 1949		

Camp Service: **Dachau, 1941**   **Auschwitz, 1942-1943**
Mauthausen, 1944

Voelkner

First Name:	Karl-Wilhelm	*National Archive File:*	A3343 SSO-207B
Birthdate:	26 Febraury 1898	*Birthplace:*	Quedlinburg
Rank:	SS-Obersturmführer	*SS Number:*	160325
NSDAP Number:	1324620	*Highest Decoration:*	War Service Cross 2nd Class
Religion:	Agnostic	*Marital Status:*	Married
Waffen-SS:	No		
Notes:	Stationed for a time at Cologne sub-camp of Buchenwald		

Camp Service: **Buchenwald, 1940-1944**
Flossenbürg, 1944

Vogdt

First Name:	Kurt	*National Archive File:*	A3343 SSO-207B
Birthdate:	6 February 1909	*Birthplace:*	Memel
Rank:	SS-Hauptsturmführer	*SS Number:*	13973
NSDAP Number:	146578	*Highest Decoration:*	War Service Cross 2nd Class
Religion:	Agnostic	*Marital Status:*	Single
Waffen-SS:	SS Infantry Regiment 4		
Notes:	Battalion commander		
	Killed in action 6 March 1942		

Camp Service: **Dachau, 1936**
Flossenbürg, 1939

Vogel

First Name:	Paul	*National Archive File:*	A3343 SSO-208B
Birthdate:	16 February 1917	*Birthplace:*	Saarbruecken
Rank:	SS-Obersturmführer	*SS Number:*	270124
NSDAP Number:	Not a member	*Highest Decoration:*	Iron Cross 2nd Class
Religion:	Agnostic	*Marital Status:*	Married
Waffen-SS:	3rd SS Division "Totenkopf", 1940-1941		
Notes:	3rd SS Totenkopfstandarte "Thüringen"		
	Killed in action, 20 October 1941 in Russia		

Camp Service: **Buchenwald, 1938-1939**

Vogler

First Name:	Wilhelm	*National Archive File:*	A3343 SSO-209B
Birthdate:	1 March 1906	*Birthplace:*	Plauen
Rank:	SS-Hauptsturmführer	*SS Number:*	1505
NSDAP Number:	15176	*Highest Decoration:*	War Service Cross 2nd Class
Religion:	Protestant	*Marital Status:*	Married
Waffen-SS:	No		
Notes:	Department IV at Stutthof; Golden Party Badge		
	Sentenced to 15 years imprisonment		

Camp Service: **Stutthof, 1943-1944**
Bergen-Belsen, 1944

Vogt

First Name:	Emil	*National Archive File:*	A3343 SSO-209B
Birthdate:	1 March 1897	*Birthplace:*	Nürnberg
Rank:	SS-Hauptsturmführer	*SS Number:*	314903
NSDAP Number:	3603834	*Highest Decoration:*	War Service Cross 2nd Class
Religion:	Agnostic	*Marital Status:*	Married
Waffen-SS:	No		
Notes:	Agricultural enterprise at Dachau camp		

Camp Service: **Dachau, 1944**

Vogtherr

First Name:	Dr. Kurt	*National Archive File:*	A3343 SSO-209B
Birthdate:	29 April 1909	*Birthplace:*	Wuerzburg
Rank:	SS-Obersturmbannführer	*SS Number:*	156330
NSDAP Number:	2948563	*Highest Decoration:*	Iron Cross 2nd Class
Religion:	Protestant	*Marital Status:*	Married
Waffen-SS:	1st SS Division "Leibstandarte Adolf Hitler", 1940-1943		
	Ist SS Corps, 1944		
Notes:	Pharmacist		
	Corps pharmacist at Ist SS Corps		

Camp Service: **Dachau, 1939**

Volkmann

First Name:	Kurt	*National Archive File:*	A3343 SSO-210B
Birthdate:	13 November 1911	*Birthplace:*	Grimmen
Rank:	SS-Obersturmführer	*SS Number:*	215329
NSDAP Number:	4407301	*Highest Decoration:*	None listed
Religion:	Agnostic	*Marital Status:*	Married
Waffen-SS:	No		
Notes:	4th Guard Company at Majdanek		

Camp Service: **Sachsenhausen, 1939-1940   Majdanek, 1943-1944**
Stutthof, 1944

Volkmar

First Name:	Horst	*National Archive File:*	A3343 SSO-210B
Birthdate:	28 January 1912	*Birthplace:*	Waltershausen
Rank:	SS-Obersturmführer	*SS Number:*	45388
NSDAP Number:	1182761	*Highest Decoration:*	War Service Cross 1st Class
Religion:	Agnostic	*Marital Status:*	Married
Waffen-SS:	No		
Notes:	Adjutant at Natzweiler		
	Work leader at Haunsteteen sub-camp of Dachau		

Camp Service: **Natzweiler, 1943   Dachau, 1944**

Wachsmann

First Name:	Herbert	*National Archive File:*	A3343 SSO-213B
Birthdate:	2 November 1914	*Birthplace:*	Goerlitz
Rank:	SS-Sturmbannführer	*SS Number:*	59944
NSDAP Number:	1268936	*Highest Decoration:*	Iron Cross 1st Class
Religion:	Agnostic	*Marital Status:*	Single
Waffen-SS:	1st SS Infantry Brigade, 1941-1942		
	7th SS Division "Prinz Eugen", 1943-1944		
Notes:	Division Operations Officer (Ia) 7th SS Division		
	Submitted for German Cross in Gold; missing in action October 1944		

Camp Service: **Dachau, 1937**

Waeckerle

First Name:	Hilmar	*National Archive File:*	A3343 SSO-214B
Birthdate:	24 November 1899	*Birthplace:*	Forchheim
Rank:	SS-Standartenführer	*SS Number:*	9729
NSDAP Number:	530715	*Highest Decoration:*	Iron Cross 1st Class
Religion:	Catholic	*Marital Status:*	Married
Waffen-SS:	5th SS Division "Wiking", 1941		
Notes:	*Kommandant* Dachau; Blood Order #305		
	Killed in action 2 July 1941		

Camp Service: **Dachau, 1933**

Wagner

First Name:	Dr. Erich	*National Archive File:*	A3343 SSO-214B
Birthdate:	15 September 1912	*Birthplace:*	Komatau
Rank:	SS-Sturmbannführer	*SS Number:*	279572
NSDAP Number:	?	*Highest Decoration:*	Iron Cross 1st Class
Religion:	Unknown	*Marital Status:*	Married
Waffen-SS:	2nd SS Division "Das Reich", 1940		
	6th SS Division "Nord", 1942		
Notes:	Camp doctor at Buchenwald		
	Wounded in action		

Camp Service: **Buchenwald, 1940**

Wagner

First Name:	Rudolf	*National Archive File:*	A3343 SSO-216B
Birthdate:	1 May 1912	*Birthplace:*	Bamberg
Rank:	SS-Hauptsturmführer	*SS Number:*	67768
NSDAP Number:	1477069	*Highest Decoration:*	War Service Cross 2nd Class
Religion:	Agnostic	*Marital Status:*	Single
Waffen-SS:	13th SS Division "Handschar", 1943		
Notes:	Department IV at Auschwitz		
	Killed in action 1943		

Camp Service: **Auschwitz, 1943**

Wagner

First Name:	Rudolf	*National Archive File:*	A3343 RS-G0535
Birthdate:	29 June 1913	*Birthplace:*	Schoenwald
Rank:	SS-Obersturmführer	*SS Number:*	104377
NSDAP Number:	812893	*Highest Decoration:*	None listed
Religion:	Agnostic	*Marital Status:*	Married
Waffen-SS:	Unknown		

Camp Service: **Dachau, 1936-1938**
Auschwitz, 1941

Waldmann

First Name:	Anton	*National Archive File:*	A3343 RS-G0552
Birthdate:	5 May 1898	*Birthplace:*	Ottobeuren
Rank:	SS-Sturmbannführer	*SS Number:*	4837
NSDAP Number:	279180	*Highest Decoration:*	None listed
Religion:	Catholic	*Marital Status:*	Married
Waffen-SS:	Unknown		
Notes:	Commander 3rd Guard Company at Natzweiler		

Camp Service: **Dachau, 1934**
Columbia Haus, 1935-1936
Sachsenhausen, 1937
Natzweiler

Waldmann

First Name:	Hans	*National Archive File:*	A3343 SSO-218B
Birthdate:	10 March 1911	*Birthplace:*	Duisburg
Rank:	SS-Obersturmführer	*SS Number:*	7531
NSDAP Number:	342427	*Highest Decoration:*	None listed
Religion:	Agnostic	*Marital Status:*	Married
Waffen-SS:	Kampfgruppe "Schuldt", 1942		
Notes:	Missing in action 19 December 1942		
	Company commander 3rd Guard Company at Neuengamme		

Camp Service: **Neuengamme, 1941-1942**

Walter

First Name:	Friedrich	*National Archive File:*	A3343 SSO-219B
Birthdate:	18 January 1891	*Birthplace:*	Danzig
Rank:	SS-Untersturmführer	*SS Number:*	90451
NSDAP Number:	2727136	*Highest Decoration:*	War Service Cross 2nd Class
Religion:	Protestant	*Marital Status:*	Married
Waffen-SS:	No		
Notes:	Iron Cross 1st Class and Wound Badge WWI		

Camp Service: **Neuengamme, 1942**

Walter

First Name:	Rudolf	*National Archive File:*	A3343 SSO-219B
Birthdate:	2 December 1911	*Birthplace:*	Oberleutensdorf
Rank:	SS-Untersturmführer	*SS Number:*	322587
NSDAP Number:	6710711	*Highest Decoration:*	None listed
Religion:	Catholic	*Marital Status:*	Married
Waffen-SS:	No		
Notes:	2nd Guard Company at Flossenbürg		

Camp Service: **Flossenbürg, 1942**
Majdanek, 1943-1944

Walther

First Name:	Richard	*National Archive File:*	A3343 SSO-220B
Birthdate:	31 December 1909	*Birthplace:*	Reinhardtsgrima
Rank:	SS-Hauptsturmführer	*SS Number:*	59768
NSDAP Number:	1064733	*Highest Decoration:*	War Service Cross 1st Class
Religion:	Agnostic	*Marital Status:*	Married
Waffen-SS:	3rd SS Division "Totenkopf", 1940-1944		
Notes:	Wounded in action		
	Served in SA 1932		

Camp Service: **Buchenwald, 1939**

Wandrei

First Name:	Arnold	*National Archive File:*	A3343 SSO-220B
Birthdate:	8 January 1915	*Birthplace:*	Metzelthin
Rank:	SS-Obersturmführer	*SS Number:*	348911
NSDAP Number:	5508231	*Highest Decoration:*	None listed
Religion:	Agnostic	*Marital Status:*	Single
Waffen-SS:	12th SS Division "Hitlerjugend", 1944		
Notes:	Served in SA 1933-1936		

Camp Service: **Mauthausen, 1944**

Warzok

First Name:	Friedrich	*National Archive File:*	A3343 SSO-221B
Birthdate:	21 September 1903	*Birthplace:*	Rogawa
Rank:	SS-Hauptsturmführer	*SS Number:*	23262
NSDAP Number:	573961	*Highest Decoration:*	None listed
Religion:	Agnostic	*Marital Status:*	Married
Waffen-SS:	No		
Notes:	Served in *Freikorps*; former stone mason		

Camp Service: **Janowska**

Wasicky

First Name:	Erich	*National Archive File:*	A3343 SSO-221B
Birthdate:	27 May 1911	*Birthplace:*	Vienna, Austria
Rank:	SS-Hauptsturmführer	*SS Number:*	298370
NSDAP Number:	197249	*Highest Decoration:*	None listed
Religion:	Catholic	*Marital Status:*	Married
Waffen-SS:	20th SS Division, 1944-1945		
Notes:	Pharmacist at Mauthausen		
	Executed 28 May 1947		

Camp Service: **Mauthausen, 1941-1944**

Weber

First Name:	Dr. Bruno	*National Archive File:*	A3343 SSO-222B
Birthdate:	21 May 1915	*Birthplace:*	Trier
Rank:	SS-Hauptsturmführer	*SS Number:*	420759
NSDAP Number:	5416695	*Highest Decoration:*	War Service Cross 2nd Class
Religion:	Catholic	*Marital Status:*	Single
Waffen-SS:	No		
Notes:	Head of SS Hygiene Institute near Auschwitz		
	Died 23 September 1956		

Camp Service: **Auschwitz, 1943**
Dachau, 1945

Wedel

First Name:	Dr. Ernst	*National Archive File:*	A3343 SSO-223B
Birthdate:	27 July 1897	*Birthplace:*	Mannheim
Rank:	SS-Hauptsturmführer	*SS Number:*	111963
NSDAP Number:	Not a member	*Highest Decoration:*	War Service Cross 2nd Class
Religion:	Protestant	*Marital Status:*	Married
Waffen-SS:	No		
Notes:	Doctor		

Camp Service: **Hinzert, 1941**
Stutthof, 1942

Wedell

First Name:	Fritz	*National Archive File:*	A3343 SSO-223B
Birthdate:	22 February 1912	*Birthplace:*	Gross Cutau, Poland
Rank:	SS-Sturmbannführer	*SS Number:*	78769
NSDAP Number:	4330458	*Highest Decoration:*	War Service Cross 1st Class
Religion:	Agnostic	*Marital Status:*	Married
Waffen-SS:	3rd SS Division "Totenkopf", 1939-1943		
	9th SS Division "Hohenstaufen", 1943		
	6th SS Division "Nord", 1943-1944		
Notes:	Awarded Close Combat Bar in Bronze and Wound Badge		

Camp Service: **Buchenwald, 1938-1939**

Wegner

First Name:	Gustav	*National Archive File:*	A3343 SSO-225B
Birthdate:	16 January 1905	*Birthplace:*	Gross-Denkte
Rank:	SS-Sturmbannführer	*SS Number:*	314183
NSDAP Number:	3278660	*Highest Decoration:*	War Service Cross 1st Class
Religion:	Protestant	*Marital Status:*	Married
Waffen-SS:	3rd SS Division "Totenkopf", 1939-1940		
	1st SS Romanian Grenadier Regiment, 1944		
Notes:	Received Iron Cross 2nd Class; Commander guard battalion at Sachsenhausen		

Camp Service: **Sachsenhausen, 1939, 1940-1943**

Weibrecht

First Name:	Hans	*National Archive File:*	A3343 SSO-226B
Birthdate:	23 September 1911	*Birthplace:*	Nürnberg-Fuerth
Rank:	SS-Sturmbannführer	*SS Number:*	55080
NSDAP Number:	1003285	*Highest Decoration:*	Iron Cross 1st Class
Religion:	Agnostic	*Marital Status:*	Married
Waffen-SS:	Unknown		
Notes:	Adjutant to Eicke; served in Einsatzkommando 10a		
	Received an Anti-Partisan Badge in Bronze		

Camp Service: **Oranienburg, 1934**
Lichtenburg, 1934

Weichselsdorfer

First Name:	Karl Theodor	*National Archive File:*	A3343 SSO-226B
Birthdate:	2 April 1909	*Birthplace:*	Passau-Eggendobl
Rank:	SS-Sturmbannführer	*SS Number:*	19619
NSDAP Number:	361431	*Highest Decoration:*	War Service Cross 2nd Class
Religion:	Agnostic	*Marital Status:*	Married
Waffen-SS:	21st SS Division "Skanderbeg", 1944		
Notes:	Administration leader at Lichtenburg and Buchenwald		

Camp Service: **Lichtenburg, 1934**
Buchenwald, 1934-1942

Weickenmeier

First Name:	Dr. Josef	*National Archive File:*	A3343 SSO-226B
Birthdate:	30 December 1912	*Birthplace:*	Murnau
Rank:	SS-Untersturmführer	*SS Number:*	229686
NSDAP Number:	7296939	*Highest Decoration:*	War Service Cross 2nd Class
Religion:	Protestant	*Marital Status:*	Married
Waffen-SS:	3rd SS Division "Totenkopf", 1944		
Notes:	Pharmacist		

Camp Service: **Dachau, 1939**
Oranienburg, 1940-1941

Weigel

First Name:	Gerhard
Birthdate:	23 February 1908
Rank:	SS-Sturmbannführer
NSDAP Number:	157375
Religion:	Lutheran
Waffen-SS:	No
Notes:	Construction engineer; Adjutant Sachsenburg

National Archive File: A3343 SSO-227B
Birthplace: Floeha
SS Number: 6089
Highest Decoration: War Service Cross 1st Class
Marital Status: Married

Camp Service: **Sachsenburg, 1935-1937**
Buchenwald, 1937-1938
Sachsenhausen, 1938

Weinhoebel

First Name:	Walter
Birthdate:	20 November 1893
Rank:	SS-Standartenführer
NSDAP Number:	952898
Religion:	Unknown
Waffen-SS:	Yes, unit unknown
Notes:	Killed in action 25 September 1944

National Archive File: A3343 SSO-229B
Birthplace: Unknown
SS Number: 277086
Highest Decoration: None listed
Marital Status: Unknown

Camp Service: **Oranienburg, 1937-1938**

Weiseborn

First Name:	Jakob
Birthdate:	22 March 1892
Rank:	SS-Sturmbannführer
NSDAP Number:	753119
Religion:	Agnostic
Waffen-SS:	No
Notes:	*Kommandant* Flossenbürg; died January 20, 1939; Iron Cross 2nd Class WWI

National Archive File: A3343 SSO-230B
Birthplace: Frankfurt
SS Number: 17063
Highest Decoration: None listed
Marital Status: Married

Camp Service: **Esterwegen, 1935** **Dachau, 1936**
Sachsenhausen, 1936-1937 **Buchenwald, 1937-1938**
Flossenbürg, 1938

Weiss

First Name:	Dr. Paul
Birthdate:	6 June 1910
Rank:	SS-Sturmbannführer
NSDAP Number:	3958926
Religion:	Agnostic
Waffen-SS:	4th SS Division "Polizei", 1942
Notes:	Leader of legal department of troop administration at KL/TV headquarters

National Archive File: A3343 SSO-231B
Birthplace: Breslau
SS Number: 195434
Highest Decoration: War Service Cross 1st Class
Marital Status: Married

Camp Service: **Oranienburg, 1938-1940**

Weiss

First Name:	Martin	*National Archive File:*	A3343 SSO-231B
Birthdate:	3 June 1905	*Birthplace:*	Weiden
Rank:	SS-Obersturmbannführer	*SS Number:*	31147
NSDAP Number:	43136	*Highest Decoration:*	War Service Cross 1st Class
Religion:	Catholic	*Marital Status:*	Married
Waffen-SS:	No		
Notes:	*Kommandant* Dachau, Neuengamme and Majdanek; Golden Party Badge		
	Executed 29 May 1946		

Camp Service: **Dachau, 1933-1940**   **Neuengamme, 1940-1942**
             Dachau, 1942-1943   **Majdanek, 1943-1944**

Weisse

First Name:	Kurt	*National Archive File:*	A3343 SSO-232B
Birthdate:	11 October 1909	*Birthplace:*	Ehrenfriedersdorf
Rank:	SS-Sturmbannführer	*SS Number:*	129822
NSDAP Number:	563159	*Highest Decoration:*	German Cross in Gold
Religion:	Agnostic	*Marital Status:*	Single
Waffen-SS:	2nd SS Division "Das Reich", 1942		
	36th SS Division "Dirlewanger", 1943-1945		
Notes:	Guard troops at Sachsenburg		

Camp Service: **Sachsenburg, 1935-1936**

Weiter

First Name:	Eduard	*National Archive File:*	A3343 SSO-233B
Birthdate:	18 July 1889	*Birthplace:*	Eschwege
Rank:	SS-Sturmbannführer	*SS Number:*	276877
NSDAP Number:	3958951	*Highest Decoration:*	War Service Cross 1st Class
Religion:	Agnostic	*Marital Status:*	Married
Waffen-SS:	5th SS Division "Wiking", 1940		
Notes:	*Kommandant* Dachau; killed 6 May 1945		
	Iron Cross 2nd Class WWI		

Camp Service: **Dachau, 1943-1945**

Weitkamp

First Name:	Dr. Ernst	*National Archive File:*	A3343 SSO-233B
Birthdate:	1 May 1908	*Birthplace:*	Quernheim
Rank:	SS-Hauptsturmführer	*SS Number:*	264024
NSDAP Number:	4444934	*Highest Decoration:*	None listed
Religion:	Protestant	*Marital Status:*	Married
Waffen-SS:	4th SS Division "Polizei", 1941		
Notes:	Camp dentist at Mauthausen		

Camp Service: **Mauthausen, 1940**

Weitzel

First Name:	Karl	*National Archive File:*	A3343 SSO-234B
Birthdate:	15 December 1901	*Birthplace:*	Frankfurt
Rank:	SS-Hauptsturmführer	*SS Number:*	8247
NSDAP Number:	230758	*Highest Decoration:*	None listed
Religion:	Agnostic	*Marital Status:*	Married
Waffen-SS:	No		
Notes:	Former businessman; SS Economic Enterprises Dachau		
	Dismissed from SS in 1944		

Camp Service: **Dachau, 1935-1939**

Wellershaus

First Name:	Hans	*National Archive File:*	No File
Birthdate:	28 January 1908	*Birthplace:*	Unknown
Rank:	SS-Sturmbannführer	*SS Number:*	2068
NSDAP Number:	194107	*Highest Decoration:*	None
Religion:	Unknown	*Marital Status:*	Unknown
Waffen-SS:	No		
Notes:	Died at Buchenwald, 3 March 1938		

Camp Service: **Buchenwald, 1937-1938**

Wendt

First Name:	Johann	*National Archive File:*	A3343 SSO-236B
Birthdate:	11 March 1888	*Birthplace:*	Greifenberg
Rank:	SS-Hauptsturmführer	*SS Number:*	113147
NSDAP Number:	1468913	*Highest Decoration:*	None listed
Religion:	Protestant	*Marital Status:*	Married
Waffen-SS:	No		
Notes:	Iron Cross 1st Class WWI		

Camp Service: **Sachsenhausen, 1939**
Neuengamme, 1942

Werner

First Name:	Bonifatius	*National Archive File:*	A3343 SSO-237B
Birthdate:	2 June 1891	*Birthplace:*	Billafingen
Rank:	SS-Obersturmführer	*SS Number:*	22052
NSDAP Number:	390565	*Highest Decoration:*	None listed
Religion:	Agnostic	*Marital Status:*	Married
Waffen-SS:	No		
Notes:	Iron Cross 2nd Class WWI		

Camp Service: **Dachau, 1940-1943**

Werner

First Name:	Dr. Jan	*National Archive File:*	No File
Birthdate:	18 January 1914	*Birthplace:*	Unknown
Rank:	SS-Hauptsturmführer	*SS Number:*	Unknown
NSDAP Number:	Not a member	*Highest Decoration:*	None listed
Religion:	Unknown	*Marital Status:*	Unknown
Waffen-SS:	Unknown		
Notes:	Worked with Josef Mengele		

Camp Service: **Auschwitz, 1943**

Werthschuetzky

First Name:	Dr. Heinz	*National Archive File:*	A3343 SSO-238B
Birthdate:	24 April 1910	*Birthplace:*	Zwotental
Rank:	SS-Obersturmbannführer	*SS Number:*	34124
NSDAP Number:	526472	*Highest Decoration:*	Iron Cross 1st Class
Religion:	Agnostic	*Marital Status:*	Single
Waffen-SS:	3rd SS Division "Totenkopf", 1940-1942		
	2nd SS Infantry Brigade, 1942		
Notes:	Doctor		

Camp Service: **Oranienburg, 1939**

Wesberg

First Name:	Dr. Walter	*National Archive File:*	A3343 SSO-238B
Birthdate:	17 June 1910	*Birthplace:*	Luedenscheid
Rank:	SS-Hauptsturmführer	*SS Number:*	112839
NSDAP Number:	Not a member	*Highest Decoration:*	War Service Cross 2nd Class
Religion:	Protestant	*Marital Status:*	Married
Waffen-SS:	4th SS Division "Polizei", 1941		
Notes:	Doctor		

Camp Service: **Oranienburg, 1940-1941**

Wessel

First Name:	Heinrich	*National Archive File:*	A3343 SSO-238B
Birthdate:	13 April 1904	*Birthplace:*	Osterberg
Rank:	SS-Obersturmführer	*SS Number:*	201029
NSDAP Number:	3566467	*Highest Decoration:*	War Service Cross 2nd Class
Religion:	Agnostic	*Marital Status:*	Married
Waffen-SS:	No		
Notes:	Adjutant in guard battalion; sentenced to 7 years		

Camp Service: **Sachsenhausen, 1939-1945**

Wetzel

First Name: Friedrich   *National Archive File:* A3343 SSO-240B
Birthdate: 14 June 1909   *Birthplace:* Enz-Kloesterle
Rank: SS-Hauptsturmführer   *SS Number:* 67959
NSDAP Number: 2340513   *Highest Decoration:* War Service Cross 1st Class
Religion: Protestant   *Marital Status:* Married
Waffen-SS: 3rd SS Division "Totenkopf", 1940-1942
Notes: Administration leader at Neuengamme and Dachau

Camp Service: **Niederhagen, 1942-1943 Neuengamme, 1943-1944
Dachau, 1944-1945**

Weyand

First Name: Dr. Walter   *National Archive File:* A3343 SSO-240B
Birthdate: 18 July 1909   *Birthplace:* Ludwigshafen
Rank: SS-Sturmbannführer   *SS Number:* 291211
NSDAP Number: 288958   *Highest Decoration:* None listed
Religion: Agnostic   *Marital Status:* Single
Waffen-SS: 6th SS Division "Nord", 1942-1943
10th SS Division "Frundsberg", 1943
Notes: Wounded in action 1944

Camp Service: **Dachau, 1938
Flossenbürg**

Weymann

First Name: Hans   *National Archive File:* A3343 SSO-240B
Birthdate: 18 June 1892   *Birthplace:* Berlin
Rank: SS-Hauptsturmführer   *SS Number:* 57002
NSDAP Number: 830391   *Highest Decoration:* None listed
Religion: Protestant   *Marital Status:* Married
Waffen-SS: No
Notes: Iron Cross 2nd Class WWI

Camp Service: **Sachsenhausen, 1939
Auschwitz, 1942**

Wickenhaeuser

First Name: Friedrich   *National Archive File:* A3343 SSO-241B
Birthdate: 30 March 1878   *Birthplace:* Heidelberg
Rank: SS-Hauptsturmführer   *SS Number:* 55359
NSDAP Number: 729573   *Highest Decoration:* War Service Cross 2nd Class
Religion: Catholic   *Marital Status:* Married
Waffen-SS: No
Notes: Iron Cross 2nd Class WWI

Camp Service: **Mauthausen, 1939**

Wicklein

First Name:	Hermann	*National Archive File:*	A3343 SSO-241B
Birthdate:	14 February 1911	*Birthplace:*	Essen-Berbeck
Rank:	SS-Obersturmführer	*SS Number:*	114870
NSDAP Number:	3670324	*Highest Decoration:*	None listed
Religion:	Protestant	*Marital Status:*	Married
Waffen-SS:	No		
Notes:	Adjutant at Ravensbrück		

Camp Service: **Ravensbrück, 1940-1941**
Herzogenbusch, 1944

Wicklmayr

First Name:	Karl	*National Archive File:*	A3343 SSO-241B
Birthdate:	12 October 1909	*Birthplace:*	Munich
Rank:	SS-Hauptsturmführer	*SS Number:*	2661
NSDAP Number:	659357	*Highest Decoration:*	None listed
Religion:	Agnostic	*Marital Status:*	Married
Waffen-SS:	No		
Notes:	Camp service not listed in personnel file		

Camp Service: **Dachau, 1933**

Wiedemann

First Name:	Karl	*National Archive File:*	A3343 SSO-242B
Birthdate:	9 April 1906	*Birthplace:*	Weilheim
Rank:	SS-Obersturmführer	*SS Number:*	92975
NSDAP Number:	5521087	*Highest Decoration:*	Iron Cross 2nd Class
Religion:	Catholic	*Marital Status:*	Married
Waffen-SS:	No		
Notes:	Served in the Navy in 1939-1940		

Camp Service: **Neuengamme, 1942**

Wiegand

First Name:	Konrad	*National Archive File:*	A3343 SSO-242B
Birthdate:	28 October 1910	*Birthplace:*	Niederurff
Rank:	SS-Untersturmführer	*SS Number:*	52809
NSDAP Number:	2560585	*Highest Decoration:*	None listed
Religion:	Agnostic	*Marital Status:*	Unknown
Waffen-SS:	No		
Notes:	Former locksmith		

Camp Service: **Auschwitz, 1944**

Wildenstein

First Name:	Karl	*National Archive File:*	A3343 SSO-246B
Birthdate:	28 July 1895	*Birthplace:*	Randern
Rank:	SS-Sturmbannführer	*SS Number:*	15153
NSDAP Number:	615678	*Highest Decoration:*	War Service Cross 2nd Class
Religion:	Agnostic	*Marital Status:*	Married
Waffen-SS:	No		
Notes:	Wounded in WWI		

Camp Service: **Hinzert, 1940-1941**

Wilken

First Name:	Peter	*National Archive File:*	A3343 SSO-246B
Birthdate:	23 February 1905	*Birthplace:*	Westerau
Rank:	SS-Sturmbannführer	*SS Number:*	7183
NSDAP Number:	137716	*Highest Decoration:*	Iron Cross 2nd Class
Religion:	Protestant	*Marital Status:*	Single
Waffen-SS:	No		
Notes:	Former farmer		
	Won Iron Cross in the army's 4th Infantry Division		

Camp Service: **Oranienburg, 1937**
Buchenwald, 1938

Wimmer

First Name:	Sebastian	*National Archive File:*	A3343 SSO-248B
Birthdate:	5 January 1902	*Birthplace:*	Dingolfing
Rank:	SS-Hauptsturmführer	*SS Number:*	264374
NSDAP Number:	Not a member	*Highest Decoration:*	None listed
Religion:	Agnostic	*Marital Status:*	Married
Waffen-SS:	2nd SS Division "Das Reich", 1942		
Notes:	Guard troops at Dachau		
	Former police officer in Munich		

Camp Service: **Dachau, 1937-1939**

Winhard

First Name:	Johann	*National Archive File:*	A3343 SSO-248B
Birthdate:	21 June 1893	*Birthplace:*	Obereichstaedt
Rank:	SS-Obersturmführer	*SS Number:*	49483
NSDAP Number:	34056	*Highest Decoration:*	Golden Party Badge
Religion:	Agnostic	*Marital Status:*	Married
Waffen-SS:	No		
Notes:	Iron Cross 2nd Class WWI		

Camp Service: **Dachau, 1939-1940**

Winkelmann

First Name:	Dr. Adolf	*National Archive File:*	A3343 SSO-248B
Birthdate:	26 March 1887	*Birthplace:*	Salzkotten
Rank:	SS-Hauptsturmführer	*SS Number:*	109112
NSDAP Number:	3101530	*Highest Decoration:*	None listed
Religion:	Catholic	*Marital Status:*	Married
Waffen-SS:	No		
Notes:	Iron Cross 2nd Class WWI		

Camp Service: **Ravensbrück, 1945**

Winkler

First Name:	Jacob	*National Archive File:*	A3343 SSO-249B
Birthdate:	24 July 1892	*Birthplace:*	Zweibruecken
Rank:	SS-Hauptsturmführer	*SS Number:*	3764
NSDAP Number:	44568	*Highest Decoration:*	Golden Party Badge
Religion:	Protestant	*Marital Status:*	Married
Waffen-SS:	No		
Notes:	Iron Cross 2nd Class WWI		

Camp Service: **Mauthausen, 1939**

Wirth

First Name:	Christian	*National Archive File:*	A3343 SSO-251B
Birthdate:	24 November 1885	*Birthplace:*	Obersalzheim
Rank:	SS-Sturmbannführer	*SS Number:*	345464
NSDAP Number:	420383	*Highest Decoration:*	None listed
Religion:	Protestant	*Marital Status:*	Married
Waffen-SS:	No		
Notes:	*Kommandant* Belzec; killed in action 26 May 1944 by partisans enroute to Fiume		

Camp Service: **Belzec, 1941-1942**   **Lublin Airfield Camp, 1942**

Wirths

First Name:	Dr. Eduard	*National Archive File:*	A3343 SSO-251B
Birthdate:	4 September 1909	*Birthplace:*	Wuerzburg
Rank:	SS-Sturmbannführer	*SS Number:*	311594
NSDAP Number:	3139549	*Highest Decoration:*	Iron Cross 2nd Class
Religion:	Catholic	*Marital Status:*	Married
Waffen-SS:	No		
Notes:	In charge of all SS physicians, dentists and sanitary orderlies at Auschwitz Suicide September 1945		

Camp Service: **Dachau, 1942**   **Neuengamme, 1942**
Auschwitz, 1942-1944   **Bergen-Belsen, 1944**
Dora, 1945

Witteler

First Name:	Dr. Willy	*National Archive File:*	A3343 SSO-002C
Birthdate:	20 April 1909	*Birthplace:*	Essen-Steele
Rank:	SS-Sturmbannführer	*SS Number:*	310314
NSDAP Number:	2137040	*Highest Decoration:*	Iron Cross 1st Class
Religion:	Catholic	*Marital Status:*	Married
Waffen-SS:	3rd SS Division "Totenkopf", 1940-1943		
Notes:	Camp doctor at Dachau; executed		

Camp Service: **Sachsenhausen, 1939-1940**
Dachau, 1944

Wittenberg

First Name:	Joachim	*National Archive File:*	A3343 SSO-002C
Birthdate:	11 September 1906	*Birthplace:*	Naumburg
Rank:	SS-Obersturmführer	*SS Number:*	382476
NSDAP Number:	Not a member	*Highest Decoration:*	None listed
Religion:	Protestant	*Marital Status:*	Single
Waffen-SS:	No		
Notes:	Former lawyer; served in SA 1923-1926 and 1933-1934		

Camp Service: **Auschwitz, 1944**

Wittig

First Name:	Oswald	*National Archive File:*	A3343 SSO-002C
Birthdate:	2 March 1903	*Birthplace:*	Kitzingen
Rank:	SS-Hauptsturmführer	*SS Number:*	28453
NSDAP Number:	747424	*Highest Decoration:*	War Service Cross 2nd Class
Religion:	Agnostic	*Marital Status:*	Married
Waffen-SS:	4th SS Division "Polizei", 1942-1943		
	VIth SS Corps, 1943-1944		
Notes:	Former salesman		

Camp Service: **Oranienburg, 1938-1940**

Wittl

First Name:	Fritz	*National Archive File:*	A3343 SSO-002C
Birthdate:	20 September 1912	*Birthplace:*	Munich
Rank:	SS-Hauptsturmführer	*SS Number:*	39517
NSDAP Number:	1283209	*Highest Decoration:*	None listed
Religion:	Agnostic	*Marital Status:*	Single
Waffen-SS:	3rd SS Division "Totenkopf", 1940-1941		
Notes:	Guard troops at Dachau and Lichtenburg; killed in action 22 August 1941		

Camp Service: **Dachau, 1933-1936**
Lichtenburg, 1936-1937
Buchenwald, 1938

Wittmann

First Name:	Dr. Leonhard	*National Archive File:*	A3343 SSO-002C
Birthdate:	31 July 1913	*Birthplace:*	Dinkelsbuehl
Rank:	SS-Hauptsturmführer	*SS Number:*	77206
NSDAP Number:	1665975	*Highest Decoration:*	None listed
Religion:	Unknown	*Marital Status:*	Single
Waffen-SS:	5th SS Division "Wiking", 1941-1944		
Notes:	Served in Hitler Youth 1929-1932		

Camp Service: **Oranienburg, 1940-1941**

Wlach

First Name:	Josef	*National Archive File:*	A3343 SSO-003C
Birthdate:	19 June 1906	*Birthplace:*	Osseg
Rank:	SS-Obersturmführer	*SS Number:*	341865
NSDAP Number:	Not a member	*Highest Decoration:*	None listed
Religion:	Catholic	*Marital Status:*	Married
Waffen-SS:	No		
Notes:	Pharmacist		

Camp Service: **Dachau, 1943-1944**

Wodraska

First Name:	Alois	*National Archive File:*	A3343 SSO-004C
Birthdate:	15 April 1909	*Birthplace:*	Neulengbach
Rank:	SS-Hauptsturmführer	*SS Number:*	301086
NSDAP Number:	1629197	*Highest Decoration:*	None listed
Religion:	Unknown	*Marital Status:*	Single
Waffen-SS:	2nd SS Division "Das Reich", 1944-1945		
Notes:	Physician assistant		

Camp Service: **Sachsenhausen, 1941**

Wohlrab

First Name:	Dr. Robert	*National Archive File:*	A3343 SSO-007C
Birthdate:	1 October 1910	*Birthplace:*	Nürnberg
Rank:	SS-Obersturmführer	*SS Number:*	289241
NSDAP Number:	Not a member	*Highest Decoration:*	Iron Cross 1st Class
Religion:	Protestant	*Marital Status:*	Married
Waffen-SS:	3rd SS Division "Totenkopf", 1942-1943		
Notes:	Doctor; Served in SA 1933-1937		

Camp Service: **Oranienburg, 1938**
Dachau, 1938-1939

Woith

First Name:	Hans Joachim	*National Archive File:*	A3343 SSO-007C
Birthdate:	25 July 1910	*Birthplace:*	Guben
Rank:	SS-Obersturmbannführer	*SS Number:*	13109
NSDAP Number:	536264	*Highest Decoration:*	German Cross in Gold
Religion:	Agnostic	*Marital Status:*	Married
Waffen-SS:	2nd SS Division "Das Reich", 1939-1940 1941-1943 3rd SS Division "Totenkopf", 1940-1941 9th SS Division "Hohenstaufen", 1944		
Notes:	Killed in action 30 June 1944 Commander 19th SS Grenadier Regiment		

Camp Service: **Oranienburg, 1937-1938**

Wolanski

First Name:	Heinz	*National Archive File:*	A3343 SSO-008C
Birthdate:	5 May 1910	*Birthplace:*	Hamburg-Altona
Rank:	SS-Hauptsturmführer	*SS Number:*	233370
NSDAP Number:	Not a member	*Highest Decoration:*	None listed
Religion:	Protestant	*Marital Status:*	Married
Waffen-SS:	4th SS Division "Polizei", 1942-1943		
Notes:	Camp dentist at Auschwitz; Auschwitz service not listed in personnel file		

Camp Service: **Auschwitz, 1940**
Ravensbrück, 1940

Wolf

First Name:	Dr. Helmut	*National Archive File:*	A3343 SSO-008C
Birthdate:	17 October 1907	*Birthplace:*	Duesseldorf
Rank:	SS-Sturmbannführer	*SS Number:*	126796
NSDAP Number:	1952114	*Highest Decoration:*	Iron Cross 2nd Class
Religion:	Agnostic	*Marital Status:*	Married
Waffen-SS:	3rd SS Division "Totenkopf", 1941-1942 9th SS Division "Hohenstaufen", 1943		
Notes:	Doctor		

Camp Service: **Columbia Haus, 1936** **Lichtenburg, 1936-1937**
Buchenwald, 1937 **Oranienburg, 1938-1941**

Wolf

First Name:	Georg	*National Archive File:*	A3343 SSO-008C
Birthdate:	11 April 1881	*Birthplace:*	Munich-Ismanning
Rank:	SS-Untersturmführer	*SS Number:*	39482
NSDAP Number:	1275315	*Highest Decoration:*	None listed
Religion:	Agnostic	*Marital Status:*	Married
Waffen-SS:	No		
Notes:	Former brewer; acting administration chief Columbia Haus		

Camp Service: **Columbia Haus, 1935-1937**
Sachsenhausen, 1937

Wolf

First Name:	Helmut	*National Archive File:*	A3343 SSO-009C
Birthdate:	22 September 1910	*Birthplace:*	Breslau
Rank:	SS-Obersturmführer	*SS Number:*	122187
NSDAP Number:	4545014	*Highest Decoration:*	None listed
Religion:	Protestant	*Marital Status:*	Married
Waffen-SS:	No		
Notes:	Former legal assistant		

Camp Service: **Buchenwald, 1941**

Wolf

First Name:	Karl-Wilhelm	*National Archive File:*	A3343 SSO-009C
Birthdate:	21 August 1914	*Birthplace:*	Halle
Rank:	SS-Hauptsturmführer	*SS Number:*	116702
NSDAP Number:	1777216	*Highest Decoration:*	Iron Cross 2nd Class
Religion:	Agnostic	*Marital Status:*	Single
Waffen-SS:	6th SS Division "Nord", 1942-1943		
	9th SS Division "Hohenstaufen", 1943		
Notes:	Severely wounded serving with the army's 30th Infantry Regiment in 1939		
	Lost parts of several fingers		

Camp Service: **Buchenwald, 1938**

Wolfmeyer

First Name:	Leopold	*National Archive File:*	A3343 SSO-011C
Birthdate:	20 May 1903	*Birthplace:*	Vienna, Austria
Rank:	SS-Obersturmführer	*SS Number:*	1529174
NSDAP Number:	897278	*Highest Decoration:*	None listed
Religion:	Unknown	*Marital Status:*	Married
Waffen-SS:	No		
Notes:	Guard troops at Dachau; IIIrd Bn, 1st Totenkopfstandarte		

Camp Service: **Dachau, 1937**

Wollweber

First Name:	Dr. Walter	*National Archive File:*	A3343 SSO-012C
Birthdate:	30 November 1911	*Birthplace:*	Muehlhausen
Rank:	SS-Sturmbannführer	*SS Number:*	310426
NSDAP Number:	Not a member	*Highest Decoration:*	Iron Cross 1st Class
Religion:	Protestant	*Marital Status:*	Married
Waffen-SS:	1st SS Division "Leibstandarte Adolf Hitler", 1940, 1943-1944		
	4th SS Division "Polizei", 1940-1943		
Notes:	Died of Wounds 8 August 1944 in France		

Camp Service: **Oranienburg, 1938**
Dachau, 1938-1940

Wolter

First Name: Dr. Andreas
Birthdate: 25 November 1903
Rank: SS-Hauptsturmführer
NSDAP Number: 3961587
Religion: Agnostic
Waffen-SS: 4th SS Division "Polizei", 1943
Notes: Dentist; served in German Army in 1938

National Archive File: A3343 SSO-012C
Birthplace: Redingen
SS Number: 112843
Highest Decoration: War Service Cross 2nd Class
Marital Status: Married

Camp Service: **Hinzert, 1940-1941**

Wolter

First Name: Dr. Waldemar
Birthdate: 19 May 1908
Rank: SS-Sturmbannführer
NSDAP Number: 3140090
Religion: Agnostic
Waffen-SS: No
Notes: Doctor; executed 28 May 1947

National Archive File: A3343 SSO-013C
Birthplace: Wuerzburg
SS Number: 104540
Highest Decoration: War Service Cross 1st Class
Marital Status: Married

Camp Service: **Dachau**, **Hinzert, 1941**, **Sachsenhausen, 1941**, **Buchenwald, 1941**, **Herzogenbusch**, **Mauthausen, 1944-1945**

Wolter

First Name: Fritz
Birthdate: 15 March 1909
Rank: SS-Untersturmführer (F)
NSDAP Number: 1995339
Religion: Agnostic
Waffen-SS: 8th SS Division "Florian Geyer", 1944
Notes: Construction Department Auschwitz, 1941-1943; guard troops Auschwitz, 1940

National Archive File: A3343 SSO-013C
Birthplace: Stendal
SS Number: 198420
Highest Decoration: None listed
Marital Status: Single

Camp Service: **Auschwitz, 1940-1943**

Wolter

First Name: Walter
Birthdate: 13 January 1897
Rank: SS-Hauptsturmführer
NSDAP Number: 4372
Religion: Agnostic
Waffen-SS: No
Notes: Probably an honorary member of the SS; Golden Party Badge

National Archive File: A3343 SSO-013C
Birthplace: Unknown
SS Number: None listed
Highest Decoration: None listed
Marital Status: Married

Camp Service: **Ravensbrück, 1944**

Worster

First Name:	Heinrich	*National Archive File:*	A3343 SSO-013C
Birthdate:	27 November 1909	*Birthplace:*	Osthofen
Rank:	SS-Hauptsturmführer	*SS Number:*	114309
NSDAP Number:	1663492	*Highest Decoration:*	War Service Cross 2nd Class
Religion:	Agnostic	*Marital Status:*	Married
Waffen-SS:	Waffen-SS Mountain Brigade 1 "Tartar", 1944-1945		
	SS Eastern People's Legion, 1945		
Notes:	Camp administration at Majdanek and Dachau		

Camp Service: **Dachau, 1937-1941**
Majdanek, 1941-1944

Wosnitzka

First Name:	Georg	*National Archive File:*	No File
Birthdate:	1911	*Birthplace:*	Kattowitz
Rank:	SS-Untersturmführer	*SS Number:*	Unknown
NSDAP Number:	Not a member	*Highest Decoration:*	None listed
Religion:	Unknown	*Marital Status:*	Unknown
Waffen-SS:	Unknown		
Notes:	Interrogations at Auschwitz		
	Died 7 November 1981		

Camp Service: **Auschwitz, 1943**

Wotke

First Name:	Dr. Karl	*National Archive File:*	A3343 SSO-013C
Birthdate:	1 June 1912	*Birthplace:*	Pressburg
Rank:	SS-Hauptsturmführer	*SS Number:*	306477
NSDAP Number:	Not a member	*Highest Decoration:*	Iron Cross 2nd Class
Religion:	Unknown	*Marital Status:*	Single
Waffen-SS:	6th SS Division "Nord", 1941-1943		
	12th SS Division "Hitlerjugend", 1944		
	27th SS Division "Langemarck", 1945		
Notes:	Doctor		

Camp Service: **Auschwitz, 1940-1941**

Woywoth

First Name:	Erich	*National Archive File:*	A3343 SSO-014C
Birthdate:	3 January 1884	*Birthplace:*	Stendal
Rank:	SS-Obersturmführer	*SS Number:*	276165
NSDAP Number:	572551	*Highest Decoration:*	War Service Cross 1st Class
Religion:	Protestant	*Marital Status:*	Married
Waffen-SS:	No		
Notes:	Iron Cross 2nd Class WWI		

Camp Service: **Buchenwald, 1944**
Gross-Rosen, 1944

Wuttke

First Name:	Dr. Herbert	*National Archive File:*	A3343 SSO-017C
Birthdate:	21 June 1905	*Birthplace:*	Juliusburg
Rank:	SS-Untersturmführer	*SS Number:*	180598
NSDAP Number:	7057411	*Highest Decoration:*	None listed
Religion:	Protestant	*Marital Status:*	Married
Waffen-SS:	No		
Notes:	Camp service not listed in personnel file		

Camp Service: **Auschwitz, 1940-1941**

Zaar

First Name:	Kurt	*National Archive File:*	A3343 SSO-017C
Birthdate:	7 January 1907	*Birthplace:*	Teschau
Rank:	SS-Obersturmführer	*SS Number:*	394248
NSDAP Number:	Not a member	*Highest Decoration:*	War Service Cross 2nd Class
Religion:	Agnostic	*Marital Status:*	Married
Waffen-SS:	9th SS Division "Hohenstauffen", 1944 IVth SS Corps, 1944		
Notes:	Spoke Polish; pharmacist		

Camp Service: **Neuengamme, 1943**

Zachmann

First Name:	Ferdinand	*National Archive File:*	A3343 SSO-017C
Birthdate:	10 June 1911	*Birthplace:*	Rosenheim
Rank:	SS-Hauptsturmführer	*SS Number:*	160982
NSDAP Number:	754140	*Highest Decoration:*	Iron Cross 2nd Class
Religion:	Agnostic	*Marital Status:*	Married
Waffen-SS:	6th SS Division "Nord", 1944 VIIth SS Corps, 1944		
Notes:	Former salesman		

Camp Service: **Lichtenburg, 1937**

Zahel

First Name:	Dr. Hans	*National Archive File:*	A3343 SSO-017C
Birthdate:	18 January 1904	*Birthplace:*	Koenigsfeld, Austria
Rank:	SS-Standartenführer	*SS Number:*	293747
NSDAP Number:	Not a member	*Highest Decoration:*	War Service Cross 1st Class
Religion:	Unknown	*Marital Status:*	Married
Waffen-SS:	3rd SS Division "Totenkopf", 1940-1941		
Notes:	Surgeon		

Camp Service: **Buchenwald, 1939-1940**

Zeitler

First Name:	Alfons	*National Archive File:*	A3343 SSO-019C
Birthdate:	26 February 1910	*Birthplace:*	Nürnberg
Rank:	SS-Sturmbannführer	*SS Number:*	1219
NSDAP Number:	91651	*Highest Decoration:*	Iron Cross 1st Class
Religion:	Agnostic	*Marital Status:*	Married
Waffen-SS:	7th SS Division "Prinz Eugen", 1943-1944		
	21st SS Division "Skanderbeg", 1944		
Notes:	Wound Badge in Silver; Golden Party Badge; battalion commander		

Camp Service: **Dachau, 1934**

Zeysing

First Name:	Hans	*National Archive File:*	A3343 SSO-020C
Birthdate:	15 February 1901	*Birthplace:*	Warweiden
Rank:	SS-Obersturmbannführer	*SS Number:*	276137
NSDAP Number:	822722	*Highest Decoration:*	Iron Cross 1st Class
Religion:	Agnostic	*Marital Status:*	Married
Waffen-SS:	4th SS Division "Polizei", 1940-1942		
	23rd SS Division "Kama", 1944		
	5th SS Division "Wiking", 1944-1945		
Notes:	Adjutant at Columbia Haus		
	Flak battalion commander in 4th SS Division		

Camp Service: **Columbia Haus, 1935-1936**
Sachsenburg, 1936-1937

Ziemssen

First Name:	Wilhelm	*National Archive File:*	A3343 RS-G5484
Birthdate:	21 February 1910	*Birthplace:*	Neuneck
Rank:	SS-Hauptsturmführer	*SS Number:*	232939
NSDAP Number:	5084030	*Highest Decoration:*	None listed
Religion:	Agnostic	*Marital Status:*	Married
Waffen-SS:	Yes, unit unknown		
Notes:	Agricultural officer at Auschwitz; killed in action 30 September 1943		

Camp Service: **Auschwitz, 1942**

Ziereis

First Name:	Franz	*National Archive File:*	A3343 SSO-022C
Birthdate:	13 August 1905	*Birthplace:*	Munich
Rank:	SS-Standartenführer	*SS Number:*	276998
NSDAP Number:	6716146	*Highest Decoration:*	War Service Cross 1st Class
Religion:	Protestant	*Marital Status:*	Married
Waffen-SS:	No		
Notes:	*Kommandant* Mauthausen		
	Apprehended by American troops near camp; died of wounds 24 May 1945		

Camp Service: **Mauthausen, 1939-1945**

Zill

First Name:	Egon	*National Archive File:*	A3343 SSO-022C
Birthdate:	28 March 1906	*Birthplace:*	Plauen
Rank:	SS-Sturmbannführer	*SS Number:*	535
NSDAP Number:	20063	*Highest Decoration:*	Golden Party Badge
Religion:	Protestant	*Marital Status:*	Married

Waffen-SS: 7th SS Division "Prinz Eugen", 1943-1944
23rd SS Division "Kama", 1944-1945

Notes: *Kommandant* Flossenbürg and Natzweiler; sentenced to life; reduced to 15 years; died 1974

Camp Service: **Lichtenburg, 1934-1937** **Buchenwld, 1937-1938**
Dachau, 1938-1939 **Ravensbrück, 1939-1941**
Natzweiler, 1942-1943 **Flossenbürg, 1943**

Zippe

First Name:	Max	*National Archive File:*	A3343 SSO-024C
Birthdate:	18 January 1871	*Birthplace:*	Berlin
Rank:	SS-Obersturmführer	*SS Number:*	9365
NSDAP Number:	437799	*Highest Decoration:*	None listed
Religion:	Protestant	*Marital Status:*	Married
Waffen-SS:	No		

Notes: Former musician; served in WWI

Camp Service: **Buchenwald, 1940** **Oranienburg, 1943**
Flossenbürg, 1944

Zoller

First Name:	Viktor	*National Archive File:*	A3343 SSO-025C
Birthdate:	22 June 1912	*Birthplace:*	Ravensburg
Rank:	SS-Hauptsturmführer	*SS Number:*	77379
NSDAP Number:	3287569	*Highest Decoration:*	None listed
Religion:	Catholic	*Marital Status:*	Single

Waffen-SS: 3rd SS Division "Totenkopf", 1942
Notes: Adjutant at Mauthausen
Executed 28 May 1947

Camp Service: **Mauthausen, 1941-1942**
Auschwitz, 1943

Zott

First Name:	Hans	*National Archive File:*	A3343 SSO-025C
Birthdate:	2 May 1908	*Birthplace:*	Munich
Rank:	SS-Untersturmführer (F)	*SS Number:*	142677
NSDAP Number:	121407	*Highest Decoration:*	None listed
Religion:	Agnostic	*Marital Status:*	Married

Waffen-SS: 4th SS Division "Polizei", 1940
Notes: Served in SA 1929-1932; Black wound badge

Camp Service: **Dachau, 1938-1939**

Zutter

First Name:	Adolf	*National Archive File:*	A3343 SSO-026C
Birthdate:	10 February 1889	*Birthplace:*	Zweibruecken
Rank:	SS-Hauptsturmführer	*SS Number:*	226911
NSDAP Number:	3543330	*Highest Decoration:*	War Service Cross 2nd Class
Religion:	Protestant	*Marital Status:*	Married
Waffen-SS:	No		
Notes:	Executed 27 May 1947		

Camp Service: **Mauthausen, 1939**

Zwerger

First Name:	Hans	*National Archive File:*	A3343 SSO-026C
Birthdate:	20 April 1903	*Birthplace:*	Unknown
Rank:	SS-Hauptsturmführer	*SS Number:*	242699
NSDAP Number:	Not a member	*Highest Decoration:*	None listed
Religion:	Unknown	*Marital Status:*	Unknown
Waffen-SS:	Unknown		
Notes:	Killed in action 15 March 1943		

Camp Service: **Dachau, 1936**

Zwirner

First Name:	Dr. Hans	*National Archive File:*	A3343 SSO-026C
Birthdate:	22 February 1906	*Birthplace:*	Waidhofen, Austria
Rank:	SS-Obersturmbannführer	*SS Number:*	309500
NSDAP Number:	Not a member	*Highest Decoration:*	Iron Cross 2nd Class
Religion:	Agnostic	*Marital Status:*	Married
Waffen-SS:	3rd SS Division "Totenkopf", 1939-1940		
Notes:	Doctor		

Camp Service: **Oranienburg, 1938-1939**

3

THE CONCENTRATION CAMP OFFICERS: AN ANALYSIS

Never forget, we are a knightly Order, from which one cannot withdraw, to which one is recruited by blood and within which one remains with body and soul so long as one lives on this earth.[1]

- Heinrich Himmler

If we were to end this book at this point, we would certainly have a valuable addition to the body of knowledge concerning the personnel assigned to the concentration camps. However, additionally, through the use of a simple computer data base management system, we can truly examine the nature of the "forest" of SS officers who served at these locations, rather than just describe the individual "trees."[2]

Two caveats are in order. First, I am not a statistician. Norms, medians and standard deviations are probably beyond my full comprehension and certainly beyond my historical interest. So the following presentations include only aggregate numbers and, in some cases, percentages, and do not delve into true *mathematica*. Second, any data base is only as good as its input. I believe that for the most part the entries within each officer's personnel file are accurate and reflect ground truth. However, occasionally an SS clerk may have made a recording error of some type. Similarly, informationally the files appear to be less complete for the period after February 1945. While I have searched numerous additional sources for information, it is quite likely that some of these SS officers received promotions, decorations, or assignments and may have even been killed in action during the last few months of the war – and such information is not reflected here.

BIRTHPLACE

In examining the birthplace for each officer assigned to the camps, the geographical distribution appears to follow what

we might expect to a point between those from urban and rural settings. The following chart shows the most frequently found places of birth for the concentration camp officers:

Table 4
CONCENTRATION CAMP OFFICERS
MOST FREQUENT PLACE OF BIRTH

Munich	39
Berlin	28
Hamburg	16
Dresden	14
Vienna	13
Nürnberg	12
Essen	11
Danzig	8
Frankfurt	8
Freiburg	7
Düsseldorf	7
Mannheim	7
Breslau	7

There are 967 officers identified in this study; 177 shown in the preceding table were born of large German and Austrian cities. From these numbers it is obvious that the vast majority of SS officers who served in the camps came from smaller cities, towns and villages, not the most populated cities, as the population from these thirteen larger cities in Germany accounts

270

for only about one-sixth of the total number of serving officers. Munich is over-represented compared to Berlin and Hamburg – when we compare overall populations for the three cities – but many early Nazi Party members came from this city in Bavaria and were thus called upon to serve in the early camps when completely reliable men were needed.

Many camp men were not born in Germany proper. Eight came from ethnic German enclaves in Romania, forty-five from Austria, two from the Netherlands, three from Russia, two from Switzerland, two from Hungary and two from Belgium. One was born to German parents in England, one in China and one in Sumatra. Several were from the Sudetenland and served in the Czech Army before Germany reoccupied this territory in 1938. However, all of these individuals grew up believing they were as German as those native born.

From small farm-towns to middle and large cities the SS concentration camp officers came from all parts of the Fatherland. Though diverse in their origins, their careers, the Nazi regime and even a small element of chance steered them to the factories of death.

AWARDS AND DECORATIONS

The concentration camp officers were a mixed lot; some had displayed bravery in World War I, some exhibited courage in front-line combat in World War II, while others received non-combat decorations for service in the camps. During World War I the basic decorations for front-line bravery were the Iron Cross 1st Class and 2nd Class. The Iron Cross 2nd Class indicated a single act of bravery in combat, while the Iron Cross 1st Class was awarded for an additional acts of valor. It was only possible for an individual to win each of the classes once. Additionally, to measure wounds received in combat, Kaiser Wilhelm II instituted the Wound Badge on March 3, 1918. Different grades were awarded based on the cumulative number of incidents in which wounds were received. The wound badge in black designated one or two wounds, the badge in white for three to four wounds, and the badge in yellow-gold for five or more wounds.[3]

In examining the concentration camp officers we find that over one hundred received the Iron Cross 2nd Class for service in World War I while a minimum of thirty-one received the Iron Cross 1st Class. Additionally, many were wounded in action during this conflict; some seriously enough to preclude further front-line service. Many more, including those too young to have seen combat in 1914, would receive decorations for World War II service.

At the outbreak of World War II the German Armed Forces re-instituted the Iron Cross 1st Class and 2nd Class. Hitler stated that the Iron Cross 2nd Class would reward a single act of bravery in combat beyond the normal requirements of duty. It could be awarded to all members of the Armed Forces or to civilians serving with the military. The Iron Cross 1st Class, also re-instituted on September 1, 1939, was usually awarded for an additional three to five significant acts of valor.[4] Recommendations for both awards went first from company to battalion to regiment, with the approving authority resting with the division commander. For non-divisional units assigned to a corps, the corps commander approved receipt of the award. Although the intent was to let an appropriate time pass between the award of the 2nd Class and the 1st Class, this could be compressed to one or two days. For soldiers who had already been awarded the Iron Cross in World War I, the actual World War II version of the decoration was not presented. Instead, they received a clasp denoting the achievement of winning the decoration again in this latest conflict.

On September 1, 1939 Hitler also instituted a new decoration, the *Ritterkreuz* (Knight's Cross of the Iron Cross) for continuous acts of exceptional bravery, or in the cases of higher ranks for successful execution of battle or for formulating outstanding battle plans.[5] Recommendation for the Knight's Cross required the endorsement of the chain of command through army commander with the final decision resting with Hitler.[6] Prerequisites included previous award of both classes of the Iron Cross. Enlisted personnel as well as officers were eligible for this award.[7] In the course of the war some 7,300 Knight's Crosses were awarded.[8] The following is a summary by rank for all 326 Waffen-SS officers who received the Knights Cross – not just former camp officers – which will help later to place this award won by men who had served in the camp system in better perspective:[9]

Table 5

ALL WAFFEN-SS OFFICER AWARDEES
OF THE KNIGHT'S CROSS[10]

SS-Untersturmführer	30
SS-Obersturmführer	69
SS-Hauptsturmführer	83
SS-Sturmbannführer	87
SS-Obersturmbannführer	40
SS-Standartenführer &	
SS-Oberführer	7
SS-Gruppenführer	4
SS-Obergruppenführer	6

Fourteen former concentration camp officers received the Knight's Cross of the Iron Cross as their highest decoration. Eight served in the 3rd SS Division "Totenkopf": *SS-*

Sturmbannführer Walter Reder and *SS-Obersturmbannführer* Ernst Häussler as a battalion commanders in the 5th Panzergrenadier Regiment "Totenkopf", *SS-Standartenführer* Kurt Launer as a battalion commander in the 6th Panzer-grenadier Regiment "Theodor Eicke" and *SS-Untersturmführer* Kurt Franke of the same regiment, *SS-Standartenführer* Eduard Deisenhofer as a battle group commander, *SS-Sturmbannführer* Adolf Pittschellis, as the commander of the division anti-tank battalion, *SS-Sturmbannführer* Azelino Masarié as the division reconnaissance battalion commander and *SS-Obersturmbannführer* Otto Kron as the commander of the division anti-aircraft battalion. *SS-Obersturmbannführer* Konrad Schellong, commander of the SS Freiwilligen Sturmbrigade "Langemarck" in the 2nd SS Division "Das Reich" and *SS-Obersturmführer* Willi Simke of the IInd Battalion Panzer Regiment "Das Reich" also won this award. So did *SS-Sturmbannführer* Rudolf Saalbach, commander of the reconnaissance battalion 11th SS Division "Nordland" and *SS-Hauptsturmführer* Josef Bachmeier, a panzergrenadier battalion commander in the same division; *SS-Standartenführer* Heinrich Petersen received the decoration as a regimental commander in the 7th SS Division "Prinz Eugen." *SS-Sturmbannführer* Johannes Göhler won the award while assigned to the 8th SS Division "Florian Geyer."[11]

On June 3, 1940 Hitler instituted the next higher grade of the Knight's Cross, the Knight's Cross of the Iron Cross with Oak Leaves (*Ritterkreuz mit Eichenlaub*). This award recognized previous winners of the Knight's Cross for continued significant bravery and initiative. Enlisted personnel, officers and foreign military personnel were eligible to receive the Oak Leaves, and by war's end 910 had done so.[12] Awards of the Oak Leaves were spread among all of Germany's Armed Forces. Seventy-seven winners of this award were from the Waffen-SS. Five former SS camp officers received the Oak Leaves as their highest decoration: *SS-Gruppenführer* Max Simon as the commander of the 16th SS Division "Reichsführer SS", *SS-Sturmbannführer* Fritz Biermeier, commander of 2nd Battalion, 3rd Panzer Regiment, *SS-Obersturmbannführer* Paul-Albert Kausch as commander of the 11th SS Panzer Regiment, *SS-Brigadeführer* Helmuth Becker as the commander of the 3rd SS Division "Totenkopf" and *SS-Obergruppenführer* Theodor Eicke, also as the commander of the "Totenkopf."[13]

One year later Hitler again introduced another higher grade of award – the Knight's Cross of the Iron Cross with Oak Leaves and Swords (*Ritterkreuz mit Eichenlaub und Schwertern*). This grade recognized previous recipients of the Oak Leaves who accomplished additional feats of military achievement. Although German military personnel of all ranks were theoretically eligible to receive this award, only 159 officers actually did.[14] *SS-Oberführer* Georg Bochmann, commander of the 18th

SS Division "Horst Wessel", was the only former camp officer to receive this award.[15] In total, twenty SS officers who served in the concentration camp system received one of the grades of the Knight's Cross – only six percent of the total of Knight's Crosses to the Waffen-SS officers as an aggregate. Certainly some former concentration camp men did win a version of this prestigious military award, but it was a very small number.

On September 28, 1941 the Germans created the War Order of the German Cross in Gold (*Kriegsorden des Deutschen Kreuzes in Gold*) to recognize a level of bravery or service above that required for an Iron Cross 1st Class but below that for the Knight's Cross. An estimated 30,000 crosses were awarded during the next three and one-half years.[16] Seventeen former concentration camp officers received this decoration as their highest award: *SS-Hauptsturmführer* Friedrich Meier, *SS-Obersturmbannführer* Wilhelm Breimaier, *SS-Obersturmbannführer* Rudolf Schneider, *SS-Obersturmbannführer* Adolf Kurtz, *SS-Sturmbannführer* Heinrich Krauth, *SS-Obersturmbannführer* Hans-Joachim Woith, *SS-Obersturmbannführer* Erich Rosenbusch, *SS-Sturmbannführer* Max Kühn, *SS-Obersturmbannführer* Franz Jakob, *SS-Sturmbannführer* Willi Hardieck, *SS-Obersturmbannführer* Wilhelm Goecke, *SS-Obersturmführer* Richard Schulze, *SS-Sturmbannführer* Hans Mützelfeldt, *SS-Sturmbannführer* Heinrich Heine, *SS-Sturmbannführer* Kurt Weisse, *SS-Oberführer* Dr. Wilhelm Fehrensen, and *SS-Sturmbannführer* Alfred Arnold. Again, considering these low figures, we can conclude that former camp officers did not figure prominently in this award.

Hitler also instituted several honors that were given for bravery or service not in a direct connection with combat.[17] Two of these were the War Service Cross 2nd Class and 1st Class (*Kriegsverdienstkreuz*). Both awards were presented in prodigious quantities. Approximately 7,600,000 War Service Cross 2nd Class were awarded while 600,000 War Service Cross 1st Class were presented.[18] The War Order of the German Cross in Silver (*Kriegsorden des Deutschen Kreuzes in Silber*) was a companion piece to the aforementioned German Cross in Gold and was presented for non-combat achievement more significant than that affiliated with the War Service Cross. The regime presented some 1,200 German Crosses in Silver during the war. Six former camp officers received the German Cross in Silver: *SS-Standartenführer* Hans Moser, *SS-Obersturmbannführer* Dr. Gustav Ortmann, *SS-Sturmbannführer* Siegfried Conrad, *SS-Sturmbannführer* Dr. Hans Stutz and *SS-Obergruppenführer* August Frank. *SS-Gruppenführer* Richard Glücks received the award in 1945 for his long-time work in the camps. The certificate read:[19]

SS-Gruppenführer Glücks has been the chief of Department D in the SS Economics and Administration Head

Office for the past two years. In this capacity, he is responsible for all matters which are connected with the concentration camp system. He does not only have to supervise the military leadership of 40,000 men who are in the camp guard system, but he is also responsible for military order and SS-like leadership of presently 15 concentration camps and 500 sub-camps with a total number of prisoners of around 750,000. In this capacity, which *SS-Gruppenführer* Glücks already had as inspector of concentration camps before becoming department chief, he has earned significant awards for the war armament because of the consistent use of prisoners in the weapons industry.

That there were no difficulties during all the years of the war and that the war industry was supplied with the demanded work force, then it was because of the efforts of *SS-Gruppenführer* Glücks. Through his accomplishments, he contributed considerably to the war supplies and with that for the conduct of the war. The amount of these contributions warrant awarding him the German Cross in Silver.

The following chart shows the overall distribution of awards for the 586 camp officers for which this information is recorded:[20]

Table 6
CONCENTRATION CAMP OFFICERS
HIGHEST DECORATION RECEIVED

DECORATION	*NUMBER*
Knight's Cross of the Iron Cross with Oak Leaves and Swords	1
Knight's Cross of the Iron Cross with Oak Leaves	5
Knight's Cross of the Iron Cross	14
Knight's Cross of the War Service Cross	1
German Cross in Gold	17
German Cross in Silver	6
Iron Cross 1st Class (includes Bar)	80
War Service Cross 1st Class	96
Iron Cross 2nd Class (includes Bar)	97
War Service Cross 2nd Class	269

Given these numbers, we can conclude that the German leadership felt that service at a concentration camp comprised both bravery and service, but was <u>not</u> directly related to combat. Every SS officer studied, who received the Iron Cross, German Cross in Gold, or one of the versions of the Knight's Cross, did so for deeds accomplished after (or before) his ser-

vice at a camp – but never for duty <u>at</u> a camp – although some senior SS officials, including *SS-Gruppenführer* Odilo Globocnik, did try to have the Iron Cross bestowed on camp personnel. In Globocnik's case, the decorations were for men involved in *Operation Reinhard* – all were disapproved.[21] For those officers who served in the camps but did not go to front-line combat with the Waffen-SS, the War Service Cross was the highest decoration they would receive. More concentration camp officers received the War Service Cross 2nd Class as their highest decoration than they did any other medal.[22] Those receiving any of the Iron Cross or Knight's Cross awards did so after their service in the camps.

In looking at the entire careers for these men through their decorations, it is obvious that many went from camp service to have distinguished records in combat. Kurt Franke, who served in the 3rd SS Division "Totenkopf" from 1940-1945, is an example. Following service at Sachsenburg and Buchenwald before the war, Franke joined the division and started a highly decorated career. He received the Wound Badge in Black on 25 may 1940 for wounds received during the campaign in France. On 22 June 1940 Franke was awarded the Iron Cross 2nd Class. The following year he received the Infantry Assault Badge in Bronze on 1 October 1941 for mechanized infantry service in Russia. On 6 October 1943 Franke was awarded the Knight's Cross for exceptional bravery and achievement. On 9 October 1943 Franke received the Close Assault Badge in Bronze – awarded to an individual for fifteen days in which close combat with the enemy (ie. grenades, bayonet attacks, hand-to-hand combat) was documented. On 20 December 1943 he received the award in silver – for a total of thirty days of this intense combat. Franke won the German Cross in Gold on 18 December 1944 before his death in action on 19 January 1945. Clearly, Franke and many others were no slackers in combat – and by any measure this combat was difficult and fierce.

SS SERVICE

Early service in the SS seems to have been a valued commodity to Heinrich Himmler and is well represented in concentration camp officers. By the end of 1929, one thousand men had joined the SS. One year later membership had risen to 2,700; by the close of 1931 there were almost 15,000 men serving in the organization. On January 30, 1933 – the day Hitler assumed the chancellorship of Germany, 52,000 men had joined. And only a year after that membership had risen to 200,000.[23] Many of these original SS members consisted of former *Freikorps* men – paramilitary units who fought Social Democrats and Communists inside Germany after World War

I, out of work intellectuals and lower-middle class Nazi Party men. Later SS members were unofficially known as "March Violets" – only coming forth after those who had served during the harsh winter – and viewed with suspicion by the veteran SS.[24]

Himmler established a silver death's head signet ring to be presented to proven SS men, regardless of rank. Initially this ring was to be limited to "old fighters" – those SS men with a membership number of below 10,000.[25]

Another indicator of the value of a low SS number is found in Nazi legal policy. On October 17, 1939 the Ministerial Council for the Defense of the Reich set up a special judicial system for cases involving members of the SS. The special SS courts were empowered to handle all military and non-military crimes committed by members of the SS or police. Infractions committed before enlistment could also be looked into. SS and police courts were located at the headquarters of each Higher SS and Police Leader (*HSSPF*).[26] There was an additional SS and police court attached to the SS Legal Department to deal with offenses of special importance where investigations were particularly difficult. Different officials could convene a court depending on the circumstances of a case. Hitler was the convening authority in the case of death sentences on death sentences of all commanders and officers or in the case of certain serious offenses by senior officials. Himmler was the convening authority on any case he reserved for himself which included cases against SS members with an SS number below 15,000. As befitting a special court, the Chief of the SS Legal Department served as the convening authority for all cases specially delegated to him by Himmler. Finally, the chief of a main department of the SS (*Hauptamt*) and commanders of HSSPF within their area of responsibility were also convening authorities when the above circumstances did not apply.[27]

An additional gauge is found in the annual SS statistics book. The *Statistisches Jahrbuch der Schutzstaffel der NSDAP 1937* indicates that 2,466 SS officers had SS membership numbers under 15,000.[28] Clearly, the SS leadership attached some importance to those who joined the movement in its early, and often difficult, days.

The following table shows a list of the twenty-four lowest SS membership numbers found for the camp men, and is followed by the distribution of concentration camp officers by SS number. One hundred thirty-seven SS officers with SS numbers lower than 15,000 served, at some point in their careers, in the concentration camp system:[29]

Table 7
CONCENTRATION CAMP OFFICERS
LOWEST SS NUMBERS

NAME	SS NUMBER
Emeran Schmid	34
Johann Beck	179
Heinrich Deubel	186
Kurt Pietzsch	249
Arno Lippmann	439
Egon Zill	535
Kurt Benz	657
Günther Tamaschke	851
Karl Möckel	908
Alfons Zeitler	1219
Arthur Rödl	1240
Willi Joachimsmeyer	1277
Hermann Dolp	1293
Hubert Karl	1339
Karl Merker	1352
Otto Sulzbach	1364
Wilhelm Vogler	1505
Fritz Miroff	1511
Johann Heidingsfelder	1537
Hans Helwig	1725
Hermann Pachen	1804
Alfred Driemel	1848
Alois Obermeier	1885
Walter Eisfeld	1996

Table 8
CONCENTRATION CAMP OFFICERS
DISTRIBUTION OF SS NUMBERS

SS NUMBER RANGE	NUMBER OF OFFICERS
1 - 1,000	9
1,001 - 5,000	58
5,001 - 10,000	38
10,001 - 15,000	32
15,001 - 50,000	131
50,001 - 100,000	106
100,001 +	554

When examining these twenty-four early entrants into the SS, it appears that most advanced reasonably well in their careers. One made *SS-Gruppenführer*, while three attained *SS-*

Oberführer, two achieved *SS-Standartenführer* and six advanced to *SS-Sturmbannführer*.

NAZI PARTY (NSDAP) SERVICE

One facet of party affiliation was the Nazi Party's highest decoration for service, "The Decoration of 9 November 1923" (*Ehrenzeichen vom 9. November 1923*) also known as the "Blood Order" (*Blutorden*).[30] Hitler created this decoration in March 1934 to commemorate the failed "Beer Hall" Putsch (attempted overthrow of the Bavarian government) on November 9, 1923 in Munich. Eligibility was initially limited to persons who had participated in the events of November 9th and who were known as "Old Comrades." In 1938 eligibility was expanded to include persons who had rendered outstanding service to the party in the 1920s and had received a Weimar court death sentence – and who had subsequently served at least one year in jail – or who had been severely wounded or killed in party service.[31]

SS men figured prominently in the award. Again, according to the *Statistisches Jahrbuch der Schutzstaffel der NSDAP 1937*, 141 SS officers were listed as recipients of this award.[32] The following table shows the twelve concentration camp officers who received the award and their first service in the concentration camp system. It is apparent from this data, that Himmler considered Blood Order recipients to be among the most reliable of officers, fully capable of helping to create the concentration camp system as evidenced by their early – with the exception of Dr. Willi Frank and Dr. Karl Gebhardt – camp service:

Table 9
CONCENTRATION CAMP OFFICERS
BLOOD ORDER RECIPIENTS

NAME INITIAL	CAMP SERVICE
Karl Bestle	Dachau, 1934
Robert Erspenmüller	Dachau, 1933
Dr. Willi Frank	Auschwitz, 1943
Dr. Karl Gebhardt	Ravensbrück, 1942
Paul Geisler	Oranienburg, 1937
Franz Kraus	Esterwegen, 1934
Christian Mohr	Columbia Haus, 1934
Josef Painter	Dachau, 1936
Eberhard Quirsfeld	Dachau, 1937
Arthur Rödl	Lichtenburg, 1934
Emeran Schmid	Esterwegen, 1935
Hilmar Wäckerle	Dachau, 1933

Another Nazi service award was the Golden Party Badge (*Goldenes Parteiabzeichen*). Hitler created this award in October 1933. To receive this award an individual must have had uninterrupted service in the Nazi Party since February 27, 1925 and who held Nazi Party membership numbers 1 to 100,000. As of December 1, 1938 1,626 SS officers had a NSDAP number below 100,000.[33] The earlier an individual joined the party, the lower the party number he would receive – the award was designed to recognize the early service of the first party members who joined before it became fashionable to do so. When both criteria were placed in effect, it was found that 22,282 – not 100,000 – persons actually qualified for the award. These individuals began to receive the Golden Party Badge on November 9, 1933 – the tenth anniversary of the failed Putsch.[34] Over one thousand SS officers wore the Golden Party Badge.[35] Within the sample of concentration camp officers, fifty-six had NSDAP membership numbers under 100,000.[36] The following two tables show the distribution of NSDAP numbers and a list of the twenty earliest camp officers who joined the Nazi Party; all had NSDAP numbers under 25,000, but not all had Golden Party Badges:

Table 10
CONCENTRATION CAMP OFFICERS
DISTRIBUTION OF NSDAP NUMBERS

NSDAP PARTY NUMBER	RANGE FREQUENCY
1 - 1,000	1
1,001 - 5,000	5
5,001 - 100,000	51
100,001 - 500,000	190
500,001 - 8,961,479	522

Table 11
CONCENTRATION CAMP OFFICERS
LOWEST NSDAP NUMBERS

NAME	NSDAP NUMBER	GOLDEN PARTY BADGE
Dr. Fritz Klein	732	Yes
Dr. Fridrich Honig	2628	No
Dr. Gustav Seifert	3388	Yes
Walter Wolter	4372	Yes
Walter Eisfeld	4802	Yes
Kurt Pietzsch	4898	No
Emeran Schmid	5428	Yes

Fritz Ritterbusch	6317	Yes	Dr. Erwin von Helmersen	SS-Hauptsturmführer
Johann Beck	6911	Yes	Erich von dem Hoff	SS-Obersturmführer
Arno Lippmann	8891	Yes	Gneomar von Hoym	SS-Sturmbannführer
Heinrich Deubel	14178	Yes	Kamillo von Knorr-Krehan	SS-Hauptsturmführer
Josef Painter	14292	Yes	Max von Lachemair	SS-Untersturmführer
Bernhard Schmidt	14699	Yes	Dr. Heinz von Lichem	SS-Obersturmführer
Wilhelm Vogler	15176	Yes	Dr. Phillip von Lützelburg	SS-Obersturmbannführer
Michael Redwitz	17607	Yes	Franz de Martin	SS-Obersturmführer
Heinrich Remmert	19110	Yes	Dr. Werner von Schenk	SS-Untersturmführer
Philipp Schmitt	19192	No		
Egon Zill	20063	Yes		
Karl D'Angelo	21616	Yes		
Karl Möckel	22293	Yes		

Equally revealing is the large number of SS camp officers who do not appear to have been members of the Nazi Party. Almost 200 officers (20.6 percent) in our sample have no party numbers listed, or any other indicator that they may have belonged to this organization. This compares with the published figure in the 1939 SS rank list of 8.3 percent of all SS officers at that time as not being party members.[37] Perhaps some of the files have clerical ommissions in this category, but clearly, a sizeable number of concentration camp officers were never members of the NSDAP.

The only similarity among these officers is their seemingly low corresponding highest rank; two *SS-Untersturmführer*, four *SS-Obersturmführer*, four *SS-Hauptsturmführer*, one *SS-Sturmbannführer*, one *SS-Obersturmbannführer* and just one *SS-Standartenführer*. Ten of the men were members of the Nazi Party but only one had an SS number below 15,000. Five were doctors, while six served in Waffen-SS units later in the war. At the conflict's conclusion, one member of this group committed suicide, one other was tried and executed, while one fled to Argentina. German nobility did not figure prominently among those who ran the concentration camps.

NOBILITY

The SS initially drew heavily from Germany's nobility. By 1938 some 18.7 percent of all *SS-Obergruppenführer*, 9.8 percent of *SS-Gruppenführer*, 14.3 percent of *SS-Brigadeführer*, 8.8 percent of *SS-Oberführer* and 8.4 percent of *SS-Standartenführer* were from the nobility hierarchy.[38] Omer Bartov, in his study of the German Army on the eastern front, defined membership in the nobility as all officers with a "von" or other prefixes of aristocratic origin attached to the family name.[39] Given this definition, we find the following thirteen members of the nobility who served as concentration camp officers:

DOCTORS

The single largest occupation – and it is overwhelmingly so – found for the concentration camp officers is the medical vocation. Doctors in Germany played a prominent role in the development and sustainment of National Socialism. More than 38,000 – nearly half of all physicians in the country – joined the Nazi Party; and doctors within the SS were represented seven times more frequently than the average for the employed male population. Jeremiah Barondess, in his *Journal of the American Medical Association* article "Medicine Against Society" states:[40]

> German physicians were attracted to the Nazi Party by promises that the National Socialists would restore Germany's power and the honor and dignity of the medical profession, and that they would be entrusted with a special role in the repair of the state...

Roger Manvell, in his work *SS and Gestapo*, states that approximately 350 doctors served in the SS.[41] He does not elaborate the sources of this figure, nor does he further divide this number into physicians or dentists. In any case, it serves as a start point to determine those in the concentration camp system. This project has found that overall, at least 285 medical officers rotated through the various camps through the war.[42]

Table 12
CONCENTRATION CAMP OFFICERS
MEMBERS OF THE NOBILITY

NAME	*RANK*
Dr. Franz von Bodmann	SS-Obersturmführer
Engelbrecht von Bonin	SS-Hauptsturmführer
Dr. Kurt aus dem Bruch	SS-Hauptsturmführer
Johann von Feil	SS-Standartenführer

We further can see the medical personnel breakdown in twelve of the major camps as shown below:

Table 13
CONCENTRATION CAMP
SS DOCTORS AND DENTISTS

	DOCTORS[43]	*DENTISTS*
Auschwitz	42	11
Buchenwald	43	8
Dachau	56	11
Flossenbürg	17	1
Gross-Rosen	8	2
Majdanek/Lublin	7	1
Mauthausen	45	7
Natzweiler	13	1
Neuengamme	16	4
Ravensbrück	20	4
Sachsenhausen	46	5
Stutthof	6	2

I believe Manville's estimate to be significantly low. So does Jack W. Robbins, J.D., who served as Legal Aide to the Chief of Counsel for War Crimes, Nürnberg, Germany, as Prosecutor in the Medical Case and as the Chief Prosecutor for the Oswald Pohl Case.[44] Whatever the total – and it is possible there were several thousand doctors in the SS – it is clear that hundreds served in the concentration camp system. Most held the rank of *SS-Hauptsturmführer* and many served in more than one camp during the period.

MARITAL STATUS

Heinrich Himmler encouraged members of the SS to marry. In a set of instructions issued in 1936, he stated "the SS man is expected to marry, preferably between the ages of 25 and 30, and found a family."[45] The SS marriage regulations gave Himmler the right to veto the marriage of an SS man, if the *Reichsführer-SS* thought the bride unsuitable. Those SS personnel already married when the regulation became effective did not have their union subject to review.[46] Not all SS officers appear to have followed the *Reichsführer-SS*'s advice; many remained single.

One might initially think that those officers attracted to concentration camp service would be socially stunted or at least not family-oriented men, but this is not the case. Of the 967 officers in this study, 777 – eighty percent – were married, with a further six engaged to be married, while thirteen had been married but were widowers.[47] Those divorced number thirteen while those listed as "single" number one hundred twelve, a percentage certainly smaller than that for single males of this age range in the population at large. Many had children and appear to have been typical family men, not only in Germany, but in any society. During this study, while I did find evidence that some – but not many – of the officers committed adultery, I did not uncover even one recorded instance of physical abuse by an officer toward his spouse.

OFFICER RANK

As a group, the SS officers who served at the concentration camps were relatively junior in rank considering the enormous tasks they were expected to accomplish. The following table presents the distribution of the highest officer ranks these individuals achieved.[48] Many of the officers actually served at a much lower rank during their camp service and achieved one or more promotions later in their career:

Table 14
CONCENTRATION CAMP OFFICERS
HIGHEST OFFICER RANK ACHIEVED

RANK	*NUMBER*
SS-Obergruppenführer	2
SS-Gruppenführer	6
SS-Brigadeführer	7
SS-Oberführer	15
SS-Standartenführer	38
SS-Obersturmbannführer	66
SS-Sturmbannführer	186
SS-Hauptsturmführer	298
SS-Obersturmführer	237
SS-Obersturmführer (F)	14
SS-Untersturmführer	93
SS-Untersturmführer (F)	3

Promotion records do not indicate that the concentration camp officers received promotions based on service at a camp. The only exception is for those men who served in the *Operation Reinhard* camps (Belzec, Sobibór and Treblinka). Most of these participants were recommended for, and received a promotion of one rank at the conclusion of this action.

RELIGION

Yisrael Gutmann, in his *Anatomy of the Auschwitz Death Camp*, explains that SS authorities insisted that all SS personnel renounce their membership in religious organizations. He maintains that while such a step was not required, the SS maintained such information in personnel files; those that did indeed abandon their previous religious beliefs were designated *"gottgläubig"*, a euphemism for atheism.[49]

I believe that perhaps "agnostic" – or "believer, but non-churchgoer" and not "atheist" would be a more accurate term for *gottgläubig*. In 1940, Theodor Eicke, chief of all concentration camps, sent the following guidance to his men:[50]

Prayer books are things for women and for those who wear panties. We hate the stink of incense; it destroys the soul as the Jews do the race. We believe in God, but not in his son, for that would be idolatrous and paganistic.

This is not a directive for atheism. Within those officers identified as having served in the camps, 264 listed Protestant as their religious faith, 166 listed Catholic and 425 listed "gottgläubig" or agnostic.[51] This category perhaps more accurately reflects what the SS personnel clerks reported under the religion category – we cannot be certain as to what the officers actually believed themselves. In 1938 the religious affiliations for all members of the SS *Totenkopf* troops were reported as: 2,211 Protestants, 632 Catholics and 6,329 Agnostics.[52]

WAFFEN-SS SERVICE

While the concentration camps did not fall under control of the Waffen-SS, it appears as though from a personnel standpoint there was a link between the two as *over forty-three percent* of all concentration camp officers served in the Armed SS. Hitler originally envisioned the Waffen-SS as an elite, militarized, politically reliable police force. The Führer maintained that this elite had to serve at the front in order to maintain its prestige. The Waffen-SS served in every theater, except Africa, and fielded the following major combat formations:

1st SS Division "Leibstandarte Adolf Hitler." The *Leibstandarte SS Adolf Hitler Regiment* was first formed August 15, 1938 in Berlin from elements of Hitler's personal SS guards. On July 15, 1942 the unit was elevated to a division in strength and named the *SS Division (motorized) Leibstandarte SS-Adolf Hitler*. On November 24, 1942 the unit underwent a further name change to *Panzergrenadier Division Leibstandarte SS-Adolf Hitler*.[53] One year later on October 22, 1943 the formation received its final unit designation – *1st SS Panzer Division "Leibstandarte-SS Adolf Hitler."*[54] The unit served in Poland, France, the Balkans, Russia, Italy, Normandy, Ardennes, Hungary and Austria.[55] Sixteen SS concentration camp officers have been identified who served with this division.

2nd SS Division "Das Reich." This unit was originally formed April 1, 1940 as the *SS Division Verfügungstruppe* which, in turn, became the *SS Division (motorized) "Reich"* on December 21, 1940. The unit received a further name change on October 15, 1942 to *SS Division (motorized) "Das Reich."* On November 9, 1942 the division was subsequently renamed *SS Panzergrenadier Division "Das Reich."* On October 22, 1943 the division acquired its final designation *2nd SS Panzer Division "Das Reich."* The Das Reich served in the Netherlands, France, the Balkans, Russia, Normandy, the Ardennes, Hungary and Bohemia.[56] Thirty-nine SS concentration camp officers served in this unit.

3rd SS Division "Totenkopf." This unit, the *SS Totenkopf Division*, was formed in Dachau on October 16, 1939 from various Totenkopf units and throughout the war maintained a close association with concentration camp personnel. On November 9, 1942 the division was renamed *SS Panzergrenadier Division "Totenkopf."* On October 22, 1943 it received its last redesignation of *3rd SS Panzer Division "Totenkopf."* The formation fought in France, Russia, Hungary and Austria.[57] One hundred fifty-nine SS concentration camp officers served, at some point in the war, in this formation.

4th SS Division "Polizei." The unit was formed on December 9, 1940 and named *SS-Polizei Division*. The division was renamed the *Polizei Panzergrenadier Division* on June 1, 1943. On October 22, 1943 it became the *4th SS Polizei Panzer-grenadier Division*. The unit fought in Russia, Greece, Yugoslavia, Hungary, Pomerania and West Prussia. Twenty-nine SS concentration camp officers served in the unit.

5th SS Division "Wiking." The division was formed November 20, 1940 as the *SS Division "Germania"* but was quickly renamed the *SS Division "Wiking."* On November 9, 1942 the division was renamed the *SS Panzergrenadier Division "Wiking."* On October 22, 1943 the unit was renamed the *5th SS Panzer Division "Wiking."* The unit fought in Russia, Hungary and Austria.[58] Forty-five SS concentration camp officers served in this division.

6th SS Division "Nord." This unit was created February 28, 1941 as *SS Kampfgruppe "Nord"* in Norway.[59] In September 1941 the unit reached division status as *SS Division "Nord."*

In September 1942 the unit became the *SS Gebirgs Division "Nord"* due to its mountain configuration.[60] On October 22, 1943 the unit was renamed as the *6th SS Gebirgs Division "Nord."* The division fought in Finland, Norway, France and Germany.[61] Fifty-seven SS concentration camp officers served in this unit.

7th SS Division "Prinz Eugen." The unit was initially formed in October 1942 and contained many ethnic Germans; its original designation was *SS Freiwilligen Gebirgs Division "Prinz Eugen."*[62] On October 22, 1943 the unit was renamed the *7th SS Freiwilligen Gebirgsjäger Division "Prinz Eugen."*[63] The unit primarily fought partisans in Serbia, Croatia and Austria.[64] Twenty-three SS concentration camp officers served in this unit.

8th SS Division "Florian Geyer." The *SS Kavallerie Division* was created in September 1942 at Debica, Poland from elements of the *SS Kavallerie Brigade.*[65] On October 22, 1943 the unit was renamed the *8th SS Kavallerie Division* and shortly thereafter became the *8th SS Kavallerie Division "Florian Geyer."* The division fought in Russia and Hungary in both front-line and anti-partisan operations.[66] Twenty-eight SS concentration camp officers served in this unit.

9th SS Division "Hohenstaufen." The unit was created on February 1, 1943 in Berlin as the *SS Panzergrenadier Division 9.* On March 1, 1943 the unit received the honorary name of "Hohenstaufen" and became the *SS Panzer Division "Hohenstaufen"* on October 3, 1943. On October 22 of that year the unit received its final designation of *9th SS Panzer division "Hohenstaufen."* The division fought in Russia, Normandy, Arnhem, the Ardennes and Hungary.[67] Twenty-two SS concentration camp officers served in this unit.

10th SS Division "Frundsberg." The formation was created on February 1, 1943 in southwest France as *SS Panzergrenadier Division 10.* On June 1, 1943 the unit was referred to as the *10th SS Division "Karl der Grosse."* On October 3, 1943 the organization became the *SS Panzer Division "Frundsberg."* Three weeks later on October 22 the unit received its last redesignation that of *10th SS Panzer Division "Frundsberg."* The unit fought in Russia, Normandy, Arnhem, the Ardennes, Pomerania and on the Oder.[68] Twenty SS concentration camp officers served in this unit.

11th SS Division "Nordland." The unit was formed at Grafenwöhr, Germany in July 1943 as *SS Panzergrenadier Division 11.* On October 3, 1943 the name changed to the *SS Freiwilligen Panzergrenadier Division "Nordland";* but this was short-lived and the formation became the *11th Freiwilligen Panzergrenadier Division "Nordland"* on October 22, 1943. The unit fought in Croatia, Russia, Courland, Pomerania, the Oder and Berlin.[69] Twelve SS concentration camp officers served in this unit during the war.

12th SS Division "Hitlerjugend." This unit began forming at Turnhout, Belgium in July 1943 from cadre from the 1st SS Division, as the *SS Panzergrenadier Division "Hitlerjugend."* On October 22, 1943 the unit became the *12th SS Panzer Division "Hitlerjugend"* – named so for its high percentage of former Hitler Youth members.[70] The division fought in Normandy, the Ardennes, Hungary and Austria.[71] Six SS concentration camp officers served in this element during the war.

13th SS Division "Handschar." This organization was created on March 1, 1943 primarily of Bosnian Muslims and was originally titled the *Kroatische SS Freiwilligen Division* (Croatian SS Volunteer Division). On July 2, 1943 the name was changed to *Kroatische SS Freiwilligen Gebirgs Division.* On October 22, 1943 the SS again changed the unit designation to that of the *13th SS Freiwilligen bosnische herzogowische Gebirgs Division (Kroatien).* In June 1944 this name was formalized to *the 13th Waffen Gebirgs Division der SS "Handschar" (Kroatien Nr. 1).* The unit fought partisans in Croatia and also served in Hungary.[72] Nine SS concentration camp officers served in this unit.

14th SS Division. The division was formed at Debica, Poland in September 1943 as the *14th Galizische SS Freiwilliger Division* of ethnic Germans and Ukrainians from the Galician district. On October 22, 1943 the unit was renamed the *14th Galizische SS Freiwilligen Infanterie Division.*[73] In August 1944 the unit again was redesignated – the *14th Waffen Grenadier Division der SS (galizische Nr. 1).* This formation fought in Russia, Slovakia and Austria.[74] Five SS concentration camp officers served in this organization.

15th SS Division. The formation was born in September 1943 as the *Lettische SS Freiwilligen Division* from the earlier *Lettische SS Freiwilligen Legion,* and was composed primarily of Latvians. On October 22, 1943 the unit was redesignated the *15th Lettische SS Freiwilligen Division.* In June 1944 the unit again was renamed, to the *15th Waffen Grenadier Division der SS (lettische Nr. 1).* The organization fought in Russia, Latvia and Pomerania.[75] Five SS concentration camp officers served in this division.

16th SS Division "Reichsführer SS." The division was formed on October 3, 1943 from the *SS Sturmbrigade "Reichsführer SS"* and received the name *16th SS Panzergrenadier Division*

"Reichsführer SS."[76] The unit fought in Italy and Austria.[77] Sixteen SS concentration camp officers served in this unit during the war.

17th SS Division "Götz von Berlichingen." This division was created on November 15, 1943 in western France as the *17th SS Panzergrenadier Division "Götz von Berlichingen."* It fought exclusively on the western front at Normandy, the Saar and Bavaria.[78] Fifteen SS concentration camp officers served in this division.

18th SS Division "Horst Wessel." This unit was formed January 25, 1944 from elements of the 1st SS Infanterie Brigade (motorized). It received the name *18th SS Freiwilligen Panzergrenadier Division "Horst Wessel."* The unit fought in Hungary, Slovakia and Silesia.[79] Seven SS concentration camp officers served in this unit.

19th SS Division. This formation entered the armed forces on January 7, 1944 as the *19th Lettische SS Freiwilligen Division* from elements of the *2nd Lettische SS Freiwilligen Brigade.* Like the 15th SS Division, the unit was composed primarily of Latvians. In June 1944 the unit was renamed the *19th Waffen Grenadier Division der SS (lettische Nr. 2).* The division fought in Latvia and Courland.[80] Three SS concentration camp officers later served in this formation.

20th SS Division. The division was created on January 24, 1944 as the *20th Estonische SS Freiwilligen Division* from elements of the *3rd Estonische SS Freiwilligen Brigade.* Both units were manned by large contingents of Estonians. In June 1944 the unit was renamed the *20th Waffen Grenadier Division der SS (estonische Nr. 1).* The unit fought in Estonia and Silesia. Six SS concentration camp officers served in this unit.

21st SS Division "Skanderbeg." This unit was formed May 1, 1944 in northern Albania as the *21st Waffen Gebirgs Division der SS "Skanderbeg" (albanische Nr. 1).* It was composed of many Muslim Albanians, and fought in Albania, Yugoslavia and Croatia.[81] Four SS concentration camp officers served in this unit during the war.

22nd SS Division "Maria Theresia." This cavalry division was formed on April 29, 1944 in Hungary as the *22nd SS Freiwilligen Kavallerie Division.* At the end of 1944 it received the honorary title of "Maria Theresia." The unit, which included many Hungarian volunteers, fought in Hungary and Budapest.[82] Three SS concentration camp officers served in this division.

23rd SS Division "Kama." This unit was formed on June 10, 1944 in Croatia and included many Croatian volunteers. The official designation of the unit was the *23rd Waffen Gebirgs Division der SS "Kama" (Kroatien Nr. 2).* The division was subsequently disbanded in December 1944. Five SS concentration camp officers served in this unit.

23rd SS Division "Nederland." This organization was formed on February 10, 1945 as the *23rd SS Freiwilligen Panzer-grenadier Division "Nederland" (niederlanische Nr. 1)* and contained many Dutch volunteers. It fought exclusively in Pomerania in the closing months of the war.[83] One SS concentration camp officer is known to have served in this unit.

24th SS Division. On August 1, 1944 this unit, the *24th Waffen Gebirgs (Karstjäger) Division der SS* was formed in northern Italy.[84] The unit may have seen very limited action against partisans in the Adriatic region.[85] One SS concentration camp officer served in this organization.

25th SS Division "Hunyadi." This unit, composed of a large number of Hungarian volunteers, was formed on November 2, 1944 as the *25th Waffen Grenadier Division der SS "Hunyadi" (ungarische Nr. 1).* It is reported to have fought in Hungary and near Nürnberg.[86] Two SS concentration camp officers served in this unit during the war.

26th SS Division. This organization was formed on January 29, 1945 as the *26th Waffen Grenadier Division der SS (ungarische Nr. 2).* It is not known if the unit saw combat.[87] Three SS concentration camp officers are believed to have served in this division.

27th SS Division "Langemarck." The division was created on October 19, 1944 at Soltau, Germany as the *27th SS Freiwilligen Grenadier Division "Langemarck."* It fought in Pomerania.[88] Five SS concentration camp officers served in this unit.

28th SS Division "Wallonien." The *28th SS Freiwilligen Grenadier Division "Wallonien"* was formed at Hannover, Germany on October 19, 1944. The formation fought in Pomerania. No SS concentration camp officers are believed to have served in the formation.

29th SS Division. The *29th Waffen Grenadier Division der SS (russische Nr. 1)* was formed in Warsaw in August 1944 from elements of the Kaminski Brigade, to combat the Warsaw Uprising. It was disbanded shortly thereafter.[89] One SS concentration camp officer served in this unit.

29th SS Division. The *29th Waffen Grenadier Division der SS (italienische Nr. 1)* was created on March 9, 1945 in Italy. It may have participated in very limited combat.[90] Two SS concentration camp officers later served in the unit.

30th SS Division. The *30th Waffen Grenadier Division der SS (russische Nr. 2)* was formed August 1, 1944. It fought near Belfort, France and the Rhine area.[91] No SS concentration camp officers are believed to have served in the unit.

31st SS Division. This division, the *31st SS Freiwilligen Grenadier Division*, was formed on October 1, 1944 from elements of the 13th and 23rd SS Divisions. It saw combat in Hungary and Silesia.[92] Two SS concentration camp officers are believed to have served in this unit.

32nd SS Division "30 Januar." The *32nd SS Freiwilligen Grenadier Division "30 Januar"* was formed on January 30, 1945. It saw action near Frankfurt a.d. Oder at the end of the war.[93] Two SS concentration camp officers are believed to have served in the unit.

33rd SS Division "Charlemagne." On February 10, 1945 the *33rd Waffen Grenadier Division der SS "Charlemagne" (franzosische Nr. 1)* was created in West Prussia. Manned by a contingent of French troops, it saw combat in Pomerania.[94] One SS concentration camp officer is believed to have served in this unit.

34th SS Division. The *34th Freiwilligen Grenadier Division "Landstorm Nederland"* was established in February 1945 from the former *SS Freiwilligen Grenadier Brigade "Landstorm Nederland."* It saw action only in the Netherlands.[95] Six SS concentration camp officers later served in the unit.

35th SS Division. The *35th SS und Polizei Grenadier Division* was formed in February 1945 from elements of *Polizei Brigade Wirth*. It fought on the Oder front. One SS concentration camp officer later served in the unit.

36th SS Division "Dirlewanger." The *36th Waffen Grenadier Division der SS "Dirlewanger"* started as a penal battalion in 1940 and was known successively as *Wilddiebkommando Oranienburg, Sonderkommando Dr. Dirlewanger, SS-Sonderbataillon Dirlewanger, Einsatz-Bataillon Dirlewanger, SS-Regiment Dirlewanger, SS-Sonderregiment Dirlewanger* and *SS-Sturmbrigade Dirlewanger*. It fought in Russia, Poland, Slovakia and Germany.[96] Seven SS concentration camp officers later served in this formation.

37th SS Division "Lützow." On February 20, 1945 the *37th SS Freiwilligen Kavallerie Division "Lützow"* was formed at Pressburg. It fought in Hungary. No SS concentration camp officers are believed to have served in this organization.

38th SS Division "Nibelungen." The *38th SS Grenadier Division "Nibelungen"* was formed in April 1945 from personnel from the SS Junkerschule Bad Tölz. It did not see combat. No SS concentration camp officers are believed to have served in this unit.

The *3rd SS Division "Totenkopf"* seems to have accounted for the lion's share of those concentration camp officers who also served in Waffen-SS units – some one hundred fifty-nine representing over sixteen percent of all concentration camp officers identified to have served in the camps. This is quite understandable as the division was formed from the *Totenkopf* units at the camps in the late 1930s, and constantly transferred men between the division and the camps during the war. The second leading unit was the *6th SS Division "Nord"*, which had fifty-seven camp officers assigned, the *5th SS Division "Wiking"* which hosted some forty-five camp officers, and the *2nd SS Division "Das Reich"*, one of the earliest and most prestigious of all SS units, which hosted some thirty-nine concentration camp officers.

Additionally, the Waffen-SS operated several corps headquarters, as well as independent regiments, brigades and specialized units. Over fifty SS concentration camp officers are believed to have served within these non-divisional organizations.

The following chart summarizes the numbers of SS concentration camp officers who also served at some point during the war in the Waffen SS divisions:

Table 15
CONCENTRATION CAMP OFFICERS
WAFFEN-SS DIVISION SERVICE

DIVISION	NUMBER CAMP OFFICERS SERVED
1st SS Division "Leibstandarte Adolf Hitler"	16
2nd SS Division "Das Reich"	39
3rd SS Division "Totenkopf"	159
4th SS Division "Polizei"	29
5th SS Division "Wiking"	45
6th SS Division "Nord"	57
7th SS Division "Prinz Eugen"	23
8th SS Division "Florian Geyer"	28

9th SS Division "Hohenstaufen"	22
10th SS Division "Frundsberg"	20
11th SS Division "Nordland"	12
12th SS Division "Hitlerjugend"	6
13th SS Division "Handschar"	9
14th SS Division	5
15th SS Division	5
16th SS Division "Reichsführer-SS"	17
17th SS Division "Götz von Berlichingen"	15
18th SS Division "Horst Wessel"	7
19th SS Division	3
20th SS Division	7
21st SS Division "Skanderbeg"	4
22nd SS Division "Maria Theresia"	3
23rd SS Division "Kama"	5
23rd SS Division "Nederland"	1
24th SS Division	1
25th SS Division "Hunyadi"	2
26th SS Division	3
27th SS Division "Langemarck"	5
28th SS Division "Wallonien"	0
29th SS Division (russische Nr. 1)	1
29th SS Division (italienische Nr. 1)	2
31st SS Division	2
32nd SS Division "30 Januar"	2
33rd SS Division "Charlemagne"	1
34th SS Division "Landstorm Nederland"	6
35th SS Division	1
36th SS Division "Dirlewanger"	7
37th SS Division "Lützow	0
38th SS Division "Nibelungen"	0

Not only did hundreds serve in front-line Waffen-SS divisions, but six former concentration camp officers also rose to become division commanders in the Waffen-SS. The following table shows the units these men commanded:

Table 16
CONCENTRATION CAMP OFFICERS
WAFFEN-SS DIVISION COMMANDERS

NAME | *UNIT (DURATION)*[97]

Theodor Eicke — 3rd SS Division "Totenkopf" (31.10.39-26.2.43)

Max Simon — 3rd SS Division "Totenkopf" (15.5.43-22.10.43); 16th SS Division "Reichsführer-SS" (22.10.43-1.7.44)

Georg Bochmann — 18th SS Division "Horst Wessel" (15.1.45-1.3.45); 17th SS Division "Götz von Berlichingen" (22.3.45-8.5.45)

Eduard Deisenhofer — 5th SS Division "Wiking" (1.8.44-15.8.44); 17th SS Division "Götz von Berlichingen" (30.8.44-15.9.44)

Heinrich Petersen — 18th SS Division "Horst Wessel" (1.4.45-8.5.45)

Helmuth Becker — 3rd SS Division "Totenkopf" (21.6.44-8.5.45)

Five different Waffen-SS divisions, the 3rd, 5th, 16th, 17th and 18th had commanders who earlier in their careers had served in the camps. Additionally, a large number of regimental and battalion commanders were also products of the concentration camp system. Those officers who went to Waffen-SS formations did so from the entire spectrum of camps rather than a specific relationship between a specific camp and unit.

CONCENTRATION CAMP SERVICE

As mentioned in the introduction, I do not believe that this investigation has uncovered one hundred percent of all the SS officers who served in the various camps in the period 1933 to 1945. But almost a thousand are known. The following is a distribution by camp of those officers who have been identified as serving at the various locations:

Table 17
CONCENTRATION CAMP OFFICERS
CAMP DISTRIBUTION

Auschwitz	161
Belsen	15
Belzec	7
Buchenwald	188
Chelmno/Kulmhof	3
Columbia Haus	32
Dachau	256
Dora	16
Esterwegen	28
Flossenbürg	69
Gross-Rosen	29
Herzogenbusch	9
Hinzert	24
Lichtenburg	47
Majdanek/Lublin	42

Mauthausen	113
Natzweiler	34
Neuengamme	61
Ravensbrück	52
Sachsenburg	47
Sachsenhausen	144
Sobibór	7
Stutthof	33
Theresienstadt	5
Treblinka	4

One additional note concerning camp distribution may be of interest. Of the total number of SS officers who worked in the camps, 554 (57%) served in one camp only. A further 229 (24%) saw service in two camps, while 69 (7%) appear to have been assigned to three camps during the period of the Third Reich. Additionally, 115 (12%) saw service in four or more concentration camps. Service at the headquarters of the concentration camp inspectorate, Oranienburg, will be discussed later.

COMBAT FATALITIES

Some SS concentration camp officers, as earlier reported, went on to serve in front-line Waffen-SS units, while others took part in anti-partisan operations behind the lines. For some SS officers, these assignments proved fatal. Of the total number of concentration camp officers identified in this work, it appears that seventy-four – or just under eight percent – were later killed in action, missing in action and presumed dead, or died of wounds.[98]

At least one source states that Heinrich Himmler issued a decree at the beginning of the war which forbade senior concentration camp officials from later serving in front-line duty. The rationale was obvious – should a former camp man be captured, he might be forced to reveal the details of the camp system.[99] This study has not been able to find such a written order; if it existed verbally – or if it existed at all – it certainly does not appear to have been very strictly enforced.

The most famous death involving a former concentration camp officer was that of *SS-Obergruppenführer* Theodor Eicke. During February 1943, the SS Division "Totenkopf" participated in the German counteroffensive that retook Khar'kov. On the afternoon of February 26, 1943 the division was involved in a lengthy pursuit of Soviet forces. A long radio silence from the division armored regiment caused Eicke, the division commander, to take to the air in his Fieseler *Storch* observation plane to attempt to gain contact with the unit. Approximately 4:30 PM, Eicke and his pilot spotted a company from the regiment in the village of Michailovka and the aircraft approached to land. Dropping to 300 feet Eicke passed over some unseen Russian positions in an adjoining village of Artelnoye. The enemy immediately opened fire with intense small arms and antiaircraft fire. The *Storch* was ripped apart in midair, crashed between the two villages and burned fiercely leaving no survivors. That night SS troops attempted to reach the wreckage with no success. The following morning, a reinforced company succeeded, and recovered the charred bodies of Eicke, his division adjutant and his pilot.[100] Many others died as well. The following is a summary of those former concentration camp officers believed to have been killed in combat:

Table 18
CONCENTRATION CAMP OFFICERS
KILLED IN ACTION

NAME	*UNIT*	*DATE KILLED*
Alfred Arnold	3rd SS Division "Totenkopf"	10 October 1944
Rudolf Bauer	3rd SS Division "Totenkopf"	24 May 1940
Richard Baumann	3rd SS Division "Totenkopf"	28 February 1942
Armin Beilhack		22 August 1943
Fritz Biermeier	3rd SS Division "Totenkopf"	10 October 1944
Dr. Erich Boose	Police Battalion 306	13 May 1942
Willi Bredemeier	5th SS Division "Wiking"	20 September 1941
Theo Bücker	3rd SS Division "Totenkopf"	28 June 1941
Heinz Büngeler	3rd SS Division "Totenkopf"	4 March 1943
Ewald Burk	6th SS Division "Nord"	14 January 1943
Eduard Deisenhofer	5th SS Division "Wiking"	31 January 1945
Alfred Driemel	8th SS Division "Florian Geyer"	9 December 1943

Theodor Eicke	3rd SS Division "Totenkopf"	26 February 1943
Herbert Eisholt	1st SS Brigade	2 September 1942
Robert Erspenmüller	2nd SS Division "Das Reich"	25 May 1940
Kurt Franke	3rd SS Division "Totenkopf"	19 January 1945
Dr. Josef Friedl	7th SS Division "Prinz Eugen"	15 November 1943
Hermann Friedrichs	10th SS Division "Frundsberg"	10 April 1944
Karl Fritzsch		May 1945
Wilhelm Goecke		22 October 1944
Heinz Goroncy	3rd SS Division "Totenkopf"	26 April 1942
Dr. Herbert Graeff	2nd SS Division "Das Reich"	5 August 1944
Adam Grünewald	3rd SS Division "Totenkopf"	1945
Adolf Haas		March 1945
Markus Habben		21 September 1941
Herbert Haenel	14th SS Division	September 1944
Willi Hardieck	12th SS Division "Hitlerjugend"	17 December 1944
Alexander Herrmann	3rd SS Division "Totenkopf"	20 October 1941
Julius Jung	6th SS Division "Nord"	2 October 1944
Hermann Kimmel	3rd SS Division "Totenkopf"	13 July 1943
Wilhelm Kleber	2nd SS Division "Das Reich"	23 July 1944
Dr. Ladislaus Konrad	Panzergrenadier Regiment 10[101]	17 February 1944
Heinrich Krauth	3rd SS Division "Totenkopf"	21 August 1943
Heinz Kuechle	6th SS Division "Nord"	19 September 1944
Karl Kuenstler		April 1945
Herbert Lange		20 April 1945
Peter Lotz	3rd SS Division "Totenkopf"	7 March 1944
Azelino Masarié	3rd SS Division "Totenkopf"	9 August 1944
Martin Melzer		24 July 1944
Hermann Michl *		21 July 1944
Dr. Gerhard Müller		Unknown
Johann Niemann *		14 October 1943
Herbert Otto		6 May 1945
Heinrich Petersen[102]	18th SS Division "Horst Wessel"	6 May 1945
Adolf Pittschellis	3rd SS Division "Totenkopf"	26 January 1945
Helmuth Rahn	6th SS Division "Nord"	24 June 1943
Emil Reichherzer		23 January 1943
Franz Reichleitner		3 January 1944
Dr. August Roschmann	2nd SS Division "Das Reich"	29 July 1944
Rudolf Saalbach	11th SS Division "Nordland"	April 1945
Albert Sauer *		3 May 1945
Max Schmid		5 January 1944
Rudolf Schneider	3rd SS Division "Totenkopf"	6 July 1943
Wilfried Schroedel	3rd SS Division "Totenkopf"	17 August 1941
Hans Schurz		December 1944
Gottfried Schwarz		19 June 1944
Anton Stehno	17th SS Division "Götz von Berlichingen"	10 July 1944
Fritz Steinert	5th SS Division "Wiking"	7 October 1942
Horst Strathmann	7th SS Division "Prinz Eugen"	26 November 1943
Walter Tietze	5th SS Division "Wiking"	January 1945
Hans-Günther Ulrich	17th SS Division "Götz von Berlichingen"	23 October 1944
Kurt Vogdt	SS Infantry Regiment 4	6 March 1942

Paul Vogel	3rd SS Division "Totenkopf"	20 October 1944
Herbert Wachsmann	7th SS Division "Prinz Eugen"	15 October 1944
Hilmar Waeckerle	5th SS Division "Wiking"	2 July 1941
Rudolf Wagner	SS Croatian Volunteer Legion	1943
Hans Waldmann	SS Kampfgruppe "Schuldt"	19 December 1942
Christian Wirth		26 May 1944
Fritz Wittle	3rd SS Division "Totenkopf"	22 August 1941
Hans-Joachim Woith	9th SS Division "Hohenstaufen"	30 June 1944
Dr. Walter Wollweber	1st SS Division "Leibstandarte Adolf Hitler"	8 August 1944
Wilhelm Ziemssen		30 September 1943
Franz Ziereis *		24 May 1945
Hans Zwerger		15 March 1943

Those notated with an asterix were killed in the vicinity of a camp.

Ten officers who are believed to have been killed in action had previously served as camp *kommandants*. Seven were physicians. Those not showing a unit in the previous table either were not assigned to a Waffen-SS unit when they were killed, or if they were assigned, it is not reflected in their personnel file. Several officers are shown to have died near the camp itself, either in the liberation of the camp by allied forces or during a prisoner revolt as in the case of Johann Niemann who was killed during the Sobibór Uprising in 1943.[103]

These deaths accurately reflect overall German losses during the war. Two of these officers were killed in action in 1940, seven in 1941, seven in 1942, sixteen in 1943, twenty-nine in 1944 and thirteen in 1945. Nineteen were serving with the 3rd SS Division "Totenkopf" at the time of their death – a unit that was involved in some of the bitterest fighting during the entire war. A review of both unit and date of death indicates that many were killed in some of the war's largest and most crucial battles such as *Operation Barbarossa* – the invasion of the Soviet Union in 1941, *Operation Zitadelle* – the offensive at Kursk in July 1943, operations against the western allies in Normandy in 1944 and the last-ditch German offensive in December 1944, which came to be known as the Battle of the Bulge. These were clearly front-line actions and indicate a degree of combat bravery we might otherwise be prone to dismiss in a population of this nature.

EPIDEMICS

The overcrowded conditions in the concentration camps enabled disease to ravage tens of thousands of prisoners. An epidemic of typhus struck Dachau in 1942 and 1944. In October 1941 the same disease prevented SS personnel from entering the main camp at Neuengamme. Dysentery hit Mauthausen in 1939, while typhoid fever plagued Majdanek/Lublin during the entire duration of the camp's existence. At Auschwitz, malaria, diphtheria, paratyphoid fever, dysentery, tuberculosis and typhus caused one epidemic after another from 1941 to 1943 – its location in a marshy area did not help matters in repelling disease. A typhus epidemic occurred in Belzec in 1942, while another hit Treblinka in 1943 – both ravaged that portion of the prisoner population who were temporarily being allowed to survive in order to assist in running the camp.[104] When such epidemics occurred, the SS would generally seal off the entire camp and enter only to conduct roll-calls.[105] But, despite these precautions, some SS troops fell victim to these diseases. Two SS officers are identified as such; Dr. Max Popiersch died on 21 April 1942 of typhus at Auschwitz, while Dr. Siegfried Schwela died of the same disease at Auschwitz on 10 May 1942.[106]

ORANIENBURG – THE CORPORATE HEADQUARTERS

At the end of 1934, Theodor Eicke had assumed the title of *Inspekteur der Konzentrationslager* and *Führer der Wachverbände* (Inspector of Concentration Camps and Leader of Guard Units).[107] In 1936 Eicke, as Inspector of Concentration Camps, began to develop a top-level administrative staff at Oranienburg to supervise the economy of the concentration camps, and to manage the increasing number of *Totenkopfverbände* troops.[108] This new staff was known as *Stab des Führers der KL und SS-TV* (Staff of the Leader of Concentration camps and SS Death's Head Units). Eicke's successor in 1939 was Richard Glücks who held the position of Inspector of Concentration Camps but not that of Leader of SS Death's Head Units. His official title was *Der Reichsführer-SS – Inspekteur der Konzentrationslager*, and he held this position until 1942.[109]

Slowly, but surely, an outside organization – initially the *Hauptamt Haushalt-und Bauten* and later its successor, the *Wirtschaftsverwaltungs-hauptamt (WVHA)*, under *SS-Gruppenführer* Oswald Pohl – began to demand economic results from the camp system. From March 1942 to the end of the war, the concentration camp administration fell under the *WVHA* as *Amtsgruppe D* (Division D). Subordinate to this level were sections D I – the Central Office, D II – Use of Prison Labor, D III – Medical and D IV Concentration Camp Administration.[110] Glücks became the chief of *Amstgruppe D*, subordinate to Pohl at the *WVHA*, which by 1944 had some 1,700 people.[111]

The inspectorate, however, did not control the operations of the *Operation Reinhard* camps – Belzec, Sobibór and Treblinka. These facilities were under the direction of the SS Leader for Lublin District in the *Generalgouvernement*.[112] Ultimate authority for the operation of these camps lay with the Führer's Chancellery (*Kanzlei des Führers – KdF*) in Berlin, via the T4 program.

One hundred eighty-seven SS officers have been identified as serving at the headquarters of the concentration camp inspectorate at Oranienburg. Of these, ninety-five also served at other camps during their careers.

GENERAL OFFICERS

Seventeen SS officers who served in the concentration camps went on to achieve general officer rank. Himmler elevated two men to the grade of *SS-Obergruppenführer*, six officers to *SS-Gruppenführer* and seven men to *SS-Brigadeführer*. These were small numbers when one considers that as of November 1944 there were ninety-two *SS-Obergruppenführer*, ninety-five *SS-Gruppenführer* and two-hundred seventy *SS-Brigadeführer* in service.[113] The following table lists these sixteen:

Table 19
CONCENTRATION CAMP OFFICERS
GENERAL OFFICERS

NAME	*GRADE*	*SS NUMBER*
Theodor Eicke	SS-Obergruppenführer	2921
August Frank	SS-Obergruppenführer	56169
Dr. Karl Blumenreuther	SS-Gruppenführer	276523
Dr. Karl Gebhardt	SS-Gruppenführer	265894
Dr. Karl Genzken	SS-Gruppenführer	207954
Richard Glücks	SS-Gruppenführer	58706
Hans Helwig	SS-Gruppenführer	1725
Max Simon	SS-Gruppenführer	83086
Helmuth Becker	SS-Brigadeführer	113174
Dr. Wilhelm Berndt	SS-Brigadeführer	229196
Dr. Carl Clauberg	SS-Brigadeführer (Honorary)	
Dr. Oskar Hock	SS-Brigadeführer	276822
Berthold Maack	SS-Brigadeführer	15690
Dr. Joachim Mrugowski	SS-Brigadeführer	25811
Karl Taus	SS-Brigadeführer	6786

It is apparent that promotion to general officer was not based solely, or even to a great degree on early membership in the SS – only three of these officers had SS numbers under 15,000. All were Nazi Party members; but only three had early party numbers under 100,000. Five of these men served at Dachau in the early to mid-1930s. Finally, nine served in the Waffen-SS later in the war.

POST-WAR JUSTICE AND PUNISHMENT

After the original International Trial of War Criminals at Nürnberg, the American Military Tribunal held twelve further trials in the same city. These judicial proceedings covered a wide variety of transgressions from the "doctors' case" to the "IG-Farben case" to the SS Economic Administrative Office. Of the 184 accused in the twelve cases, the court sentenced 24 defendants to death and a further 20 to life imprisonment.[114] American military tribunals also prosecuted 1,021 personnel for concentration camp activities at Dachau, Buchenwald, Mauthausen, Dora-Mittelbau and Flossenbürg. Of these defendants 885 were convicted. In total, American military tribunals of all cases sentenced 324 persons to death and 247 to life imprisonment.[115]

British military tribunals were also quite busy during the post war period. British authorities brought legal proceedings against concentration camp personnel who served at Auschwitz, Bergen-Belsen and Natzweiler. Of 1,085 defendants accused in all British military tribunals, 240 received the death sentence.[116]

French military tribunals handled various cases to include proceedings against personnel who served at Natzweiler. In total, these French proceedings convicted 2,107 persons and sentenced 104 to death. Belgium convicted 75 persons, of whom 10 received death sentences. Poland convicted 5,358 German nationals, although we do not know the exact breakdown of sentences.[117]

Germany tried several thousand individuals for Nazi-crimes beginning in 1958. None of the defendants were sentenced to death, while 79 appear to have received a sentence of life imprisonment.[118]

Many of the sentences of life imprisonment were later reduced. Some death sentences were also commuted. Most never faced judicial proceedings of any sort after the war. It appears in this study that 63 concentration camp officers actually were put to death as shown in the following table:

Table 20
CONCENTRATION CAMP OFFICERS
SENTENCED AND EXECUTED

NAME	*DATE EXECUTED*
Johann Altfuldisch	28 May 1947
Hans Aumeier	1948
August Blei	28 May 1947
Heinrich Eisenhöfer	April 1947
Dr. Friedrich Entress	28 May 1947
Otto Förschner	28 May 1946
Dr. Karl Gebhardt	2 June 1948
Amon Goeth	13 September 1946
Maximilian Grabner	12 December 1947
Hermann Grossmann	19 November 1948
Johannes Grimm	27 May 1947
Dr. Erwin von Helmersen	12 April 1947
Dr. Wilhelm Henkel	28 May 1947
Rudolf Höss	16 April 1947
Franz Hössler	13 December 1945
Dr. Waldemar Hoven	2 June 1948
Josef Jarolin	28 May 1946
Dr. Willi Jobst	28 May 1947
Heinrich Josten	Unknown
Dr. Bruno Kitt	8 October 1946
Max Koegel	27 April 1947
Josef Kramer	13 December 1945
Dr. Eduard Krebsbach	28 May 1947
Walter Langleist	28 May 1946
Arthur Liebehenschel	24 January 1948
Arno Lippmann	29 May 1946
Julius Ludolph	27 May 1947
Gerhard Maurer	2 April 1953
Hans Merbach	14 January 1949
Theodor Meyer	13 August 1947
Fritz Miroff	19 November 1948
Karl Möckel	Unknown
Hans Moeser	Unknown
Dr. Joachim Mrugowski	2 June 1948
Max Pauly	October 1948
Max Pausch	12 November 1948
Alex Piorkowski	22 October 1948
Karl Rahm	1947
Michael Redwitz	29 May 1946
Dr. Werner Rohde	11 October 1946
Wilhelm Ruppert	28 May 1946
Walter Schmiedetzki	Unknown
Hans Schmidt	7 June 1951
Phillipp Schmitt	1950
Kurt Schmutzler	29 October 1948
Max Schobert	19 November 1948
Karl Schöpperle	12 November 1948
Vinzenz Schoettl	28 May 1946
Heinrich Schwarz	20 March 1947
Ludwig Schwarz	3 October 1947
Johann Schwarzhuber	3 May 1947
Dr. Siegfried Seidl	February 1947
Bruno Skierka	3 October 1947
Fritz Suhren	12 June 1950
Anton Thernes	3 December 1944
Richard Thomalla[119]	12 May 1945
Anton Thumann	8 October 1946
Alfred Trzebinski	8 October 1946
Dr. Helmuth Vetter	2 February 1949
Erich Wasicky	28 May 1947
Martin Weiss	29 May 1946
Dr. Waldemar Wolter	28 May 1947
Viktor Zoller	28 May 1947
Adolf Zutter	27 May 1947

In examining the data concerning executions, we find that twenty-one officers served at Auschwitz at some time, seventeen at Dachau, twelve at Mauthausen, eight at Majdanek/Lublin, seven at Sachsenhausen and six each at Buchenwald, Flossenbürg and Neuengamme. Eight of those executed were doctors and fourteen had served as camp *kommandants*.

THE *KOMMANDANTS*

No analysis of this population can be complete without a discussion of the highest members of the camp supervision – the *kommandants*. As previously mentioned, the *kommandant* had overall responsibility for the camp, and therefore, it is believed that *SS-Reichsführer* Heinrich Himmler personally interviewed and approved each prospective *kommandant* – at least for those of primary camps – before his appointment to the position.[120] The following seventy-four officers are known to have served in this position:

Table 21

CONCENTRATION CAMP KOMMANDANTS

NAME	*CAMP*
Herbert Andorfer	Sajmiste
Richard Baer	Auschwitz, Dora
Hermann Baranowski	Lichtenburg, Sachsenhausen
Hans Bothmann	Chelmno
Paul Brinkmann	Esterwegen, Boergermoor
Otto Brossmann	Blechhammer sub-camp
Anton Burger	Theresienstadt
Karl D'Angelo	Osthofen
Erich Deppner	Westerbork
Heinrich Deubel	Dachau, Columbia Haus
Irmfried Eberl	Treblinka
Johann Eichelsdorfer	Kaufering sub-camp
Theodor Eicke	Dachau
Walter Eisfeld	Sachsenhausen
Emil Faust	Neusustrum
Willi Fleitmann	Boergermoor
Hermann Florstedt	Majdanek
Otto Foerschner	Dora, Kaufering sub-camp
Kurt Franz	Treblinka
Karl Fritzsch	Flossenbürg
Albert Gemmeker	Westerbork
Walter Gerlach	Columbia Haus
Wilhelm Gideon	Gross-Rosen
Wilhelm Goecke	Kauen
Hans Griem	Husum-Schwesing sub-camp
Friedrich Hartjenstein	Birkenau, Flossenbürg, Natzweiler
Johannes Hassebroek	Gross-Rosen
Walter Heinrich	Amersfoort
Hans Helwig	Ankenbuck, Sachsenhausen
Gottlob Hering	Belzec
Paul Hoppe	Stutthof
Hans Hüttig	Natzweiler, Herzogenbusch
Anton Kaindl	Sachsenhausen
Rudolf Kinne	Elbing sub-camp
Kurt Klipp	Blechhammer sub-camp
Karl Otto Koch	Columbia Haus, Esterwegen, Sachsenhausen, Majdanek, Buchenwald
Max Koegel	Flossenbürg, Ravensbrück, Majdanek
Josef Kramer	Birkenau, Natzweiler, Belsen
Karl Künstler	Flossenbürg
Herbert Lange	Chelmno
Walter Langleist	Kaufering sub-camp
Arthur Liebenhenschel	Auschwitz, Majdanek
Michael Lippert	Sachsenhausen
Arno Lippmann	Kaufering sub-camp
Hans Loritz	Papenburg, Esterwegen, Dachau, Sachsenhausen
Julius Ludolph	Melk sub-camp
Max Pauly	Neuengamme, Stutthof
Bruno Pfuetze	Jaworzno sub-camp
Alex Piorkowski	Dachau
Hermann Pister	Buchenwald
Karl Rahm	Theresienstadt
Otto Reich	Lichtenburg
Franz Reichleitner	Sobibór
Alexander Reiner	Columbia Haus, Sachsenburg
Arthur Roedl	Lichtenburg, Gross-Rosen
Albert Sauer	Mauthausen, Riga, Bad Sulza, Ravensbrück
Wilhelm Schitli	Arbeitsdorf
Bernhard Schmidt	Lichtenburg, Sachsenburg
Heinrich Schwarz	Natzweiler, Auschwitz-Monowitz
Ludwig Schwarz	Hersbruck sub-camp
Siegfried Seidl	Theresienstadt
Paul Sporrenberg	Hinzert
Franz Stangl	Sobibór, Treblinka
Karl Streibel	Trawniki
Anton Streitweiser	Melk sub-camp
Arnold Strippel	two sub-camps of Neuengamme
Fritz Suhren	Ravensbrück
Hilmar Wäckerle	Dachau
Jakob Weisseborn	Flossenbürg
Martin Weiss	Dachau, Neuengamme, Majdanek
Eduard Weiter	Dachau
Christian Wirth	Belzec
Franz Ziereis	Mauthausen
Egon Zill	Flossenbürg, Natzweiler

Four of the *kommandants* hailed from Munich, more than any other birthplace. Twenty-one held SS numbers under 10,000, almost twenty-nine percent. Ten held NSDAP numbers under 100,000. The vast majority – sixty-eight – were married, with two others widowers and three divorced. Thirty-one *kommandants* professed to be agnostic, with eighteen listed Catholic and twenty-two Protestant as their religious faith. Twenty served at some point during the war in the Waffen-SS. One received the Knight's Cross with Oak Leaves, one the German Cross in Gold, nine the Iron Cross 1st Class, twenty-one the War Service Cross 1st Class, four the Iron Cross 2nd

Class and ten the War Service Cross 2nd Class. Ten of the *kommandants* were killed in action during the war, two were executed by the SS near the end of the war, two died of natural causes while serving as *kommandants*, four committed suicide shortly before or after the war, four died in prison and sixteen were executed by the allies after the conflict.

CONCLUSIONS

While each individual officer possessed unique characteristics, with a sample this size it is possible to develop a profile for those men who served in the camps. A "typical" SS officer from the camps seems to have been relatively young, in his early thirties, and likely to have been born somewhere other than one of Germany's largest cities – if he did come from a large city, it was most probably Munich or Berlin. He was overwhelmingly likely to be married and presumably professed to be agnostic, although his actual religious convictions in private may have been closer to the religion in which he grew up. The "typical" officer most likely served in one camp – Dachau would be the highest probability – and if he served in the Waffen-SS later in the war, it was most likely with the *3rd SS Division "Totenkopf."* He would have been of relatively low commissioned rank, *SS-Hauptsturmführer* or *SS-Obersturmführer.* Not well decorated, his highest award probably was the War Service Cross 2nd Class. While some officers appear to have been punished for various disciplinary infractions during the war, most had spotless records and seem to have been model citizens by the standards of any society. The "typical" camp officer stood a good chance of surviving the war and almost an equally good chance of avoiding serious judicial proceedings in the post-war years. While many civilian occupations are represented in this population, service related to the medical field seems to figure prominently. Given the actuarial tables for men in the twentieth century, it is most likely that our "typical" officer resumed civilian life in Germany or perhaps Austria after the war, raised a family, and died in the 1970s or 1980s.

Based on the analysis of data I would like to propose two conclusions made possible by looking at the aggregate statistics of this large SS officer sample. The first conclusion is quite obvious; the other is, at this point, still in speculation and requires further research beyond the scope of this book.

THE STRONG LINK BETWEEN CAMP AND WAFFEN SS SERVICE

The indictments at Nürnberg were designed to charge both individuals – such as Goering, Kaltenbrunner, Hess, etc., and organizations such as the SS, the Gestapo and the Nazi "Leadership Corps." Lawyers for the defense attempted to separate sub-organizations within the SS (*Waffen-SS* versus *Allgemeine-SS*) to limit the condemnation to the general SS, the overall body of the SS, as distinct from the Waffen-SS as shown in the following exchange:[121]

PRESIDENT OF THE COURT: What can you tell us about the task of the Death's-Head [Totenkopf] units"?

WITNESS BRILL: The tasks of the Death's Head units were laid down in the basic decree of August 1938. At times they furnished guards for the concentration camps, although they had no permission to enter the camps. Their replacements were recruited among the German youth or among men who had already served their term of military service. Their training was not supervised by the Armed Forces but it was on military lines.

Paul Hausser testified at the Trial of the Major War Criminals before the International Military Tribunal at Nürnberg. Born October 7, 1880 in Brandenburg, Hausser was one of the most respected commanders in the Waffen-SS. He retired from the *Reichswehr* as a major general in 1932, and joined the SS two years later. During World War II he commanded *SS Division "Das Reich",* the SS Panzer Corps, and the 7th Army. One of the highest decorated soldiers in the Reich, he was a recipient of the Knight's Cross with Oak Leaves and Swords.[122] Hausser's image was that of a true "front-line" soldier, never personally involved in anything but front-line operations. In the following testimony at Nürnberg in 1946, he and others described the relationship – or lack thereof – between the concentration camps and the *Waffen-SS*:[123]

LAWYER PELCKMANN: Did the *Waffen-SS* furnish the guard units and the so-called command personnel for the concentration camps?

HAUSSER: The guards of the concentration camps and the personnel in the command did not belong to the *Waffen-SS.* Only in the course of the war were these units designated as *Waffen-SS* in order to release them from military service and give them freedom to carry out their police duties. The members of the *Waffen-SS* considered this measure, which they learned of only after the war, a deliberate deception on the part of Himmler. We did not have anything to do with the men of the concentration camps and the guard personnel.

In his own mind, perhaps Hausser did believe "his men" had nothing to do with concentration camps. But we now know that at least thirty-nine officers in Hausser's division – and hundreds in the *Waffen-SS* as a whole – had, in fact, served in the camps, even if Hausser maintained he was unaware of this actuality.[124]

After the war many German politicians attempted to rehabilitate the image of the *Waffen-SS*. The August 1956 issue of *Deutsche Soldatenzeitung* (German Soldiers' Newspaper) for example, reported that Konrad Adenauer, the Federal Chancellor, said at a public speech in Hannover "The men of the *Waffen-SS* were soldiers, just like the others..."[125]

Post-war literature has frequently mirrored public opinion in Germany. The official history of the *5th SS Division "Wiking",* for example, fails to mention the presence in the unit of one *SS-Hauptsturmführer* Josef Mengele, whose infamous existence was so notorious when the history was written, he would be hard to overlook.[126] Jost Schneider, in his *Their Honor was Loyalty!*, a book on Knight's Cross winners in the *Waffen-SS*, summarizes Theodor Eicke – often known as the father of the concentration camp system – as follows:[127]

> To the end, Eicke believed in and lived by the code: 'Right or wrong – my country!'

These views are not limited to German authors.[128] Richard Landwehr, an American, in his work *Fighting For Freedom: The Ukrainian Volunteer Division of the Waffen-SS*, has this to say about the organization:[129]

> Let us hope that someday soon there will no longer be any need to 'apologize' for service in the *Waffen-SS*, or to belittle someone else for having served in it. The *Waffen-SS* was a unique experiment that fostered international unity, high ideals and valiant sacrifice against what can be termed the somewhat less than high-minded forces of Soviet Communism and its assorted capitalist allies.

Even many impartial scholars have omitted elaborating on the larger link between the *Waffen-SS* and concentration camp personnel. Robert Lewis Koehl, in his work *The Black Corps*, states the following:[130]

> An additional irony which confuses matters further is the policy begun in 1940 of inducting the camp administrators into the *Waffen-SS* to keep them from being drafted

for the Wehrmacht. While some of these persons certainly saw service at the front, it was not possible for Himmler to pursue his policy of wholesale rotations of even top officers through all branches of SS activity. Once absorbed into the rapidly growing system, the concentration camp SS tended to remain there, while correspondingly only a fraction of the *Waffen-SS* had any official contact with the concentration camps.

I believe that the statistics for the SS concentration camp officers do show a link with the *Waffen-SS* which is far greater than "only a fraction." At least 419 of the SS officers who served in the concentration camps, were assigned to *Waffen-SS* units at some point during the war. Twenty one-time camp officers won one of the grades of the prestigious Knight's Cross, while seventeen received the German Cross in Gold. Six former camp officers rose to become *Waffen-SS* division commanders. Additionally, it appears the concentration camps served as a definitive training ground for SS medical officers who later served in combat units of the *Waffen SS* – 152 medical officers who went on to serve in the *Waffen-SS*, previously spent time in one or more camp. The transfer of SS guard personnel between concentration camps was always directed through the *Führungshauptamt/Kommandoamt* of the Waffen-SS – due, quite naturally, to the fact that the Concentration Camp Inspectorate of the *SS Hauptamt* was transferred to the *Waffen-SS* headquarters. On March 16, 1942 the department was again transferred to the *WVHA*; but the *SS Führungshauptamt* still maintained responsibility for training and equipping the guard personnel.[131] If nothing else, this study blurs the boundary between those who served in the camps and those who fought in the *Waffen-SS* – if there indeed was a boundary at all.

THE MYSTERIOUS FATE OF OPERATION REINHARD OFFICERS

Something is missing as we examine the later careers of the SS officers who were assigned to the camps associated with *Operation Reinhard* – Belzec, Sobibór and Treblinka. When asked to sort officers who were later killed in action, the computer model found that camp officers associated with this action were over six times as likely to have later been killed in action than the rest of the studied population. It is possible that the high battlefield fatality rates for these officers are perfectly within the norm and that the many absent personnel files for these men are simply the result of human error – either during the war by SS clerks or after the conflict in the preservation of the records within the archival system. Or perhaps, there is another conclusion that can be drawn.

Many aspects of the concentration camp system were considered Top Secret. But the secrecy for the camps associated with *Operation Reinhard* was even more stringent. All SS members of *Operation Reinhard* had to declare and sign the following oath of secrecy:[132]

I have been thoroughly informed and instructed by *SS-Hauptsturmführer* Höfle, as Commander of the main department of *Einsatz Reinhard*[133] of the SS and Police Leader in the District of Lublin:

1. That I may not under any circumstances pass on any form of information, verbally or in writing, on the progress, procedure or incidents in the evacuation of Jews to any person outside the circle of the *Einsatz Reinhard* staff;

2. That the process of the evacuation of the Jews is a subject that comes under "Secret Reich Document," in accordance with censorship regulation.

3. That there is an absolute prohibition on photography in the camps of *Einsatz Reinhard*;...

I am familiar with the above regulations and laws and am aware of the responsibilities imposed upon me by the task with which I have been entrusted. I promise to observe them to the best of my knowledge and conscience. I am aware that the obligation to maintain secrecy continues after I have left the Service.

The Germans made other attempts to keep much of the killing operations a secret. At the beginning of the summer of 1942, Gestapo chief Heinrich Müller appointed *SS-Standartenführer* Paul Blobel, the outgoing commander of *Sonderkommando 4a* of *Einsatzgruppe C*, to head *Aktion 1005* – the operation to remove all traces of mass murder in the east. In July 1942, Blobel organized the nucleus of what would be called *Sonderkommando 1005*. During the fall of that year Blobel's men began to disinter corpses at Chelmno for destruction by burning and conducted a similar undertaking at Auschwitz – where the *Sonderkommando* burned 107,000 corpses through November. Additionally, from the autumn of 1942 to March 1943, Blobel's charges unearthed and burned some 500,000 bodies at Sobibór and Belzec. The SS also carried out destruction operations at Treblinka during this period.[134] Franz Stangl described the technique:[135]

It must have been at the beginning of 1943. That's when excavators were brought in. Using these excavators, the corpses were removed from the huge ditches which had been used until then. The old corpses were burned on the roasters, along with the new bodies. During the transition to the new system [Christian] Wirth came to Treblinka. As I recall, Wirth spoke of a *Standartenführer* who had experience in burning corpses. Wirth told me that according to the *Standartenführer's* experience, corpses could be burned on a roaster, and it would work marvelously. I know that in the beginning [at Treblinka] they used rails from the trolley to build the cremation grill. But it turned out that these were too weak and bent in the heat. They were replaced with real railroad rails.

A Jewish survivor witnessed such operations and presented an even more graphic account.[136]

The SS "expert" on bodyburning ordered us to put women, particularly fat women, on the first layer on the grill, face down. The second layer could consist of whatever was brought – men, women, or children – and so on, layer on top of layer...Then the "expert" ordered us to lay dry branches under the grill and to light them. Within a few minutes the fire would take so it was difficult to approach the crematorium from as far as 50 meters away...The work was extremely difficult. The stench was awful. Liquid excretions from the corpses squirted all over the prisoner-workers. The SS man operating the excavator often dumped the corpses directly onto the prisoners working nearby...

Gassings ceased in Belzec in mid-December 1942; by March 1943 exhumations and cremations of the corpses was pretty much complete. The decision to close Treblinka was taken after the prisoner revolt of 2 August 1943. Sobibór continued to function until the revolt of 16 October 1943. But by these dates, most of the Jews in the General Government were already dead – and the Auschwitz-Birkenau complex was by now in full operation, able to meet any future needs.[137]

The German intent was to not only erase all traces of their crimes at the three locations, but also to hide the very existence of the installations. To this end the SS removed all equipment from Belzec at the end of April 1943 after the last Jews had been killed or transported to Sobibór. Then the SS dismantled all the camp buildings. But this was not enough. Soon thereafter, neighboring Poles began diggings and searches of the area to attempt to find buried valuables. So the Germans returned, and by the end of October 1943 built a farm, installed a Ukrainian guard and planted trees over the former camp. At the end of October 1943, Kurt Franz applied the same methodology in removing all traces of Treblinka, and by the end of December the SS closed Sobibór in a similar manner.[138]

On three occasions there occurred ominous foreshadowing of what might lie ahead for the perpetrators associated with the extermination camps. At Treblinka an enlisted SS man requested a transfer away from the camp from the *kommandant*. *SS-Hauptsturmführer* Franz Stangl denied the request saying that "the circle of those who knew [about the camp] could not be increased." At Auschwitz, an SS man told a Jewish work gang at the crematoria "Good evening, children, you are all going to be killed very soon but after that it will be our own turn."[139]

Josef Oberhauser and Franz Suchomel, a non-commissioned officer at Treblinka, testified that in Poland in 1943 there was a rumor among the *Operation Reinhard* personnel that Berlin intended to eliminate them all. They reported that Christian Wirth gave a speech to the SS at Treblinka to the effect that "the Jews have come here to die, the Ukrainian guards will be eliminated after the operations, and maybe we too will have to die." The Treblinka garrison became so demoralized that Wirth accosted Werner Blankenburg, a high ranking official from the *KdF* on a visit to Lublin. Oberhauser stated that Blankenburg "turned a glaring red and was speechless." The impression of the moment indicated that Blankenburg knew exactly what Wirth was talking about – that there was a plan in Berlin to eliminate the SS men.[140]

Speculation was rampant among the Operation Reinhard personnel. The most frequent rumor had it that all SS and Police involved in the operation would be treated to a *Kraft durch Freude* (Strength through Joy) sea cruise designed to improve morale. Once at sea, the cruise liner would subsequently be torpedoed by a U-boat, and no one allowed to survive.[141]

Perhaps it would not be a cruise, but something else. Many of the SS personnel involved in *Operation Reinhard* were transferred in the fall of 1943 to the Dalmatian coast to operate a holding center for Jews enroute to Auschwitz, and to exterminate Italian and Yugoslav partisans in the area. Christian Wirth was the operational commander under Odilo Globocnik; he divided the group into three teams – R1 in San Saba, a suburb of Trieste, R2 in Fiume and R3 in Udine. The SS men set up R1 as an interrogation center in a former rice warehouse called "the Risera." Wirth ensured the group had a mobile gassing van. His mission was to expedite the transportation of Italian Jews, kill Jewish mental patients in asylums in Trieste and Venice and execute persons suspected of partisan activities.[142] Other Italian-Jewish mental patients were deported from Trieste to the T4 killing center at Schloss Hartheim in Austria, which functioned until December 1944.[143] It is estimated the group killed at least 5,000 people.

Franz Stangl recalled the dread that he and other former *Operation Reinhard* perpetrators felt in northern Italy:[144]

My first assignment in Trieste and for the first three months to December, was 'Transport Security'. I realized quite well and so did most of us, that we were an embarrassment to the brass: they wanted to find ways to 'incinerate' us. So we were assigned the most dangerous jobs – anything to do with anti-partisan combat in that part of the world was very perilous.

It was perilous indeed. Christian Wirth quickly became a fatality. Again, Stangl comments on what transpired:[145]

I saw him [Wirth] dead. They said partisans killed him but we thought his own men had taken care of him.

According to research done by historian Michael Tregenza at the Slovenian State Arcives at Ljubljana, there is a strong possibility that Wirth was killed on orders from Berlin. By the time of his death, Wirth was totally out of control – so much so that the HSSPF in Trieste, Odilo Globocnik, ordered him to cease his "private" killing operations. Globocnik, who feared Allied revenge for his atrocities in Poland – he had experienced a nervous breakdown earlier in Lublin – by this time even refused to admit Wirth to his office. Wirth's movements could have been betrayed to the local partisans by an Italian customs official employed in San Saba who periodically travelled outside Trieste on fortifications work and thus had the opportunity to contact Yugoslav partisans. Wirth drove into a carefully planned ambush on a country road – nineteen guns, including four heavy machine-guns, assorted sub-machine-guns and rifles riddled his body "until their magazines were empty."[146]

It is unclear exactly what happened to the officers of *Operation Reinhard* as a whole. Their rate of fatalities in later combat and partisan action is significantly higher than that for the group of all SS concentration camp officers – *a full fifty percent of these officers were killed in action compared to less than eight percent for all other SS concentration camp officers!* They also have a higher rate of missing personnel files – either their files were not maintained and preserved during the war, by random chance the Berlin Document Center (BDC) lost them or the National Archives did not microfilm these files.[147] The following table shows the wartime fate of these officers:

Table 22
CONCENTRATION CAMP OFFICERS
OPERATION REINHARD COMBAT FATALITIES

NAME	*CAMP*	*WARTIME FATE*
Josef Oberhauser	Belzec	Survived
Gottfried Schwarz	Belzec	KIA 1944
Gottlob Hering	Belzec	Died 1945[148]
Christian Wirth	Belzec	KIA 1944
Kurt Franz	Sobibór/Treblinka	Survived
Franz Stangl	Sobibór/Treblinka	Survived
Franz Reichleitner	Sobibór	KIA 1944
Richard Thomalla	Sobibór	KIA 1945[149]
Josef Niemann	Sobibór	KIA 1943
Dr. Irmfried Eberl	Treblinka	Survived
Herbert Lange	Chelmno[150]	KIA 1945
Hans Bothmann	Chelmno	Survived

There are three plausible explanations for what may have happened. First, there is a possibility that nothing untoward occurred; the increased fatalities just happened. War is a dangerous occurrence – World War II was especially bloody – and under this sequel these men simply were a few of the many victims. The second possibility is that the SS hierarchy deliberately placed the men in a particularly dangerous and confusing theater of operations and let events happen on their own. This would indicate a realization on the part of Odilo Globocnik, and even perhaps Heinrich Himmler, that the fewer of these *Operation Reinhard* men that survived, the better. In a brutal partisan warfare, such as that in Yugoslavia, prisoners of war were seldom taken by either side. A captive German officer would meet a quick death and would be in no position to bargain information he possessed to gain better treatment in confinement which was at least theoretically possible if captured by conventional forces.[151] Interestingly enough, Globocnik was reassigned after the conclusion of the killing operation, to be the Higher SS and Police Leader for the Adriatic Coast (headquartered in Trieste) – a position in which he would continue to oversee many of the *Operation Reinhard* participants. Finally, the third possibility is that the SS, in some way, actually took active measures to silence some of their own. A plan of this nature would have been approved only at the highest levels, and even then probably never in writing. The fact that every *Operation Reinhard* officer was not killed does not decrease the possibility of this alternative; perhaps senior SS leaders had a plan to eliminate the officers over a lengthy period of time to preclude suspicion on the part of the survivors. I believe that the second possibility is the most likely – that senior SS officials placed the men in particularly lethal environments where the likelihood of becoming a living prisoner of war was low and the probability of combat death was high – but clearly research and work in this area needs to be done beyond the scope of this enterprise.

THE FINAL WORD

This finally leads back to our introduction as to the value that the preceding compendium of SS concentration camp officers has to the history of World War II and the Holocaust. Justice Robert H. Jackson, chief American prosecutor at the International Military Tribunal, during the 1946 Trials of Major War Criminals in Nürnberg stated the worth of such an investigation:[152]

The wrongs which we seek to condemn and punish have been so calculated, so malignant, and so devastating, that civilization cannot tolerate their being ignored because it cannot survive their being repeated.

Based on our profile of the "typical" SS officer who served in the concentration camps, after fifty years the time for earthly punishment has probably passed – since all but a handful of these men have gone to their ultimate judgment by this time. However, since the qualities and characteristics of these officers are indeed <u>so typical</u> – not only of men at that particular time in Germany, but also for men under the right conditions today and tomorrow throughout the world – the time for ignoring the crimes, and the camp men who committed them, should not and cannot be over.

Notes:

[1] Peter Padfield, *Himmler: Reichsführer-SS.* (New York: Henry Holt and Company, 1990), p.139.

[2] Microsoft Access, Version 2.0.

[3] John R. Angolia, *For Führer and Fatherland; Military Awards of the Third Reich (Volume 1-2).* (San Jose, CA: R. James Bender, 1976) Vol 1, pp. 256, 337 and 343.

[4] Ibid.

[5] Ibid. pp. 356-357.

[6] Martin van Creveld, *Fighting Power.* (London: Arms and Armour Press, 1983), p.126.

[7] The Knight's Cross of the War Service Cross was a comparable award to the Knight's Cross of the Iron Cross, with the exception that the former award was bestowed for non-combat accomplishments. One concentration camp officer, Karl Gebhardt, received the Knight's Cross of the War Service Cross.

[8] John R. Angolia, *On The Field of Honor, A History of the Knight's Cross Bearers (Volume 1-2).* (San Jose, CA: R. James Bender, 1980), Vol 1, pp. 14-22.

[9] *Ordensgemeinschaft der Ritterkreuzträger,* 1 January 1980.

[10] Rank at date of award.

[11] Jost Schneider, *Their Honor was Loyalty!* (San Jose, CA: R. James Bender Publishing, 1977), pp.61, 137, 198-199, 218, 329-330.

[12] Ibid., pp. 108 and 125.

[13] Ibid., pp.31-32, 85-89, 361-364.

[14] Angolia, *For Führer, Vol 1,* pp. 366-367.

[15] Schneider, *Their Honor was Loyalty!,* pp.38-39.

[16] Angolia, *For Führer, Vol 1,* pp. 330-331.

[17] In reviewing the award of the War Service Cross in other services, we find that it was given to medical personnel, mechanics, transportation troops and other logistical staff.

[18] Ibid., pp.300-302.

[19] Personalakt Richard Glücks, Washington, D.C: National Archives Microfilm Publication A3343, Records of SS Officers from the Berlin Document Center, Roll SSO-017A.

[20] While not recorded in many of the files, I believe that many more officers actually received awards and decorations and it was due to clerical error or faulty reporting that the files are missing this information.

[21] Odilo Globocnik, the Higher SS and Police Leader of Lublin, Poland, was born in Trieste April 21, 1904. He entered the Nazi Party in 1931 and received a party number of 412,938. The following year he joined the SS. An Austrian, who had received a prison sentence in 1933 for the murder of a Viennese Jew, he served as the *Gauleiter* for Vienna from May 1938 to January 1939. However, he continued his criminal activities and in 1939 the Nazi Party stripped him of all honors for illegal speculation in foreign currency. However, Himmler pardoned his old friend and installed him as the highest SS authority in the Lublin district. Globocnik frequently circumvented the head of the General Government (formerly the bulk of Poland) Governor General Hans Frank, as he developed extensive SS economic enterprises in the Lublin area. He later organized the *Operation Reinhard* death camps at Belzec, Sobibór and Treblinka and in 1943 went to Italy as the Higher SS and Police Leader for the Adriatic coast. Odilo Globocnik committed suicide on May 31, 1945 to avoid capture by the British.

[22] Award of the War Service Cross was frequently done on September 1, April 20 and January 30, the anniversaries of the beginning of the war, Hitler's birthday and the Nazi seizure of power, respectively.

[23] Segev, *Soldiers of Evil,* p.54.

[24] Höhne, *The Order of the Death's Head,* pp.134-135.

[25] This was gradually expanded to include more senior SS commanders regardless of membership number.

[26] HSSPF – *Höhere SS und Polizeiführer,* Higher SS and Police Leader, Himmler's regional commander in an area. Directly responsible to Himmler for the implementation of all measures related to the security of the state and the treatment of dangerous elements within their realm.

[27] Helmut Krausnick & Hans Buchheim, Martin Broszat and Hans-Adolf Jacobsen. *Anatomy of the SS State.* (New York: Walker and Company, 1968), pp. 250-253.

[28] *Statistisches Jahrbuch der Schutzstaffel der NSDAP 1937.* (Berlin, 1938).

[29] SS numbers are unknown for 39 officers in the study. Other than a small number who were honorary SS officers, the officers must each have had a number.

[30] The Blood Order had many different unofficial names to include: *Blutorden vom 9. November 1923, Ehrenzeichen am Band vom 9. November 1923, Erinnerungszeichen für aktive Kämpfer der nationalen Erhebung 1923* and *Ehrenzeichen cer NSDAP vom 9. November 1923.*

[31] French MacLean, "The Unknown Generals – German Corps Commanders in World War II." (Masters Thesis, United States Army Command and General Staff College, 1988.)

[32] *Statistisches Jahrbuch der Schutzstaffel der NSDAP 1937.* (Berlin, 1938.)

[33] *Dienstalterssliste der Schutzstaffel der N.S.D.A.P., Stand vom 1. December 1938.* Berlin: Personalkanzlei des Reichsführers-SS, 1939.

[34] John Angloia, *For Führer and Fatherland: Political & Civil Awards of the Third Reich.* (San Jose, CA: R. James Bender Publishing, 1978), p. 178.

[35] *Statistisches Jahrbuch der Schutzstaffel der NSDAP 1937.* (Berlin, 1938.)

[36] 198 SS officers in the sample appear to either not have been members of the NSDAP; or if they were, it is not annotated in their files – an item which should have been known early in an officer's career.

[37] *Dienstalterssliste der Schutzstaffel der N.S.D.A.P., Stand vom 1. December 1938.* Berlin: Personalkanzlei des Reichsführers-SS, 1939.

[38] Höhne, *The Order of the Death's Head,* p.135.

[39] Omer Bartov, *The Eastern Front, 1941-1945, German Troops and the Barbarization of Warfare.* (New York: St. Martin's Press, 1986), p.172.

[40] Jeremiah A. Barondess, "Medicine Against Society - Lessons From the Third Reich." *JAMA, The Journal of the American Medical Association.* (Chicago, IL: American Medical Association, Vol 276, No.20, November 27, 1996), pp.1658-1659.

[41] Roger Manvell, *SS and Gestapo.* (New York: Ballentine Books, 1969), p.100.

[42] For the purposes of this study, I have defined medical personnel to be doctors, dentists or pharmacists.

[43] Includes physicians and pharmacists.

[44] Discussion with Jack W. Robbins, J.D. at the *Nuremberg Code and Human Rights: Fiftieth Anniversary of the Doctors Trial Conference,* United States Holocaust Memorial Museum, Washington, D.C., Decmber 9 and 10, 1996.

[45] Höhne, *The Order of the Death's Head,* p. 156.

[46] Koehl, *The Black Corps,* p.51.

[47] Marital status is unknown for 46 of the officers.

[48] At least through February 1945. The personnel files do not appear to have been adequately updated after this period.

[49] Gutman and Berenbaum, eds. *Anatomy of the Auschwitz Death Camp,* p.298.

[50] Sydnor, *Soldiers of Destruction,* p.29.

[51] While most information concerning religious affiliation came from the officer's SS personnel file, some conversions back to religious faith appear to have occurred in many men sentenced to death after the war.

[52] *Statistisches Jahrbuch der Schutzstaffel der NSDAP 1938.* (Berlin, 1939.)

[53] *Panzergrenadier* (Armored Infantry).

[54] *Panzer* (Armored).

[55] Georg Tessin, *Verbände und Truppen der deutschen Wehrmacht und Waffen-SS im Zweiten Weltkrieg 1939-1945, Band I - XVI.* (Osnabrück, FRG: Biblio Verlag, 1979.), Band XIV, pp.151-153 & Band II, pp.144-145.

[56] Ibid., Band XIV, pp. 213, 214, 248, 249 & Band II, pp.144-145.

[57] Ibid., Band XIV, pp.241-242 & Band II, pp.212-213.

[58] Ibid., Band XIV, pp.108, 259, 260 & Band II, pp.321-322.

[59] *Kampfgruppe* (Battle Group).

[60] *Gebirgs* (Mountain).

[61] Ibid., Band XIV, pp.183-184 & Band III, pp.44-45.

[62] *Freiwilligen* (Volunteer).

[63] *Gebirgsjäger* (Mountain-Hunter).

[64] Ibid., Band III, pp.83-84.

[65] *Kavallerie* (Cavalry).

[66] Ibid., Band III, pp.119-120.

[67] Ibid., Band III, pp.156-157.

[68] Ibid., Band III, pp.188-189.

[69] Ibid., Band III, pp.223-224.

[70] *Hitlerjugend* (Hitler Youth).

[71] Ibid., Band III, p.257.

[72] Ibid., Band III, pp.283-284.

[73] *Infanterie* (Infantry)

[74] Ibid., Band III, pp.313-314.

[75] Ibid., Band IV, pp.21-22.

[76] *Sturmbrigade* (Storm Brigade).

[77] Ibid., Band IV, pp.47-48.

[78] Ibid., Band IV, p.77.

[79] Ibid., Band IV, pp.108-109.

[80] Ibid., Band IV, p.127.

[81] Ibid., Band IV, p.173.

[82] Ibid., Band IV, pp.188-189.

[83] Ibid., Band IV, p.205.

[84] *Karstjäger* (Rough Hill Hunters).

[85] Ibid., Band IV, p.220.

[86] Ibid., Band IV, p.234.

[87] Ibid., Band IV, p.248.

[88] Ibid., Band IV, p.259.

[89] Ibid., Band IV, p.280.

[90] Ibid., Band IV, pp.280-281.

[91] Ibid., Band IV, p.291.

[92] Ibid., Band V, pp.11-12.

[93] Ibid., Band V, pp.22-23.

[94] Ibid., Band V, p.33.

[95] Ibid., Band V, p.42.

[96] Ibid., Band V, p.62.

[97] Dates in this table shown in style day, month, year.

[98] Killed in Action (KIA) refers to an individual who is killed outright in combat or who dies shortly thereafter on the battlefield. Missing in Action (MIA) is generally categorized when a body is not recovered. An individual classified as Died of Wounds (DOW) is one who expires after reaching medical attention.

[99] Gutman, Israel, and Michael Berenbaum, eds. *Anatomy of the Auschwitz Death Camp.* (Bloomington, IN: Indiana University Press in association with the United States Holocaust Memorial Museum, 1994), p.292.

[100] French L. MacLean, *Quiet Flows the Rhine: German General Officer Casualties in World War II.* (Winnipeg, Canada: J.J. Fedorowicz, 1996), pp. 69-70.

[101] Panzergrenadier Regiment 10 was an Army not a Waffen-SS unit.

[102] Possible suicide.

[103] On October 14, 1943 inmates at Sobibór revolted, set the camp on fire and killed eleven SS personnel, to include Niemann. 300 prisoners escaped initially; 100 were recaptured and shot. The camp was closed shortly thereafter.

[104] Letter from Michael Tregenza to the author, February 1998.

[105] Sofsky, *The Order of Terror*, pp. 206-213.

[106] Hermann Baranowski, Walter Eisfeld and Andreas Unsin also died while on duty at a concentration camp, but their deaths were ruled to be from natural causes.

[107] Helmut Krausnick & Hans Buchheim, Martin Broszat and Hans-Adolf Jacobsen. *Anatomy of the SS State*, p. 443.

[108] Koehl, *The Black Corps*, p.134.

[109] Helmut Krausnick & Hans Buchheim, Martin Broszat and Hans-Adolf Jacobsen. *Anatomy of the SS State*, p. 461.

[110] Ibid.,pp.298-299.

[111] Paul Berben, *Dachau 1933-1945.* (London: The Norfolk Press, 1975), p.21.

[112] Sofsky, *The Order of Terror*, p.39.

[113] *Dienstaltersliste der Schutzstaffel der N.S.D.A.P., Stand vom 9. November 1944.* (Reprinted by INFORA Establishment, Vaduz Fürstentum, Lichtenstein, 1985.)

[114] Of the 24 death sentences, only 12 were actually carried out.

[115] Adalbert Rückerl, *The Investigation of Nazi Crimes, 1945-1978: A Documentation.* Translated by Derek Rutter. (Hamden, Connecticutt: Archon Books, 1980), p.28.

[116] Ibid., p.29.

[117] Ibid., pp. 29-31.

[118] Ibid., pp.122-123.

[119] Thomalla was executed by the NKVD shortly after capture; there were probably no legal proceedings followed.

[120] Segev, *Soldiers of Evil*, p. 23.

[121] International Military Tribunal Nürnberg. *Trial of the Major War Criminals before the International Military Tribunal,* Volume XX (30 July - 10 August 1946), (Nürnberg, Germany: Allied Control Authority for Germany, 1948.), pp. 360-369.

[122] Schneider, *Their Honor was Loyalty!*, pp. 147-150.

[123] International Military Tribunal Nürnberg. *Trial of the Major War Criminals before the International Military Tribunal,* Volume XX (30 July - 10 August 1946), (Nürnberg, Germany: Allied Control Authority for Germany, 1948.), pp. 360-369.

[124] In his defense, very few division commanders would know the background of any but the most senior officers arriving to the division (primary division staff officers, battalion commanders and higher), especially with the turnover experienced in wartime.

[125] George H. Stein, *The Waffen SS: Hitler's Elite Guard at War, 1939-1945.* (Ithaca, NY: Cornell University Press, 1966), p.254.

[126] Posner, Gerald L. and John Ware. *Mengele: The Complete Story.* (New York: McGraw-Hill, 1986), p.17.

[127] Schneider, *Their Honor was Loyalty!*, p.89.

[128] Or to publishers for that matter. In a previous work by this author, a non-German publisher rejected the manuscript as "not being favorable enough to the Waffen-SS."

[129] Richard Landwehr, *Fighting For Freedom: The Ukrainian Volunteer Division of the Waffen-SS.* (Silver Spring, MD: Bibliophile Legion Books, 1985), p.14.

[130] Koehl, *The Black Corps*, p.168.

[131] Helmut Krausnick, Hans Buchheim, Martin Broszat and Hans-Adolf Jacobsen. *Anatomy of the SS State.* (New York: Walker and Company, 1968), p.273.

[132] Yitzak Arad, *Belzec, Sobibór, Treblinka: The Operation Reinhard Death Camps.* (Bloomington, IN: Indiana University Press, 1987.), p. 18.

[133] *Einsatz Reinhard* is the German term for *Operation Reinhard*.

[134] Shmuel Spector, "Aktion 1005", *Holocaust and Genocide Studies*, Vol.5 No.2. (Oxford, England: Pergamon Press, 1990), pp.157-161.

[135] Arad, *Belzec, Sobibór, Treblinka: The Operation Reinhard Death Camps*, p.174.

[136] Ibid., p.175.

[137] Letter from Michael Tregenza to the author, February 1998.

[138] Ibid., pp.370-373.

[139] Gerald Reitlinger, *The Final Solution.* (Northvale, NJ: Jason Aronson Inc., 1987), p.143.

[140] Letter from Michael Tregenza to the author, February 1998.

[141] Ibid.

[142] Michael Burleigh, *Death and Deliverance*, pp.234-235.

[143] Letter from Michael Tregenza to the author, February 1998.

[144] Gitta Sereny, *Into That Darkness.* (New York: Vintage Books, 1983), p.261.

[145] Ibid., p.262.

[146] Letter from Michael Tregenza to the author, February 1998.

[147] Dr. Irmfried Eberl and Franz Reichleitner have no personnel file on microfilm at the National Archives. Theft is another occurrence. Heiner Meyer, in his book *Berlin Document Center: Das Geschäft mit der Vergangenheit*, states that 80,000 documents have been stolen from the BDC over the years – stolen for resale to military autograph collectors and stolen to conceal events concerning the lives of former SS personnel living in Germany. Those personnel files held by the *KdF* or *T4* in Berlin were in part burned at Schonfliess in 1945 – Christian Wirth's file is heavily damaged. The files of many *Operation Reinhard* men were transferred with them to Italy; many of these files were destroyed at Tolmezzo. According to historian Michael Tregenza, there was a letter from Globocnik to Himmler urging the destruction of everything and anything connected with *Operation Reinhard*.

[148] Hering died in the Katharinen Hospital, Steltin-im-Remstal, Württemburg presumably of a heart attack. His death certificate does not list a cause of death – making it a legally <u>invalid</u> document. Source: Michael Tregenza.

[149] Thomalla was executed by the Soviet NKVD on 12 May 1945 at Jicin, Czechoslovakia.

[150] Chelmno was technically not a part of *Operation Reinhard* but had the same level of secrecy.

[151] The most notable group in the category of collaborators was the National Committee for a Free Germany formed in July 1943 from German emigres and prisoners of war held in the Soviet Union.

[152] Office of United States Chief of Counsel For Prosecution of Axis Criminality, *Trials of War Criminals Before The Nuernberg Military Tribunals Under Control Council Law No. 10, Volume I.* (Washington: United States Government Printing Office, 1949), p.28.

APPENDICES

APPENDIX 1: SS RANKS

SS-Reichsführer (Reichsführer-SS)	Reichs Leader
SS-Oberstgruppenführer	General
SS-Obergruppenführer	Lieutenant General
SS-Gruppenführer	Major General
SS-Brigadeführer	Brigadier General
SS-Oberführer	Senior Colonel
SS-Standartenführer	Colonel
SS-Obersturmbannführer	Lieutenant Colonel
SS-Sturmbannführer	Major
SS-Hauptsturmführer	Captain
SS-Obersturmführer	First Lieutenant
SS-Untersturmführer	Second Lieutenant
SS-Sturmscharführer	Sergeant Major
SS-Hauptscharführer	Master Sergeant
SS-Oberscharführer	Sergeant First Class
SS-Scharführer	Staff Sergeant
SS-Unterscharführer	Sergeant
SS-Rottenführer	Corporal
SS-Sturmmann	Acting Corporal
SS-Oberschütze	Private First Class
SS-Schütze	Private

APPENDIX 2: SS PERSONNEL GLOSSARY

The following glossary of German terms – many of which are used throughout the personnel files of the SS camp officers – and their English translations, are provided to facilitate further research:

Abschied – discharge/resignation

Akten – documents, records, files

Allgemeine SS – the general SS, the overall body of the SS, distinct from the Waffen-SS.

Alter Kämpfer – old fighter, early member of the party or SS

Amt – bureau, office

Anwärter – candidate; **SS-Junker** – SS officer candidate

ärztliche untersuchung – medical examination
    Arbeitsverwendungdfähig (a.v.) – fit for labor duty only
    Arbeitsverwendungsfähig in der Heimat (a.v. Heimat) – fit for labor duty in the zone of interior only
    Garnisonsverwendungsfähig Feld (g.v.F.) – fit for garrison duty in the field
    Garnisonsverwendungsfähig Heimat (g.v.H.) – fit for garrison duty in the zone of the interior
    Kriegsverwendungsfähig (k.v.) – fit for active service (highest medical classification)
    Körperliche Eignumg – physical aptitude

Arzt – medical doctor
    Apotheker – pharmacist
    Sanitätsoffizier – doctor
    Sanitätsoffizier des zahnärtlichen Dienstes – dentist
    Standortarzt – station surgeon (chief physician)
    Zahnarzt – dentist
    Veterinär – veterinary

Ausbildung – training; **Lehrgänge** – schools, training courses

Ausstossen – expel, cashier (stronger dismissal than **Abschied**)

Auszeichnung – awards and decorations

Beförderung – promotion; **Letzte Beförderung** – last promotion date

Beruf (erlernt) – civilian trade
    Ingenieur (Dipl.-Ing.) – engineer
    Kaufmann – salesman
    Student – student
    Polizei – police official
    Bankbeamter – bank clerk
    Rechstanwalt / Jurist – lawyer
    Landwirt – farmer

Mechaniker / Handwerker / Maschinist – mechanic
Elektriker – electrician
Lehrer – teacher

Beurteilung – efficiency report
    durchschnitt – average
    sehr gute Ausfüllung – very good performance
    Schwachen und Fehler – poor characteristics (followed by a description)

degradiert – demoted, reduced in rank
    Abtreibung – abortion
    Sexualverbrechen – sex crimes
    Veruntreuung – embezzlement
    Pflichtvergessen / Fahrlässigkeit – negligence
    Ungehorsam – disobedience
    Nichtachtung / Missachtung – disrespect
    Alkoholiker / trunksucht – alcoholic / alcoholism
    Gehorsamsverweigerung – insubordination

Dienstgrad – rank (See Appendix 1)

Dienststellungen – duty positions
    Zugführer – platoon leader
    Kompanie-Chef – company commander
    Abteilungs-Kommandeur (Abt.-Kdr.) – detachment/battalion commander
    Regiments-Kommandeur (Rgt.-Kdr.) – regimental commander
    Intendant – official in charge of rations, clothing, equipment, pay, etc **Verbindungsoffizier** – liaison officer
    Verflegungsoffizier – rations/mess officer
    Vernehmungsoffizier – interrogation officer

Ehefrau – wife
    verheiratet – married
    ledig – single
    geschieden – divorced
    verwitwet – widowed
    kinder – children
    Mädchenname der Frau – wife's maiden name

Einheit – unit

Einsatzgruppe – battalion-size mobile extermination group on the eastern front, primarily Security Police and SD officials.

Einsatzkommando – subordinate command of an **einsatzgruppe**, normally company-size.

Eintritt in die Partei – date entered Nazi Party

Eintritt in die SS – date entered SS

Endlösung – final solution, the German euphemism used here to indicate the extermination of the Jewish race.

Freiwilliger – volunteer

Frontkämpfer – combat veteran

Gauleiter – highest ranking Nazi Party official in a district. Germany was composed of forty-two Nazi Party districts.

Geburtstag / Geburtsort – date of birth / place of birth

Geheim – secret

Geheime Staatspolizei (Gestapo) – the secret police dedicated to the preservation of the Nazi regime.

Hauptamt SS Gericht – the SS Legal Department.

Höhrere SS und Polizeiführer (HSSPF) – Higher SS and Police Leader, Himmler's regional commander in an area. Directly responsible to Himmler for the implementation of all measures related to the security of the state and the treatment of dangerous elements within their realm.

im Felde gefallen / vor dem Feind gefallen – killed in action
    erschiessen – killed by shooting
    erschlagen – killed by blows
    leichtverwundundet (le.V.) – slightly wounded
    schwerverwundet – seriously wounded
    vermisst – missing in action
    kriegsbeschädigt – disabled on active duty
    Unfall – accident
    Beschädigung – injury
    Blutvergiftung – blood-poisoning, infection, gangrene
    krank – sick, ill

konfession – religion
    (ev.) – Protestant
    (k.) – Catholic
    (ggl. or **gg.)** – Agnostic

Konzentrationslager (KZ, KL) – concentration camp

Kraftfahrwesen – motor transport

Kriminalpolizei (Kripo) – criminal police under the control of the SD.

Nachrichtenabteilung – signal detachment

Ordnungspolizei (Orpo) – order police, consisting of uniformed police forces in the Third Reich. While separate from the Gestapo and Criminal Police, they handled routine police business and sometimes assisted in carrying out mass executions.

Rassisches Gesamtbild – racial makeup

Reichsführer-SS (RFSS) – Reich Leader Heinrich Himmler

Sicherheitsdienst (SD) – the intelligence branch of the SS.

Sicherheitspolizei – Security Police; a fusion of various criminal police forces and state political police separate from the SS, but closely linked to the SD.

Sonderkommando – special commando

SS-Führungshauptamt (SS-FHA) – SS Leadership Main Office, the headquarters of the Waffen-SS; designed to control the organization of field units of the SS and to monitor the training and replacement units of the Waffen-SS. It additionally looked after training schools of the Waffen-SS. The **SS-FHA** was independent of the SS Main Office.

SS-Hauptamt (SS-HA) – SS Main Office, evolved in the mid-1930s and controlled such functions as personnel, administration, medical, physical training, education, communications and so forth.

SS und Polizeiführer (SSPF) – SS and Police Leader, district commander subordinate to an **HSSPF**.

Stammrolle – personnel roster

Sturmabteilung (SA) – Storm Detachment, the early private army of the Nazi party.

Totenkopf – Death's Head, units which guarded concentration camps. Also the 3rd Waffen-SS Division.

Verfügungstruppe – the first Waffen-SS field troops.

Wachbataillon – guard battalion

Waffen-SS – SS field troops

Wirtschaftliche Verhältnisse – personal financial situation

Wirtschafts und Verwaltungshauptamt (WVHA) – Economics and Administration Head Office of the SS charged with the administration of the concentration camps.

Wohnort – current place of residence

SOURCES

Published Sources

Aly, Götz. *Aktion T4*. Berlin: Edition Hentrich, 1989.

Angolia, John. *Cloth Insignia of the SS*. San Jose, CA: R. James Bender Publishing, 1983.

Angolia, John. *For Führer and Fatherland: Military Awards of the Third Reich*. San Jose, CA: R. James Bender Publishing, 1976.

Angolia, John. *For Führer and Fatherland: Political & Civil Awards of the Third Reich*. San Jose, CA: R. James Bender Publishing, 1978.

Antoni, Ernst. *KZ von Dachau bis Auschwitz*. Frankfurt: Röderberg Verlag, 1979.

Arad, Yitzhak. *Belzec, Sobibor, Treblinka: The Operation Reinhard Death Camps*. Bloomington, IN: Indiana University Press, 1987.

Barondess, Jeremiah A. "Medicine Against Society - Lessons From the Third Reich." *JAMA, The Journal of the American Medical Association*. Chicago, IL: American Medical Association, Vol 276, No.20, November 27, 1996.

Bartov, Omer. *The Eastern Front, 1941-1945, German Troops and the Barbarization of Warfare*. New York: St. Martin's Press, 1986.

Bauche, Ulrich and Heinz Brüdigam, Ludwig Eiber, Wolfgang Wiedey. *Arbeit und Vernichtung: Das Konzentrationslager Neuengamme, 1933-1945*. Hamburg: VSA Verlag, 1986.

Bembeneck, Lothar and Frank Schwalba-Hoth. *Hessen hinter Stacheldraht*. Frankfurt: Eichborn Verlag, 1984.

Berben, Paul. *Dachau 1933-1945*. London: The Norfolk Press, 1975.

Bornus, Aleksy et al. *Majdanek 1941-1944*. Lublin, Poland: Wydawnictwo Lubelskie, 1991.

Breitman, Richard. *The Architect of Genocide*. New York: Alfred A. Knopf, 1991.

Burleigh, Michael. *Death and Deliverance*. Cambridge, England: Cambridge university Press, 1994.

Ciechanowski, Konrad, et al. *Stutthof: hitlerowski oboz koncentracyjny*. Warsaw: Aydawnictwo Interpress, 1988.

Creveld Martin van, *Fighting Power*. London: Arms and Armour Press, 1983.

Czech, Danuta. *Auschwitz Chronicle, 1939-1945*. New York: Henry Holt, 1990.

Dienstalterliste der Schutzstaffel der N.S.D.A.P., Stand vom 1. Oktober 1934. Berlin: Personalkanzlei des Reichsführers-SS, 1935.

Dienstalterliste der Schutzstaffel der N.S.D.A.P., Stand vom 1. Juli 1935. Berlin: Personalkanzlei des Reichsführers-SS, 1935.

Dienstalterliste der Schutzstaffel der N.S.D.A.P., Stand vom 1. December 1936. Berlin: Personalkanzlei des Reichsführers-SS, 1937.

Dienstalterliste der Schutzstaffel der N.S.D.A.P., Stand vom 1. December 1937. Berlin: Personalkanzlei des Reichsführers-SS, 1938.

Dienstalterliste der Schutzstaffel der N.S.D.A.P., Stand vom 1. December 1938. Berlin: Personalkanzlei des Reichsführers-SS, 1939.

Dienstalterliste der Schutzstaffel der N.S.D.A.P., Stand vom 9. November 1944. Reprinted by INFORA Establishment, Vaduz Fürstentum, Lichtenstein, 1985.

Distel, Barbara and Ruth Jakusch, eds. *Concentration Camp Dachau, 1933-1945*. Brussels: Comité International de Dachau, 1978.

Donat, Alexander. *The Death Camp Treblinka*. New York: The Holocaust Library, 1979.

Drobisch, Klaus and Günther Wieland. *System der NS-Konzentrationslager, 1933-1939*. Berlin: Akademie Verlag, 1993.

Edelheit, Abraham J. and Hershel. *History of the Holocaust*. Boulder, CO: Westview Press, 1994.

Feig, Konnilyn G. *Hitler's Death Camps*. New York: Holmes & Meier Publishers, 1981.

Freund, Florian. *Arbeitslager Zement*. Vienna: Verlag für Gesellschaftskritik, 1989.

Geyer, Michael. "German Strategy in the Age of Machine Warfare, 1914-1945," in *Makers of Modern Strategy* ed. Peter Peret. Princeton, NJ: Princeton University Press, 1986.

Graber, G.S. *History of the SS*. New York: David McKay, Inc., 1978.

Grabowska, Janina. *K.L. Stutthof*. Bremen, Germany: Edition Temmen, 1993.

Gutman, Israel, and Michael Berenbaum, eds. *Anatomy of the Auschwitz Death Camp*. Bloomington, IN: Indiana University Press in association with the United States Holocaust Memorial Museum, 1994.

Hackett, David A., ed. *The Buchenwald Report*. Boulder, CO: Westview Press, 1995.

Heigl, Peter. *Konzentrationslager Flossenbürg*. Regensburg, FRG: Mittelbayerische Druckerei, 1989.

Hilberg, Raul. *The Destruction of the European Jews*. New York: Holmes & Meier, 1985.

Höhne, Heinz. *The Order of the Death's Head*. Translated by Richard Barry. New York: Coward-McCann, 1970.

Höss, Rudolf, Pery Broad and Johann Paul Kremer. *KL Auschwitz Seen by the SS*. Warsaw: Interpress, 1991.

Hüser, Dr. Karl. *Wewelsburg 1933-1945: Kult- und Terrorstätte der SS*. Paderborn, FRG: Verlag Bonifatius, 1987.

International Auschwitz Committee. *Nazi Medicine*. New York: Howard Fertig, 1986.

International Military Tribunal Nürnberg. *Trial of the Major War Criminals before the International Military Tribunal*. Volume XX (30 July - 10 August 1946), Nürnberg, Germany: Allied Control Authority for Germany, 1948.

Isbach, Karl. *Kemna: Wuppertaler Konzentrationslager 1933-1934*. Wuppertal, FRG: Peter Hammer Verlag, 1981.

Karny, Miroslav and Vojtech Blodig, Margita Karna. *Theresienstadt*. Prague: Edition Theresienstadter Initiativ, 1992.

Kater, Michael H. *Das Ahnenerbe der SS, 1935-1945*. Stuttgart, FRG: Deutsche Verlags-Anstalt, 1974.

Klopp, Eberhard. *Hinzert – kein Richtiges KZ?* Trier, FRG: Editions Treves, 1983.

Koehl, Robert Lewis. *The Black Corps: The Structure and Power Struggles of the Nazi SS*. Madison, WI: The University of Wisconsin Press, 1983.

Kogon, Eugen, Hermann Langbein and Adalbert Rückerl. *Nazi Mass Murder: A Documentary History of the Use of Poison Gas*. New Haven, CN: Yale University Press, 1993.

Kolb, Eberhard. *Bergen Belsen*. Hannover, FRG: Verlag für Literatur und Zeitgeschehen, 1962.

Krausnick, Helmut, Hans Buchheim, Martin Broszat and Hans-Adolf Jacobsen. *Anatomy of the SS State*. New York: Walker and Company, 1968.

Krausnick, Helmut and Hans-Heinrich Wilhelm. *Die Truppe des Weltanschauungs-krieges: Die Einsatzgruppen der Sichersheitpolizei und des SD 1938-1942*. Stuttgart: Deutsche Verlags-Anstalt, 1981.

Kumm, Otto. *Prinz Eugen: The History of the 7th SS Mountain Division "Prinz Eugen."* Winnipeg, Canada: J. J. Fedorowicz, 1995.

Landwehr, Richard. *Fighting For Freedom: The Ukrainian Volunteer Division of the Waffen-SS*. Silver Spring, MD: Bibliophile Legion Books, 1985.

Le Chene, Evelyn. *Mauthausen*. London: Methuen & Co., 1971.

Lerner, Daniel. *The Nazi Elite*. Stanford, CA: Stanford University Press, 1951.

MacLean, French. *Quiet Flows the Rhine: German General Officer Casualties in World War II*. Winnipeg, Canada: J.J. Fedorowicz, 1996.

Manvell, Roger. *SS and Gestapo*. New York: Ballentine Books, 1969.

Marsalek, Hans. *Die Geschichte des Konzentrationslagers Mauthausen*. Vienna: Oesterreichische lagergemeinschaft Mauthausen, 1980.

Marszalek, Józef. *Majdanek: Konzentrationslager Lublin*. Warsaw: Interpress, 1984.

Meyer, Heiner. *Berlin Document Center: Das Geschäft mit der Vergangenheit*. Frankfurt, FRG: Ullstein, 1988.

Mollo, Andrew. *Uniforms of the SS: Volume 4 - SS-Totenkopfverbände 1933-1945*. London: Historical Research Unit, 1971.

Moldawa, Mieczyslaw. *Gross Rosen*. Warsaw: Wydawnictwo Bellona, 1980.

Musiol, Teodor. *Dachau 1933-1945*. Katowice, Poland: Instytut Slaski W Opolu, 1971.

Naumann, Bernd. Translated by Jean Steinberg. *Auschwitz*. New York: Frederick A. Praeger, 1966.

Office of United States Chief of Counsel For Prosecution of Axis Criminality. *Nazi Conspiracy And Aggression, Volume I*. Washington: United States Government Printing Office, 1946.

Office of United States Chief of Counsel For Prosecution of Axis Criminality. *Trials of War Criminals Before The Nuernberg Military Tribunals Under Control Council Law No. 10, Volume I*. Washington: United States Government Printing Office, 1949.

Padfield, Peter. *Himmler: Reichsführer-SS*. New York: Henry Holt and Company, 1990.

Patzwall, Klaus D. *Der Blutorden der NSDAP*. Hamburg, FRG: Verlag Militaria-Archiv Klaus D. Patzwall, 1985.

Perk, Willy. *Hölle im Moor: zur Geschichte der Emslandlager 1933-1945*. Frankfurt: Röderberg-Verlag, 1979.

Posner, Gerald L. and John Ware. *Mengele: The Complete Story*. New York: McGraw-Hill, 1986.

Preradovich, Nikolaus von. *Die Generale der Waffen-SS*. Berg am See, FRG: Kurt Vowinckel Verlag, 1985.

Pressac, Jean-Claude. *Die Krematorium von Auschwitz*. Munich: Piper, 1993.

Reitlinger, Gerald. *The Final Solution*. Northvale, NJ: Jason Aronson Inc., 1987.

Reitlinger, Gerald. *The SS: Alibi of a Nation*. London: Arms and Armour Press, 1981.

Rückerl, Adalbert. *The Investigation of Nazi Crimes, 1945-1978: A Documentation*. Translated by Derek Rutter. Hamden, Connecticutt: Archon Books, 1980.

Schelvis, Jules. *Vernietigingskamp Sobibor*. Amsterdam: De Bataafsche Leeuw, 1993.

Scheurig, Bodo. *Free Germany; The National Committee and the League of German Officers*. Middleton, CN: Wesleyan University Press, 1969.

Schneider, Jost. *Their Honor was Loyalty!* San Jose, CA: R. James Bender Publishing, 1977.

Schwarz, Gudrun. *Die nationalsozialistischen Lager*. Frankfurt: Campus, 1990.

Segev, Tom. *Soldiers of Evil*. New York: McGraw-Hill Book Company, 1987.

Sereny, Gitta. *Into That Darkness*. New York: Vintage Books, 1983.

Shelley, Lore. *Auschwitz: The Nazi Civilization*. Lanham, Maryland: University Press of America, 1992.

Shelley, Lore. *Criminal Experiments on Human Beings in Auschwitz and War Research Laboratories*. San Francisco: Mellen Research University Press, 1991.

Snyder, Louis L. *Encyclopedia of the Third Reich*. New York: McGraw-Hill, 1976.

Sofsky, Wolfgang. *The Order of Terror: The Concentration Camp*. Translated by William Templer. Princeton, NJ: Princeton University Press, 1997.

Sofsky, Wolfgang. *Die Ordnung des Terrors: Das Konzentrationslager*. Frankfurt: S. Fischer Verlag, 1993.

Spector, Shmuel. "Aktion 1005", *Holocaust and Genocide Studies*, Vol.5 No.2. Oxford, England: Pergamon Press, 1990.

Statistisches Jahrbuch der Schutzstaffel der NSDAP 1937. Berlin, 1938.

Statistisches Jahrbuch der Schutzstaffel der NSDAP 1938. Berlin, 1939.

Stein, George H. *The Waffen SS: Hitler's Elite Guard at War, 1939-1945*. Ithaca, NY: Cornell University Press, 1966.

Supreme Headquarters Allied Expeditionary Force, G-2. *Basic Handbook on KL's (Konzentrationslager) – Axis Concentration Camps and Detention Centers Reported as Such in Europe*. Wiltshire England: Antony Rowe Ltd, (republication), 1996.

Sydnor, Charles W. Jr. *Soldiers of Destruction*. Princeton, NJ: Princeton University Press, 1977.

Tessin, Georg. *Verbände und Truppen der deutschen Wehrmacht und Waffen-SS im Zweiten Weltkrieg 1939-1945, Band I - XVI*. Osnabrück, FRG: Biblio Verlag, 1979.

United States Holocaust Memorial Museum. *Historical Atlas of the Holocaust*. New York: Macmillan Publishing USA, 1996.

Weinmann, Martin, Anne Kaiser and Ursula Krause-Schmitt. *Das national-sozialistische Lagersystem*. Frankfurt: Zweitausendeins, 1990.

Wiesenthal, Simon. *The Murderers Among Us*. New York: McGraw-Hill, 1967.

Yerger, Mark. *Allgemeine-SS: The Commands, Units and Leaders of the General SS*. Atglen, PA: Schiffer Publishing, 1997.

Zörner, G. *Frauen-KZ Ravensbrück*. Berlin: VEB Deutscher Verlag der Wissenschaften.

Unpublished Sources

MacLean, French. "The Unknown Generals – German Corps Commanders in World War II." Masters Thesis, United States Army Command and General Staff College, 1988.

National Archives of the United States, Washington D. C. Microfilm Publication A3343 Series SSO, Records of SS Officers from the Berlin Document Center.

The Nuremberg Code and Human Rights: Fiftieth Anniversary of the Doctors Trial Conference, United States Holocaust Memorial Museum, Washington, D.C., Decmber 9 and 10, 1996. Discussion during the conference between the author and Jack W. Robbins, J.D.

Summary sheet from *Ordensgemeinschaft der Ritterkreuzträger*, 1 January 1980.

Discussions by the author with Dr. Robert Jan van Pelt and Dr. Deborah Dwork, authors of *Auschwitz: 1270 to the Present*, 1997.

Letters to the author from Michael Tregenza, 1997-1998.

PHOTO SECTION

March 1936, Otto Reich (left) in discussion with Theodor Eicke (center). (USHMM)

March 1936, Theodor Eicke (center). (USHMM)

1936, Theodor Eicke (center) reviews Totenkopf troops. (USHMM)

March 1936, Theodor Eicke (2nd from left) and Otto Reich (3rd from left) during a visit to Lichtenburg. (USHMM)

March 1936, SS officers "clown" for the camera during a visit to Lichtenburg. (USHMM)

May 1936, Heinrich Himmler (center) and Reinhard Heydrich (right of Himmler) visit Dachau. (USHMM)

Above: Hans Baranowski. (BDC)

Left: Richard Baer. (BDC)

Above: Hellmut Becker. (BAK [84/58/21a])

Above right: Georg Bochmann. (BAK [78/105/3a])

Right: Carl Clauberg, SS physician who performed sterilization experiments on Jewish and Gypsy women in Auschwitz and Ravensbruck. (USHMM)

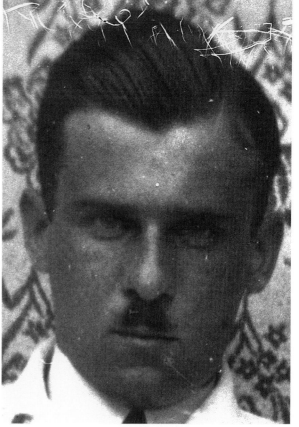

Above: Heinrich Deubel. (BDC)

Above right: Erwin Ding-Schuler, member of the SS Totenkopfverbande and a concentration camp physician at Buchenwald. (USHMM)

Right: SS-Unterstrumführer Irmfried Eberl (1910-1948) joined the NSDAP on December 8, 1931 while studying medicine. On February 1, 1940, when he was only twenty-nine years old, Eberl became the director of the Brandenburg "killing facility," part of the Euthanasia program. In the fall of 1941, he assumed control of the Benberg "euthanasia facility," and in late summer 1942, became the commandant of Treblinka when Operation Reinhard commenced. Eventually, however, he was soon replaced for incompetence. The SS leadership was particularly concerned with the "indescribable conditions" that existed in the camp. Erbel repeatedly ordered the gassing of Jews before the prior group of bodies was removed, thus destroying any notion that the Jews were merely being made to take a shower, a deception the SS wanted to protect. Erbel committed suicide while in investigative detention. (BDC)

This page and opposite: Theodor Eicke. (BAK [73/107/13] - [119/2115/10])

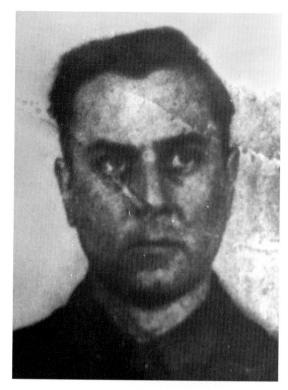

Right: Hans Eisele, SS-Untersturmführer physician at Buchenwald. (USHMM)

Below: Walter Eisfeld. (BDC)

Below right: Hermann Florstedt. (BDC)

Left: Karl Fritsch. (BDC)

Below left: Johann Göhler. (Private Source)

Below: Adolf Haas. (BDC)

Friedrich Hartjenstein. (BDC)

Hans Helwig. (BDC)

SS-Obersturmführer Gottlied Hering (right), camp commandant of Belzec, drinking with SS-Oberscharführer Heinrich Gley. (USHMM)

Above left: Paul Hoppe. (BDC)

Above: Hans Hüttig. (BDC)

Left: Anton Kaindl. (BDC)

Above: Max Koegel. (BDC)

Right: Josef Kramer (1907-1945), commandant of Birkenau and Bergen-Belsen, was assigned to Dachau, Esterwegen, Sachsenhausen, and Mauthausen before becoming Rudolf Höss' adjutant in 1940. Kramer accompanied Höss to the site of the Auschwitz camp in 1940 and became commandant of Auschwitz II, the Birkenau concentration camp. Then, in 1943, he was made commandant of Natzweiler, where he was personally involved in the gassing of eighty female prisoners whose skeletal remains were to be used for "anatomical studies." In 1944, Kramer returned to Auschwitz to help with the extermination of Hungarian Jews who had just been deported, but left again on December 1, 1944 to take command of Bergen-Belsen. Kramer transformed the formerly "privileged" camp into a center for sick and dying persons from all over Europe, swelling the population to over 60,000. With the camp filled beyond capacity, Kramer let the inmates starve to death, which earned him the nickname "Beast of Belsen" from the British who liberated the camp. He joined the British soldiers inspecting the camp, casually guiding them through the carnage. In his trial at Lüneburg, he described with indifference how his training allowed him to carry out mass murders without thinking. He was sentenced to death on November 17, 1945, and was executed on December 13 of that year. (BDC)

Photo Section

Left: Arthur Liebehenschel. (BDC)

Max Pauly. (BDC)

Josef Mengele (1911-1979?), German physician and SS-Hauptsturmführer. Mengele received a degree in philosophy from Munich and his medical degree from the University of Frankfurt am Main. He joined the NSDAP in 1937 and the SS in 1938. Prior to World War II, Mengele served as a research fellow and staff member of the Institut fur Erbbiologie und Rassenhygiene (Insitute for Heredity Biology and Race Research) specializing in the study of twins and family lineage. Following the outbreak of war, Mengele joined the Waffen-SS and in 1941 was named battalion physician for the "Viking" Division. Wounded on the Eastern Front in 1943, Mengele was given the position of SS garrison physician (Standortartz) of Auschwitz. In that capacity, he was responsible for the differentiation and selection of those fit to work and those destined for gassing. Also, Mengele carried out human experiments on camp inmates, especially twins. Following the end of the war, Mengele, after spending a short time in a British internment camp, went into hiding. Through a network of Vatican sympathizers, he was able to reach South America. In the 1950s, Mengele's deeds at Auschwitz became known and he was sought for arrest by prosecutors in West Germany. In 1985, Israel set-up a special court for the sole-purpose of pronouncing his guilt. By the spring of that year however, investigators learned that Mengele had, in all likelihood, died in a swimming accident in Brazil in 1979. The story was confirmed by the Mengele family and the body was exhumed. After being examined by sixteen forensic experts, it was announced that "within a reasonable scientific certainty" that the body was Mengele's. (BDC)

Left: Alex Piorkowski. (BDC)

Below left: Hermann Pister. (BDC)

Below: SS-Obersturmbannführer Arthur Rödl, commandant of Gross-Rosen. (USHMM)

844527912254292279252222227222222222

Above: Albert Sauer. (BDC)

Above right: Norbert Scharf. (BDC)

Right: Franz Stangl. (BDC)

Fritz Suhren. (BDC)

Richard Thomalla. (BDC)

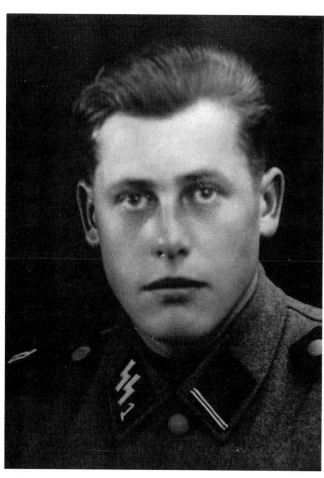

Jakob Weiseborn. (BDC)

Martin Weiss. (BDC)

Christian Wirth. (BDC)

Christian Wirth (left) and Gottlieb Hering (right) in northern Italy, 1944, after conclusion of Operation Reinhard. (Zentrale Stelle der Landesjustiz-verwaltungen)

Franz Ziereis. (BDC)

Egon Zill. (BDC)

Auschwitz, 1941: SS ceremony on Hitler's birthday. (USHMM)

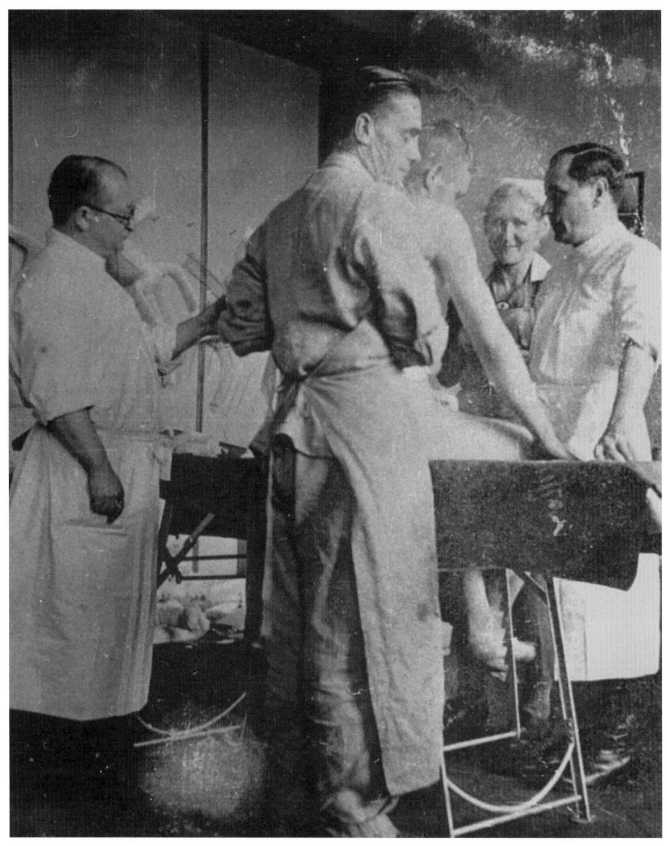

Auschwitz: Dr. Clauberg (left) at Block 10. Clauberg experimented with non-surgical methods of sterilization on Jewish female prisoners in Auschwitz I. (USHMM)

Auschwitz-Monowitz, July, 1942: Himmler (right) on visit; Rudolf Höss is third from right. Manager of building operations for IG-Farbenindustrie in Monowitz-Buna, Max Faust is first from the left. (USHMM)

Auschwitz-Monowitz, July 1942: Himmler and IG Farben supervisor, Max Faust, tour factory. (BAK [79022/2])

Auschwitz-Monowitz, July 1942: Himmler reviewing camp plans. (USHMM)

Auschwitz-Monowitz, July 1942: Himmler taking a break. (USHMM)

Auschwitz-Monowitz, July 1942: Himmler tours. (USHMM)

Auschwitz-Monowitz, July 1942: Himmler greets SS officer. (USHMM)

Auschwitz-Birkenau, May, 1944: Hungarian Jewish men and women await selection on the ramp. (USHMM)

Auschwitz-Birkenau, 1944: New prisoners on selection ramp; left column will head to gas chambers. (BAK [E0317/07/1])

Auschwitz-Birkenau: Prisoner selection under the supervision of Dr. Heinz Thilo. (BAK [0718/42/1])

Auschwitz-Birkenau: Arrival of new prisoners on selection ramp. (BAK [P0410/360])

Opposite: Auschwitz-Birkenau, May 1944: The Birkenau arrival ramp was completed only weeks before this photo was taken. Formerly the transport trains arrived at a ramp half a mile away. The members of the SS "ramp" team take their stations in front of each boxcar of the newly arrived train on the right. On command they will unbolt all the doors. Due to the unprecedented crush of transports destined for the ramp in the late spring of 1944 two trains were often alongside simultaneously, with others backed up and waiting for a day or longer. (Yad Vashem)

Above: Belzec, 1942: SS Guards stand in formation behind outside the commandant's house in the Belzec death camp. Pictured (in front row from right to left): SS-Rottenführer Heinrich Barbl and Wachtmeister Artur Dachsel; (second row) SS-Hauptscharführer Lorenz Hackenholt, Ernst Zierke, Karl Gringers (front), and Fritz Tauscher (second from the left). (USHMM)

Buchenwald: SS men begin construction of a gallows just outside the camp. (USHMM)

Buchenwald: SS and police officials in discussion. (USHMM)

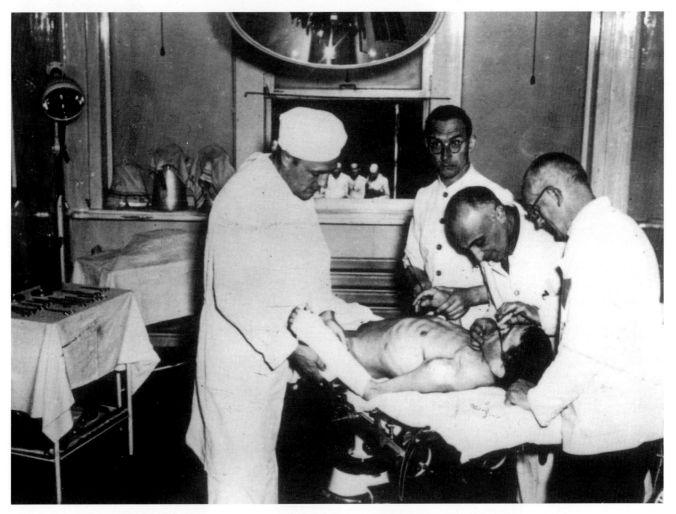

Buchenwald: SS medical personnel operate on a prisoner. (La Documentation Francaise. [B223-34/1c])

Dachau, 1933: SS personnel. (BAK [119/P52/1])

Dachau, 1933: Early guards. (BAK (152/1/17)

Dachau, 1933: Release of prisoners at Christmas. (BAK [1984/0823/500])

Dachau, 1933: Release of prisoners. (BAK [183/H29240])

Dachau, 1933: Prisoners to be released approach front gate. (BAK [H29241])

Dachau, 1933: SS guard bids farewell to released prisoner. (BAK [1987/0527/503])

Dachau: Visit by Dr. Robert Ley, German Labor Front, (third from right) with Theodor Eicke (second from right). (BAK (152/6/27])

Dachau: Visit by Dr. Robert Ley. (BAK [152/5/10])

Dachau: Dr. Ley reviews SS troops. (BAK [152/5/21])

Dachau: Visit by Dr. Ley; Theodor Eicke speaks. (BAK [152/5/36])

Dachau: Visit by Dr. Ley. (BAK [152/5/3])

Dachau, January 20, 1941: Heinrich Himmler, Rudolf Höss (second from left) and Richard Glücks (with gray lapels). (USHMM)

Dachau, January 20, 1941: (left to right) Oswald Pohl, Anton Mussert, Heinrich Himmler, Karl Wolff and Rudolf Höss. (Rijksinstituut voor Oorlogsdocumentatie)

Dachau, January 20, 1941: Camp commandant Alex Piorkowski (left) greets Heinrich Himmler. (USHMM)

Dachau, January 20, 1941: Himmler visit; Richard Glücks on far left. (Rijksinstituut voor Oorlogsdocumentatie)

Dachau, May 15, 1941: SS officers discuss recent shooting. Two of the SS pictured who participated in the killing are Egon Zill and Franz Johann Hofmann. A large labor kommando can be seen in the distance. (USHMM)

Gross-Rosen: Visit by SS-Oberführer Loritz. (Private Source)

Gross-Rosen: Karl Rödl. (Private Source)

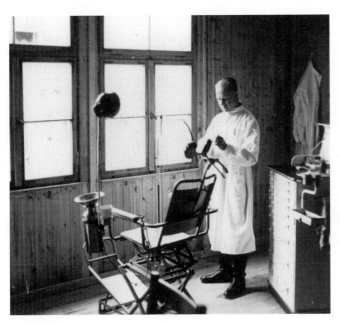

Gross-Rosen: Dentist, Dr. Kruncik. (Private Source)

Gross-Rosen: SS officers relax. (Private Source)

Gross-Rosen: Rudolf Suttrop on left. (Private Source)

Gross-Rosen: Visit of SS-Brigadeführer Glücks. (Private Source)

Gross-Rosen: Visit of SS-Brigadeführer Glücks. (Private Source)

Gross-Rosen: Visit of SS-Brigadeführer Glücks; SS-Untersturmführer Kuno Schramm is third from left. (Private Source)

Gross-Rosen: Visit of SS-Oberführer Schmauser; Karl Rödl second from right. (Private Source)

Gross-Rosen: Visit of SS-Obersführer Schmauser; Karl Rödl in right foreground. (Private Source)

Gross-Rosen, January 1942: Kommandant Rödl. (Private Source)

Gross-Rosen: Camp adjutant on right. (Private Source)

Gross-Rosen: SS officers relax. (Private Source)

Gross-Rosen: SS officers with visitors. (Private Source)

Gross-Rosen: Camp staff. (Private Source)

Gross-Rosen: Arthur Rödl in white tunic. (Private Source)

Gross-Rosen: (front row, left to right) Kuno Schramm, Arthur Rödl and Georg Güssregen. (Private Source)

Gross-Rosen: SS officers with camp dog. (Private Source)

Gross-Rosen: Anton Thumann. (Private Source)

Right: Janowska: SS troops and guard dog. (USHMM)

Below: The Janowska camp orchestra of prisoner-musicians, conducted by the director of the Lvov opera, Yakub Munt and Prof. Schtiks. The orchestra played while the inmates set out to work and when they returned, the Nazis ordered the orchestra to perform a specially composed melody entitled "Tango of Death," which was performed when prisoners were tortured and executed. On the right (in the light uniform) is the camp commandant. (USHMM)

Janowska: SS guard company commander passes the main gate of the camp. (USHMM)

Majdanek/Lublin, July 1944: SS enlisted men display canisters of Zyklon-B to Russian troops after camp liberation; both were subsequently hanged. (USHMM)

Majdanek/Lublin, August-September 1944: Russian officers interrogate SS-Obersturmführer Anton Thernes after liberation of the camp. (USHMM)

Mauthausen: Franz Ziereis is third from right. (Yivo Institute)

Mauthausen, April 27, 1941: Heinrich Himmler; Karl Wolff is second from left. (USHMM)

Mauthausen: (from left to right) two unidentified Hauptsturmführer, Standartenführer Franz Ziereis (the camp commandant), Sturmbannführer Krebsbach (the camp doctor), unidentified, unidentified. (USHMM)

Mauthausen, 1941: Heinrich Himmler tours camp; Franz Ziereis, camp commandant, on right. (BAK [44969/9])

Mauthausen, April 1941: (front row from left) Ernst Kaltenbrunner, Franz Ziereis, Heinrich Himmler, Karl Chmielewski, George Bachmayer, and Nazi Party District Leader Eigruber. (USHMM)

Mauthausen, April 1941: Heinrich Himmler listens to Franz Ziereis with Ernst Kaltenbrunner. (USHMM)

Above: Mauthausen: SS officers; personnel in rear are captured Russian soldiers. (BAK [44736/1])

Right: Mauthausen: Kommandant Franz Ziereis. (BAK [44969/5])

Mauthausen, 1941: Heinrich Himmler tours the camp; officer on far right is Karl Wolff. (BAK [45534/4])

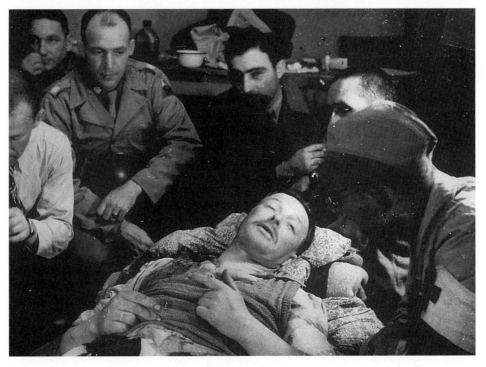

Mauthausen, May 24, 1945: Franz Ziereis on his deathbed, mortally wounded by American troops. (USHMM)

Neuengamme, November 1943: SS troops observe 20th anniversary of Nazi "Beer Hall" Putsch. (USHMM)

Neuengamme, December 1943: SS camp personnel with wives celebrate Christmas. (USHMM)

Neuengamme, 1943: SS guards oversee prisoners. (USHMM)

This page: Amon Leopold Goeth (1908-1946), was responsible for the liquidation of the ghettoes and labor camps in Bochnia, Tarnow, and Krakow, among others. In February 1943 he was appointed commandant of Plaszow, where he remained until September 1944. After the war he was tried and executed in Krakow. (USHMM)

Plaszow, 1944: SS enlisted guards; man on right has received an Iron Cross First Class for front-line Waffen-SS service. (USHMM)

Ravensbrück, 1941: Visit by Heinrich Himmler. (USHMM)

Sachsenhausen, August 1933: Early SA guard personnel. (BAK [R88978])

Sachsenhausen: Visit by Interior Minister Wilhelm Frick (light tunic); Heinrich Himmler walks with him while Richard Glücks leads party. (BAK [41630/1])

Sachsenhausen: SS-Hauptsturmführer Campe gives instructions to other non-commissioned officers. (BAK [78612/10])

Stutthof, 1941: Visit by Heinrich Himmler (middle); to the right Karl Wolff, to the left Max Pauly. (USHMM)

Sobibór: SS non-commissioned officers Alexander Kaiser, Franz Hödl and Hubert Gomerski. (USHMM)

Stutthof, November 1941: Heinrich Himmler inspects honor guard. (USHMM)

Stutthof, November 1941: Camp commandant Max Pauly delivers welcoming address for Heinrich Himmler. (USHMM)

Stutthof, November 1941: Himmler at breakfast table talks with Max Pauly. (USHMM)

Stutthof, November 1941: Himmler visits camp officers. (USHMM)

Stutthof, November 1941: Commandant Max Pauly. (USHMM)

Right: Franz Stangl (left) and Kurt Franz (deputy commandant) in front of the commander's hut in Treblinka. Stangl holds a horsewhip, "a favorite status symbol of the German cadre personnel." Stangl was the second commandant of Treblinka, arriving in August 1942 from Sobibór. (USHMM)

MAPS

CONCENTRATION CAMPS IN AUSTRIA

1 MAUTHAUSEN

2 MAUTHAUSEN-GUSEN I

3 MAUTHAUSEN-GUSEN II

4 MAUTHAUSEN-GUSEN III

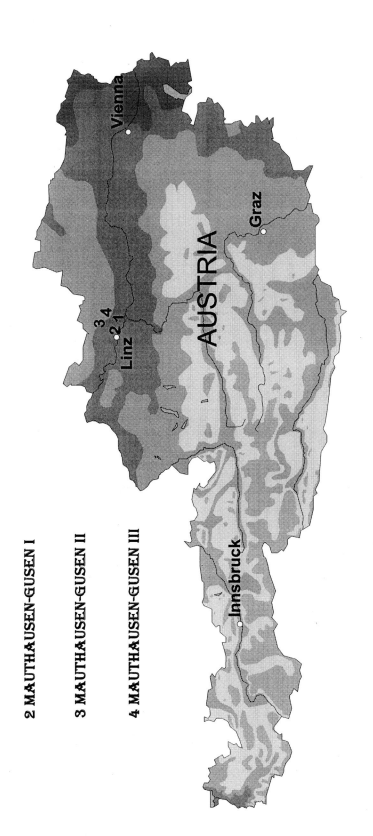

CONCENTRATION CAMPS IN BELGIUM

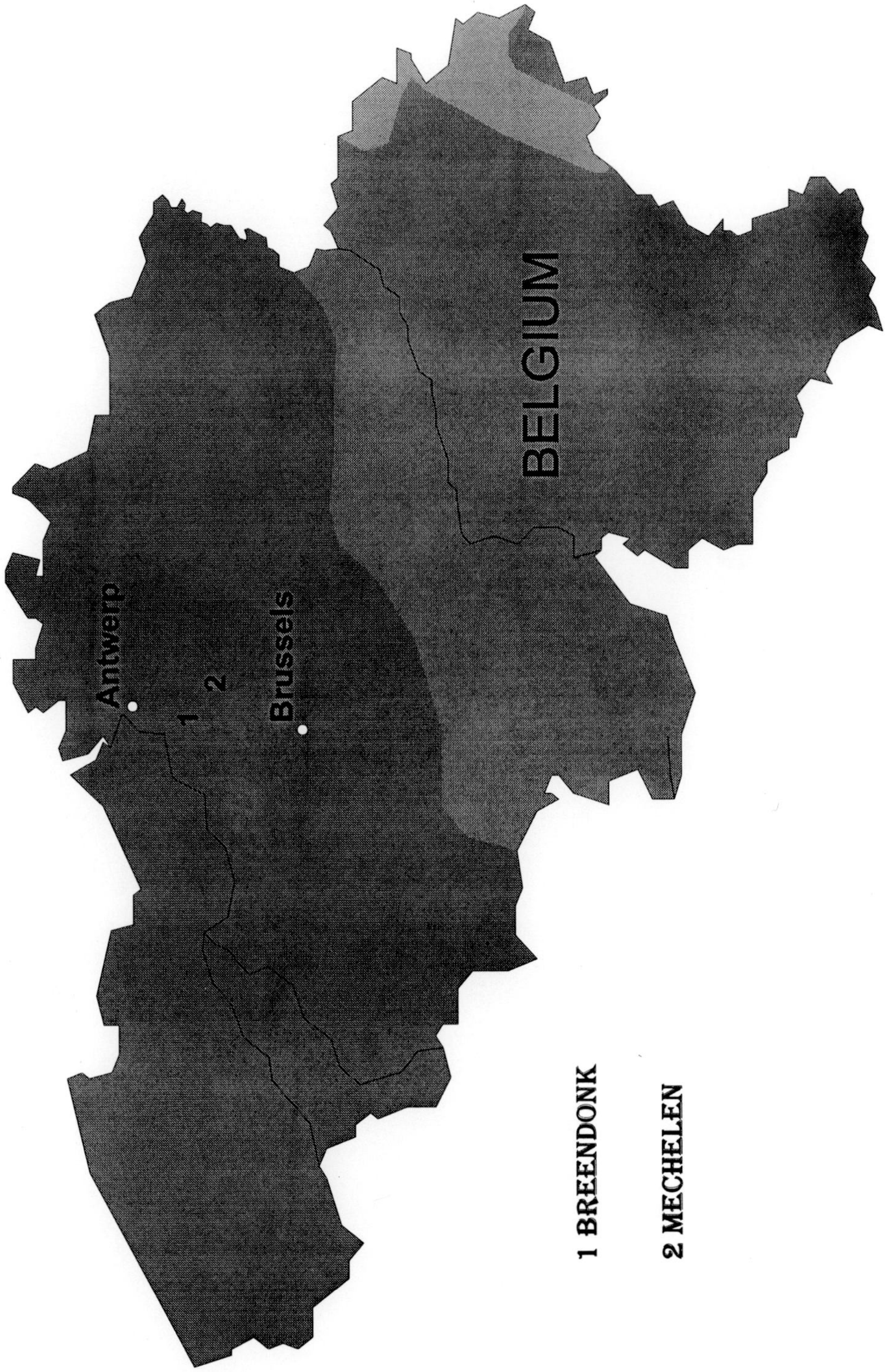

BELGIUM

Antwerp

1
2

Brussels

1 BREENDONK

2 MECHELEN

CONCENTRATION CAMPS IN CZECH REPUBLIC

1 THERESIENSTADT

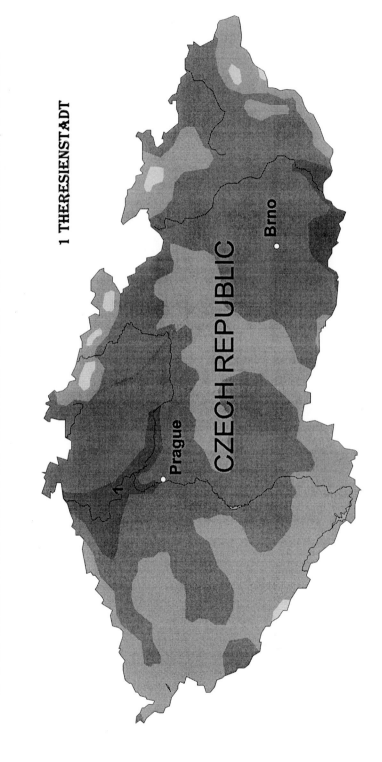

CZECH REPUBLIC

Prague

Brno

CONCENTRATION CAMPS IN ESTONIA

1 VIAVARA

2 KLOOGA

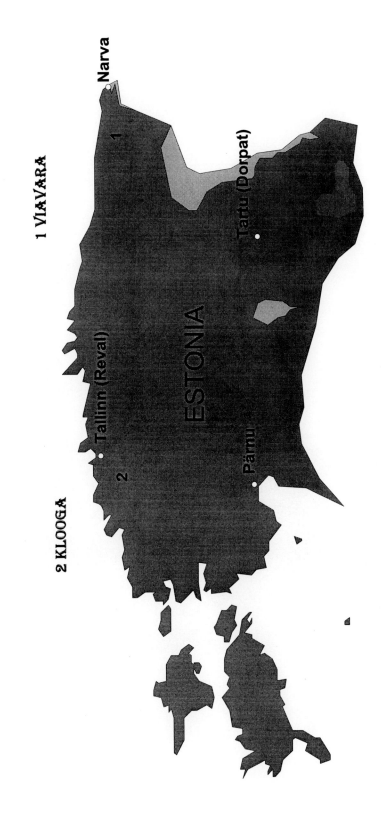

Narva

Tartu (Dorpat)

ESTONIA

Tallinn (Reval)

Pärnu

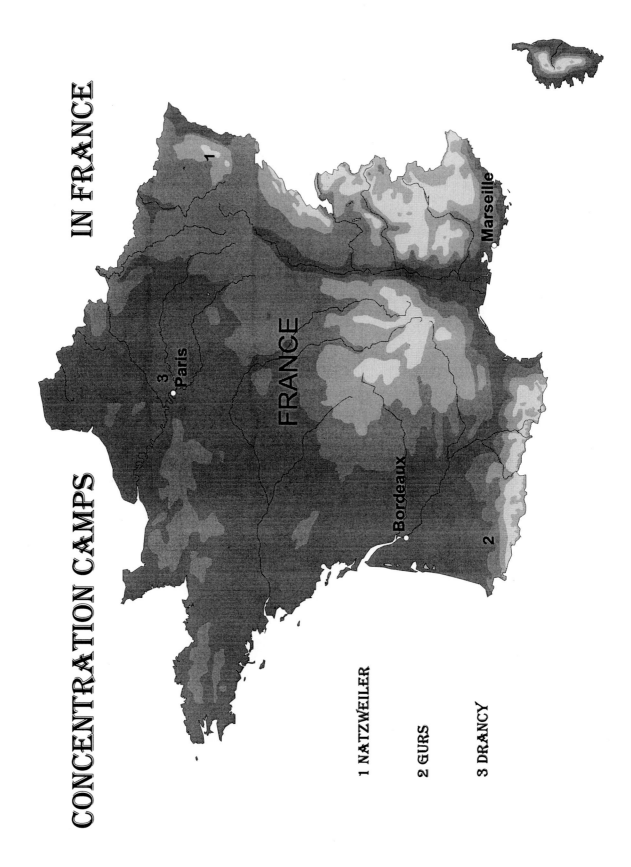

CONCENTRATION CAMPS

IN FRANCE

FRANCE

Paris

Bordeaux

Marseille

1

2

3

1 NATZWEILER

2 GURS

3 DRANCY

CONCENTRATION CAMPS IN LATVIA

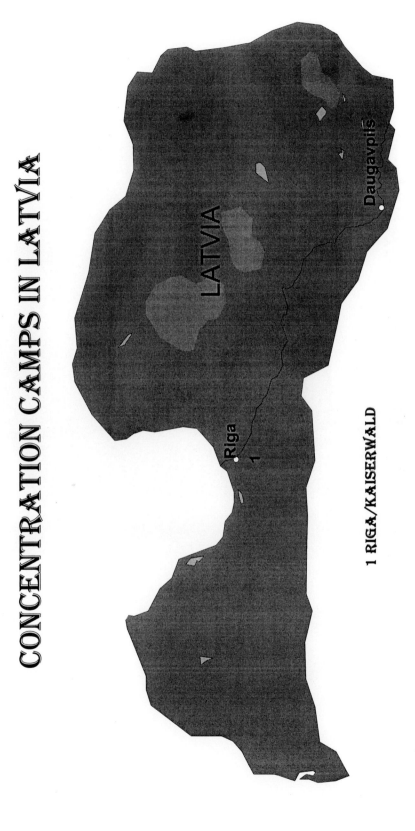

LATVIA

Daugavpils

Riga
1

1 RIGA/KAISERWALD

CONCENTRATION CAMPS IN LITHUANIA

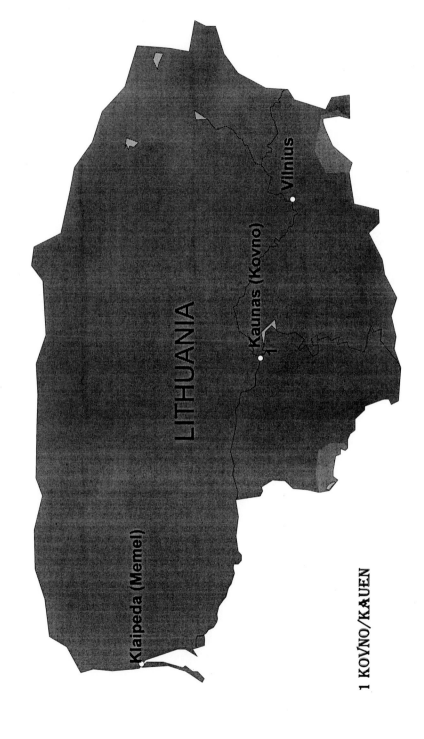

LITHUANIA

Klaipeda (Memel)

Kaunas (Kovno)

Vilnius

1 Kovno/Kauen

CONCENTRATION CAMPS IN THE NETHERLANDS

1-HERZOGENBUSCH-VUGHT

2-WESTERBORK

3-AMERSFOORT

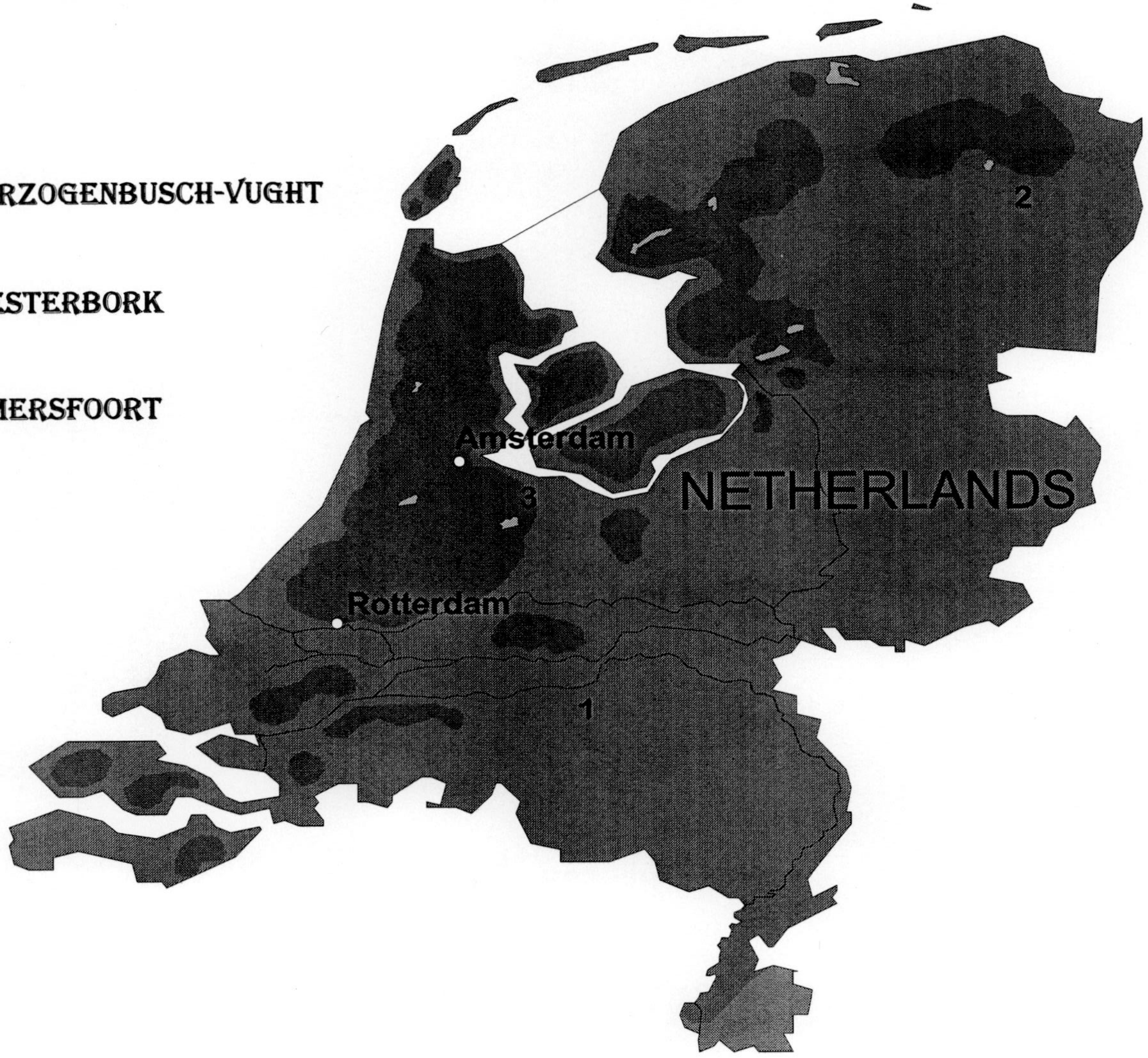
2
Amsterdam
3
NETHERLANDS
Rotterdam
1

CONCENTRATION CAMPS IN POLAND

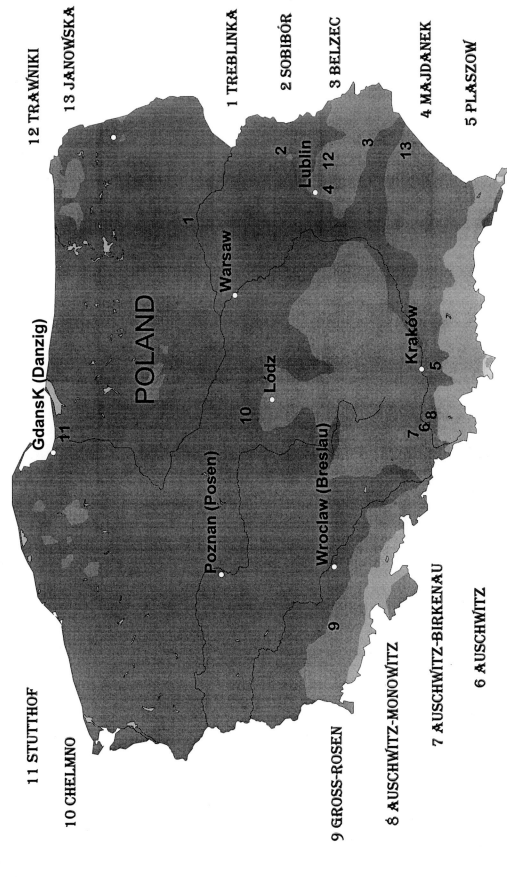

1 TREBLINKA
2 SOBIBÓR
3 BELZEC
4 MAJDANEK
5 PLASZOW
6 AUSCHWITZ
7 AUSCHWITZ-BIRKENAU
8 AUSCHWITZ-MONOWITZ
9 GROSS-ROSEN
10 CHELMNO
11 STUTTHOF
12 TRAWNIKI
13 JANOWSKA

WARTIME CONCENTRATION CAMPS

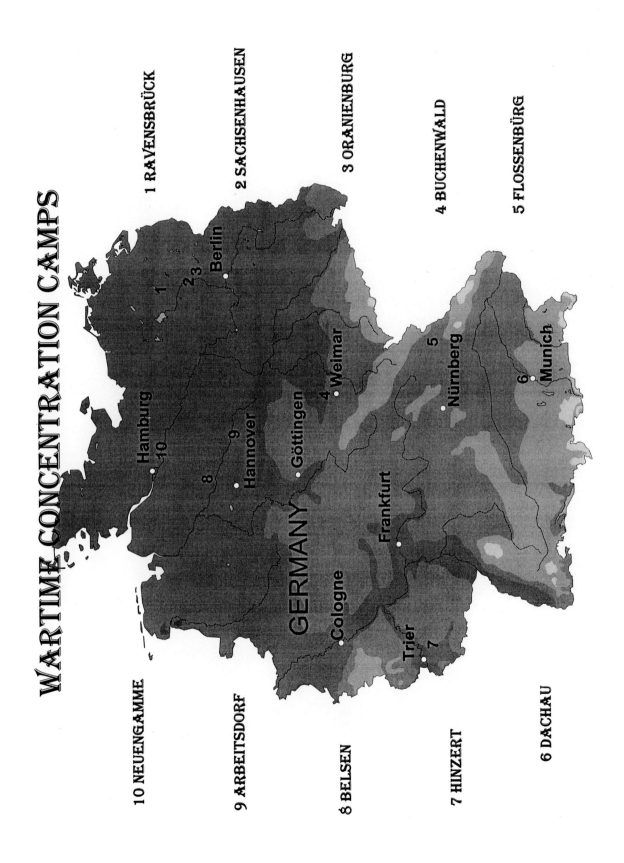

1 RAVENSBRÜCK
2 SACHSENHAUSEN
3 ORANIENBURG
4 BUCHENWALD
5 FLOSSENBÜRG
6 DACHAU
7 HINZERT
8 BELSEN
9 ARBEITSDORF
10 NEUENGAMME

GERMANY

Berlin
Hamburg
Hannover
Göttingen
Weimar
Nürnberg
Munich
Frankfurt
Cologne
Trier

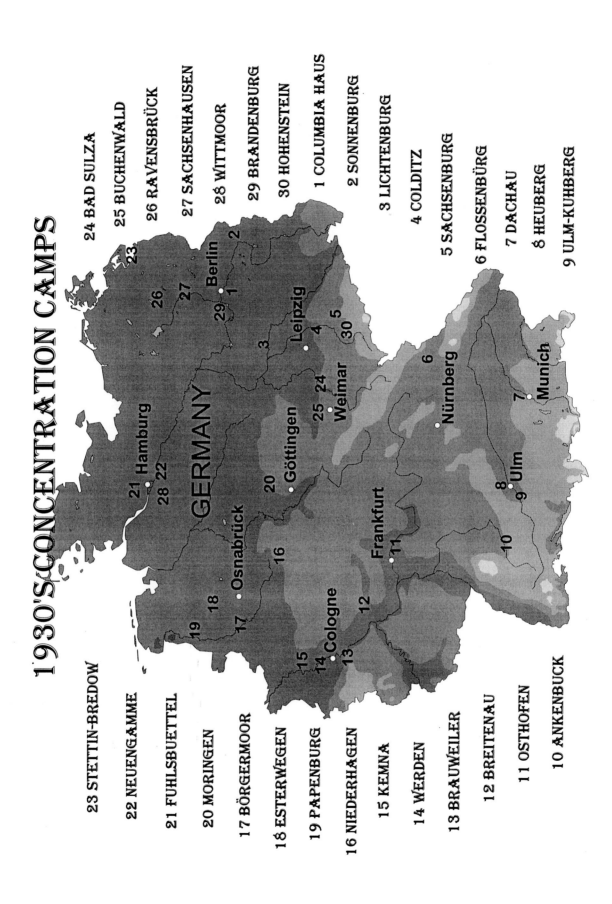

1930's CONCENTRATION CAMPS

24 BAD SULZA
25 BUCHENWALD
26 RAVENSBRÜCK
27 SACHSENHAUSEN
28 WITTMOOR
29 BRANDENBURG
30 HOHENSTEIN
1 COLUMBIA HAUS
2 SONNENBURG
3 LICHTENBURG
4 COLDITZ
5 SACHSENBURG
6 FLOSSENBÜRG
7 DACHAU
8 HEUBERG
9 ULM-KUHBERG

23 STETTIN-BREDOW
22 NEUENGAMME
21 FUHLSBUETTEL
20 MORINGEN
17 BÖRGERMOOR
18 ESTERWEGEN
19 PAPENBURG
16 NIEDERHAGEN
15 KEMNA
14 WERDEN
13 BRAUWEILER
12 BREITENAU
11 OSTHOFEN
10 ANKENBUCK

NOTES

NOTES

NOTES

NOTES